Building Strong Banks

Through Surveillance and Resolution

Editors
Charles Enoch
David Marston
Michael Taylor

International Monetary Fund
Washington, D.C. 2002

© 2002 International Monetary Fund

Production: IMF Graphics Section
Cover design: Lai Oy Louie
Cover photo: Craig Stewart/SolusImages

Library of Congress Cataloging-in-Publication Data

Building strong banks through surveillance and resolution / editors Charles Enoch, David Marston, Michael Taylor.
    p. cm.
    Includes bibliographical references (p.).
    ISBN 1-58906-043-1

    1. Banks and banking—Government policy. 2. Banks and banking—State supervision. 3. Financial institutions—Government policy. 4. Financial institutions—State supervision. 5. Monetary policy. 6. International Monetary Fund. I. Enoch, Charles. II. Marston, David. III. Taylor, Michael (Michael W.), 1962–

HG1551 .B85 2001
332.1—dc21

2001039741

Price: $38.00

Address orders to:
External Relations Department, Publication Services
International Monetary Fund, Washington D.C. 20431
Telephone: (202) 623-7430; Telefax: (202) 623-7201
E-mail: publications@imf.org
Internet: http://www.imf.org

Contents

	Page
Foreword	v
Acknowledgments	vii

1. Introduction
   Charles Enoch, David Marston, and Michael Taylor 1

PART I: ISSUES IN SURVEILLANCE

2. Loan Review, Provisioning, and Macroeconomic Linkages
   Luis Cortavarria, Claudia Dziobek, Akihiro Kanaya, and Inwon Song 11

3. Domestic Lending in Foreign Currency
   Fernando L. Delgado, Daniel S. Kanda, Greta Mitchell Casselle, and R. Armando Morales 40

4. Toward a Framework for Systemic Liquidity Policy
   Claudia Dziobek, J. Kim Hobbs, and David Marston 69

5. Emergency Liquidity Support Facilities
   Dong He 106

6. Issues in the Unification of Financial Sector Supervision
   Richard Abrams and Michael Taylor 146

7. The Financial Sector—The Responsibilities of the Public Agencies
   Peter Hayward 180

PART II: RESOLUTION STRATEGIES

8. Addressing the Prudential and Antitrust Aspects of Financial Sector Mergers and Acquisitions
   Michael Andrews 201

9. Guidelines for Bank Resolution
   David S. Hoelscher 243

10. Two Approaches to Resolving Nonperforming Assets During Financial Crises
    David Woo 265

11. Recapitalizing Banks with Public Funds: Selected Issues
    Charles Enoch, Gillian Garcia, and V. Sundararajan 308

12. An Operational Framework for Addressing the Public Costs of Systemic Bank Restructuring
    Priya Basu 368

List of Authors 388

Foreword

The International Monetary Fund occupies a unique vantage point from which to survey the economic and financial systems of its 184 members. In recent years its role in financial sector surveillance has expanded significantly, reflecting increased recognition of the important interactions between financial (especially banking) system soundness and macroeconomic stability. Moreover, a number of member countries have called on the IMF's advice and assistance to help resolve banking sector problems, often in the context of IMF-supported programs. Staff of the Monetary and Exchange Affairs Department (MAE) have been at the forefront of the IMF's efforts in these areas. In consequence, they have built up a great reserve of expertise on some highly specialized issues in both financial sector surveillance and the resolution of banking sector problems.

This book forms part of the ongoing effort of the IMF to explain the standards and principles that guide it in its work. Many chapters have their origin in papers written for internal use as a means of sharing valuable expertise among a group of colleagues. While some were subsequently revised and published in the IMF Working Paper series, many have not previously been made publicly available. Their publication in the present volume is intended to disseminate them to the largest possible audience, and we hope that the principles and policy advice they contain will be widely discussed and analyzed.

Policy advice needs to be tailored to the circumstances of individual member countries, and there can be no off-the-peg or "cookie cutter" solutions to the issues discussed in this book. On the other hand, a sound financial system is like a safe automobile: whatever the differences in styling and design between different models, safety is a function of a set of basic, unvarying principles. Therefore, although policy advice may differ from country to country, it also needs to be based on a set of common principles, which are in turn supported by sound arguments and strong evidence. The chapters of this book attempt to set out some of those principles.

The range of issues with which MAE staff have dealt over recent years is very extensive, and only a small sample of them can be considered in the space of this book. Over the coming years, the IMF will continue to work with its members to help enhance financial sector stability. In the long run our aim must be to ensure that all financial systems are sufficiently robust and supervisory capacity is sufficiently well-developed to reduce the frequency of banking problems. However, even if this goal can be achieved, there will always be a role for the kind of special expertise that the IMF's MAE department has developed. Continuing to develop and refine its work in this area represents a major task for the staff of this Department.

STEFAN INGVES
Director
Monetary and Exchange
Affairs Department, IMF

Acknowledgments

This book would not have been possible without the contribution of many people, both within the Monetary Exchange Affairs Department (MAE) and in other Departments of the International Monetary Fund. It is, first of all, one of the fruits of MAE's ongoing work on banking sector issues, conducted first under the general guidance and supervision of the late Mr. Manuel Guitián, Director between 1995–98, and subsequently of Mr. Stefan Ingves, Director since 1999. We especially wish to record our thanks to Mr. V. Sundararajan, Deputy Director of MAE, for overseeing this project in his capacity of editor of the Operational Papers series in which many of the chapters first appeared. The individual chapters have also benefited from the comments of reviewers too numerous to mention here. However, among those who have offered comments on many—if not most—of the chapters of the book are Messrs. Tomás Baliño and Carl-Johan Lindgren. The contributions of other reviewers are recognized in each individual chapter. In addition, completion of the book has been greatly assisted by the support and encouragement offered by Mr. David Hoelscher, Mr. Marc Quintyn, and Ms. Claudia Dziobek, the last having played an especially valuable role by coordinating work on the Operational Papers. The book has also gained greatly from the editorial work performed on it by Ms. Natalie Baumer and by Mr. Jeffrey Hayden of the External Relations Department, who also coordinated the book's production. Finally, we would like to thank Lidia Tokuda, Funke Fasalojo, Magally Bernal, and Sandra Solares for their excellent assistance in producing this volume.

1

Introduction

CHARLES ENOCH, DAVID MARSTON, AND MICHAEL TAYLOR

The twin themes of this book—surveillance and resolution—involve issues that are at the core of the IMF's recent work on the financial sector. Although the intensity of this work is relatively new, the IMF has long recognized that an appropriate macroeconomic policy stance alone is not sufficient to maintain balance in an economy; sound underlying microeconomic conditions are also vital. In no area is this more important than in monetary policy. Maintaining a monetary policy stance geared to price level stability requires a sound and competitive banking system to transmit policy signals and to ensure the efficient allocation of financial resources. Moreover, maintaining openness to international capital markets requires a sound and well-regulated banking system through which these flows can be intermediated. The IMF helps to promote bank soundness through its surveillance, lending, and technical assistance activities.

In its surveillance activities, the IMF aims to improve the macroeconomic environment and structural framework in which banks operate. In its discussions with member countries, the IMF calls attention to emerging macroeconomic problems and structural deficiencies and recommends appropriate policy actions. The IMF's efforts to strengthen member countries' banking systems are also reflected in the design of IMF-supported lending programs and technical assistance, which in recent years has focused increasingly on banking legislation, regulation, and supervision and on the design of bank safety nets, including lender-of-last-resort facilities and deposit insurance schemes.

Since the mid-1990s, partly in response to the Mexican and Asian crises, the IMF has kept a watchful eye on financial sector issues, paying greater attention to the banking sector, the sustainability of capital flows, and situations where crises could spill over into other markets. At its April 1998 meeting, the IMF's governing body, the Interim Committee (now the International Monetary and Financial Committee), set a demanding agenda for the IMF's work, including the central role to be played by the IMF in crisis prevention through its surveillance and its role in encouraging members to strengthen their macroeconomic policies and financial sectors. The Interim Committee also called upon the IMF to help members strengthen their domestic financial systems by encouraging them to develop supervisory and regulatory frameworks that are consistent with internationally accepted best practices, as well as strengthened standards for bank and nonbank institutions. Subsequently, the IMF has enhanced its surveillance of the financial sector through the Financial Sector Assessment Program (FSAP) conducted jointly with the World Bank.

In addition to its surveillance and institutional development work, the IMF has also provided extensive technical assistance to member countries in banking system restructuring—the management and resolution of banking sector problems. IMF staff has been actively engaged in assisting member countries in reestablishing their banking and financial sectors on a sound basis both during and immediately after financial crisis, frequently in the context of IMF-supported programs. Given the relatively high number of the IMF's 184 member countries that have experienced significant banking sector problems during the last decade, this has provided IMF staff with a unique vantage point from which to consider the issues involved in bank system restructuring and to gain a comparative perspective on the effectiveness of crisis management and resolution arrangements.

In recent years the IMF has spent a good deal of time developing "best practice" standards that allow it to judge the strength of banking systems and of the related bank safety net. Moreover, the IMF staff has also sought to reflect upon the expertise it has developed in assisting member countries to resolve their banking sector problems in the aftermath of financial crises. The present volume can be viewed as one outcome of this ongoing effort, in that it is concerned primarily with the practical lessons that can be drawn in building a sound financial sector and in both the prevention and management of banking system instability. It represents a distillation of the collective experience of the staff of the Monetary and Exchange Affairs Department (MAE), which has primary responsibility within the IMF for these areas. Given the breadth of the subjects considered, the present volume can inevitably only deal with selected issues.

The first part of this volume examines IMF surveillance and the best practice standards that serve as a benchmark for judging financial systems. Key prerequisites for banking system soundness are high standards of prudential supervision and regulation. The IMF's work, through the FSAP process and through its technical assistance program, which is increasingly shaped by the outcome of the resulting Financial Sector Stability Assessments, aims to help member countries raise their standards of supervision. In this way, member countries enjoy both improved access to international capital markets and an improved ability to manage the resulting capital flows. The IMF's work in this area is supported by the now well-established body of international best practice standards for banking supervision, with the work of the Basel Committee at its center. The key document of these standards is the Committee's *Core Principles for Effective Banking Supervision*, although the work of other financial organizations also has a direct bearing on the development of these best practice standards.

One important issue highlighted by the IMF's experience is that the existing body of international capital standards for banks presuppose adequate and comprehensive rules on the recognition and valuation of assets and liabilities, as well as the adequacy of rules for making provisions for impaired assets. Although a number of crisis-hit countries appeared to include banks that were well-capitalized according to international standards, their capital adequacy was overstated by the failure to recognize adequately (and hence provision for) nonperforming loans. Hence a robust system of loan classification and provisioning must be at the center of any system of banking supervision. The second chapter by Luis Cortavarria, Claudia Dziobek, Akihiro Kanaya, and Inwon Song reviews this important issue.

Foreign currency–denominated lending lies as the heart of the linkage between currency vulnerabilities and financial sector weakness. As a number of recent financial crises have demonstrated, foreign currency lending to domestic residents by domestic financial institutions can destabilize the banking system if such lending is not properly monitored and controlled. In the third chapter, Fernando Delgado, Daniel Kanda, Greta Mitchell Casselle, and R. Armando Morales argue against placing too much emphasis on outright restrictions on this type of lending. Instead, bank regulators and firm management need to pay close attention to developing internal control systems to ensure that banks are able to identify and control their risks.

Another form of risk at the micro-institutional level that can rapidly be translated into banking system instability at a macro level is the risk of illiquidity. Indeed, one of the primary reasons why special regulation of banks is necessary is because they engage in a process of maturity transformation, turning short-term liabilities into long-term assets. The robustness of banking systems, and of the financial sector more generally, can be enhanced if banks have access to deep and liquid money markets. Although the conditions for the existence of these markets are often taken for granted, they form an essential component of financial sector soundness. The fourth chapter by Claudia Dziobek, J. Kim Hobbs, and David Marston reviews some of the issues in establishing a sound infrastructure for liquidity management.

The framework for a systemic liquidity policy should be supplemented by emergency liquidity support, both for individually distressed institutions and for systemic disruptions. Emergency lending to one or a few nonsystemic institutions will necessarily differ from the support given to systemically important institutions, whose troubles could threaten serious banking sector instability. But in Chapter 5, Dong He argues that properly designed lending procedures, together with clearly laid out authority and accountability and disclosure rules, are all central to a well-functioning lender-of-last-resort function.

The final two chapters of Part I focus on the institutional structure of regulation. The lack of comprehensive consolidated supervision has been at the root of a number of banking sector problems. Some have argued that some of these problems might have been avoided if a single integrated regulatory agency had existed that could have surveyed the entire financial sector. Many IMF member countries have recently taken steps to create this very kind of integrated agency, thus attracting widespread international interest. In the sixth chapter, Richard Abrams and Michael Taylor review this trend and consider the circumstances in which the integrated approach might be adopted. They argue that the decision will rest on a complex matrix of factors that will vary according to the circumstances of particular countries.

In addition to the regulatory function itself, many countries distribute the responsibility for ensuring the soundness of the financial system among a variety of bodies. These include the government (usually the ministry of finance), the central bank, the supervisory agency (or agencies), and sometimes a deposit insurance agency as well. In times of crisis, a dedicated crisis resolution body is also often established. The extent to which these institutions are allocated clearly defined responsibilities and how they coordinate their activities can have important implications for the soundness of the financial system as a whole. In

Chapter 7, Peter Hayward seeks to set out some guiding principles concerning the respective roles of these different bodies, so as to achieve the efficient allocation of their responsibilities and to ensure effective coordination.

Part II is concerned with banking system "restructuring." This term does not necessarily refer to the bank consolidation that is being observed in many countries around the world, but with the *management* and *resolution* of banking sector instability. Since in most countries serious banking sector problems are a rare event, the expertise and specialist knowledge concerning the most efficient mechanisms for resolving banking crises can rarely be found within a single country. A sense of what constitutes "best practices" in bank crisis resolution requires the degree of specialization and cross-country experience that the IMF is perhaps uniquely placed to provide.

Even the best-regulated and managed banking system can be overwhelmed by a sufficiently severe macroeconomic shock such as a sudden drop in currency values. In managing and resolving banking sector instability, one needs to bear in mind that the best practice in normal times may not represent the best practice in a crisis. This distinction runs through many of the chapters contained in Part II. Nonetheless, all the papers have as an overarching concern the need to minimize moral hazard, the notion that "bailouts" (or a promise of support) prompt recklessness among investors.

Countries whose banking systems have suffered only modest damage can cope by encouraging bank mergers and the acquisition of weaker banks by stronger ones. This technique raises important antitrust issues that exist in a particularly acute form in banking, especially because there is a prudential dimension to mergers and acquisitions in the financial sector that does not exist in mergers in other sectors of the economy. Thus, in considering mergers in the banking sector, there is a need to consider the interaction between competition law and prudential supervision. Michael Andrews examines in Chapter 8 some of the issues that arise in this comparatively neglected area and attempts to provide an overview of the principles and best practices that should be applied to financial sector mergers and acquisitions.

Where attempts to rehabilitate insolvent banks fail or are not feasible, then the banks should be liquidated. As insolvency laws differ among countries, universally applicable procedures for bank liquidation cannot be developed. However, there are a number of issues that must be addressed, irrespective of the legal environment, including the treatment of shareholders, the respective responsibilities of the central bank and the supervisory agency (where these are different), and the role and responsibilities of the bank liquidator. These issues are considered by David Hoelscher in Chapter 9, which also seeks to lay out specific procedures to be followed at each stage of the liquidation process.

Where the financial crisis has led to a collapse of asset values, a dislocation of secondary markets, and widespread real sector insolvency, a range of different techniques for banking sector restructuring and resolution is required. Chapter 10 by David Woo reviews two further possible approaches to resolving a systemic crisis—the creation of asset management companies and the creation of out-of-court centralized corporate debt workout frameworks—that have come to define the core asset management infrastructure of countries most seriously affected by recent financial crises. In addition to investigating their respective roles and evaluating their strengths and weaknesses, his chapter also seeks to develop benchmarks for assessing best practice in their design.

In several recent cases, the resolution of banking sector problems has involved the use of substantial amounts of public funds to permit banks to write off bad debts and to be returned to capital adequacy. Recapitalizing banks is a complex process that requires significant government intervention and careful management at both the strategic and individual bank levels. Chapter 11 by Charles Enoch, Gillian Garcia, and V. Sundararajan highlights the range of operational and strategic issues to be addressed and the institutional arrangements needed to foster an effective banking system restructuring and to maximize the return on the government's investment. The approaches to recapitalization have varied, with different countries choosing different mixes of capital injections and asset purchase and rehabilitation. The choice of an appropriate mix is critical to minimizing the expected present value of government outlays net of recoveries.

Where banking system restructuring has involved public funds, it will have often required the issuance of vast quantities of public debt. While government support to bank restructuring through the issuance of public debt can help address the immediate crisis, it can result in escalating costs to the government, raising significant—and often unanticipated—medium-term risks related to fiscal and debt sustainability and financial stability. Priya Basu in Chapter 12 concludes this volume by presenting a simple operational framework for quantifying, analyzing, and reducing such costs on an ex post basis.

As already noted, this volume has a strong practical flavor with most chapters growing out of the authors' close involvement in dealing with these issues in the context of IMF programs or technical assistance. Many of the chapters have appeared as Operational Papers of MAE or Working Papers of the IMF. As their name suggests, Operational Papers are intended to provide practical advice to experts working in the field, and are authored by MAE staff based on their own extensive practical experience of the subject under review. By including these papers as chapters of the present volume we hope to make this important body of work available to a wider audience.

Part I

Issues in Surveillance

2

Loan Review, Provisioning, and Macroeconomic Linkages

LUIS CORTAVARRIA, CLAUDIA DZIOBEK, AKIHIRO KANAYA, AND INWON SONG

Recent banking crises have highlighted the importance of macroprudential indicators as a basis to assess financial stability. Of particular concern are indicators such as nonperforming or restructured loans, measures of bank capitalization, profitability, and the quality of collateral. This chapter explores the underpinnings of these concepts.

Well-managed banks invest considerable resources in the review of loan performance. Loan-loss provisions (an expense set aside as an allowance for bad loans) are a way to adjust the balance sheet consistent with the results of loan review. Both are elements of a credit management framework for banks and also constitute important tools for prudential oversight. Using country examples, this chapter describes how bank supervisors use credit management systems to assess bank soundness.

Loan valuation relies on complex techniques and tools. In a highly stylized fashion, the various elements of credit risk management can be described as a chain of events, starting with loan review and classification, entailing, in some cases, the placement of a loan on a nonaccrual (cash) basis. Criteria for classification range from ex post (payments overdue) to more *forward-looking elements*, involving, where appropriate, empirical data for loan default probabilities. Collateral also plays an important role for valuing loans; its valuation adds a further layer of complexity and source of estimation errors, sometimes with systemic consequences. Classification may require further action in the form of establishing appropriate provisions. Adequate levels of provisions can be set by the authorities or by banks, ideally at levels approximating loss experience. In this regard, important incentives stem from a supportive tax treatment of provisions. Provisions in turn reduce income and therefore a bank's capital, thus disclosing important information about the banks' condition to the public.

Loan valuation produces important information on the value of the stock of outstanding credit. Since bank loans are in most cases not traded, they have no market price. Secondary markets for loans, particularly mortgage loans, exist in some countries, but the depth and liquidity of those markets vary and may be thin. Sometimes, market prices can be synthesized from the quotes in the credit derivative market, but the depth and liquidity of the derivative market may also be an issue. For the majority of banks, loan valuation is the main vehicle for tracking the value of a loan portfolio. Thus, valuation can be considered a substitute for market pricing of loans.

Loan valuation has direct implications for macroeconomic analysis, in particular estimates of aggregate credit. Timely valuation adjustments are a precondition for accurate data. Under conditions of macroeconomic instability, or during times of banking sector distress, loan valuation becomes more difficult and lags in loan review can produce distortions.

Other aggregate effects may arise—for instance, when credit risk management systems are biased to ex post loss recognition. Recent banking crises in many countries have triggered a debate about whether current practices of provisioning (estimating the value of bad loans) are biased to produce procyclical bank behavior with macroeconomic effects, and whether more anticipatory approaches to provisions should be developed to neutralize such effects. Empirical evidence reviewed in this paper does not support a clear link between provisioning and business cycles. Nevertheless, from the perspective of financial soundness, a case can be made for more forward-looking valuation approaches.

The terms used in this chapter are defined as follows. *Loan review* is an ongoing monitoring process, which relies on classification of loans into various categories of performance as an analytical tool. Classification is also often used by bank supervisors as a benchmark in assessing a bank's soundness. The results of a loan review may translate into adjustments of loan values through allowances or provisions. For example, if a loan review reveals a loss of value, the loss would be recognized as an expense to the bank by establishing a provision. This, in turn, is reflected in the bank's capital ratio which, as illustrated in this chapter, most likely falls as provisions increase. Loan review and provisioning are key ingredients of capital ratio calculation. Of course, when losses identified in loan review do not translate into provisions, there would be no measurable impact on capital. Banks may publish information about the ratio of nonperforming loans but this does not necessarily imply that appropriate provisions have been established.[1]

Well-designed and consistently applied procedures on loan review and provisioning are important from a prudential regulatory perspective and for all market participants for comparability of balance sheets. Ineffective rules reduce the meaningfulness of bank balance sheet data, including that of capital ratios. Regulators in most Group of Ten (G-10) countries place great emphasis on judgmental factors and grant banks considerable latitude in using internal models for loan valuation. By contrast, many emerging market countries apply more formal systems with relatively greater emphasis on objective factors. While there is no international best practice system of loan classification and provisioning, cross-country comparisons show that many countries, including the larger emerging market countries, employ somewhat similar loan classification systems and have somewhat similar guidelines for adequate levels of provisioning.

Loan Review and Classification

In most countries, banks value their loans at historic cost (the face value of the loan as noted in the loan contract) and make periodic adjustments to the value based on loan valuation. Loan valuation of a portfolio of loans can be done by classifying loans into different categories that reflect different default risk profiles. But the world lacks a uniform loan classification technique or a standard procedure to assess loan risk. In some countries, banks determine their own systems of classification. In other countries, the bank regulatory agency sets detailed rules on loan classification. Although a loan review can provide a good estimate of a bank's loan portfolio, it does not necessarily provide for a cross-country comparison of such figures. The following principles and guidelines can be considered desirable but actual implementation varies widely.

Broad categorization of loans for review

A sound loan classification system should have the following features:
- Individual large loans should be analyzed separately. Key criteria comprise (1) the overall financial condition and resources of the

---

[1] This paper is focused on loans but in many respects applies to bank assets; more generally "loans" and "assets" are sometimes used interchangeably. The authors recognize that the economic terminology is not always fully in line with accounting terms. For example, "provision" and "allowance for loan losses" are used synonymously. Also, the term "nonperforming loan" is used interchangeably with "impaired loan," the accounting term.

borrower measured by the current and stabilized cash flow (repayment capacity); (2) the credit history of the borrower; (3) the borrower's character; (4) the purpose of the credit; and, as appropriate, (5) the types of secondary sources of repayment available, such as a guarantor support and/or collateral.
- Pools of similar loans with small denominations, for which a loan-by-loan analysis is too costly, could be analyzed collectively using statistical methods (e.g., such a procedure could be applied to housing and consumer loans). The same criteria as for large loans apply.
- Other groupings of loans may be appropriate (e.g., real estate, agricultural, commercial loans).

Subjectivity and objectivity

A loan classification process inevitably includes an element of judgment by credit analysts, and internal or external auditors. Subjective factors comprise experience and knowledge of the credit reviewer; macroeconomic or sectoral forecasts; value of collateral; market sentiment; and the borrower's character.

In many developing countries the credit staff at banks and bank supervisors may have a weak background in judging loans. Similarly, in highly unstable economies establishing a good basis for judgment is difficult. Moreover, under such conditions banks may be reluctant to use their own judgment to adversely classify a loan and establish provisions on the basis of subjective judgment. Supervisory authorities often find it useful to rely primarily on more standardized factors that can be applied routinely in the classification process. The application of rules-based criteria by the supervisory authorities, as well as by banks, can be a useful second best practice.

A Useful Classification System

To assess loan quality, credit analysts segregate bank loan portfolios into risk categories according to certain specifications.[2] The U.S. guidelines are a good example of a relatively simple and transparent grid. The system includes five categories—standard, special mention, substandard, doubtful, and loss.[3]

---

[2]Some countries allow *split classification* of a loan when there is more certainty regarding the collectibility of a portion of a loan than the remaining balance. However, credit risk classification is usually done by borrower, not by loan.

[3]U.S. Federal Reserve System, 2000; see the Internet at www.federalreserve.gov/boarddocs/supmanual.

- Standard assets. Loans in this category are performing and have sound fundamentals. (Fundamentals include the borrower's overall financial condition, resources and cash flow, credit history, and character. They also include the purpose of the loan, and types of secondary sources of repayment.)
- Special loans. This is a protected category but includes potentially weak loans that, if not corrected, may deteriorate and damage the bank's asset quality. Examples are credit that the lending officer is unable to properly supervise; an inadequate loan agreement; and uncertainty of the condition of collateral, or other deviations from prudent lending practices.
- Substandard loans. The loans in this category have well-defined weaknesses, where the current sound worth and paying capacity of the borrower is not assured. Orderly repayment of debt is in jeopardy.
- Doubtful loans. Doubtful loans exhibit all the characteristics of substandard loans, with the added characteristics that collection in full is highly questionable and improbable. Classification of "loss" is deferred because of specific pending factors that may strengthen the asset. Such factors include merger, acquisition, or liquidation procedures, capital injection, perfecting liens on additional collateral, and refinancing plans.
- Loss loans are considered uncollectible and of such little value that their continuance as bankable assets is not warranted. This classification does not mean that the asset has absolutely no recovery or salvage value, but rather that it is not practical or desirable to defer full provision or writing off this basically worthless loan. Partial recovery may be effected in the future.

While the U.S. Examination Manual uses multiple criteria to determine an appropriate classification, banks and regulators in many countries often use delinquency as the main benchmark, measured as the number of days or months loan payments are past due.

Past due and forward-looking criteria

As shown in Table 2.1, many countries refer to the above-mentioned classification system. Often, regulators set guidelines in terms of past-due payments. Special mention tends to be for past-due loans up to three months (Kuwait, Philippines, Slovak Republic). Some countries do not use this category at all or may have other categories not detailed in this table. Substandard loans tend to be those with overdue payments of up to six months (Argentina, the Central Bank of West African States or BCEAO, Colombia, Kuwait, Malaysia, Rwanda, Slovak Republic), while doubtful loans are clustered around 6–12 months overdue (Argentina,

Table 2.1. Past-Due Criteria in Selected Loan Classification Systems, 2000[1]
(In months)

Country	Special Mention	Substandard	Doubtful	Loss
Argentina	Up to 3	3–6	6–12	Over 12
Bangladesh	Up to 12	12–36	37–60	61
BCEAO[2]	n.a.	Up to 6	Over 6	n.a.
Chile (Consumer)	Up to 2	2	4	5
Colombia				
Consumer	Up to 2	2–3	3–6	6–12
Other	Up to 4	4–6	6–12	Over 12
Czech Republic	Up to 3	3	6	12
India	n.a.	Up to 18	Over 18	n.a.
Korea[3]				
Secured portion	Up to 3	3	n.a.	n.a.
Unsecured portion	n.a.		3	3
Kuwait	Up to 3	3–6	6–12	Over 12
Malaysia	n.a.	3–6	6–9	Over 9
Mexico (credit card)	1	2	3–6	Over 7
Peru				
Consumer	Up to 1	1–2	2–4	Over 4
Mortgage	Up to 3	3–4	4–12	Over 12
Philippines	Up to 3	Over 3	Over 6[4]	Over 6[5]
Poland	Up to 1	1 or qualitative	3	6; borrower in bankruptcy
Rwanda	Up to 3	3–6	6–12	Over 12
Russia	Up to 5 days	Up to 1	1–6	Over 6
Saudi Arabia	Up to 1	1	3–6	n.a.
Slovak Republic	1–3	3–6	6–12	Over 12

Sources: IMF staff; and Moody's Investor Services
Notes: n.a. means "not applicable."

[1] Other criteria, such as repayment capacity, may also apply to loan classification (as shown, e.g., in the case of Poland). Several of the countries listed additionally use "pass" and "special mention" as categories above substandard. Group of Ten (G-10) countries use complex systems, a mix of formal rules, and management discretion. See Appendix. In general, banks are expected to use internal models subject to prudential oversight and in accordance with applicable accounting principles and rules. Principles such as "true and fair presentation, consistency, and prudence" are used in all G-10 countries.

[2] Central Bank of West African States. Members are Benin, Burkina Faso, Côte d'Ivoire, Guinea-Bissau, Mali, Niger, Senegal, and Togo.

[3] The secured portion can be classified as substandard. The unsecured portion may be classified either doubtful or loss depending on the possibility of collection.

[4] A past due unsecured loan can be classified as "doubtful" if it was classified as "substandard" in the previous examination, and the principal has not been reduced at least 20 percent during the previous 12 months.

[5] Six months overdue for an unsecured loan, or six months for a secured loan not in the process of collection and interest unpaid for six months, and loans classified as "doubtful" on which no payment has been done for the last 12 months. Past due loans that are well secured may be classified as substandard-secured.

Colombia, Czech Republic, Kuwait, Peru, Rwanda, Slovak Republic). Loss category tends to refer to past due beyond one year.

Relying solely on past due introduces a strong bias to recognize losses at a late rather than an early stage. Past due is sometimes used as a proxy when other information is not sufficiently objective, or as a reference to other laws and regulations (i.e., commercial or accounting laws). Many countries recognize that loan classification should go beyond this ex post indicator and take into account more forward-looking criteria, particularly repayment capacity and cash flow of the borrower (Basel Committee, 1999b). For that reason, the U.S. guidelines outlined above stress various factors in addition to past due information. In January 2000, Korea introduced forward-looking criteria to reflect borrowers' capacity to repay (FSS, 2000). Previously, loan classification guidance was based mainly on delinquency and the presence of collateral, rather than repayment capacity of the borrower (Song, 1998). A more in-depth discussion of forward-looking criteria can be found later in the section on forward-looking provisioning and accounting principles.

Classification of Off-Balance-Sheet Items

Off-balance sheet activities are commitments or obligations by a bank to provide funds or loans under certain conditions. Typical off-balance sheet items are loan commitments, commercial letters of credit, stand-by letters of credit, and guarantees. Off-balance sheet transactions involve credit risks arising from the possibility that the creditworthiness of the customer will deteriorate between the time the commitment is made and the loan takedown occurs. The 1988 Basel Capital Accord (and its current draft revision) incorporates off-balance sheet items as additional risk for banks requiring capital. Considering that off-balance sheet activities hold credit risk, they should be treated the same as loans for classification. When evaluating off-balance sheet items for the purpose of valuation, careful consideration should be given as to whether the bank is irrevocably committed to advance additional funds under the credit agreement. Good practice requires that if there is a defined weakness that jeopardizes repayment of a commitment, the amount of the commitment be classified accordingly. It should be separated into two components: the direct amount (the amount that has been already advanced) and the indirect amount (the amount that must be advanced in the future).

In some derivatives—for example, swaps—where the credit risk is limited to the replacement cost, the maximum loss is only the cost of replacing the contract. In those cases, banks can classify the credit equivalent of off-balance sheet items by using the Basel conversion factors.

Classification of Restructured Loans

Restructured (troubled) loans are loans that have been modified at favorable terms and conditions for the borrower owing to the borrower's financial condition or ability to repay. Restructuring (sometimes also referred to as "workout") may include modification of terms—for example, a reduction in the interest from that amount originally agreed to or a reduction in the principal amount. It may also involve the transfer from the borrower to the bank of such assets as real estate, receivables from third party, other assets (e.g., additional collateral), or an equity interest in the borrower in full or partial satisfaction of the loan.[4]

In addition to the prospects and viability of the restructured debtor, the bank's workout capability is an important factor in determining whether a restructured loan agreement is viable. The ultimate loss to the bank may be higher than the losses incurred if the bank had taken early action to seize and liquidate collateral. Credit analysts of banks that classify restructured loans should ensure that restructuring is based on sound underwriting standards such as effective workout plans and internal controls.

Table 2.2 surveys some country practices. A restructured loan might generally be classified as substandard (as done for example in Czech Republic) or in the same category as prior to restructuring (as done in the Philippines). If justified, a classification as special mention or pass might be considered (Thailand).[5] Then, after a reasonable period of demonstrated payment performance (e.g., six months), banks would upgrade a restructured loan. However, if the restructured loan again runs into difficulties, it would also be appropriate to classify a formally restructured loan according to the classification grades.

The Notion of "Nonperforming Loans"

The notion of nonperforming loans or assets is often used as a proxy for asset quality of a particular bank or banking system. Although there is no uniform definition of nonperforming assets, in many countries, including most Group of Ten (G-10) countries, assets are considered to be nonperforming when principal or interest is due and unpaid for 90 days or more; or interest payment equal to 90-day interest or more has been capitalized, refinanced, or rolled over. As shown in Table 2.3, for countries that are using standard classification systems, nonperforming is often (but not always) defined as loans in the three lowest categories (*substandard, doubtful, loss*). Nevertheless, as illustrated in Table 2.1, the definitions of loan classification vary across countries.

---

[4] A loan extended or renewed at a stated interest rate equal to the current interest rate for new debt with similar risk is not a restructured troubled loan.

[5] For example, when a new credible debtor replaces the original borrower. If additional loans are extended to borrowers with restructured loans outstanding, new loans may be subject to the same loan classification category as the restructured loans consistent with the idea that credit risk classification should be done by borrower and not by loan.

Table 2.2. Classification of Restructured Loans in Selected Countries

Czech Republic	Classified as "substandard."
Indonesia	A restructured loan is classified based on the borrower's ability to pay under the new terms, but "substandard" at best. After *three payments* under the restructured terms, the loan can be reclassified into higher categories.
Italy[1]	Only the portion subject to restructuring is classified. After 12 months, banks must verify whether restructured loans should be classified as "bad debt" or "substandard."
Korea	A restructured loan is classified as "special mention," "substandard," "doubtful," or "loss" based on forward-looking criteria recently adopted (June 2000).
Malaysia	A restructured loan stays at the same classification as before. After the borrower has serviced the loan for *six months,* the loan can be reclassified as "performing."
Philippines	A restructured loan generally stays at the same classification as before.[2] After the borrower has serviced the loan for *three consecutive months,* the loan can be reclassified as "performing."[3]
Singapore	Restructured loans remain "nonperforming" and when the borrower has serviced the loan for *six months,* the loan may be reclassified as "performing."
Thailand	Under certain conditions (approval by the Corporate Debt Restructuring Advisory Committee, CDRAC or a Court) a restructured loan can be classified immediately as "performing."[4]

Sources: IMF, 1999b; and staff estimates.
[1]European Monetary Institute (1996).
[2]Loans not classified at time of restructuring become "special mention." Loans with capitalized interest and loans restructured a second time are classified substandard or below.
[3]Six months are required for loans not fully secured by real estate and where loan value is up to 60 percent of appraised value of real estate.
[4]CDRAC was formed by the Bank of Thailand and representatives from debtor and creditor groups to facilitate debt restructuring. See IMF, 1999b, p. 42.

For cross-country data comparability, a common definition of nonperforming loans is necessary (Institute of International Finance, 1999). Data comparison of nonperforming loans should also consider the level of specific provisions currently in place to cover losses. In some countries, the legal system makes it difficult for banks to write off nonperforming loans even when banks have established sufficient provisions.[6] In such cases, a figure of nonperforming loans may be misleading. Adjusting nonperforming loan figures for specific provisions would provide a better basis of analysis, especially for cross-country comparisons.

---

[6]For example, in some countries tax legislation prevents banks from writing off bad loans without a court decision on bankruptcy. Write-offs may be impeded by time-consuming bankruptcy procedures as well as by inefficient judicial systems.

Table 2.3. Nonperforming Loan Definitions in Selected Asian Countries, 1999

India	Assets overdue six months.
Indonesia	*Substandard, doubtful, loss* (over three months overdue).
Korea (2000)	Loans overdue more than three months plus nonaccrual loans.
Malaysia	*Substandard* (optional), *doubtful, loss* loans with principal or interest overdue by three or by six months (at banks' discretion).
Philippines	*Substandard, doubtful, loss* loans payable in monthly installments more than three months overdue and loans repayable on other terms if one month overdue.
Singapore	*Substandard* loans and below are those three months overdue.
Thailand	*Substandard, doubtful,* and *loss* loans are those three months overdue.

Source: IMF staff.

Actual levels of nonperforming assets in selected countries

The proportion of nonperforming loans during banking crises in emerging market countries has generally been much greater than in the industrial world (Alexander and others, 1997). Peak levels of nonperforming loans (in percent of total loans) in the banking sector were about 49 percent in Indonesia, 48 percent in Thailand, 19 percent in Malaysia, and 8 percent in Korea. In Nordic countries, at the peak of their crises, nonperforming loans reached about 10 percent of total loans; in the United States, during its savings and loans crisis, the shock of nonperforming loans was approximately 4 percent; and estimates for Japan were at 8 percent (using national definitions) (Barth, Nolle, and Rice, 1997; and BIS, 1998).

During normal times, the ratio of nonperforming loans relative to total assets for a sample of large banks in industrial countries is even lower—Canada, 1.92 percent; Denmark, 0.19 percent; France, 0.26 percent; Italy, 1.91 percent; Spain, 1.78 percent; and the United Kingdom, 4.62 percent (Barth, Nolle, and Rice, 1997, based on 1993 data).

Collateral

Collateral constitutes a claim by the lending bank on the debtor's assets in case of default or insolvency. Collateral often but not always plays a role in lending decisions and provisioning. Excessive reliance on collateral can be counterproductive, particularly if it substitutes for adequate credit analysis (Federal Deposit Insurance Corporation, 1997, p. 58; Herring and Wachter, 1999). Bank supervisors sometimes argue that bankers tend to manage uncollateralized loans with more care and more successfully than those secured by collateral.

The most common collateral for commercial or housing loans is real estate. Because property prices may change over time, many supervisors issue guidelines on the ratio of loan value to collateral. For example, several supervisory authorities limit mortgage loans to around 70 percent of valuation (Hungary, Indonesia, Slovak Republic, and Thailand).

The value of collateral is normally not sufficient for determining whether a loan is impaired. Weaknesses in the legal systems and other obstacles make it difficult to ensure rights in foreclosing and disposing of collateral. This should be taken into account in the valuation of collateral. Collateral should be taken into account in establishing provisions. In calculating provisions, a conservative value of the collateral could be deducted from the loan amount. When other sources of repayment become inadequate over time, the importance of the collateral value in the analysis increases.[7]

A credit quality review focuses on two items: the original source of repayment, and the borrower's ability and intent to fulfill the obligation without liquidating the collateral that was used to secure the loan. The lending institution must have sufficient information concerning the condition, location, liquidity, and marketability of collateral to demonstrate the collateral's capacity to allow full repayment of the obligation. Collateral should be conservatively valued by reliable, independent experts, and, in general, little or no value should be ascribed to items such as plant and machinery, because the resale value is often subject to rapid changes.

Loan-Loss Provisioning

Loan-loss provisioning is the vehicle for adjusting the value of loans so as to reflect loan review and classification.[8] For example, when a review shows that a loan value has become "doubtful," a provision needs to be established to reflect the loss of loan value. In some respects, provisioning is similar to the concept of depreciation of the property and equipment for nonbanks (Dziobek, 1996). The cost of provisions constitutes a normal business expense and reduces bank profit. From a prudential perspective, an important distinction is made between specific and general provisions. This is discussed in the following section. This section also provides some country examples.

---

[7]This factor would have been different for failed banks during banking crises in Latin America and Asia, where a large amount of connected lending was not collateralized.

[8]For accounting purposes, it is important to differentiate clearly between the expense associated with provisioning (an income statement item that represents the write-off or charge off to recognize an impairment loss), and the resulting balance sheet item (a stock concept, referred to as an "allowance account" in recent international accounting standards). In this chapter, the term "level of provisioning" is used to refer to the balance sheet item, and provision for the income item.

General and Specific Provisions

The Basel Capital Accord and subsequent amendments differentiate between general and specific provisions. The main difference is that general provisions are for possible or latent losses not yet identified, whereas specific provisions reflect identified losses. In some countries, banks are required to hold general provisions as a certain percentage of total loans or assets. Such a requirement may be based on a global analysis of past loss experience rather than on (specific) identified losses.

Specific provisions are based on loan classification as described earlier. These reflect losses already identified. The level of such provisions typically varies with the degree of loan value deterioration as illustrated in the following paragraphs. The definitions and rules concerning general and specific provisions vary across countries, but banks should be familiar with the important conceptual difference between a provision for latent losses versus provision for already discovered losses. The conceptual distinction matters for the bank's calculation of capital. Specific provisions should never be considered bank capital, while general provisions can, to some extent, be considered bank capital.

Levels of Required Provisions in Selected Countries

General or specific provisions should reflect the probability of loss or the actual reduction in value, given the loan review. To arrive at such exact measures, however, significant information and experience are necessary, and such knowledge is not always available to many banks or in most countries. Levels of losses can also change over time, depending on the overall economic condition, the evolution of a credit culture, contract law, and court systems' efficiency.

In most G-10 countries banks decide the level of provisions, while external auditors and the banking authority assess the adequacy of banks' allowance for bad debts. As shown in Table 2.4, in many countries bank supervisors establish required levels of provisions. Standard levels seem to gravitate toward 20 percent of loans for the substandard category, 50 percent for doubtful, and 100 percent for loss. In some countries banks are also required to hold a general provision, which may be considered as a proxy for more forward-looking approaches to provisioning. The summary in Table 2.4 does not necessarily reflect the full detail of existing rules. Aspects such as value of collateral or differentiation of required provision by type of loans are in place in many countries. Nevertheless, Table 2.4 provides a broad idea of the levels currently in force in a range of countries. G-10 countries do not publish comparable data.

Table 2.4. **Levels of Required Provisions in Selected Countries, 2000**[1]
(In percent)

Country	Pass[2]	Special Mention[3]	Substandard	Doubtful	Loss
Argentina	1	5	25	50	100
BCEAO[4]	n.a.	n.a.	50	100	n.a.
Chile	0	1	20	60	90
Colombia	0	1	20	50	100
Czech Republic	2	5	20	50	100
India	0.25	n.a.	10	20–100	100
Indonesia	1	5	15	50	100
Korea[5]	0.5	2	20	50	100
Kuwait	2	Management decision	20	50	100
Malaysia[6,7]	1.5	n.a.	20	50	100
Mexico	0.5	10	45	65–85	100
Peru	1	3	30	60	100
Philippines[7]	2	5	25	50	100
Poland	0	5	20	50	100
Russia	1	n.a.	20	50	100
Rwanda	n.a.	n.a.	20	50	100
Slovak Republic	0	5	20	50	100
Thailand	1	2	20	50	100

Sources: IMF (1999a) p. 45; Moody's Banking System Outlook; BIS (1998).

[1]For commercial loans, G-10 countries do not have such general guidelines. Banks are expected to develop suitable and appropriate levels of provisioning based on loss experience and accounting practices.

[2]Considered general provision in Czech Republic, India, Indonesia, Korea, Kuwait, Malaysia, Philippines, Singapore, and Thailand.

[3]Considered general provision in Korea and Thailand.

[4]Central Bank of West African States. Members are Benin, Burkina Faso, Côte d'Ivoire, Guinea-Bissau, Mali, Niger, Senegal, and Togo.

[5]That portion of a loan classified doubtful or loss that is fully secured will normally be classified substandard to the extent of the market value of collateral.

[6]Computed against total outstanding loans, including interest, and net of interest in suspect and specific provisions.

[7]Provision computed against uncollateralized portion, in case of doubtful and loss.

Phasing in provisions

Should a new (tighter) provision requirement be phased in over time, giving banks a chance to plan for this additional expense, or should provisioning rules be fully applied without a phase-in period to show the actual level of capital and to increase transparency? A less than full application of provisioning rules may weaken the transparency of capital ratios, arguing for instant application of (tighter) rules, even if capital ratios fall drastically. Such a move might be accompanied by a policy of phasing in capital requirements over time.

A number of countries, including Japan, opted for the immediate application of provisioning requirements without a phase-in period. By contrast, in several Asian countries, the authorities devised systems to phase in more stringent provisioning requirements. For example, in the Philippines, a general provision was phased in starting from 1 percent in October 1998 to 1.5 percent six months later, and to the full level of 2 percent another six months later, by October 1999. Similarly, in Thailand, provisions were phased in over two-and-a-half years (July 1998 until the end of 2000). In countries where phase-in periods were established, the authorities placed great emphasis on setting an explicit time schedule of introducing the more stringent loan classification and provisioning requirements, as well as capital adequacy requirements.

Income and Expense Recognition

Loan classification can directly affect a bank's income statement. For example, the classification of a given loan may lead to a change from accrual-based to cash-based income recognition. As illustrated in this section, this may reduce income and, hence, profits and capital. Provisions constitute a business expense and thus enter directly into a bank's income statement. Improper loan valuation often leads to an overstatement of income. Similarly, insufficient provisions translate into underestimation of business costs. Both lead to overstatements of a bank's profits and its capitalization, and may entail higher-than-reasonable tax payments. These issues are explained in the remainder of this section.

Accrual versus Cash

Loan contracts generally involve ongoing payments of interest and principal until repayment or renegotiation. It is customary for banks to recognize income on an accrual basis, which means expected payments are booked as income. Cash accounting, on the other hand, is frequently used for nonperforming loans, where income is entered only when it is actually received. Switching accounting practices for a loan from accrual to cash accounting might therefore be considered a signal of loan deterioration.

Such a change may reflect a deterioration of the loan value but it does not, by itself, change the legal contract underlying a loan. Interest and principal, and possibly penalty fees, continue to accrue for the borrower while the bank begins to make adjustments for potential losses.[9] In other words, a move to cash accounting for impaired loans appropriately reduces a bank's income flow (as well as tax and dividend obligations) but allows the bank to take action to collect on it.

---

[9]When a loan is placed on cash accounting, interest capitalization should also be ceased. However, accrual of interest, penalty fees, etc., should be maintained in a separate account.

Where uncollected interest on nonperforming assets is added to income, the bank's true profits will be overstated and, thus, ultimately so will its capital and reserves. A bank might pay taxes on income that it has not actually received and is not likely to receive in the future. This leads to the payment of taxes and dividends on income unlikely to be earned. Inappropriate income recognition policies can rapidly distort banks' financial statements, especially when nominal interest rates are high.

To avoid these pitfalls, policies should define nonperforming assets and require the suspension of interest or cessation of accrual on such assets. For this reason, nonperforming assets should be placed on a nonaccrual status so that income is recorded only when it has actually been received in cash. Income adjusted in this way is the proper measure of profit for both prudential and taxation purposes.

The criteria for determining whether interest should cease to be recognized on nonperforming loans vary across countries. In some countries (e.g., Canada and the United States), interest is not normally recognized when the payment of interest and principal is 90 days or more overdue. Some countries (the Netherlands) leave interest recognition to the discretion of banks, and accrued interest is reviewed as part of the determination of provisions. Table 2.5 provides some examples. In France, the switch to cash accounting is made as soon as a loan is impaired, generally at 90 days or earlier. (Alternatively, if accrual continues, an allowance covering the entire amount must be established, which is equivalent to cash accounting.)

Tax Deductibility of Loan-Loss Provisioning

Provisions are regular business expenses and their tax treatment is an important policy issue. Well-designed systems for tax recognition of loan-loss provisions provide a strong incentive for banks to adequately provision and to do so in a timely fashion. Such a system should permit banks to deduct loan-loss provisions from taxable income as a normal operating expense in a manner similar to the depreciation, depletion, or amortization of other assets, provided that banks apply consistently and strictly the system of loan-loss provisioning based on the reasonable way of estimating loss probabilities (Dziobek, 1996). General provisions are often not tax deductible.

In some countries tax authorities allow tax deductibility only when the bank has declared a "write-off" or the borrower has declared bankruptcy. This restrictive practice suggests that provisions are not recognized as tax deductible on a timely basis (because bankruptcy is generally the final stage of an ongoing process of deterioration that should be recognized by loan valuation systems). Such

Table 2.5. When Is a Nonperforming Loan Placed on Cash Accounting? Some Country Examples

Country	Debt Payments Overdue[1] (Number of Days)
Argentina	90
Brazil	60
Canada	90
Chile	1
France	90
Korea	30
Singapore	90

Sources: Goldman Sachs (2000); Basel Committee (1998a).
[1] Other criteria may also apply.

restrictive tax systems also weaken banks' incentives to provision adequately even when prudential rules require provisioning.

Of course, in well-functioning financial markets, the role of external audit evaluation is an important one as well in determining provisioning expenses. In this context, if bank management fails to properly recognize loan impairment because of tax-based rules, the bank supervisor or the external auditor would be expected to suggest that there be an accounting adjustment to ensure proper valuation of assets. Similarly, in highly efficient markets, disclosure of accounting policies would push banks to publish the true value of assets. Box 2.1 summarizes some principles on disclosure of provisioning.

Linkages with Capital Adequacy

Loan valuation and capital adequacy are closely linked. This section provides a simplified mechanical description of the linkages between loan valuation, provisioning, and capital adequacy. It highlights that capital ratios are only meaningful when their components are well defined.

In a highly simplified form, a capital ratio is measured by comparing eligible capital to eligible assets. Following the Basel Capital Accord, capital is divided into Tier 1 and Tier 2 components (Tier 3 market-risk component is not considered in these examples). Tier 1 is paid-in capital, or shares and retained earnings. Tier 2 includes various debt elements and to some extent general provisions. Total assets may be risk weighted, although simple "leverage" ratios (without differential risk-weights) are also meaningful and are often used.

Capital is of crucial importance to banks because prudential corrective action is often based on capital performance. For instance, supervisors usually take corrective action if a bank's capital falls below the minimum required level. The following discussion of accounting practices provides some further details on how provisions may affect capital ratios.

> **Box 2.1. Public Disclosure of Loan Provisioning**
>
> As market forces are growing in prominence worldwide, the traditional emphasis on official oversight and safety nets has shifted toward increased reliance on market discipline.
>
> A bank should disclose to the public information about the composition of the loan portfolio based on a meaningful categorization of borrowers (e.g., commercial loans, consumer loans, and related parties); the number of nonperforming loans and of past-due loans by major categories of borrowers; and restructured loans.
>
> Information should also be provided on all significant accounting policies for the loans, nonperforming loans, and loan classification system; past-due loans; related provisions; income recognition on nonperforming loans; written-off loans; and accounting for recoveries. Disclosed information on loan-loss provisions, if presented in a constant and reliable format, constitutes an important indicator by which market participants can judge the condition of a bank.
>
> Information should be provided on a consolidated basis.
>
> Source: Basel Committee (1999b), pp. 31–37.

General provisions and capital

Using the Basel definition, general provisions are a cushion for unforeseen losses. In this sense, general provisions have some similarity with capital. Nevertheless, general provisions do reflect potential (as yet unspecified) losses and are therefore not fully included as capital. The Basel Capital Accord allows banks to include general provisions in Tier 2 capital, up to 1.25 percent of (risk) assets. Country practices vary and some countries do not allow banks to count general provisions toward regulatory capital.

Concerning the denominator of a capital ratio, a common practice in G-10 countries is not to change the value of assets when general provisions are established. The rationale is that a general provision does not refer to an identified loss.

Specific provisions and capital

Following a common accounting method, used in virtually all G-10 countries, specific provisions reduce income and are not included in capital. This practice is based on the logic that capital adequacy ratios should be a mirror of banks' ability to absorb *unexpected losses*. Specific provisions are established for an *expected loss* and, hence, should be excluded from capital.

Most G-10 countries require that banks deduct specific provisions from loans, which reduces the value of total assets and, hence, the value

Table 2.6. How Specific and General Provisions May Impact a Bank's Capital Ratio[1]

	Initial Capital Ratio Is Assumed to Be 10 Percent
Example 1	General provision of 2 deducted from income and fully included as (Tier 2) capital. Capital ratio: (100−90−2+2)/(100)= 10.0 percent
Example 2	General provision of 2 deducted from income and partially included as (Tier 2) capital (applying Basel limit of 1.25 percent of assets). Capital ratio: (100−90−2+1.25)/(100)= 9.25 percent
Example 3	Specific provision of 2, deducted from income and from loans (not included as capital). Capital ratio: (98−90)/(100−2) = 8.16 percent
Example 4	Specific provision of 2, deducted from income (not included as capital). Capital ratio: (100−90−2)/(100) = 8.00 percent

[1]Initial capital ratio is 10 percent. In each example, initial assets are 100, liabilities are 90, and the provision is 2, and a simple capital-to-asset ratio is calculated. Thus, before provisions, the ratio is (100−90)/100 = 10 percent. (Capital is calculated as a residual—that is, assets minus liabilities.)

of capital, which is a residual (assets minus liabilities). Applying this method, specific provisions reduce the numerator as well as the denominator of the capital ratio. The following simplified examples in Table 2.6 illustrate how general and specific provisions may affect a bank's capital ratio (capital divided by assets). The result depends on the nature and level of provision. As explained above, specific provisions are usually deducted from assets and general provisions are not, leaving the value of assets unchanged. Similarly, the inclusion in capital depends on the nature of provisions. The examples below are for a hypothetical bank with initial assets of 100, liabilities of 90, and capital (calculated as assets minus liabilities) of 10. A simple capital ratio for this bank equals 10. The first two examples assume a general provision of 2, leaving total assets unchanged at 100. In one case the provision is fully included in the capital, and in the other case it is not fully included in the capital (in observation of the Basel limit of 1.25 percent of capital). In the first example, the capital ratio remains unchanged at 10, and in the second example the ratio falls to 9.25.[10]

The impact of specific provisions on capital ratios is illustrated in Examples 3 and 4, in Table 2.6. The capital-to-asset ratio falls (because the numerator is always smaller than the denominator). The same logic applies to write-offs of nonperforming loans. Example 3 illustrates a case where specific provisions are not deducted from loans, an accounting practice commonly found outside the G-10.

---

[10]The value of total assets remains unchanged, however. Since total assets are often looked upon as an indicator of bank size and market share, this is a noteworthy aspect of general provisions.

> ### Box 2.2. Tax Deductibility of Provisions and Capital
>
> In the aftermath of the Asian crisis, a number of countries have opted for mandatory general provisions as a percentage of total loans. The following example illustrates the importance of its tax treatment.[1]
>
> Assumptions:
> 1. Income (before general provision) and before tax is 2.
> 2. Tax rate is 50 percent.
> 3. General provision is tax deductible.
>
> Value of assets remains unchanged.
>
> Case 1: before general provision.
>
> Income increases capital (retained earnings) by 1 after tax payment.
>
> Capital ratio: (100−90+1)/(100)= 11 percent.
>
> Case 2: making general provision of "1."
>
> General provision of 1 deducted from income and included as (Tier 2) capital (below Basel limit of 1.25 percent of assets). "Income after general provision and tax" increases capital (retained earnings) by 0.5.
>
> Capital ratio: (100−90 + 0.5 + 1)/(100) = 11.5 percent.
>
> By making a general provision, banks can increase the capital ratio, because they can reduce the tax payment by the amount of (general provision * tax rate). Therefore, banks have a strong incentive to make general provision up to 1.25 percent of assets.
>
> ---
> [1]This example assumes congruence of tax and prudential accounting, not usually found in practice.

In analyzing the impact of provisions on capital, the role of taxes must also be considered. Box 2.2 illustrates that tax deductibility can increase the capital ratio. This case may be applicable in emerging market countries that require banks to maintain a minimum level of general provisions, often as part of a more forward-looking approach to provisioning. Under such circumstances, the tax deductibility of general provisions can increase capital to asset ratios, providing a strong incentive to banks to comply.

Macroeconomic Aspects

Loan valuation and provisioning can have direct or indirect macroeconomic linkages. For example, on the fiscal side, the tax treatment of loan-loss provisions is important, as discussed in the previous section.

On the monetary side, loan classification and provisioning are incorporated in aggregate measures of credit to the economy. The number of nonperforming loans are also increasingly viewed as a measure of a bank's soundness. In the wake of systemic banking crises in many emerging market countries, figures on restructured loans are used as indicators of success in crisis management.

More broadly, the possible procyclical macroeconomic effects of classification and provisioning systems have been the subjects of recent debate. Some argue, for example, that provisioning practices with a focus on ex post factors may have played a role in amplifying financial crises, and regulators in many countries are encouraging banks to use more forward-looking loan valuation. The remainder of this section examines the monetary issues and discusses procyclical aspects in more depth.

Enhanced Data on "Credit to the Economy"

In many countries figures on domestic credit to nonbanks, a core component of monetary analysis, are reported on a gross basis, including provisions. Many industrialized countries now collect and analyze aggregate credit data on a net basis, subtracting specific provisions, because the use of gross-credit figures can distort results, especially in times of rapid deterioration of asset quality. Under such conditions, banks may incur significant losses and establish provisions that are not reflected in aggregate credit growth. This can distort macroeconomic relationships involving credit variables. Similarly, with high levels of nonperforming loans, liquidity management by banks and central banks becomes more difficult. This should be considered in interpreting monetary data. Frécaut and Sidgwick (1998) provide some empirical evidence for these mechanisms. The ongoing work on macroprudential indicators at the IMF addresses the issues in more depth.

In this regard, additional information on loan classification and provisions would be important to obtain a fuller picture of the quality of credit growth. This allows for an adjustment of credit for provisions (subtracting provisions from the figure of credit to the economy), and an analysis of credit growth on a net basis (Frécaut and Sidgwick, 1998). Of course a one-time adjustment should not necessarily be interpreted as a contraction as it may simply show that the actual level of outstanding credit (adjusted for loan-loss provisions) is lower than previously thought.

Procyclical Aspects of Provisioning and Empirical Evidence

Classification and provisioning methods that emphasize ex post criteria, such as interest past due, could have a procyclical economic impact, an issue that has been raised in the context of the financial stability forum (Basel, 2000, and Commission Bancaire, 2000). Procyclical effects could be transmitted through several different channels.

For example, during an expansion, default rates typically fall, and banks relying mainly on ex post criteria respond by reducing the level of provisions, showing higher profits, and distributing more dividends. During the next contraction, when default rates rise, banks are suddenly faced with the need for higher provisions, reducing capital, lowering the banks' financial strength, and reducing their ability to lend, thus contributing to a protracted downturn. An amplified effect could result when lending behavior changes over the course of the business cycle. For example, during a protracted expansion, the quality of new loans may decline because banks become too optimistic about borrowers' repayment capacity. In this case, loan review and provisioning systems based on ex post criteria may fail to register the decline in asset quality while the expansion is ongoing. During the following contraction, banks may then experience a disproportionate rise in nonperforming loans.

The effect might also come through a different channel. Regulators sometimes react to systemic weakness by swiftly tightening provisioning regulations. This can have procyclical effects similar to the ones described above. In theory these appear to be pervasive mechanisms, but the empirical evidence is less convincing. Bank behavior seems to have macroeconomic effects but not necessarily procyclical ones.

Empirical evidence of procyclical effects of ex post provisioning

The following selective review of the literature illustrates that it is difficult to establish empirically that bank behavior has procyclical macroeconomic effects and even more difficult to prove that deficient provisioning plays an important role. Thus, proposals to design "anticyclical" provisioning requirements would appear to be virtually impossible to operationalize. There is, however, evidence for cyclicality of bank behavior, and ex post provisioning practices may provide incentives for banks to engage in such behavior. Some country studies show that loan standards loosen during expansions and ex post provisioning systems would typically fail to detect deteriorating asset quality on a timely basis. More forward-looking analyses would be able to capture changes in lending behavior and changes in asset quality at an early date and would, therefore, be a useful tool for managing risk. This conclusion supports the view held by the Basel Committee (1999a).

In a study of procyclicality of risk-based capital ratios, the Basel Committee (1999a) examined potential procyclical effects of capital requirements. It noted that in times of recession banks are likely to incur higher levels of loan losses and, consequently, higher levels of loan-loss provisions (reducing capital) than when the economy is strong. Retained earnings from bank profits, which add to Tier 1 capital, also tend to rise in boom periods and fall during recessions. But cause and effect remain indeterminate.

The literature on cyclical bank behavior and credit crunch provides some empirical evidence of cycles of bank behavior. An example is a large panel data analysis covering over two million bank loans by 580 U.S. banks from 1977–93 (Asea and Blomberg, 1998). This study shows an impact on aggregate economic activity, but not necessarily a procyclical one. A German-U.S. comparison of bank lending behavior suggests that German banks show less variability in lending patterns than U.S. banks (Grossl-Gschwendtner, 1993).

The credit crunch literature postulates that a shortage of bank capital leads to downward shifts in the supply of credit and finds considerable evidence for procyclical bank behavior. Given the close linkages between capital and provisioning, the credit crunch hypothesis would appear to be consistent with ex post provisioning systems.

Some studies find credit crunches in the United States during the 1990–91 recession and in Japan in the recession after 1991. In the United States, a sharp credit slowdown was recognized before and during the 1990–91 recession. A complicating factor, however, in almost all studies is the regulatory response during banking distress (when regulations are often tightened)—a factor that may itself have produced a procyclical effect during the downturn. However, from a policy perspective, this may be intended in order to bring credit expansion to a more sustainable path.

For example, in the United States, banking regulations were tightened during the early 1990s.[11] Bernanke and Lown (1991) found a positive correlation between loan growth from the second quarter of 1990 through the first quarter of 1991 and capital ratios at the beginning of the periods, whereas Peek and Rosengren (1992) found that banks in New England that were the target of formal regulatory actions substantially reduced their lending following such actions.

In Japan, starting in 1989, banks were faced with high levels of nonperforming loans in the aftermath of the stock market crash and subsequent decline of property prices after 1992 (Kanaya and Woo, 2000). Though banks charged off nonperforming loans aggressively during the 1990s, the amount of nonperforming loans stayed at a high level. During the same period, Japan experienced the longest recession in

---

[11]The BIS risk-based capital standards began to phase in at the end of 1990 and were fully implemented in 1992. Also, in 1991, the Financial Deposit Insurance Corporation Improvement Act of 1991 codified Prompt Corrective Action, especially the mandatory closure of institutions when their capital ratios fall below 2 percent.

modern times. Several major financial institutions went into bankruptcy in 1997. The securities market scrutinized the conditions of financial institutions more severely, and the depositors, both institutional and retail, became conscious about risks. Supervisory authorities introduced stricter regulations in loan classification, including self-assessment schemes and the rules on restructured loans, as well as loan provisioning. Prompt corrective action was announced in 1997 and formally introduced in 1998. Bayoumi and Morsink (2001) find support for the credit crunch hypothesis in Japan. Although the evidence is mixed whether there was a capital crunch in Korea or Indonesia after the Asian financial crisis started in July 1997 (IMF 1999a and b, and Chan-Lau and Chen, 1998), banks in those countries found difficulties in complying with capital adequacy requirements under stricter loan classification and loan-loss provisioning rules.

In retrospect, it appears that in countries with systemic financial crisis, banks tended to underprovide against potential loss in their assets and, hence, overvalue their assets. In hindsight, loan values (and capital) were vastly overstated. This calls for more emphasis on accuracy in loan valuation and provisioning, including the use of more forward-looking methods. However, another lesson may be contained in the timing and phase in of more stringent rules. Overly ambitious timetables may unduly impede the economic recovery and slow down the return of the banking sector to solvency and soundness.

Emphasis on more forward-looking loan valuation to counteract bank myopia

There appears to be a broad move to incorporate more forward-looking (ex ante) factors in provisioning techniques to reflect more accurately the current economic value of a loan. Table 2.7 lists some examples of criteria for *ex post* versus forward-looking classification.

More forward-looking approaches to provisioning could help raise the overall level of bank soundness and hence a bank's ability to withstand economic shocks or cyclical trends. For example, Korea has opted explicitly for this approach. Supervisors and banks in many countries note the practical difficulties in implementing more forward-looking systems. Requiring general provisions for all loans, in addition to application of straight loan valuation and specific provisions, is a simple way of introducing forward-looking elements that may be effective. Several countries use this instrument (see Table 2.4). In industrial countries, general provisions are not usually a prudential requirement, although they are widely used voluntarily by banks to better cushion unforeseen shocks. A large Australian bank has adopted "Dynamic Provisioning," a model that focuses on anticipatory and forward-looking criteria in es-

Table 2.7. Ex Ante Versus Ex Post Criteria for Loan-Loss Recognition

Ex Post Criteria (Examples)	Ex Ante Criteria (Examples)
• Interest and/or principal past due. • When the loss has been confirmed as a legal event.	• A loss is probable based on statistical analysis (including arrears, aging of balances, past loss experience, current economic conditions). • Credit quality has deteriorated because the lender no longer has reasonable assurance of collection in accordance with the terms of the contract. • Loss is probable based on credit rating information. • Losses attributable to seasonal factors (annual fluctuations around an expected mean of losses over an economic cycle). • Inherent risk.

tablishing provisions. After some years of experience, the bank's management concludes that this model is a good one, evoking discipline and consistency in risk measurement and raising bank competitiveness. (Westpac, 1999). The forward-looking approach to provisioning raises some accounting and shareholder concerns that are discussed below.

Forward-Looking Provisioning and Accounting Principles

Consistency of forward-looking (ex ante) approaches to provisioning from a prudential and accounting perspective is an important issue that remains part of the public debate. From an accounting perspective, such practices raise a question about the nature of such provisions, and whether they can be clearly differentiated from "income smoothing" practices, which might give banks undue discretion in hiding or showing profits. The relevant standard is International Accounting Standard (IAS) 39 on Financial Instruments. According to this standard, impairment is deemed to have occurred when the carrying value of an asset exceeds the estimated recoverable amount. Objective evidence of impairment (or uncollectibility) generally tends to be based on observation of events that have occurred, rather than those that might occur. Paragraph 110 notes, however, that impairment might also consider whether a historical pattern of collections indicates that the entire face value of a portfolio of accounts receivable will not be collected. Impairment may be measured and recognized individually for financial assets that are individually significant, but it may also be measured and recognized on a portfolio basis for a group of similar financial assets.

IAS 39, therefore, does leave some room for ex ante provisioning; for example, in the form of general loan-loss allowances for a class or portfolio of assets. Accounting policies would need to be based on very sound criteria that are applied consistently from one accounting period to another to avoid the possibility of manipulation. The important issue from an accounting and transparency perspective is that such amounts can be clearly identified in the bank's capital.

Summary and Conclusions

Loan review and provisioning are important elements of bank-risk management systems and they are also used for bank supervision. In G-10 countries, banks are expected to use internal systems of loan valuation, although supervisors and auditors may also use various grids and systems to verify adequacy and application. Supervisors in many emerging market countries rely on standard systems of loan classification and set standard provisioning levels. Systems should have a forward-looking focus, considering such factors as borrower repayment capacity and economic conditions, as well as ex post factors such as interest past due. Due recognition should be given to off-balance sheet items. Collateral values should be considered but not overrated. A tax system that supports timely recognition of loan losses further supports a forward-looking system of loan valuation.

From a macroeconomic perspective, several observations can be made. In many non-G-10 countries aggregate measures of credit fail to take into account nonperforming loans and provisions. Given the actual levels of nonperforming loans, especially during financial distress, this can lead to considerable errors in policy analysis. Additional aggregate information on provisions and nonperforming loans would allow a fuller analysis of credit flows, particularly in countries with macroeconomic instability or systemic banking distress. Furthermore, the notion of nonperforming loans, an often-cited indicator of systemic bank soundness, does not have a uniform definition. Consequently, it should be used cautiously for cross-country comparisons.

Finally, a focus in many countries on ex post factors in analyzing loan quality and in taxation of bank profits can jeopardize systemic soundness, particularly during economic contraction. Best practices already stress forward-looking approaches to loan classification and provisioning. However, because of the operational difficulties of implementation, some countries use mandatory general provisions as a way to incorporate more anticipatory loan valuation. An interesting debate on the viability of up-to-date approaches to risk management, incorporating macroeconomic information, is ongoing.

Appendix: Loan Valuation in 12 Member Countries of the Basel Committee

1. When is impairment recognized?

    • When a loss is probable. 4 countries France, Italy, Sweden, United States

    • When there has been a deterioration in the credit quality of the loan to the extent that the lender no longer has reasonable assurance of collection in accordance with the terms of the contract. 5 countries Canada, Italy, Japan, Switzerland, United States

    • One of the above and management discretion. 5 countries Belgium, Germany, Luxemburg, Netherlands, United Kingdom

2. How is loan loss recognized in the financial statements?

    • Reducing the carrying amount of the loan and recognizing a charge in the statement of income. 12 countries

    • Setting up a liability and charge to income (one country permits both). 1 country Switzerland

3. How is each loan loss allowance presented in the balance sheet?

    • Loan loss allowance as deductions from assets. 12 countries

    • Loan loss allowances as liabilities (one country permits both). 1 country Switzerland

4. What conditions require cessation of accrual of interest?

    • Lender no longer has reasonable assurance of timely repayment. 7 countries Belgium, Canada, France, Japan, Luxemburg, Sweden, United States

    • Payment is contractually a certain period in arrears (unless collateral is sufficient). 5 countries Canada, France, Japan, Switzerland, United States

    • Lender has strong assurance that the full amount will not be paid. 2 countries Germany, Luxemburg

    • Management discretion/other. 5 countries Germany, Italy, Luxemburg, Netherlands, United Kingdom

Appendix: Loan Valuation in 12 Member Countries of the Basel Committee *(continued)*

5. Does the regulator have a system for classifying loans?

No.	3 countries	Netherlands, Switzerland, United Kingdom
Yes, conform with accounting.	2 countries	Belgium, Sweden
Yes.	8 countries	Canada, France, Germany, Italy, Japan, Luxemburg, Sweden, United States

Categories used:

Satisfactory/Pass.	Canada, United States
Loans involving no apparent risk.	Germany
Special mention.	Canada, United States
Loans involving increased latent risk.	Germany
Past due, secured.	Japan, Sweden
Loans with reduced interest.	Sweden
Sub-standard.	Canada, Italy, Japan, United States
Doubtful.	Canada, France, Japan, Luxembourg, Sweden, United States
Bad debts.	Italy
Value-adjusted loans.	Germany
Irrecoverable.	Canada, Japan, Luxembourg, United States
Restructured loans.	Italy, Japan
Loans being restructured.	Italy

Source: Basel Committee, 1998b.

References

Alexander, William E., Jeffrey M. Davis, Liam P. Ebrill, and Carl-Johan Lindgren, 1997, *Systemic Bank Restructuring and Macroeconomic Policy* (Washington: International Monetary Fund).

Asea, Patrick K., Brock Blomberg, 1998, "Lending Cycles," *Journal of Econometrics*, March–April 1998.

Bank for International Settlements (BIS), 1998, *Bank Restructuring in the Emerging Market* (Basel: Bank for International Settlements).

Barth, James, Daniel Noelle, and Tara N. Rice, 1997, "Commercial Banking Structure, Regulation and Performance: An International Comparison," March (Washington: Office of the Comptroller of the Currency).

Basel Committee on Banking Supervision, 2000, *Financial Stability and the Basel Capital Accord*, FSF Meeting (Basel: Bank for International Settlements).

———, 1999a, *Capital Requirements and Bank Behavior: The Impact of the Basel Accord* (Basel: Bank of International Settlements).

———, 1999b, *Sound Practices for Loan Accounting and Credit Risk Disclosure and Related Matters*, October (Basel: Bank for International Settlements).

——— 1998a, *Survey of the Valuation of Loans, Loan-Loss Provisions and Related Matters in Basel Committee Member Countries*. (Basel: Bank for International Settlements).

———, 1998b, *Ongoing Work in the Basel Committee's Accounting Task Force* (Basel: Bank for International Settlements).

Bayoumi, Tamim and James Morsink, 2001, "A Peek Inside the Black Box: The Monetary Transmission Mechanism in Japan," *IMF Staff Papers*, International Monetary Fund, Vol. 48, No. 1, pp. 22–57.

Bernanke, Ben S., and Cara S. Lown, 1991, "The Credit Crunch," *Brookings Papers on Economic Activity 2*, Brookings Institution, pp. 205–248.

Chan-Lau, Jorge A., and Zhaohui Chen, 1998, "Financial Crisis and Credit Crunch as a Result of Inefficient Financial Intermediation—with Reference to the Asian Financial Crisis," IMF Working Paper No. 98/127 (Washington: International Monetary Fund).

Commission Bancaire, 2000, "From Expected Loss to Dynamic Provisioning," (Paris: Commission Bancaire).

Dziobek, Claudia, 1996, "Regulatory and Tax Treatment of Loan Loss Provisions," IMF Paper on Policy Analysis and Assessment No. 96/6 (Washington: International Monetary Fund).

European Monetary Institute, 1996, "Definition of Bad and Doubtful Loans."

Federal Deposit Insurance Corporation, 1997, *History of the Eighties—Lessons for the Future*, Vol. II (Washington: FDIC).

Financial Supervisory Service Republic of Korea (FSS), 2000, Weekly Newsletter Vol. I, No. 11 (http://www.fss.or.kr).

Frécaut, Olivier, and Eric Sidgwick, 1998, "Systemic Banking Distress: The Need for an Enhanced Monetary Survey," IMF Paper on Policy Analysis and Assessment No. 98/9 (Washington: International Monetary Fund).

Goldman Sachs, 2000, *Latin American Financial Services Monthly*, May 10 (New York: Goldman Sachs Global Equities Research).

Grossl-Gschwendtner, Ingrid, 1993, "Regulation of the Financial System and the Stability of the Banking Sector: A Comparison between the United States and Germany," *Konjunkturpolitik*, Vol. 39, No. 5, pp. 286–314.

Herring, Richard J. and Susan Wachter, 1999, "Real Estate Booms and Banking Busts: In International Perspective," Working Paper No. 99–27 (Pennsylvania: University of Pennsylvania: Wharton School Financial Institutions Center).

Institute of International Finance (IIF), 1999, *Report of the Working Group on Loan Quality*, July (Washington: Institute of International Finance, Inc.).

International Monetary Fund, 1999a, *Financial Sector Crisis and Restructuring—Lessons from Asia*, Occasional Paper No. 188, by Carl-Johan Lindgren, Tomás Baliño, Charles Enoch, Anne-Marie Gulde, Marc Quintyn, and Leslie Teo (Washington: IMF).

———, 1999b, *IMF-Supported Programs in Indonesia, Korea, and Thailand: A Preliminary Assessment*, Occasional Paper No. 178, by Timothy Lane, Atish R. Ghosh, Javier Hamann, Steven Phillips, Marianne Schulze-Ghattas, and Tsidi Tsikata (Washington: IMF).

Kanaya, Akihiro, and David Woo, 2000, "The Japanese Banking Crisis of 1990s: Sources and Lessons," IMF Working Paper No. 00/7 (Washington: International Monetary Fund).

Moody's Banking System Outlook (New York, various issues).

Peek, Joe, and Eric S. Rosengren, 1992, "The Capital Crunch in New England," *New England Economic Review*, pp. 21–31 (Massachusetts: Federal Reserve Bank of Boston).

Song, Inwon, 1998, "Korean Banks' Responses to the Strengthening of Capital Adequacy Requirements," Pacific Basin Working Paper Series No. PB 98-01, (California: Federal Reserve Bank of San Francisco).

U.S. Federal Reserve System, 2000, Commercial Bank Examination Manual, Section 2060.1 (March).

Westpac Bank, 1999, *Annual Financial Review* (Sydney: Westpac Bank).

3

Domestic Lending in Foreign Currency

FERNANDO L. DELGADO, DANIEL S. KANDA,
GRETA MITCHELL CASSELLE, AND R. ARMANDO MORALES

The availability of foreign currency loans to domestic borrowers has expanded as a natural result of increased global liquidity and the liberalization of domestic financial systems. These loans have also expanded because of negative incentives resulting from implicit government guarantees on the exchange rate or the expectation of governmental support of certain financial institutions and because of a supervisory environment that did not fully incorporate all relevant risks into lending decisions. Moreover, some stabilization policies have often resulted in relatively higher interest rates on domestic currency loans, which along with somewhat stable exchange rates made it attractive for domestic agents to borrow in foreign currency even when their businesses essentially dealt in domestic currency (see Bank for International Settlements, 1998). Banks generally transfer currency risk to customers who commit to debt service payments in foreign currency, regardless of the currency denomination of their revenues, in the expectation that the currency risk element implicit in domestic interest rates will not materialize during the term of the loan. Concerns about the potential sudden deterioration in bank portfolios during currency crises have led policymakers to consider prudential

---

The authors would like to thank the comments and assistance from the staff of the IMF's Monetary and Exchange Affairs Department (MAE), in particular participants in the MAE seminar on the subject, and from Richard K. Abrams, Daniel Dueñas, Claudia Dziobek, Charles Enoch, Huw Evans, Peter Hayward, Alain Ize, David Marston, Elizabeth Milne, Thordur Olafsson, Mark Stone, and Delisle Worrell, and from Natalie Baumer for her editorial assistance.

instruments that would discourage banks from lending to agents whose revenue is not denominated in the currency in which they borrowed, while encouraging them generally to manage foreign exchange and credit risks more actively.

In economies whose currencies are not internationally accepted, economic factors that undermine credibility in the domestic currency will condition the assessment of risks and will further affect the choice of the currency of financing. The issue of bank domestic lending in foreign currency can then be re-addressed as one of borrowing in a currency accepted by others for international transactions by agents whose revenue is denominated in a currency only accepted domestically.[1] The continuous uncertainty about potentially high expected depreciation may lead to equally high real interest rates in domestic currency, a factor that in turn makes borrowing in a foreign currency dangerously attractive and raises the likelihood of systemic banking problems. Box 3.1 illustrates the limits to which bank lending in foreign currency can reach following a sudden depreciation of the domestic currency.

This chapter focuses on when supervisory limits to banks' domestic lending in foreign currency are appropriate, considering both economic and supervisory grounds, and when internal policies and prudential measures are acceptable to address these risks. Particular attention is given to characterizing the nature of risk exposure and differentiating between prudential limits and discriminatory standards or indirect capital controls. Following the chapter's introduction, the second section describes the nature of the risks involved in foreign currency lending, whereas the next section discusses the incentives to assume currency and credit risk and the need for prudential guidelines. The following section describes best practices in terms of risk management guidelines, internal policies, and prudential and supervisory measures. The final section provides conclusions based on the preceding analysis.

Risks of Banks' Domestic Lending in Foreign Currency

Compound Credit and Currency Risk

The compounding of credit and currency risks inherent in banks' domestic lending in foreign currency results from counterparty exposure.

---

[1]Hard currencies of worldwide acceptance include the U.S. dollar, the euro, the yen, and the British pound. Currencies with regional acceptance could be hard currencies relative to those only accepted in the home country. Pegged currencies, to the extent that they are subordinated to a third party's currency, are in principle weaker, as their sustainability depends on the availability of the third party's currency in central bank reserves.

Box 3.1. The Effect of U.S. Dollar Lending in Ecuadorian Domestic Markets on the Banking Crisis

Ecuador maintained the exchange of the sucre within a bank that was kept relatively stable for several years, while fiscal imbalances resulted in rates on sucre-denominated deposits and loans that were substantially higher than those denominated in U.S. dollars (see the first figure). As a result, a large number of households and corporations, even those without dollar-denominated income, decided to borrow in U.S. dollars, on the expectation that reduced interest rates would compensate the possible exchange rate depreciation during the life of the loan. Banks also favored domestic lending in U.S. dollars in order to reduce their consolidated depreciation during the life of the loan. Banks also favored domestic lending in U.S. dollars in order to reduce their consolidated foreign exchange exposure, since a sizable share of their funding was in dollar-denominated deposits through their off-shore subsidiaries.[1] By January 1999, over 70 percent of total banking sector credit was denominated in U.S. dollars.[2]

The compound credit risk created by the high volume of the U.S. dollar-denominated lending was not appropriately assessed by bank risk management systems, nor did the bank supervisory authority introduce appropriate regulations. As a consequence, reserves and provisions of the banks were grossly inadequate to confront a large depreciation of the sucre. From January to December 1999 the sucre/U.S. dollar exchange rate depreciated by 191 percent (see the second figure).

Interest Rates
(Annual percentage)

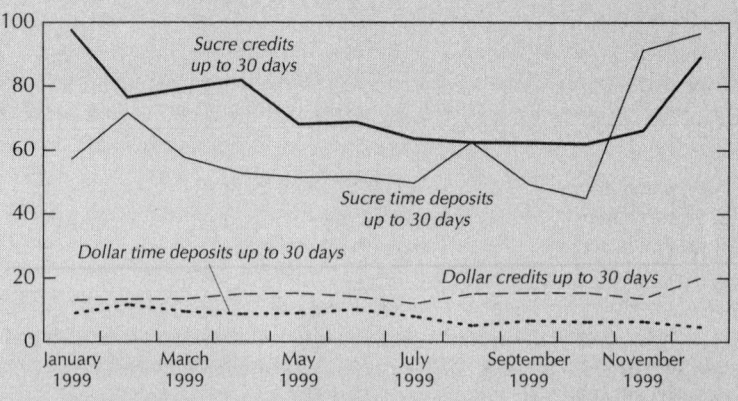

---

[1] Early in 1996, Ecuador introduced limits on banks' foreign exchange net open positions.
[2] Although there is no statistical data, it is estimated that approximately three-fourths of borrowers in U.S. dollars did not have U.S. dollar-denominated income.

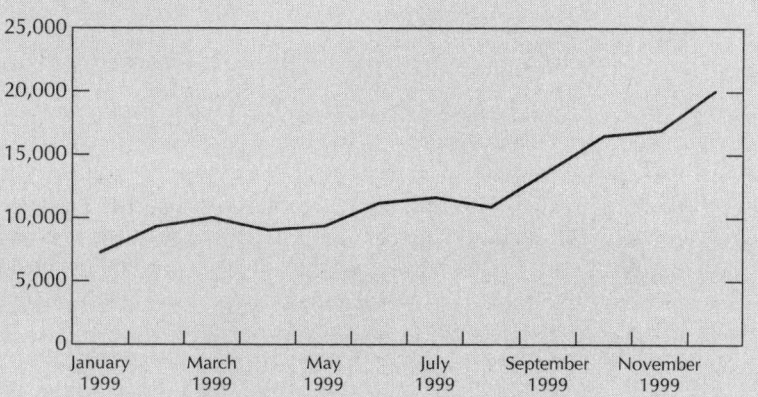

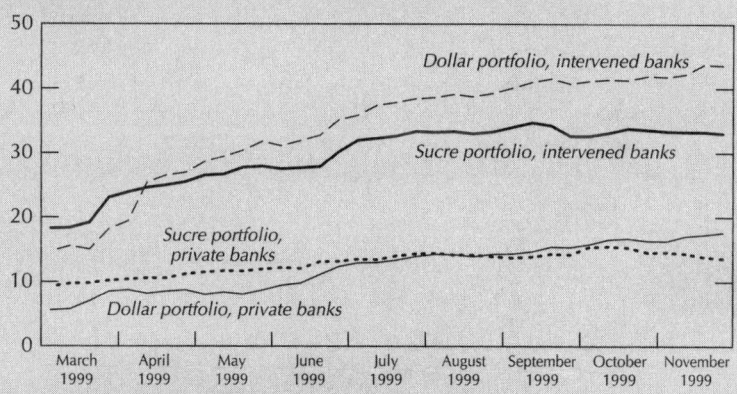

A number of other factors, ranging from external shocks affecting the productive sector[3] to the freeze of most of the banking system deposits, also contributed to reducing liquidity of Ecuadorian corporations and resulted in a substantial increase in the nonperforming loan ratio, which jumped from 10 percent in December 1998 to over 40 percent in December 1999. Nonperforming loan ratios of U.S. dollar-denominated portfolios increased well above those denominated in sucres (see the third figure), illustrating how the compound risk involved in foreign exchange lending to domestic borrowers could be a major force behind banking crisis.

---

[3]These included El Niño floods, white spot epidemic affecting shrimp production, and other similar shocks.

This exposure may result from a counterparty cash flow that is predominantly in domestic currency—for example, in the case of import financing of capital goods in foreign currency for the production of nontradable goods, which only generate domestic currency revenue. Import financing expressed in foreign currency is customary, especially when financial institutions are concerned about potential convertibility problems at the time of settlement. However, by not refinancing or hedging the obligations, the borrower remains exposed to an exchange rate risk, which translates into a credit risk for the financing institution. Counterparty exposure also results from risk that the domestic currency market value of the collateral backing the obligations to the bank declines below what is required to cover the obligations—for example, the use of real estate assets as collateral for the financing of an export activity. In this case, the borrower does not face direct exchange rate risk; however, the bank is exposed to a potential credit risk that would be triggered by industry- or firm-related adversities, when, in addition, the value of the collateral declines below the value of the related obligation. Because the same demand factors support domestic activities and asset prices, it is not unusual that countries experience both types of effects simultaneously.

Other Risks

Other risks particular to bank domestic lending in foreign currency include *currency* and *transfer* risks. *Currency risk* (a type of market risk) results from the probability of immediate large losses associated with the impact of exchange rate instability inherent in the foreign exchange business.[2] This type of risk may also affect those institutions that lend in foreign currency with a balanced foreign exchange position. For example, this situation would occur if a bank sets a loan-loss provision because of increased currency risk, which would subsequently decrease the value of its assets, thus creating an open position. Therefore, the incorporation of an exchange rate risk may turn an ex ante balanced foreign exchange position into an ex-post-uncovered open position.[3] This type of risk has been analyzed particularly in connection with open foreign exchange positions (Basel Committee on Banking Supervision, 1980).

Transfer risk derives from lending in a currency other than that of the country in which the borrower resides. This risk arises from the ability

---
[2]Currency risk is also denoted as exchange rate risk for the purpose of this chapter.
[3]Discrepancies of ex ante and ex post open foreign positions could be dramatic as illustrated by the case of Chile in the early 1980s.

of borrowers to obtain the foreign exchange necessary to repay the debt. It includes the risk that, due to lack of foreign currency reserves (usually caused by a currency or debt crisis), a borrower's local currency holdings and cash flow could not be converted into a sufficient quantity of foreign currency to repay their loans.[4]

Foreign currency loans also entail additional risks, which are the same potential concerns seen in any typical lending product. Those common risks may be captured in three broad categories: *credit, market* (interest rate and liquidity), and *compliance* (internal policies and procedures, operational and legal) risks. Because of their commonality with other lending products, these risks will not be addressed in this chapter.

Borrower and Lender Incentives to Assume Credit and Currency Risk

Credit Risk, Exchange Rate Risk, and Arbitrage

Ideally, complete and continuous arbitrage across currencies should lead to perfectly equivalent ex ante and ex post financial costs of borrowing in domestic or foreign currency in conditions of perfect competition, complete information, full flexibility of prices, and full capital mobility. However, the timing, duration, and magnitude of exchange rate instability have proven extremely difficult to anticipate across exchange rate regimes—a situation that complicates the measurement of foreign exchange risk. Thus, even in the best of conditions, perfect arbitrage would not be possible at all times or within short-term periods.[5]

In this context, risks may not be fully internalized by economic agents. Banks may not fully assess credit risk, and borrowers may misperceive exchange rate risk. However, even if supervisors have reason to believe that the lack of internalization of risks is a severe problem, inappropriate attempts of correction may lead to disproportional limits to arbitrage opportunities. In the extreme, innovation in the financial market may be arrested, the allocation of financial resources may be suboptimal, and competitiveness may be diminished,

---

[4]A measure of transfer risk is a comparison of a country's ability to meet its external debt obligations from foreign currency reserves, cash flow, credit lines, salable assets, and its access to new foreign currency borrowing. However, it also relates to market arrangements to access foreign exchange and to capital controls.

[5]A recent study by MacDonald and Nagayasu (1999) shows that a relationship between real exchange rates and real interest rate differentials is more of a long-term nature.

especially if limits are introduced in the context of market-unfriendly government measures.[6]

Arbitrage could also be affected by the design of monetary instruments. Countries restrict coverage of deposit insurance for some types of foreign currency deposits, especially if they are not significant.[7] Countries issuing currency accepted for international transactions and many transition economies prefer reserve requirements on foreign currency deposits held in domestic currency, unlike countries experiencing protracted stabilization efforts and currency weakness.[8] Countries perceiving a recovery in demand for home currencies may prefer nonsterilized intervention to sterilization (see Marston, 1995). This may result in unbalanced incentives to borrow or lend in either domestic or foreign currency.

Borrower Incentives to Demand Foreign Exchange Credit

A borrower's preference for financing in either currency may be related to strategic decisions or to various cost incentives. The latter may result from imperfect arbitrage, policy-induced costs, or the inadequate incorporation of risks into the borrower's cost-benefit considerations.

Strategic incentives

In more developed financial markets, swap opportunities result from differences in comparative advantage for economic agents when borrowing in foreign currency and in domestic currency. This makes it sensible for both types of borrowers to exploit this advantage by borrowing and swapping the obligations.[9] This development could only result from allowing borrowers access to financing in different currencies.[10] Other strategic incentives to borrow in foreign currency for borrowers with domestic currency revenues may be related to the time structure of repayments and the possibility of indirect natural hedging.

---

[6]In March 1999, the Central Bank of Egypt restricted bank lending in dollars to borrowers with dollar revenues in parallel with the imposition by the government of trade restrictions and exchange controls.

[7]This is true for 21 countries out of a sample of 61—see Garcia (1999).

[8]In Eastern European economies, quick removal of inadequate incentives in favor of foreign currency deposits permitted some reversal of dollarization in the context of adequate macroeconomic policies. This may prove difficult for countries experiencing a long-standing preference for foreign currency. See Ize (1995).

[9]Thus, a company whose revenues are in domestic currency may still borrow in foreign currency and, by swapping the obligations, contract a liability in domestic currency.

[10]As the scope of the chapter is related to unhedged positions, swaps are not further analyzed.

- *Time structure incentives.* Because exchange rate depreciation directly affects the domestic value of the principal, the domestic value of repayments increases throughout the repayment period. For loans in foreign and domestic currency in equivalent terms, an increase in the rate of exchange rate depreciation matched by a higher interest rate would result in a more acute skewness of the repayment schedule for foreign currency loans expressed in domestic currency.[11]
- *Indirect natural hedging.* Economic sectors benefiting from an exchange rate depreciation compensate higher financial costs with additional revenue from a favorable switch in demand. Domestic providers of tradable goods and services to the domestic market would hedge against an increase in financial costs by borrowing in foreign currency, since a depreciation allows them to capture additional domestic and foreign demand.

Strategic incentives do not require supervisory response. Borrowers may have legitimate reasons to take advantage of a loan with back-loaded repayments, since further back loading constitutes a reasonable escape valve in times of distress. Economic sectors benefiting from the depreciation of the exchange rate could make legitimate and reasonable use of the hedging protection that results from borrowing in foreign exchange. However, inflationary processes may justify additional supervisory concerns. Since a back-loaded debt repayment schedule becomes even more attractive, uncertainty surrounding an inflationary period may lead borrowers to use back loading as a means to facilitate the delay of default.

Cost-benefit incentives to foreign exchange borrowing

Even in reasonably efficient financial markets, arbitrage is not perfect as a result of the economic distortions affecting financial cost equivalence across currencies.[12] Imperfect arbitrage will be reflected on

---

[11]The ratio of initial-final repayment quotas for domestic currency loans against foreign currency loans increases from 1.069 to 1.166 for a rise in the lending interest rate in domestic currency from 15 to 30 percent paired by an equivalent acceleration of exchange rate depreciation at a 5 percent interest rate in foreign currency.

[12]In other words, uncovered interest rate parity may not hold, among other reasons, on account of (1) imperfect markets, including incomplete liberalization of the capital account, insufficiently open financial systems, price rigidities, significant transaction costs, lack of competition, and limited information; (2) time-varying risk premiums, lack of risk neutrality, or irrational expectations of some sort (Frankel and Froot, 1990); (3) continuous policy shocks as a reaction of the monetary authorities to undesired exchange rate fluctuations (McCallum, 1994); (4) predominant impact of real disturbances on exchange rate volatility (Meese and Rogoff, 1988); or (5) slow convergence to equilibrium in the long term (Meredith, 1998; and Edison and Pauls, 1993). The list is by no means exhaustive. It is intended to include the main factors that may be relevant for the operational aspects of domestic lending in foreign currency.

a lag between the incorporation of expectations into interest rates and actual exchange rate changes. Even agents envisaging an exchange rate depreciation may prefer to borrow in foreign currency, especially on a short-term basis, if they perceive that the exchange rate would not change according to expectations at least until after the loans are repaid. Thus, borrowing in foreign currency might still be preferred even in times of increasing risk. In periods of liquidity problems, better informed agents modify their risk preferences faster, and they may reduce the range of alternatives for less-informed agents to adjust their own risks subsequently.

Continuous and uninterrupted convertibility and the associated market arrangements ensures the presence of a degree of credibility in internationally accepted currencies. As a result, overall risk neutrality between financing alternatives in different currencies is achieved. Unbalanced incentives are more likely in situations of protracted and severe instability combined with external vulnerability. To compensate for the long-lasting expectations of a large depreciation or even inconvertibility (transfer risk), governments frequently embark on a policy mix that combines a stable exchange rate with higher interest rates. For countries with a long history of instability, slow convergence of the real exchange rate to its equilibrium level in the context of high domestic interest rates may result in more costly domestic currency lending, regardless of the exchange rate regime.[13]

Lender Incentives to Supply Foreign Exchange Credit

The motivation to lend in foreign currency is related to the availability of foreign exchange resources and risk management considerations. The sources of financing may be long-term lines of credit, short-term capital inflows, or foreign currency deposits.[14] In all these cases, availability of resources may prevail over risk management con-

---

[13]Deviations from purchase power parity (PPP) may last on average between six to eight years. See MacDonald (1995).

[14]Banks' domestic lending in foreign currency is frequently related to dollarization, as the most obvious example of its unavoidable widespread practice, connected with the ample availability of deposits in foreign currency by residents. However, it is by no means the only case, neither the most dramatic. The collapse of the banking system in Chile in the early 1980s was the result of widespread lending in foreign currency financed with external loans. Chile converted 47 percent of bank loans originally denominated in foreign currency into domestic currency, and at the same time turned bank private external debt into sovereign debt. Dollarization remained low throughout that period. Cost-benefit incentives related to a fixed exchange rate regime had a more important role in encouraging this practice.

siderations in developing economies, as a result of one or more of the following factors:
- *Lack of medium-term sources of financing in domestic currency.* Foreign currency borrowing by banks or intermediated or guaranteed by the government normally complements domestic savings and may be the only available option for long-term financing in less developed financial markets. In such markets, and in the absence of government intermediation or guarantees, the banking system may well face the dilemma of lending in foreign currency without coverage or not lending, which may leave unsatisfied a particular demand for financing (especially long-term financing).[15]
- *Dollarization.* High inflation, negative real interest rates on domestic-currency-denominated assets, and frequent exchange rate devaluations can contribute to the rise of the ratio of foreign currency deposits over total deposits (see Baliño, Bennett, and Borensztein, 1999). The larger availability of deposits in foreign currency leaves few options to domestic banks than to on-lend these resources domestically.
- *Speculative capital inflows.*[16] Banks and foreign investors may have a common interest in channeling foreign exchange flows in some periods, attracted by high interest rates on a nonrisk-adjusted basis in terms of foreign currency. However, these high interest rate differentials may be the result of a low risk premium on foreign exchange resources, resulting in turn from the discount of implicit government guarantees, as a government embarked on enhancing its credibility would resist any possibility of default on these transactions. On the assumption that exchange rate stability would be preserved within the investment maturity time frame, such a decision artificially increases the availability of foreign exchange resources, especially at times of low interest rates in developed markets.[17] Even in cases where exchange rate flexibility is nominally allowed, the government may limit it to a

---

[15]If the government provides direct intermediation or guarantees for foreign credit lines, it may still undermine credibility in the domestic currency by increasing the public debt, even if the additional debt is hedged in international markets through swap or swap options. Industrial economies such as Germany, Japan, and the United States do not issue sovereign foreign currency debt, and the United Kingdom has only issued such debt in European currency units. Canada, Belgium, Denmark, and New Zealand have stopped issuing it. See Cassard and Folkerts-Landau (1997).

[16]See Johnston and Otker-Robe (1999) for a discussion of policy mix consistency and how it could affect capital flows.

[17]In addition, it is usually difficult to ascertain which factors are at work: See Marston (1995).

minimum precisely in periods when the currency is under pressure because of its impact on the real sector and on expectations.[18]

The Nature of the Problem

Banks' domestic lending in foreign currency is not a problem as such. As was stated previously, the availability of multiple sources of financing in terms of currency facilitated the development of swaps, related to the development of other derivative products in international financial markets. Because of strategic motives, this type of lending may exceed the borrowing requirements of economic agents whose revenue is in foreign currency. The preceding section illustrates that the problem of banks' domestic lending in foreign currency arises when the allocation of credit is not based on an adequate assessment of risks, which in turn would make this lending unduly inexpensive in times of exchange rate stability. In the extreme, this distortion may lead to a significant allocation of lending to borrowers whose activities appear profitable only because of the apparent low cost of credit.

Table 3.1 provides some indicators for a sample of countries with available data related to the analysis in this chapter. First, the share of foreign currency loans appears closely related to the share of foreign currency deposits, but there are cases where wide differences between both variables are observed (such as Belarus, Estonia, Hungary, and Mexico). Second, the share of exports to GDP does not show a close relationship with lending in foreign currency, which could be a rough signal that this type of lending is not predominantly allocated to activities generating foreign currency revenue.[19] Third, for some countries showing a large availability of foreign loans to banks to GDP (such as El Salvador, Malaysia, and Thailand), the share of foreign currency loans made by banks domestically appears surprisingly modest. Fourth, the last column shows casual evidence of the importance of cost-benefit factors: The apparent significance of the number of years out of the last five when borrowing in foreign currency has been less costly than

---

[18]Or alternatively, it may limit interest rate fluctuations. In Costa Rica, in the early 1990s, direct central bank control of interest rates on domestic currency deposits led to higher returns on foreign currency deposits, contributing to a rapid increase in foreign currency denominated deposits and encouraging foreign currency lending.

[19]A cross-section regression using this data shows that lending to agents that do not generate foreign currency revenue (proxied by foreign currency loans to total loans standardized by exports over GDP) is explained by both the availability of foreign currency deposits and the length of the period when borrowing in foreign exchange was less costly. These results are only illustrative.

Table 3.1. Indicators of Bank Foreign Currency Operations, 1999

	Share of Foreign Currency Deposits to Total Deposits	Share of Foreign Currency Loans to Total Loans	Exports of Goods and Services/GDP	Foreign Loans to Banks/GDP	Number of Years when Foreign Currency Loans were less costly[1]
Argentina	56.4	68.2	9.8	4.5	5
Belarus	70.7	38.1	61.8	2.0	2
Bolivia	92.6	96.2	19.7	10.5	5
Chile	10.5	9.15	30.4	4.4	4
El Salvador	8.6	13.8	18.2	11.7	5
Estonia	31.1	76.1	78.0	7.0	2
Haiti	33.7	37.3	13.3	0.8	3
Hungary	19.7	35.3	26.4	8.7	2
Indonesia	19.2	38.3	35.0	9.3	3
Israel	31.6	36.2	38.2	2.0	4
Malaysia	1.7	2.2	121.2	20.0	2
Mexico	8.2	34.0	31.2	3.2	4
Peru	77.8	81.7	13.6	5.5	5
Russia	44.6	45.6	45.0	18.7	4
South Africa	3.5	6.0	25.4	6.7	3
Thailand	1.4	8.8	58.9	22.8	3
Uruguay	83.0	59.5	17.1	14.9	5

Source: International Financial Statistics, EDSS, and BIS.
[1] For the years 1995–1999, considering end-of-period interest rate differentials and subsequent annual exchange rate depreciation.

borrowing in domestic currency, considering the interest rate differential at the beginning of the period and the exchange rate depreciation in the subsequent year.

Internal Policies, Supervisory, and Prudential Best Practices

The Need for Guidelines

Because lending in foreign currency has not been a matter of concern for industrial countries, industrial-country bank regulations have not served as a reference for developing economies. In the absence of a framework to address this problem, developing countries have frequently resorted to exchange restrictions to forcefully limit these operations during crises. Practices followed by the countries reporting to the IMF's *Annual Report of Exchange Arrangements and Exchange Restrictions* (see Appendix) show that, while degree and form of restriction on capital transactions varies, such restrictions are more common among developing and transition economies than among industrial countries.

The way in which developing countries and transition economies have addressed this issue depends also on several factors, such as the level of dollarization, the availability of foreign exchange, and concerns related to trade flows. Heavily dollarized economies can only impose some quantitative limits. Other developing countries allow only on-lending of credit from abroad to discourage domestic banks from competing to attract deposits in foreign currency from residents. Concerns about the continuous availability of loanable resources in foreign exchange seem to be behind "official approval requirements" as the favored restrictive tool. When limitations are based on the use of resources, the motivation appears more related to concern about affecting trade flows than to an intention to restrict the use of these resources to economic agents generating foreign currency revenue.

The trend toward the removal of capital controls and the globalization of financial flows will tend to limit the use of these restrictions. Recently, prudential mechanisms have been used to induce an effective internalization of foreign exchange risks in banks' decisions. This mechanism has been used with a high degree of improvisation and without direct practical references from industrial economies. This section presents guidelines that banks and supervisors could consider to manage this risk. Although most of the measures included in the guidelines are common to industrial and developing countries, they would be particularly relevant in countries with a large availability of foreign exchange resources from dollarization and short-term capital inflows relative to savings in domestic currency (particularly long-term).

The following set of guidelines are derived mainly from the limited experience of measures taken by countries after a banking crisis where domestic lending in foreign currency has played a major role and from extrapolating banks' exchange risk management and prudential measures to bank customers. The guidelines have been classified in two broad groups: internal policies and procedures for risk management; and supervisory and prudential guiding principles for banks' domestic lending in foreign currency.

Internal Policies and Procedures

The evaluation of bank policies, practices, and procedures and a bank's adherence to them, together with adequate management information systems, should be assessed in ensuring adequate internal oversight of domestic lending in foreign currency.[20] Fundamental to the success of banks' domestic lending in foreign currency is the strength of banks' respective management information systems and risk management systems.

---

[20]See Principles 11, 12, and 13 in Basel Committee on Banking Supervision (1997).

Regarding management information systems, banks should determine that such systems monitor: (1) the relative and absolute exposure related to foreign exchange to unhedged domestic borrowers, including the share in total lending and on total foreign currency deposits and other funding; (2) open positions and maturity structure of foreign currency assets and liabilities, including net lending in foreign exchange to domestic hedged and unhedged borrowers, and corresponding bank hedging positions; (3) hedging positions (including "natural hedges")[21] of borrowers in foreign exchange at an individual level, and the aggregated foreign exchange exposure of the corporate and household sectors and their corresponding hedging positions; (4) compliance with limits and procedures set in the risk management system; and (5) the direct and indirect impact of exchange rate fluctuations on future earnings.

Banks' risk management systems in this area share the same building blocks as the management of overall foreign exchange risk—namely, written policies and procedures; sound internal controls, accounting procedures and rules resulting in accurate valuation of assets and liabilities; formulas to allow the accurate measurement of the various forms of risk; steps to ensure that unexpected shocks do not unduly undermine the individual institution; and the availability of timely and accurate information on each specific risk (see Abrams and Beato, 1998).

Written policies and procedures should include specific provisions to manage the compound risk of domestic lending in foreign currency. Among the specific main guiding principles for risk management in banks' domestic lending in foreign currency are: (1) limits to unhedged foreign exchange open positions should be set "net of provisions" for counterparty risk derived from bank domestic lending in foreign currency to reduce the chances of a sudden exposure of a bank's position in case of a counterparty's default (the corresponding capital requirements would apply); (2) credit in foreign currency to activities generating foreign currency revenue should be categorized according to the standard classification criteria of a bank's asset portfolio, which should include an assessment of the eventual impact of the exchange rate on profitability driven by consequent changes in relative prices; (3) proper counterparty risk evaluation systems should be applied in the assessment of credits in foreign exchange to nonforeign exchange earners, interest rate spreads applied should reflect the compound risk,[22] additional guarantees should

---

[21] Borrowings for which the adverse exchange rate impact on domestic currency obligations is compensated by a positive impact on revenue and profitability.

[22] Appropriate pricing systems should be applied in which lending rates to unhedged borrowers are inclusive of the implicit or explicit incremental counterparty risk hedging costs for the banks.

be required if necessary, and conservative loan classification criteria should be applied particularly during periods of high exchange rate volatility; (4) appropriate limits on foreign currency loan concentration should be made; (5) collateral denominated in currencies different from the one in which the loans are expressed should be valued conservatively, allowing for a margin for exchange rate movements and providing for reappraisals in the face of eventual but substantial exchange rate changes; (6) maximum use of available hedging mechanisms should be pursued, as should their frequent reassessment, both for the bank and borrowers in foreign exchange; and (7) the viability of projects should be assessed independently of the currency of financing.

As part of internal risk management, banks should have hedging techniques appropriate to address exposures from foreign currency lending to domestic borrowers. In addition, banks should introduce clear written procedures that critically evaluate a borrower's ability to withstand adverse exchange rate changes, and protect banks from excessive exposure to direct exchange rate risk.[23] Limits on foreign currency lending to various types of borrowers should be clearly specified in written policies. Moreover, the Basel Committee on Banking Supervision recommends establishing a "maturity ladder" approach to future cash inflows and outflows over a series of specified time periods, taking into account the complicating factor of differences in currencies.[24] In addition, banks should analyze the results of "alternative scenarios," including the effects of higher interest rates or depreciation of the exchange rate.[25]

Sophisticated risk management systems include provisions for stress testing loans, foreign exchange exposures, and other activities.[26]

---

[23]For example, such procedures might include monitoring the size and trend of the borrowers' foreign exchange profits and cash flow, and requesting additional collateral or constituting appropriate provisions on unhedged foreign exchange loans to borrowers with domestic currency-denominated income, according to the magnitude of exchange rate depreciation.

[24]Basle Core Principles 6, 12, and 13 apply, in this case, related respectively to capturing market risk with respect to capital adequacy, maintaining appropriate systems to measure, monitor, and adequately control market risks, and establishing an overall risk management process.

[25]Recent events in Korea provide an illustration. Prior to the Asian financial crisis, Korea had a very crude liquidity requirement, like many other developing economies. In the context of technical assistance, the IMF recommended and Korea adopted a cash flow approach along the lines described above. Banks are now required to analyze the maturity of their assets and liabilities in foreign exchange and ensure that negative mismatches do not exceed certain limits.

[26]Stress testing may involve the results of performance under extreme, perhaps improbable scenarios. Line personnel and a bank's auditing unit should both conduct stress testing to provide independent oversight and integrity to the process.

Stress testing provides banks with insights into levels of risk consequent on various changes in the economy, like currency depreciation, which can then be used in evaluating total risk exposure. The results of stress testing allow bank management to decide whether potential losses identified through the process are acceptable. Stress testing models for monitoring foreign currency loans to domestic borrowers could include, among other things, vulnerability to scenarios such as a sharp depreciation in currency, foreign exchange movements of international reserves (and foreign exchange in regional currencies), and related changes in other relevant prices. Banks should consider placing either absolute limits or management action triggers on the size of losses they will tolerate due to foreign currency lending to domestic borrowers. Depending on the potential losses revealed by the stress tests and the anticipated likelihood of occurrence, bank management should consider appropriate risk-reducing actions.

Supervisory and Prudential Guidelines

This section contains a discussion on the negative effects of an outright prohibition (or limitation) to a bank's domestic lending in foreign currency.[27] Currently a large number of countries (see Table 3.3 in the Appendix) resort to prudential measures—including prudential currency matching mechanisms—aimed at eliminating the risk-enhancing incentives to borrow in foreign exchange. To the extent that these measures tend to correct incentive biases arising from other sources, they should not be considered as capital control devices.

Specific measures along these lines should include the following: (1) incentives for unhedged domestic borrowers to borrow in foreign exchange that are introduced by an inconsistent monetary and exchange rate policy mix or the design of monetary instruments (for example, differential reserve requirements) should be discussed between supervisors and monetary authorities, to avoid unintended negative effects on loan allocation; (2) prudential currency-matching mechanisms, such as additional capital requirements or additional provisions, may be used to offset currency biases introduced by the overall macroeconomic policy in coordination with the monetary authority; or required in periods of prolonged discrepancy between expected exchange rate changes embedded in interest rates and actual exchange

---

[27]In addition, these measures are usually difficult to implement effectively and uniformly, thus aggravating their negative impact.

rate changes;[28] (3) value-at-risk models with a proven track record should be used if banks have sound risk management systems, skilled staff, and are made subject to stress tests;[29] if this is not the case, a generic provision on all foreign exchange loans to unhedged domestic borrowers should be applied preferably; (4) while domestic lending in foreign currency should not be prohibited, lending in foreign currency to sectors naturally hedged against exchange rate fluctuations should probably benefit from a better loan classification; and (5) the banking system should be allowed without restriction (other than prudential regulations) to invest abroad foreign exchange resources from their depositors.

To be able to promptly and accurately assess the compounded risk generated by domestic lending in foreign currency, the supervisory authorities should monitor, on an aggregated basis, the trend of the share of foreign currency loans of the banking system to total loans and to total foreign currency deposits (and other funding) over certain time periods—at least on quarterly basis. Accounting system requirements should be set up so as to allow the supervisory authorities to track the counterparty risk assumed by banks as a result of foreign exchange lending to domestic unhedged borrowers. In addition, selected information should be disclosed to the public to promote market discipline. Supervisors in some Latin American countries provide quarterly bulletins that detail individual bank and aggregate bank data, including the amount of foreign currency liquid assets, loans and liabilities (see Edmonds, 2000). Supervisors should also monitor corporate foreign currency debt (on an aggregated and disaggregated basis) since significant currency depreciation could put severe pressure on those banks whose clients have large external burdens.

---

[28]Raising capital requirements domestically for foreign exchange operations, which in turn raises bank costs that will be passed on to customers, may provide an incentive to shift foreign exchange borrowing from on-shore to off-shore institutions. Hence, there is a limit to how much arbitrage opportunities should be introduced through this mechanism.

[29]Supervisors are responsible for evaluating each bank's overall foreign exchange risk profile; the potential impact on future earnings of foreign exchange fluctuations, including the effect induced through mismatching maturities in foreign-denominated assets and liabilities (taking into account the compounded risk of net unhedged domestic lending in foreign currency); and the bank management's ability to measure and manage these risks (including the appropriateness of vector autoregression (VAR) models and stress test to incorporate the links between the macroeconomic policies and the compounded risk of domestic lending in foreign exchange). General supervisory principles call for more frequent information on foreign exchange operations given that changes in risk exposure can take place rapidly (see Folkerts-Landau and Lindgren, 1998).

Concluding Remarks

After analyzing the risks involved in banks' domestic lending in foreign currency, the following concluding remarks could be made:
- Banks and supervisory authorities should be aware of the compounding of risks involved in foreign exchange-denominated lending to domestic borrowers who are not hedged against currency risk. For a particular country, macroeconomic volatility, the consistency of the monetary and exchange rate policy mix, the scope to diversify risks, the quality of bank management, and the quality of supervision determine the complexity and the potential severity of problems arising from banks' domestic lending in foreign currency. Supervisors should be alert to policies that undermine the safety and soundness of the banking system (Basel Committee on Banking Supervision, 1997).
- Special care should be used in redressing perverse incentives and establishing the adequate internal policies and procedures, oversight, and regulatory systems in countries whose currencies are not internationally accepted, as the compound risk introduced by foreign exchange-denominated lending to domestic borrowers who are not hedged against currency risk is more likely to materialize.
- The domestic borrower's demand for foreign exchange-denominated loans is determined by preferences that ultimately respond to a set of economic incentives. Some of these incentives contribute to the stability of the banking system (e.g., borrowing in foreign exchange to hedge against negatively correlated risks), while some other incentives result from market imperfections (e.g., those resulting in imperfect arbitrage) or inadequate policies (e.g., inconsistent monetary and exchange rate policy mix) and thus have a negative effect on the stability of the banking system. It is primarily by redressing these latter perverse incentives that the problem of compound risk introduced by foreign exchange-denominated lending to domestic borrowers should be addressed.
- Prohibiting foreign exchange-denominated lending to domestic borrowers would be difficult to enforce, would result in nonoptimal allocation of financial resources, could hamper financial innovation, and would introduce a competitive disadvantage for domestic banks.
- To the extent that negative incentives could not always be eliminated and new ones may emerge, the banks and the supervisory authorities should develop adequate systems to deal with the risks

introduced by foreign exchange-denominated lending to domestic borrowers. These systems should be based on sound internal policies and procedures for banks, adequate oversight by the supervisory authorities, and a comprehensive prudential regulation framework (see Table 3.2 for a summary of these mechanisms). To the extent that prudential measures are aimed at eliminating asymmetrical incentives to borrow in foreign exchange, prudential currency-matching mechanisms should not be considered as capital control devices, since asymmetric prudential mechanisms are appropriate for asymmetric risks. To the extent that different mechanisms are applied for different types or risk, these instruments would not imply discriminatory standards for different stages of development. Because of the dynamic nature of foreign exchange risk, these mechanisms should be adaptable to changing circumstances, but they should not be expected to change frequently to avoid obscure signals.

Table 3.2. Risk Management, Internal Policies and Procedures, and Supervisory and Prudential Guidelines for Banks' Domestic Lending in Foreign Currency

	Foreign Exchange Position	Loan Policies and Procedures	Other Specific Measures
Risk management guiding principles	- Position limits net of provisions for counterparty risk should be incorporated. - Maximum use of available hedging and frequent reassessment should be exercised.	- Loan classification should account for economic impact of possible adverse exchange rate move. - Projects should be viable regardless of currency of financing. - Collateral should be valued conservatively, allowing for margins and reappraisals after exchange rate movements.	- When demand for domestic currency is low or declines, loan classification may still reflect a preference for allocating foreign currency loans to domestically oriented sectors potentially benefiting from an exchange rate devaluation. - Banks should be allowed to invest part of foreign exchange resources abroad in first quality, liquid instruments. - Inadequate incentives introduced by the design of monetary instruments should be continuously reassessed.
Governance guidelines	- Written policies and procedures, along with sound internal controls should be employed. - Accounting procedures should allow accurate valuation of assets and liabilities. - Formulas should allow an accurate measurement of various forms of risks. - Timely and accurate information on each specific risk should be included.	All banks should: - Adopt written procedures on evaluation of borrowers' ability to withstand adverse exchange rate changes, along with written procedures on limits on foreign currency lending should be used. - Avoid facilitating currency switching to refinance loans as a device to delay potential defaults. - Monitor trends and maturity structure of hedged and unhedged share of foreign currency loans to total loans. - Ensure that stress testing indicates absolute limits and management action triggers - Differentiate by currency in "maturity ladders" of future cash flows. - Adopt a policy favoring foreign currency lending to borrowers that follow hedging practices.	- VAR models of risk management should be used if systems and skilled staff allow it.
Supervisory guidelines	Banks should: - make provisions to incorporate corrections in the cost of borrowing for exchange rate risks that may have been neglected. - evaluate interest and exchange rate incentives introduced by macroeconomic policy.	Banks should: - monitor share of foreign exchange loans to total loans.	
Prudential Guidelines	- Supervisors should require additional capital requirements for foreign exchange positions.	- Supervisors may also require provisions if unexpected discrepancies between interest rate and exchange rate movements are prolonged.	- Supervisors may also require additional capital requirements when inadequate incentives from macroeconomic policy are evident (fixed exchange rates, currency boards).

Appendix: Current Practices for Domestic Lending in Foreign Currency

Patterns Observed in the Restrictions Used to Limit Banks' Domestic Lending in Foreign Currency

Main restrictions on banks' domestic lending in foreign currency, as reported for the IMF's 1999 *Annual Report of Exchange Arrangements and Exchange Restrictions* related to the Article VIII,[30] show the following patterns (see Table 3.3):

Currency-related patterns
- Industrial countries do not report restrictions. This is consistent with the fact that banks' domestic lending in foreign currency are perceived as a problem mainly by developing economies. Continuous and sizable cost-benefit incentives for borrowers to increase foreign exchange borrowing are unlikely in these economies.
- Dollarized economies tend to have no restrictions. The group of countries without restrictions includes Argentina, Bolivia, Ecuador, Indonesia, Peru, Poland, Russia, and Uruguay, all of them showing some degree of dollarization. The large availability of foreign exchange resources severely limits the possibility of effectively restricting the domestic allocation of these resources significantly. Some countries set quantitative limits to the amount that can be lent domestically, without restricting the use of resources (Bahrain, Honduras, Jordan, Lebanon, and Mexico).
- Some restrictions aim at favoring the use of domestic currency over foreign currency. In some cases, only the on-lending of credit from abroad is allowed (Algeria and Brazil). Residents may relate this to an intention to discourage domestic banks from competing to attract deposits in foreign currency.

Capital-Control Related Patterns
- Outright prohibitions are rare. Even in developing economies, considerations of the negative effects on arbitrage and efficiency seem to have prevailed in limiting the use of outright prohibitions to this type of operation. Countries reporting such a limitation are Dominica, Macedonia, and Pakistan. Some countries only allow

---

[30]Some additional information was incorporated to the list, mainly from the Occasional Paper, "Monetary Policy in Dollarized Economies" (Baliño, Bennett, and Borensztein, 1999).

foreign currency loans to nonresidents (Belarus, Bangladesh, and Sri Lanka) and some others only for trade-related purposes (Morocco).
- An approval by an official entity is the main control mechanism. A large number of countries require an approval by an official entity, which allows the government to impose ad hoc restrictions when deemed necessary. This apparently aims at having the possibility to adapt restrictions to specific needs related to the evolution of capital flows. Countries that show these restrictions include The Bahamas, Benin, China, Cyprus, Fiji, Niger, Papua New Guinea, San Marino, Togo, and Zimbabwe.

Patterns Related to the Use of Resources
- Some countries restrict the use of resources to foreign exchange payments, while others allow foreign exchange borrowing to finance foreign exchange payments regardless of the source of revenue of the borrower. Countries reporting this practice include Korea, Moldova, Morocco, Ukraine, and Vietnam. Rather than hedging considerations, these restrictions may be explained by an intention to limit foreign exchange financing to facilitate trade.
- Some countries restrict the use of resources based on the source of revenue of the borrower. Some countries report that natural hedging considerations are the main reason to restrict banks' domestic lending in foreign currency, such as Croatia, Dominican Republic, Egypt, Philippines, St. Kitts, and Turkey.

Table 3.3. Restrictions on Foreign Exchange Lending

No Restrictions	Outright Prohibition	Other Specific Restrictions[1]	Description
		Albania	Bank of Albania may impose credit ceilings on outstanding stock of credits for each commercial bank.
		Algeria	Banks and financial institutions may on-lend foreign funds borrowed abroad.
Argentina			
		Bahamas	Exchange control approval is required to make loans to residents.
		Bahrain	Lending is limited to 15 percent of each bank's capital base.
		Bangladesh	Lending is subject to prior approval by the Bank of Bangladesh.
		Belarus	Permitted for settlements with nonresidents.
		Belize	Unspecified restriction reported.
		Benin	Domestic lending denominated in foreign exchange or purchases of foreign currency-denominated securities issued in Benin require prior authorization by the Ministry of Finance.
		Bosnia and Herzegovina	Unspecified restriction reported.
Bolivia			
		Brazil	All contracts, securities, or other documents, as well as any obligations executable in Brazil that require payment in foreign currency, are null and void. Consequently, banks are prohibited from granting foreign currency loans within Brazil. However, this regulation does not apply to the on-lending of external foreign currency loans.
		Burkina Faso	The same regulations apply as for lending to nonresidents.
		Burundi	Unspecified restriction reported.
		Chad	Unspecified restriction reported.
Chile			
		China	Lending is mainly subject to review of qualifications by the PBC and to asset-liability ratio requirements. Borrowers need to register ex post the transaction with the SAFE and should get a permit from the SAFE to repay the principal.
		Colombia	Unspecified restriction reported.
		Croatia	Domestic commercial banks may not give foreign exchange credits to resident natural persons. Commercial banks may, under certain circumstances, give foreign exchange credits to juridical persons for activities they are registered for. Foreign commercial banks may extend credit in foreign exchange to both natural and juridical persons.

Table 3.3. (continued)

No Restrictions	Outright Prohibition	Other Specific Restrictions[1]	Description
		Cyprus	Authorized dealers may grant certain short-term credit facilities in foreign currency (e.g., discounting bills of exchange) to residents without reference to the Central Bank of Cyprus. For other lending to residents in foreign currency, prior approval of the Central Bank of Cyprus is required. Such approval is usually granted for the following purposes: to finance transit trade, to provide working capital for resident oil companies or for industries operating in the industrial free zone, to meet the financial needs of Cyprus Airways, and to finance other desirable productive projects.
Czech Republic			
		Djibouti	Unspecified restriction reported.
	Dominica		These transactions are generally not permitted.
		Dominican Republic	Banks authorized to offer services may grant loans in dollars to the sectors exporting goods and services to finance activities specific to their functions and to the importing sectors to cover payments abroad for the acquisition of goods and services.
Ecuador			
		Egypt	Bank lending in foreign exchange restricted to borrowers with foreign exchange revenue, and other related exchange controls.
		Equatorial Guinea	Unspecified restriction reported.
		Eritrea	Unspecified restriction reported.
		Ethiopia	Domestic banks may grant personal loans to staff members of international institutions.
		Fiji	The banks and nonbank financial institutions may not lend foreign currency to any resident of Fiji without the specific permission of the Reserve Bank of Fiji.
		Georgia	Unspecified restriction reported.
		Ghana	Unspecified restriction reported.
		Guinea	Unspecified restriction reported.
Guinea-Bissau			
		Guyana	Unspecified restriction reported.
		Honduras	Financial institutions may lend 50 percent of their foreign exchange deposits locally in foreign exchange.
Indonesia			
		Jordan	Licensed banks are permitted to lend up to 50 percent of their foreign exchange deposits.

Table 3.3. *(continued)*

No Restrictions	Outright Prohibition	Other Specific Restrictions[1]	Description
Kazakhstan			Authorized banks are entitled to provide credits in foreign currency to resident and nonresident juridical persons only, in accordance with non-cash procedures. There are no controls on credits extended to natural persons.
		Republic of Korea	There are no controls on loan ceilings, but there are some restrictions on the use of loans.
		Lebanon	No restrictions. However, banks may only on-lend up to 65 percent of FCD.
	Former Yugoslav Republic of Macedonia		
		Malawi	Unspecified restriction reported.
Malaysia			Authorized dealers and merchant banks are allowed to lend in foreign currency to residents.
		Mexico	There are limits on the amount that banks may lend to individual borrowers and on the open foreign exchange position of banks.
		Moldova	Authorized banks are permitted to lend in freely convertible currencies only to importers that are resident juridical persons.
Morocco			Moroccan banks may grant foreign exchange loans to residents for the financing of foreign trade operations and investment.
Namibia			
		Niger	There are no controls on these operations when they involve commercial credits; the prior authorization of the MOFERP is required for loans, financial credits, and purchases of securities issued abroad.
	Pakistan		
		Papua New Guinea	Subject to presentation of commercial invoices for bona fide transactions.
		Paraguay	Unspecified restriction reported.
Peru			
		Philippines	The following foreign currency loans may be granted by foreign currency deposit units (FCDUs) of commercial banks without prior BSP approval: (1) private sector loans, if they are to be serviced using foreign exchange to be obtained outside the banking system; (2) short-term loans to financial institutions for normal interbank transactions; (3) short-term loans to commodity and service exporters, and producers/manufacturers, provided that the loan proceeds are to be used to finance the import costs of goods and services necessary in the production of goods. Regular units of commercial banks may also grant foreign currency loans to residents involving trade transactions.

Table 3.3. *(continued)*

No Restrictions	Outright Prohibition	Other Specific Restrictions[1]	Description
			Commercial banks may grant: (1) private sector loans if serviced using foreign exchange to be sourced outside the banking system; (2) short-term loans to financial institutions for normal interbank transactions; and (3) short-term loans to commodity and service exporters and to importers. In practice, this regulation does not restrict FCL.
Poland			
Russia			Only authorized banks are allowed to lend to residents in foreign exchange.
		Samoa	Unspecified restriction reported.
Sierra Leone			Banks are not engaged in this lending.
		San Marino	The granting of financial credits of a considerable amount is subject to authorization.
Singapore			
Slovak Republic			
		Solomon Islands	Unspecified restriction reported.
		South Africa	Unspecified restriction reported.
		Sri Lanka	Commercial banks may grant foreign currency loans to experts.
		St. Kitts and Nevis	Ministry of Finance approval is required, which is granted only in the case of projects generating foreign exchange to service the loan. The purchase of locally issued securities denominated in foreign currencies requires Ministry of Finance approval.
		Sudan	Unspecified restriction reported.
		Swaziland	Unspecified restriction reported.
		Tajikistan	Unspecified restriction reported.
		Thailand	Commercial lending to particular industries denominated in foreign currencies can be partially (50 percent) included as foreign assets in order to recognize the potential risk that banks may not be fully repaid as exchange rate risk is heightened.
		Togo	Local lending in foreign exchange or purchases of securities issued locally and denominated in foreign exchange requires prior authorization by the MEF.
		Tunisia	Resident banks may freely extend credit to finance import and export operations. They may also lend their foreign currency surpluses to other resident banks and to their correspondent banks, in exchange for loans in another currency with the same maturity.

Table 3.3. *(concluded)*

No Restrictions	Outright Prohibition	Other Specific Restrictions[1]	Description
		Turkey	Resident banks may not extend credits to residents in foreign exchange except to exporters, investors, financial leasing firms, Turkish entrepreneurs working abroad, residents who are conducting business related to international tenders held in Turkey, and residents who are conducting business related to defense industry projects that have been approved by the Undersecretariat of the Defense Industry.
		Turkmenistan	Unspecified restriction reported.
		Ukraine	This may be done only for financing a limited range of "critical imports." The provision of foreign exchange to service private sector loans contracted by residents may not be made at an interest rate higher than 20 percent.
Uruguay			
Uzbekistan			
		Vietnam	Permission is given only for import purposes. Domestic lending in foreign currency may be done only for trade-related financing.
		Democratic Republic of the Congo (Zaire)	Unspecified restriction reported.
		Zimbabwe	Subject to exchange control rules and regulations.

Sources: IMF's 1999 *Annual Report of Exchange Arrangements and Exchange Restrictions* (AREAER); IMF, Exchange Arrangements and Exchange Restrictions Database; and Baliño, Bennett, and Borensztein, 1999.

[1]Other restrictions different from those defined by the banking license, prudential regulations applied to domestic loans, and capital/open position limits.

References

Abrams, Richard, and Paulina Beato, 1998, "The Prudential Regulation and Management of Foreign Exchange Risk," IMF Working Paper No. 98/37 (Washington: International Monetary Fund).

Baliño, Tomás J.T., Adam Bennett, and Eduardo Borensztein, 1999, "Monetary Policy in Dollarized Economies," IMF Occasional Paper No. 171 (Washington: International Monetary Fund).

Bank for International Settlements, 1998, *68th Annual Report* (Basel: BIS).

Basel Committee on Banking Supervision, 1980, *Supervision of Banks' Foreign Exchange Positions* (Basel: BIS).

———, 1997, *Core Principles for Effective Banking Supervision* (Basel: BIS).

Cassard, Marcel, and David Folkerts-Landau, 1997, "Risk Management of Sovereign Assets and Liabilities," IMF Working Paper No. 97/166 (Washington: International Monetary Fund).

Edison, Hali, and B. Dianne Pauls, 1993, "A Re-Assessment of the Relationship Between Real Exchange Rates and Real Interest Rates: 1974–1990," *Journal of Monetary Economics*, Vol. 31 (April), pp. 165–87.

Edmonds, Howard, 2000, *Bank Supervision as a Tool to Reduce Risks in Foreign Currency Funding to Emerging Markets*, Office of the Comptroller of the Currency (Washington: U.S. Office of the Comptroller of the Currency).

Folkerts-Landau, David, and Carl-Johan Lindgren, 1998, *Toward a Framework for Financial Stability*, World Economic and Financial Surveys (Washington: International Monetary Fund).

Frankel, Jeffrey A., and Kenneth Froot, 1990, "Exchange Rate Forecasting Techniques, Survey Data, and Implications for the Foreign Exchange Market," NBER Working Paper No. 3470 (Cambridge, Mass.: National Bureau of Economic Research).

Garcia, Gillian G.H., 1999, "Deposit Insurance: A Survey of Actual and Best Practices," IMF Working Paper No. 99/54 (Washington: International Monetary Fund).

Ize, Alain, 1995, "Reserve Requirements of Foreign Currency Deposits," Monetary and Exchange Affairs Department Operational Paper No. 95/1 (Washington: International Monetary Fund).

Johnston, Barry, and Inci Otker-Robe, 1999, "A Modernized Approach to Managing Risk," IMF Policy Discussion Paper No. 99/6 (Washington: International Monetary Fund).

MacDonald, Ronald, 1995, "Long-Run Exchange Rate Modeling," *IMF Staff Papers*, International Monetary Fund, Vol. 42 (September), pp. 437–89.

———, and Jun Nagayasu, 1999, "The Long-Run Relationship Between Real Exchange Rates and Real Interest Rate Differentials: A Panel Study," IMF Working Paper No. 99/37 (Washington: International Monetary Fund).

Marston, David, 1995, "Short-Term Absorption of Capital Inflows," Monetary and Exchange Affairs Department Operational Paper No. 95/3 (Washington: International Monetary Fund).

McCallum, Bennett, 1994, "A Reconsideration of the Uncovered Interest Parity Relationship," *Journal of Monetary Economics*, Vol. 33 (April), pp. 105–32.

Meese, Richard, and Kenneth Rogoff, 1988, "Was It Real? The Exchange Rate-Interest Differential Relation Over the Modern Floating-Rate Period," *Journal of Finance*, Vol. 43 (September), pp. 933–48.

Meredith, Guy, 1998, "Long-Horizon Uncovered Interest Parity," NBER Working Paper No. 6797 (Cambridge, Mass.: National Bureau of Economic Research).

4

Toward a Framework for Systemic Liquidity Policy

CLAUDIA DZIOBEK, J. KIM HOBBS, AND DAVID MARSTON

The capacity for banks to access liquid funding markets and their use of effective liquidity management techniques are important aspects of financial intermediation in that they contribute to financial sector resilience. Without ready access to funding, market participants would be severely constrained in managing payments, transforming maturities, and managing interest rate risk, thus undermining prudent intermediation. Where foreign currency transactions are significant, liquidity management can be complicated by the ease with which funds can be converted from one currency to another, a factor that is linked to the credibility of the exchange rate regime.

An environment allowing sound liquidity management is also essential for effective monetary policy implementation. Where markets are liquid and deep, price discovery and determination will be more efficient, thereby improving the information content of market yields to guide monetary operations. These markets also facilitate effective transmission of central bank intervention from the initial market subset to broader financial markets without undue price volatility. The adequacy

---

The authors would like to thank William E. Alexander and V. Sundararajan for initiating the research project and providing valuable comments. This paper has also benefited from comments by staff of the Central Bank of Argentina and the Central Bank of Mexico, and by Edward Frydl, Eliot Kalter, Meral Karasulu, Elizabeth Milne, Gabriel Sensenbrenner, Mark Swinburne, Bob Traa, and other colleagues during a seminar sponsored by the IMF's Monetary and Exchange Affairs Department. Research assistance was provided by Jahanara Begum and Anil Bhatia.

of procedures for smooth liquidity management operations are often tested in periods of stress. Under such conditions, rigidities or poorly specified arrangements can have adverse implications for the payment system and bank soundness.

The importance of liquidity for sound banking practice is well established at both the theoretical and operational levels. Market microstructure theory has long focused on liquidity issues in equity and securities markets. However, there is also a growing body of academic and empirical literature concerning the importance of money market liquidity, although many of these studies focus on industrial countries where bank liquidity management takes place against the background of a developed infrastructure.[1] In part, renewed interest emanates from the experience of financial market crises and the stresses of illiquidity associated with these episodes at both the national banking and international levels. In the context of strengthening the architecture of the international monetary system, there is now a concerted effort by national authorities and international organizations to reinforce financial systems and their resilience to shocks. With this in mind, the role of strong liquidity and currency risk management, among other items, has been acknowledged.

Systemic liquidity refers to adequate arrangements and practices that permit efficient liquidity management, and that provide a buffer during financial distress. Systemic liquidity is viewed as the combination of bank liquidity management practices and the supporting liquidity infrastructure. This chapter explores a framework for assessing the adequacy of arrangements for market liquidity with a view to evolving elements of a systemic liquidity policy. It argues that robust arrangements for liquidity are crucial to resilience and effective monetary operations and must provide confidence that liquidity can be mobilized and repaid on demand in a predictable and transparent manner. Such liquidity arrangements include several institutional elements that are described in the chapter and involve a role for national authorities in promoting their adoption.

Bank Portfolio and Liquidity Operations

Bank liquidity can be defined as the degree to which a financial institution is able to meet its obligations under normal business conditions. Liquidity is closely linked with confidence because its most

---

[1]See Basel Committee on Banking Supervision (1993); Bank for International Settlements (1999); O'Hara (1995); and Dattels (1995).

generic function is to provide the bank and its customers with the reassurance that the bank's liability obligations can be met as they become due without necessarily having to roll these over or postpone access to credit. For this reason, an important objective of liquidity management operations is to engage in confidence-enhancing practices (Bundesbank, 1982; U.S. Federal Reserve, 1990; Group of Twenty-two, 1998). The core issue of bank vulnerability to sudden and sustained loss of liquidity (and loss of confidence) emanates from the volatility of funding relative to the liquidity of bank assets. In such circumstances of market uncertainty, market participants become less willing to trade or commit funds, and the decline in activity results in a loss of market liquidity. The following sections discuss funding volatility and asset liquidity, respectively.

Determinants of funding volatility

Funding volatility reflects how sensitive depositors or creditors are to events that undermine confidence. More specifically, it refers to the likelihood that bank depositors or creditors will, in a short period of time, withdraw their funds (or fail to roll them over at maturity) in response to a perceived weakness in an individual bank or banking system. The volatility of a particular liability is a function of institutional and economic factors. Typically, the key variables used to define the extent of volatility can be grouped into three broad areas: type of depositor or creditor, insurance coverage, and maturity.

Type of depositor or creditor. The volatility or stability of a bank's liabilities depends on the nature of the depositor or creditor. Institutional investors are relatively sophisticated, have access to banks' financial information, and have a fiduciary responsibility to safeguard their assets. As a result, they are prone to shifting investments and, hence, such investments are volatile. By contrast, household depositors tend to be more complacent, often because of their confidence in deposit insurance, but also because of their lower awareness of risk. Commercial depositors fall between the two groups in terms of volatility. While more aware of bank risk than household depositors, they are less able to act on these fears than institutional investors, since doing so typically requires unwinding and replacing complex banking relationships.[2]

Insured and collateralized liabilities. Instruments covered by deposit insurance can be considered stable sources of funding, with the important

---

[2]The volatility of bank creditors will also be influenced by the unique experiences of creditors. For example, creditors who have experienced bank runs or state confiscation of deposits may be more sensitive to perceived risk than those whose experience is limited to a more stable environment.

caveat that insurance schemes that are not credible may not have this effect. Large deposits can be indicative of volatility, if the holder is either an institution or a relatively sophisticated individual. Foreign currency deposits may be volatile if they are large or if they are excluded from deposit insurance or if there is uncertainty about their coverage.[3] However, as illustrated below, no a priori judgment about funding volatility can be made on the basis of currency denomination.

In the case of larger denomination instruments, uncollateralized liabilities are more volatile than those backed by collateral, assuming the pledge mechanism is credible to the creditor. An important precondition is that asset pledging is allowed and protected under the law. In the event of the borrower's bankruptcy or failure to comply with contractual terms in a collateralized transaction, the rights of the pledgee (lender) must be must be protected and be beyond doubt to provide confidence even under circumstances of stress (see Box 4.1). There must also be adequate market acceptance of assets as collateral, and trading and custody practices must carry no unusual risks to the lender. Collateralized transactions may be hampered by practices that constrain the execution of collateral or that affect the price of collateralized transactions—for example, by requiring reserve holdings against repurchase transactions.[4]

Instrument maturity. On instrument maturity, it is generally held that the longer the time before a liability matures, the more stable (less potentially volatile) it is, on the presumption that the depositor is unlikely to leave until the deposit matures. In this regard, the *remaining* maturity is a superior measure to *original* maturity, although data for the former are often difficult to obtain. There is no standard maturity cut-off that divides volatility from stability, although some supervisory bodies use a one-year benchmark. Even so, in countries where banks are obligated by law to meet early withdrawal requests with only minor penalties, maturity may be less relevant to determining volatility.

Liability management

Liability management aims at controlling liquidity risk by limiting volatility gaps between asset and liabilities, and by assuring access to funding markets. In broad terms, techniques of limiting liquidity

---

[3] The exchange rate regime and its credibility influence the liquidity properties of foreign exchange deposits. In some highly dollarized economies, foreign currency deposits may be more stable than local currency deposits.

[4] Many analysts view such assets as liquid if the volatility of their associated liabilities are properly captured (as liquid) in overall measures of liquidity. Balance sheet data do not necessarily distinguish between assets that are pledged and those that are not.

> **Box 4.1. The Liquidity of Pledgeable Assets**
>
> *The pledging of bank assets.* Banks pledge assets to obtain liquidity from illiquid assets (e.g., consumer and residential mortgage loans) or to diversify sources of liquidity. Asset pledging can diversify the funding because it attracts buyers who differ from outright buyers of an asset and from potential depositors. Asset pledging can also serve to obtain liquidity without triggering the recognition of a loss that might occur under a sale.
>
> *Perfecting the pledging process.* For most bank assets, perfection requires that the creditor take possession. Pledged securities (whether physical or book-entry) might be held in custody by the creditor or by its custodial agent. For some bank assets (real estate, fixed assets, mortgage loans) the bank continues to hold the asset but a creditor's lien is noted legally. Perfection in this case involves a notification process (e.g., via official registration, notification attached to an underlying document, or public announcement).
>
> *Valuation practices.* Market practice should routinely ensure an appropriate relationship between the market value of collateral and the loan (e.g., a margin that reflects the terms of the repurchase agreement and price volatility of the underlying collateral). Valuation should include accrued interest.
>
> *Custody practices.* If perfection involves possession of the collateral, this should be done by routine processes. There should be adequate safeguards against double-pledging of the same collateral.
>
> *Effective enforcement of creditor legal rights in the event of default.* In case of collateralized borrowing, the lender should be able to liquidate the collateral immediately and not be subjected to a lengthy bankruptcy process.
>
> *Pledging limited to liquidity management.* Pledging should only be permitted in connection with liquidity management. The legal framework must ensure that pledging does not impinge on depositor rights.

mismatches aim at extending the maturity of liabilities and increasing stable "core" deposits. A second group of techniques aims at assuring and improving funding market access. By diversifying funding sources by market segment, banks can reduce their vulnerability to market or counterparty disruptions and increase the probability that funding can be retained or replaced if there is a disruption. In managing funding relations, banks also establish contingency arrangements and often have bilateral/correspondent and last-resort arrangements from which funds can be raised on a temporary basis (Dacey and Bazel-Horowitz, 1990).

Asset liquidity

The liquidity of assets can be defined in close analogy to funding volatility. Negotiability, maturity, as well as the type of borrower, collateralization, and currency denomination are key components of asset liquidity, just as they are with funding volatility. An important difference is that assets are less likely to be covered by explicit insurance.

Asset liquidity can be obtained by holding liquid paper, by managing the maturity distribution of nonliquid assets with a view toward the bank's liquidity needs, or by selling outright (or lending) collateralized claims on a repurchase basis. In this context, market arrangements for asset pledging are important. If an asset can reliably be pledged as collateral for a new liability, the asset can be treated as liquid.

Effective commercial liquidity management requires that sufficient liquid assets be held to meet normal business requirements (including reserve requirements) and that excess balances be minimized. Liquid assets, primarily cash and readily marketable securities, generally offer lower yields than other portfolio choices. Thus, under normal conditions, holding liquid assets is costly in terms of reduced profitability.[5] The types of adjustment banks will consider in managing their assets will depend mainly on the magnitude of the deviation from desired balances, the asset's likely duration, the relative yields available on alternative types of investment and on the costs of different sources of funds. If the transaction costs of making an adjustment are large compared to the interest that could be earned on surplus balances or to the size of the penalty on a deficiency, the incentive to make the adjustment will be less.

Measuring Funding Volatility: An Aggregate Balance Sheet Approach

Funding volatility of a bank can be judged by comparing liquid assets (including off-balance sheet items) to overall funding.[6] In Figure 4.1 below, balance sheets for banks at two extremes are presented. On the left is a bank that relies on volatile funds to finance its investment in non-liquid assets. On the right is a bank with a significant margin of surplus stable funds (e.g., core deposits) to invest. Under liquidity stress, the bank that relies primarily on volatile funding is vulnerable to illiquidity and may become insolvent if creditors permanently move their funds elsewhere. The bank with a low level of confidence-sensitive

---

[5]However, yields on liquid (government) securities may be higher than a reasonable return on investments; and under such circumstances, it may be highly profitable for banks to hold liquid assets.

[6]Another standard indicator is a loan-to-deposit ratio that shows the extent to which a bank has committed its stable funds to clients in the form of loans. When loan commitments are low relative to the banks' stable source of funds, liquidity may be described as ample and vice versa. See, for example, Basel Committee (1993). Other measures of funding volatility include direct empirical estimation of the volatility of liabilities, or analysis of interest spreads to derive a liquidity risk premia.

Figure 4.1. Funding Volatility Concepts Focus on the Gap Between Liquid Assets and Volatile Liabilities Relative to Illiquid Assets

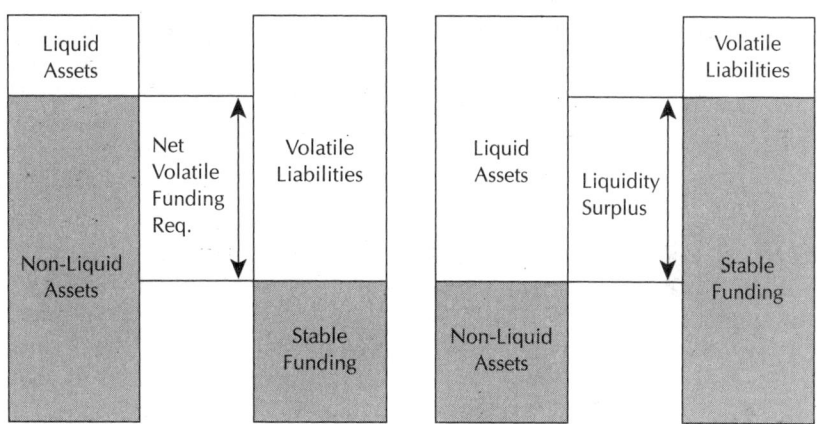

Illiquid Bank (vulnerable)   Liquid Bank (comfortable)

funds is less affected by liquidity stress because of the relative inertia of its depositors and because of the large portfolio of liquid assets.

At the level of the individual bank, cash flow models are often used, which gauge cash inflows relative to cash outflows over different time horizons. Cash flow models allow for a dynamic analysis of liquidity, which complements the static (balance sheet-based) approach taken here. However, in the absence of sufficiently detailed data, it is very difficult to use cash flow models for analysis of the entire banking system; moreover, balance sheet data are more readily available.

The balance sheet-based approach to assessing liquidity can be expressed in terms of the volatility ratio shown below. This volatility indicator measures the extent to which banks rely on confidence-sensitive or volatile funds to finance its assets. Naturally, volatility analysis should fully incorporate any off-balance sheet items (e.g., contingent credit lines), which often play an important role in liquidity management strategies.

Funding volatility ratio: $\dfrac{VL - LA}{TA - LA} = \dfrac{\text{(volatile liabilities)} - \text{(liquid assets)}}{\text{(total assets)} - \text{(liquid assets)}}$

Prudent liquidity management implies that a bank maintain at least sufficient liquid assets to cover volatile liabilities. In this case, the ratio is zero. More prudent banks would be expected to maintain liquid assets

Table 4.1. Interpreting the Funding Volatility Ratio[1]

Value	Occurs when Volatile Liabilities	Indicates
>0	are not fully covered by liquid assets	High risk[2]
0	are fully covered by liquid assets	Intermediate risk
<0	are more than fully covered by liquid assets	Low risk

[1] (VL–LA)/(TA–LA) where VL=Volatile Liabilities; LA=Liquid Assets; and TA=Total Assets.
[2] Can be corrected by raising stable funds (e.g., building domestic deposit base) and by reducing the share of illiquid assets (e.g., sale, maturing, or pledging).

in excess of volatile liabilities. In this case, the ratio is negative. Less prudent banks, those that rely heavily on confidence-sensitive funds, will have volatility ratios above zero (Table 4.1).

The ratio is scaled by illiquid assets in the denominator, which mirror volatility more accurately than if total assets were the scale factor. For example, if a bank's liquidity is measured as $(VL-LA)/TA$ and the ratio is significantly positive, the bank can reduce the ratio merely by borrowing and investing more (raising volatile liabilities and liquid assets). In this case, the numerator stays unchanged but the denominator rises, lowering the overall ratio without lowering the bank's dependence on confidence-sensitive funds. If illiquid assets are used as the scale factor, however, a positive ratio cannot be reduced by such window dressing operations. Total assets and liquid assets would grow by the same amount, leaving the difference unchanged.

While liquidity and volatility ratios are conceptually well understood, difficulties arise in applying these ratios in practice. The major problem is that it is not clear a priori which assets should be classified as liquid and which liabilities should be classified as volatile. This depends on the liquidity infrastructure. Available balance sheet data are generally more focused on providing information on the value of assets and liabilities rather than on liquidity. Moreover, rapid change in financial products makes it difficult to know what the liquidity properties are of a given instrument.[7]

The liquidity properties of assets and liabilities depend on the institutional setting. In this regard, considerations of the existence of legal contract rights, the design of prudential and monetary instruments, foreign exchange regulations, as well as the overall variability of interest rates, and exchange rates, are important. These can be summarized as the liquidity infrastructure.

---

[7] For example, in many countries, a mortgage loan would be considered an illiquid asset. However, if there is a well-developed secondary market for mortgage loans, a mortgage loan may be a liquid asset since it can easily be sold for cash.

Table 4.2. Components of a Balanced Liquidity Infrastructure

Day-to-Day Liquidity Management Support	Safety Net Support
Information disclosure	Credible deposit insurance
Prudential liquidity rules	Lender of last resort
Creditor rights	
Monetary instruments, payments, microstructure	
Foreign exchange liquidity	

Infrastructure for Short-Term Liquidity Management

Effective liquidity management tools require explicit and developed contract law as well as other economic and institutional factors. Studies of liquidity management often take these factors for granted, and, hence, the infrastructural prerequisites are a neglected dimension of liquidity management (de Villiers, 1996; Group of Twenty Two, 1998).

A good liquidity infrastructure should allow banks to operate in a reliable and transparent ("confidence-enhancing") environment. Table 4.2 lists key components that are grouped into two broad categories. A balanced infrastructure needs to provide for the day-to-day liquidity management activities as well as for a suitable support network for emergencies. For each category, key factors are cited. These are not exhaustive but cover major aspects that are of particular relevance from a systemic liquidity perspective.

Day-to-Day Liquidity Management Support

The modalities of market structures to facilitate the recycling of liquidity have an important bearing on the capacity for liquidity management. Microstructures for interbank and secondary trading of securities must provide efficient price discovery and facilitate reasonable trading costs. The platform for these features is broad-based and, even where necessary features exist (as discussed below), structural issues such as ownership patterns in the banking system, the types of creditors or debtors, and the degree of competition in markets will impact on the infrastructure, thereby affecting the depth of markets.

Market framework issues affecting liquidity

Information disclosure. A basic underpinning for a good infrastructure relates to a requirement for efficient rules and practices for information disclosure. Public disclosure refers to the timely publication of meaningful financial data and for the purpose of informing market participants.[8] Lack of disclosure and uncertainty about the true conditions of counterparties are invariably the main factors underlying market segmentation because the absence of regular and reliable information concerning the financial condition of financial institutions reduces the ability to assess counterparty risk. More generally, efficient dissemination of financial information also affects the interaction between informed and uninformed participants, thereby affecting price determination. Information can also affect the degree of market integration. Without this integration, orders arriving in the market will be sporadic and uneven and, thus, not fully representative of underlying supply and demand conditions.[9]

Prudential liquidity requirements. In many countries, banks are subject to prudential rules on liquidity. These rules should be designed to compel banks to engage in prudent liquidity management, and are, thus, an important component of systemic liquidity infrastructure. Useful liquidity requirements provide market participants with a minimum acceptable standard of liquid assets relative to liabilities, defining assets and liabilities in terms of actual properties that reflect the prevailing institutional and legal framework.

Liquidity rules vary widely across countries, ranging from those that rely primarily on banks' own self-assessment of required liquidity to more rigid rules. Sometimes, liquid asset requirements are put in place primarily to create a captive market for hard-to-sell government bonds (Gulde, 1995). Such rules may well reduce the level of public confidence in bank soundness, and, hence, tend to be detrimental to the liquidity infrastructure.

Creditor rights. An environment of confidence requires an effective legal and judicial structure supporting creditor rights.[10] If creditor rights are well developed and creditors are confident that they will be given fair treatment in the event the bank experiences problems, all banks will find it easier to attract funds. In this regard, insolvency or default

---

[8]Information in this regard can either be public (available to all market participants, such as publicly announced statistics) or private (not available to all market participants, but only to traders).

[9]Integration has to be seen in the context of concentration of market liquidity. Notwithstanding the availability of many assets of different maturities and product design, market liquidity is usually concentrated in relatively few assets.

[10]See Claessens, Djankov, and Leora (1999) and La Porta and others (1997). Most of the literature on creditor rights refers to nonbank enterprises. Nevertheless, the criteria used to assess creditor rights are relevant for banking. These are the timetables (number of days) for reaching judgment, the rights of management during resolution, high priority for secured creditors, and automatic stay for assets. Similarly, criteria for court efficiency (costs, duration, etc.) have been established.

procedures must meet criteria of predictability. Relevant risk allocation rules should be clearly specified and applied consistently by the implementing institutions. While all creditors should receive equitable treatment, this does not necessarily mean equal treatment. Different creditors may have struck different arrangements with the debtor, for example, through the granting of collateral. For the benefit of all creditors, however, procedures must address issues of fraud and favoritism that arise in the context of financial distress.[11] Creditor rights to information on proceedings dealing with the resolution of the affected institution and information on the debtor institution to ensure that decisions are informed are both critical elements of a confidence-enhancing framework.

Monetary instrument design affects liquidity

Prevailing monetary arrangements, design aspects of central bank instruments, and arrangements for payments and money market operations bear directly on banks' ability to manage short-term liquidity.[12] High transactions costs, for example, arising from rigid instrument design and trading rules, and infrequent clearing arrangements can discourage trades and contribute to price volatility (Dattels, 1995). The relevant design features of instruments affecting liquidity management include reserve averaging and rules of access, as well as volume, maturity, and rates of interest on standing facilities. Another significant design feature is the extent to which instruments place restrictions on the asset/liability management of banks.

Reserve requirements. The role of reserve requirements in liquidity management depends on the rules of reserve accounting (averaging provisions, contemporaneous or lagged reserve accounting, and carry-over provisions). More generally, reserve requirements are most compatible with liquidity management where banks hold reserve assets with liquidity characteristics that correspond to their needs. As noted earlier, effective cash management requires that sufficient liquid assets are held to meet normal business requirements. Where this voluntary demand for liquid assets coincides with the requirement for reserve holdings, the requirement does not constitute a problem for banks if they are generally able to mobilize these required reserves for liquidity management purposes. If reserve requirements are set very low, banks have less leeway through averaging to manipulate their reserve positions without the risk of incurring the penalty of non-compliance.

---

[11] Given the importance of international finance, it is essential that there is no discrimination against foreign creditors.

[12] See, for example, Bank of England (1981); Bundesbank (1982).

In such cases, banks would have to voluntarily maintain higher levels of reserves so as to meet the requirements.[13]

Contemporaneous measures of reserve requirements closely link the requirement with movements in bank deposits and so provide liquidity managers with immediate information on funding needs. The disadvantage, however, is that banks do not know their exact reserve requirement until the testing date. This could be problematic for banks that have difficulties in consolidating their daily positions or where intrabank accounting systems and methods of transferring funds between branches are weak. For these reasons, a lagged measure of reserve requirements may actually help banks to determine their reserve requirements more precisely, hence improving liquidity management.

Differentiated reserve requirements complicate liquidity management to the extent that they could induce banks into assuming maturity and interest rate structures for their portfolio that could be suboptimal or at least require them to manage potential mismatches. (Prestopino, 1994).

Standing facilities. Standing facilities, which are accessed at the initiative of commercial banks, provide liquidity, usually against collateral, to meet transitional liquidity needs of banks. In settlement facilities and in some rediscount arrangements, credit is provided at market or below market rates. In the latter case, many central banks establish volume limits on access to this window or alternately limit usage through moral suasion. For commercial bank liquidity, management, rules of access, the volume of credit allowed, maturity, and rates of interest on the credit available are all relevant design features. In this regard, many countries operate standing credit facilities most often with unlimited volumes of credit at market or above-market rates. In the case of rediscount operations, the bulk of credit is restrained by penalty rates of interest rather than volume restrictions. Some countries restrict the number of banks that can access overnight standing facilities, the frequency of access, the intervals between access, or have cumbersome application procedures that sometimes result in delays in the receipt of value. Naturally, such restrictions reduce the usefulness of standing facilities for liquidity management.

Asset/liability restrictions. Restrictions on the asset side of portfolios cover practices affecting the volume of asset trading allowed, including restrictions that create captive markets for government securities and those affecting the development of markets in securities and other assets.

---

[13]The maturity profile of a bank's liability often understates actual liquidity since deposits are normally not demanded at the end of term. See U.S. Federal Reserve Bank of New York (1990).

Where securities qualify as a reserve asset to meet reserve requirements, banks hold a certain proportion of liabilities in the form of securities. The same applies when using a strict liquid assets ratio with government securities as the main eligible asset. These restrictions (if binding) limit the volume of securities that can be readily used to realize liquidity in the short run. Some countries impose restrictions on the loan portfolio of banks by stipulating proportions to be lent to particular sectors or set absolute quantitative ceilings on outstanding credit. In the former case, the restriction limits the ability of banks to sell loans affected by the stipulation, while in the latter case income is constrained and so reduces the incentive to sell these assets in the event that liquidity is needed. Ceilings on loan rates or interest spreads reduce the flexibility to price loan assets for sale.

Similarly, several countries have restrictions on liability management. Interest rate ceilings on deposits restrict the ability of banks to mobilize funds in general. Differential reserve requirements could also increase the costs of mobilizing particular deposit maturities, as would marginal requirements, which could affect the costs of all incremental deposits mobilized. Some countries also place restrictions on the geographical domain of business for banks. While such restrictions can arise purely from a market response to a bank not well known outside of its main locale, restrictions on branching and those on domain add to these difficulties. Several countries also place restrictions on interbank activity, either through taxing interbank trading (by applying reserve requirements) or by directing portions of interbank trade. This tax not only increases the price of interbank transactions but also can affect their maturity.[14] In other cases, central banks have encouraged sound banks to dedicate a portion of reserve holdings to interbank placements to assist banks facing liquidity problems.

Payment system arrangements

An integral part of the decision framework for bank management of short-run liquidity relates to the technical and institutional characteristics of payment and settlement arrangements, including the central banks' attitude toward end-of-day marginal financing. In this regard, the design of standing facilities and modalities of reserve requirements have important bearing on liquidity funding decisions.

---

[14]If the liability to which reserve requirements apply is measured periodically (as opposed to being averaged), banks would have an incentive to avoid the tax on the day of measurement. This could lead to transaction maturities of a length only within the measurement period. On the day of measurement, volumes traded could fall and the price of interbank trades could rise, leading to spikes in interbank rates around the period of measurement.

In the arrangements for payments and settlement, at least three factors help reduce the need for precautionary balances (Borio, 1997). First, settlement procedures should be designed to allow banks to borrow and lend among themselves toward the end of the day after settlement positions are known or can be estimated with a comparatively small margin of error.[15] If this is allowed then, provided the interbank market among participants works smoothly, the institutions can be reasonably confident of obtaining funds at the going market rate. A second factor relates to the expectation of being able to finance imbalances at a rate with no penalty. Many central banks seek to ensure that sufficient funds are available in the system so that participants do not need to turn to them for end-of-day assistance, which is then only provided at penalty rates. Finally, this arrangement, if supported by moral suasion discouraging banks from turning to the central bank, in turn will encourage the development of interbank markets.[16]

Foreign exchange liquidity

International banks operate in more than one currency, and must, therefore, include foreign exchange considerations in their liquidity management. Access to liquidity in foreign exchange is affected by a number of factors different from those affecting liquidity in domestic currency. In this regard, banks operating in highly dollarized economies are faced with special challenges. For example, deposits in domestic currency may prove less stable than those denominated in dollars.

Similarly, several countries have restrictions on liability management. Interest rate ceilings on deposits restrict the ability of banks to mobilize funds in general. Differential reserve requirements could also increase the costs of mobilizing particular deposit maturities, as would marginal requirements, which could affect the costs of all incremental deposits mobilized. Some countries also place restrictions on the geographical domain of business for banks. While such restrictions can arise purely from a market response to a bank not well known outside of its main locale, restrictions on branching and those on domain add to these difficulties. Several countries also place restrictions on interbank activity, either through taxing interbank trading (by applying reserve requirements) or by directing portions of interbank trade. This tax not only increases the price of interbank transactions but also can

---

[15]The same effect could be achieved but with increased payments risk by extending the settlement period to next-day settlement, for example.

[16]The Lamfalussy Report (1990) and its recent update BIS (1999) spell out in more depth the framework for best practice payment systems.

> **Box 4.2. Should Local and Foreign Currency Liquidity Be Analyzed Separately?**
>
> When the involved currencies are *fully convertible* and can easily and *reliably* be converted, liquidity measures can be viewed in the aggregate. In essence, this requires a well-established, credible exchange regime. A sudden need to pay off liabilities of one currency can be met by issuing new liabilities or liquidating assets of another currency.
>
> For *thin currency markets* or markets with *limited foreign currency availability*, interbank foreign exchange lines are limited and vulnerable to disruption. When *forward hedging is unavailable*, the fungibility (convertibility) assumption may be unwarranted for liquidity management purposes. Sufficient currency may not always be available. Alternatively, spot transactions can be performed, but the banks may find themselves unable to hedge against the resulting net foreign exchange positions. The unhedged use of "cross-currency liquidity" might well be viewed as an unacceptable risk, whether or not there are formal limits on foreign exchange open positions. *If fungibility is not assured, currency-specific measures of liquidity should be used in addition to the aggregate figures.*
>
> There may be other reasons for keeping separate accounts. The volatility of liabilities and liquidity of assets may vary by currency. Foreign-currency creditors are often more volatile than their domestic counterparts. This may be either because foreign currency holders may have more choices or are more vulnerable themselves to competitive pressures.

affect their maturity. In other cases, central banks have encouraged sound banks to dedicate a portion of reserve holdings to interbank placements to assist banks facing liquidity problems.

Specific market and institutional factors affecting foreign exchange liquidity include linkages between local and external financial markets, which will have an important impact on liquidity in the local foreign exchange market. A network of correspondent relationships or cross-border banking networks involving domestic and foreign banks and, in particular, foreign bank branches and subsidiaries can improve domestic access to foreign exchange liquidity. However, at the same time, correspondent relationships are costly (see Box 4.2).

Access to liquidity in foreign exchange and the transferability of liquidity between domestic and foreign currencies will be reduced by capital controls (e.g., gross limits on the size of banks' external correspondent balances and required approvals for borrowing abroad), either in the home country or in the currency issuing country. The design of prudential controls on open foreign exchange positions can also have an impact on access to foreign exchange liquidity. For example, very tight limits on the foreign exchange net position can constrain banks' ability to manage liquidity through currency conversion. Separate limits on net spot and forward transactions or other types of restrictions on the use of derivatives will also limit the incentive for developing hedging mechanisms that can improve management of liquidity and other types of risk.[17]

Safety Net Infrastructure

Deposit insurance and emergency credit provisions are part of the safety net that plays a role when banks are experiencing liquidity or solvency difficulties. A system of depositor protection that guards the holders of small deposits when their bank fails has in recent years become part of safety net arrangements in a number of countries. A well-designed deposit insurance system can strengthen incentives for efficiency and good governance for banks. With strong incentives for bank owners, managers, depositors, borrowers, and regulators to keep the system sound, a well-designed insurance scheme can encourage capitalization and discourage excessive risk taking by charging risk-adjusted premiums. Such systems should also encourage sophisticated depositors to exert market discipline by demanding disclosure of reliable information on the condition of banks (Garcia, 1999). This can be achieved by appropriate caps on insurance coverage.

Some central bank regulations include emergency credit arrangements to lend to banks perceived to be solvent but illiquid. These are distinct from normal standing facilities that provide overnight support to facilitate interbank settlement or to maintain interbank interest rates within a corridor. In fact, emergency credit arrangements are sometimes separate from the central bank and may take the form of liquidity consortia, called upon short notice. Most commonly, in order to minimize moral hazard, however, there is no ex-ante specification of such facilities.[18] Where such emergency facilities exist, the focus is on early assessment of the solvency of the affected institution. Such lend-

---

[17]The design of monetary instruments can also affect foreign exchange liquidity. For example, a requirement to hold required reserves on foreign currency deposits in foreign, rather than domestic, currency will provide a greater liquidity cushion against large deposit withdrawals in foreign exchange. Such a requirement will also eliminate the demand for additional liquidity to meet reserve requirements in the event of a depreciation of the domestic currency.

[18]In this regard a notable exception is the Federal Reserve Board's description of facilities under its discount window.

ing can only be a stopgap measure since the credit risk assumed by the central bank can be significant.

In periods of banking stress, the factors precipitating emergency central bank liquidity support and recycling arise from a desire to avert systemic settlement failure, or as emergency support to banks experiencing deposit runs. Both conditions often arise from real or prospective flight of depositors to quality assets and institutions, and the inability of the troubled bank to either liquidate sufficient assets or raise new liabilities in the money market at a pace sufficient to match the outflow of funds, with resulting threats to the payment system.

In providing support, the central bank implicitly assumes the market risks that either depositors or money market lenders have been unwilling to bear. Support is given on the presumption that this minimizes costs that would arise in case of wide-scale disruption to the intermediation process. To minimize credit risk, these facilities are invariably collateralized—even where the collateral is not as liquid as that which the market would have required for short-term transactions. The overarching caveat to such operations is the need to rapidly determine prospective solvency.[19]

The Importance of a Balanced Liquidity Infrastructure

A balanced liquidity infrastructure should primarily rely on factors for day-to-day liquidity management (as outlined in Table 4.2) and rely on safety-net features for emergencies only. A balanced infrastructure allows systemic resilience to shocks. In many countries rigidities exist in the factors necessary for smooth day-to-day operations. In some cases, the authorities hope to counterbalance the shortcomings in the financial infrastructure by providing overly generous guarantees and support mechanisms. Infrastructures relying heavily on crisis control are weak relative to those with more balanced qualities. The measure of funding volatility and the factors that affect a balanced infrastructure are very closely linked. Dysfunction in the infrastructure could induce a need for larger holdings of liquidity. In this situation, the funding volatility ratio may appear sufficiently negative, masking underlying low resilience to shocks.

---

[19]Even where the modalities of safety nets are not explicitly defined ex ante, they can support confidence in the market. This can be beneficial in facilitating excess reserve recycling outside the central bank. Nonetheless, significant moral hazards can be inherent, if these arrangements are badly designed. Good banks (or depositors) could lose the incentive to monitor troubled banks and price their credit risk appropriately.

The importance of a balance is highlighted in the two in-depth case studies of Argentina and Mexico during 1994–95, included later in this chapter. While volatility ratios were high in both countries, Mexico's banks operated in a very weak and unbalanced infrastructure that relied heavily on the safety net. Argentina's infrastructure also had significant shortcomings and completely lacked a safety net. However the emphasis on day-to-day factors helped Argentina avert a more serious financial crisis in 1994.

Systemic Liquidity Framework: Stylized Application

In applying and interpreting the framework developed, a group of 14 countries was chosen, all with relatively developed financial markets and with reasonably large internal markets.[20] The countries were chosen to represent countries with and without recent systemic liquidity crises.[21] Data availability and IMF experience with the countries' financial market structure were important considerations in choosing the sample.

Volatility Ratio of 14 Countries

In approximating a volatility ratio, a private database containing bank by bank data (Thomson Bankwatch) was used. This database covers the three elements of the volatility ratio, total assets, volatile liabilities, and liquid assets. In the database, *total assets* are defined as reported assets plus off-balance sheet items, consumer liabilities on acceptance, and bills rediscounted. *Liquid assets* are those on- and off-balance sheet items immediately available as cash, or quickly convertible into cash (e.g., cash, trading securities, government securities, claims due from banks, and short-term marketable securities). *Volatile liabilities* are approximated using "total borrowed funds," which include average liabilities of interbank borrowings, notes, bills, bonds, and other debt instruments issued plus other borrowings, regardless of maturity.

The volatility ratio was calculated for each country. Available data cover cross-country data for a seven-year time period from 1992–98. Table 4.3 shows the results and Figure 4.2 displays the average values for volatility indicators for each country, where the countries are in ascending order of their volatility ratios. The data show that the ratio

---

[20]The countries are: Argentina, Brazil, Canada, Germany, France, India, Indonesia, Japan, Korea, Malaysia, Mexico, Thailand, United Kingdom, and United States.

[21]Systemic liquidity crises were experienced in Indonesia, Japan, Korea, Mexico, and Thailand.

Table 4.3. Volatility Ratios for Selected Countries' Commercial Banks[1]

	Industrial Countries						Other Countries						
Year	Canada	France	Germany	Japan	United Kingdom	United States[2]	Argentina	Brazil	India	Indonesia	Korea	Malaysia	Mexico	Thailand
1998	-0.13	-0.25	-0.05	0.01	-0.26	0.09	0.11	0.04	-0.71	-0.10	0.08	-0.24	0.03	-0.23
1997	-0.15	-0.22	-0.03	0.02	-0.31	-0.08	0.09	0.05	-0.66	0.14	0.10	-0.33	0.03	-0.12
1996	-0.15	-0.24	-0.04	0.01	-0.32	-0.09	0.09	0.08	-0.57	0.04	0.08	-0.32	0.07	0.02
1995	-0.22	-0.16	-0.04	-0.02	-0.31	-0.08	0.15	0.03	-0.63	0.08	0.07	-0.38	0.20	0.02
1994	-0.20	-0.11	-0.03	-0.04	-0.36	0.01	0.07	0.19	-0.70	0.07	0.07	-0.52	0.07	0.01
Average	**-0.17**	**-0.19**	**-0.04**	**0.00**	**-0.31**	**-0.07**	**0.10**	**0.08**	**-0.66**	**0.05**	**0.08**	**-0.36**	**0.08**	**-0.06**
Standard Deviation	0.04	0.06	0.01	0.02	0.03	0.04	0.03	0.06	0.06	0.09	0.01	0.10	0.07	0.11
Dispersion Indicators[3]														
Average	-0.31	-0.56	-0.18	0.02	-0.49	-0.36	-0.08	0.09	-0.64	0.14	0.13	-0.32	0.14	-0.02
Standard Deviation	0.48	1.92	0.34	0.09	0.93	0.44	1.37	0.59	0.24	0.38	0.13	0.17	0.35	0.26

Sources: Bankstat and Thomson BankWatch, Inc.
[1]Data for 1998 are incomplete. Volatility ratio is calculated as $V=(VL-LA)/(TA-LA)$, where VL= Volatile Liabilities (or "Borrowed Funds"); LA=Liquid Assets; and TA=Total Assets.
[2]U.S. estimates are based on holding companies.
[3]Unweighted average of volatility ratios, 1997. Dispersion is a measure of differences among banks.

Figure 4.2. Average Highest and Lowest Values of Volatility Ratios for Selected Countries During 1992–98
(In percent)

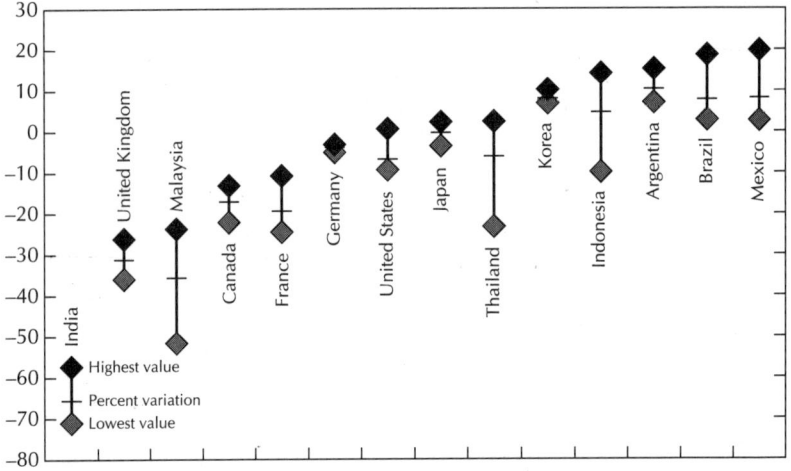

is negative in India, Malaysia, and the industrial countries except for Japan, reflecting relatively conservative (prudent) liquidity management for the banking sectors taken as a whole. By contrast, for Argentina, Brazil, Japan, Mexico, Thailand, and Indonesia, the ratios were positive, indicating higher risk profiles.

In addition, a dispersion indicator was calculated to measure differences among banks within the banking sector. Dispersion was measured as an unweighted average of volatility ratios in one year (1997). For most countries, the dispersion indicator confirms the findings of the aggregate picture. However, for Argentina, the dispersion volatility ratio is negative because the majority of banks has negative ratios, while the large banks have positive ratios. This could be a sign that larger banks are more exposed to confidence-sensitive funding than smaller banks. In Malaysia and Thailand, the aggregate (multiyear) figures yield almost the same results as the bank-by-bank dispersion ratio. This may suggest greater homogeneity in bank behavior than in other countries.

Several shortcomings of the data must be taken into account. Aggregate data on all commercial banks often hide very substantial discrepancies within the banking sector between strong and weak banks. In some countries, the banking sector is segmented and vulnerabilities arise from weaknesses of some institutions. Furthermore, the database does not differentiate between domestic and foreign currency. For reasons discussed above in many cases, this may introduce a bias in favor of stability. The following section illustrates how additional information can be used to fine-tune volatility ratios. In both case studies the more in-depth study of volatility ratio components leads to upward revisions (more volatility).

Systemic Liquidity Infrastructure

As discussed above, volatility ratios should be interpreted in the context of the infrastructure for liquidity management. Table 4.4 attempts to map the liquidity infrastructure of the selected countries at the end of 1997. The observations shown in this table are rough approximations of the factors discussed above. This reflects the difficulty in producing comparable data. For example, to make judgments on disclosure quality countries' adherence to International Accounting Standards (IAS) could be a benchmark. However, adherence to IAS is not monitored in a consistent way and a database maintained by the International Accounting Standards Committee contained only a few self-assessments. Therefore, no measure for disclosure could be included. Prudential liquidity was measured by whether or not banks are required to maintain liquid reserves relative to some measure of illiquid assets. No attempt was made to assess the adequacy of prudential liquidity rules, except to ensure that the rules are written from a prudential point of view, rather than liquid asset requirements, which force banks to purchase government bonds.

The third column shows observations on creditor rights and the efficiency of court systems. This issue has received considerable attention in the wake of the recent financial crises and, as noted above, empirical studies of creditor rights and court system efficiency in various countries. For Asian countries, two recent surveys of bankruptcy codes are available, one from the World Bank (La Porta, and others, 1997; and Claessens, Djankov, and Leora, 1999). For some other countries, the World Bank and International Finance Corporation (IFC) have produced studies of bankruptcy procedures and creditor rights. Naturally, these studies constitute first attempts to "rate" countries in these respects and the results must, therefore, be considered with great caution. Table 4.4 reproduces judgments from the above sources. In the absence of such studies, no entries were made. This does not indicate a deficiency of creditor rights.

The confidence-enhancing aspects of instruments, payments, and microstructure were approximated using two separate indicators, one to mirror market depth and one to indicate any restrictions on liquidity

Table 4.4. Liquidity Infrastructure of 14 Selected Countries, 1997

Criteria Countries	Prudential Liquidity Rules[1]	Creditor Rights and Court Efficiency[2]	Central Bank Instruments, Payments, Microstructures[3]			Explicit Deposit Insurance[5]
			Government securities market turnover	Portfolio restrictions	Foreign Borrowings[4]	
Industrial						
Canada	Yes	Well developed.	21.9	None.	19.3	Yes
France	Yes	Well developed.	33.8	Liquid asset ratios.	32.1	Yes
Germany	Yes	Well developed.	...	None.	17.7	Yes
Japan	No	Well developed.	6.9	None.	10.2	Yes
United Kingdom	No	Well developed.	7.0	None.	51.4	Yes
United States	No	Well developed.	22.0	None.	9.4	Yes
Developing						
Argentina	Yes	Strengthened in 1995.	...	None.	18.8	Yes
Brazil	No	Concordata delays action, reduces value of claims.	10.3	Differential reserve requirements.	13.2	Yes
India	Yes	n.a.	3.6	Deposit rate ceilings, liquid asset ratios/, secondary reserve requirements.	4.1	Yes
Indonesia	No	Insolvency law and courts weak, rarely used in practice.	n.a.	Ill-designed standing facilities.	14.2	No
Korea	Yes	Well developed but inexperienced with restructuring.	8.3	Deposit rate ceiling.	8.7	Yes
Malaysia	Yes	Legal system developed but procedures not well established.	4.0	Interest spread restriction, limited Reserve averaging, Liquid asset req., limited collateral.	8.5	No
Mexico	Yes	"Suspension" practice strongly favors debtors, reform in preparation (1999).	n.a.	None.	3.3	Yes
Thailand	No	Very slow process. No commercial courts exist.	n.a.	None.	15.9	Yes

[1]Canada: Part X485 Banking Law; France: Regulation 88-01; Germany: Banking Act Section 10; India: Banking Act Art. 24; Korea: just introduced in 1999; Malaysia, Article 38 Banking Act; Mexico Bank of Mexico regulation.

[2]Criteria as discussed in the third section. Sources: Canada, France, Germany, United Kingdom, and United States (White, 1993); Brazil (Mendes,1995), Indonesia, Japan, Korea, Malaysia, Thailand (Claessens, Djankov, and Leora 1999 and World Bank/IFC Documents); Mexico (Lubrano 1996); Argentina (IFC).

[3]Sources: BIS (1999) and; Central bank reports. In cases the data could include repo transactions. India: treasury-bills only.

[4]Source: IFC Statistics. 1988 Foreign liabilities of money center banks in percent of total liabilities (excluding interbank claims). India: Foreign currency liabilities (IMF staff estimates).

[5]Garcia (1999).

transformation imposed by the authorities. Market depth was approximated using data on turnover in markets for government securities.

Ideally, foreign currency borrowings would be represented as a ratio of foreign currency liabilities relative to total bank assets. However, this information is just beginning to be published in the IMF's *International Financial Statistics* (IFS) and is not available for the full sample of countries. As a proxy, therefore, Table 4.4 shows foreign liabilities (liabilities to foreign residents) of money center banks relative to total liabilities (but excluding interbank deposits). In the same table, foreign liabilities play a significant role for most countries in the sample, thus adding complexity to liquidity management for banks. Foreign liabilities are modest (at or below 10 percent) in India, Japan, Korea, Malaysia, Mexico, and the United States.

In the case of deposit insurance, the guiding criterion was whether an explicit scheme was in place (Garcia, 1999). No attempt was made to determine whether these schemes are credible, and, hence, effective in making covered deposits a stable base of funding. Lender-of-last-resort arrangements were not mapped because often these were not specified ex ante as discussed above.

Summarizing Information on Systemic Liquidity Frameworks

With more reliable information on volatility ratios and the liquidity infrastructure, a quantification of systemic liquidity could be established with a view of rank ordering the countries in the sample group. The observations in Tables 4.3 and 4.4 could be aggregated into a composite indicator that could be used to rank the countries by strength of systemic liquidity environment. Table 4.5 lays out conceptually how countries could be grouped into four broad categories without attempting to place individual countries. The table measures the volatility ratio along the vertical axis and the infrastructure on the horizontal axis. The lower right-hand quadrant, marked as "double plus" would be the best-case scenario, where good bank liquidity management (represented by negative volatility ratios) is supported by a strong and balanced infrastructure. As discussed above, this finding would have to be supported by a relatively homogeneous and unfragmented financial sector.

The upper left-hand quadrant is the weakest scenario, where high-level exposure to funding volatility coexists with a weak liquidity infrastructure, indicating systemic vulnerability. The lower right-hand quadrant represents the most robust structure where banks are prudent managers of their exposure to confidence-sensitive funds and operate in a supportive infrastructure. On the upper right-hand quadrant, banks

Table 4.5. Classifying Systemic Liquidity Environments

– – (double minus) Systemic Vulnerability Exposure to Volatile Funding: High Infrastructure: Weak	+ or – Weakness of Management Exposure to Volatile Funding: High Infrastructure: Balanced
+ or – Weakness of Infrastructure Exposure to Volatile Funding: Low Infrastructure: Weak	+ + (double plus) Systemic Robustness Exposure to Volatile Funding: Low Infrastructure: Balanced

are operating in a supportive infrastructure but liquidity management of banks displays excessive exposure to volatile funding, thus jeopardizing systemic stability. Conversely, the lower left quadrant is the case where banks are conservatively managed but operating in a weak infrastructure. This may indicate particular vulnerability to contagion. With more reliable and uniformly applicable information, it may be possible to establish empirically whether infrastructure is more important than volatility ratios of banks.

Systemic Liquidity Framework: Case Studies of Mexico and Argentina

The systemic liquidity framework can be used for an in-depth study of country practices as illustrated in the following two case studies. The experience of Mexico and Argentina during 1994–95 further elaborate the findings of the previous section, which suggested that both countries had similar vulnerabilities in their respective liquidity frameworks. The case studies allow a refined analysis of the bank balance sheets and of the institutional structure underlying the systemic liquidity infrastructure. The analysis can be used to identify weaknesses and ways to overcome them.

Mexico, 1994–95

In 1991–92, Mexico re-privatized 18 commercial banks that had been nationalized 10 years earlier. The prices paid were high, often at multiples of three to four times book value. Bank managers found themselves under immediate pressure to generate high earnings to justify such high prices, and assets continued to grow rapidly at what appeared to be healthy spreads. However, rapid growth was accompanied by asset quality deterioration, which was not disclosed due to weak accounting practices. While bankers concentrated on the asset side of their balance sheets, few invested in the infrastructure and product development nec-

Table 4.6. Mexico: Commercial Banks' Liabilities: September 30, 1994
(In percent of total assets)

	All Currencies			Foreign Currency Denominated Only		
	Total	Stable	Volatile	Total	Stable	Volatile
Sight deposits	14	7	7	1	...	1
Direct funding	31	9	22	4	...	4
Repurchase agreements	21	...	21	—	...	—
Interbank liabilities	9	...	9	7	...	7
Bonds, acceptances, other	17	13	4	3	...	3
Subtotal	**92**	**29**	**63**	**15**	...	**15**
Capital, subordinated debt	8	...	...	...	...	...
Total	100					

Source: Comisión Nacional Bancaria y de Valores, Boletín Estadístico de Banca Múltiple, March 1995.

essary to build a deposit franchise, focusing instead on raising funds in the domestic and foreign wholesale money markets. The result was that as banks funded their deteriorating assets with volatile deposits, vulnerability to a loss of confidence grew.

In December of 1994, after a year of political uncertainty and a drain on the Banco de Mexico's dollar reserves, the government devalued the peso by 15 percent. This encouraged more speculative attacks, and a few days later Mexico allowed the peso to float freely. It fell to 56 percent of its early December value. Peso interest rates rose sharply, from 13.7 percent (28-day treasury bills) on December 15 to 31.0 percent at year end and then to over 80 percent a few months later. Both dollar and peso deposits declined, although, as discussed below, the impact on bank liquidity was somewhat divided between dollar and peso liabilities, as the figures are sometimes, erroneously, interpreted as showing that pesos are more stable than dollars. Extensive emergency financial support eventually stabilized the banks sufficiently to allow the broader task of restructuring the banking system (Carstens and Schwartz, 1998).

Bank liabilities

A simplified picture of Mexican bank liabilities just prior to the crisis is shown in Table 4.6. Liabilities are classified as stable and volatile, based on standard characteristics discussed in the first section and some additional institutional factors that played a role in Mexico.

Sight deposits, which can easily be moved but may benefit from some inertia were evenly divided into stable and volatile. With better knowledge of depositor behavior and types of depositors (institutional,

Table 4.7. Mexico: Commercial Banks' Assets: September 30, 1994
(In percent of total assets)

	All Currencies			Foreign Currency Denominated Only		
	Total	Illiquid	Liquid	Total	Illiquid	Liquid
Government securities	0.4	...	0.4	...	...	...
Fixed income securities	5.6	...	5.6	...	...	...
Foreign securities	10.7	...	10.7	...	...	...
Securities receivable, under repo	9.3	...	9.3	...	...	...
Repo receivables	...	...	...	...	...	...
Cash	2.1	2.1	...	0.6	0.6	...
Loans (performing)	54.9	54.9	...	12.0	12.0	...
Loans (past due)	5.8	5.8	...	...	...	...
Other	10.6	10.6	...	5.2	5.2	...
Total	100.0	73.4	**26.6**	19.2	17.8	1.4

Source: Comisión Nacional Bancaria y de Valores, Boletín Estadístico de Banca Múltiple, March 1995.

commercial, government, etc.), more accurate classification would be possible. Non peso accounts were assumed to be volatile, although this may exaggerate the volatility. Of the banks' direct funding, about 70 percent were large, negotiable peso-denominated promissory notes. Foreign currency funding are euro CDs, which were favored because of their liquidity.

Repurchase agreements were classified as volatile due to their short-term nature. Accordingly, the underlying assets, mainly government securities were classified as liquid (Table 4.7).

Interbank borrowings were also classified as volatile. Banks' borrowings from other banks— about 42 percent of the September 1994 balances were borrowed by offshore branches of Mexican banks— were confidence-sensitive and volatile. The remainder (including some foreign currency-denominated liabilities) were obligations of domestic offices, but included borrowings from both domestic and foreign banks. Bonds are classified as mostly nonvolatile, although more information on maturity would permit a more accurate classification.

Bank assets

A simplified picture of Mexican bank assets just prior to the crisis is shown in Table 4.7. In classifying various items as liquid or illiquid, no special assumptions were made in the case of domestic and foreign securities, although the liquidity of domestic securities may be somewhat overstated.

Fixed income securities tend to have short maturities, and they are both salable and can be repoed. Securities receivable under repurchase agreements (repos) are securities that have been sold and are awaiting repurchase. There may be more of such securities, but Mexican accounting rules in effect at the time permitted limited netting against other transactions. Repo receivables arise from a purchase-and-resale transaction (a reverse repo), and the balance is viewed as liquid, given its short maturity.

Cash includes cash in the vault, and correspondent and central bank accounts. Since these are vital in order to support intra day teller transactions and interbank payments, any balance reductions must be made up quickly for the bank to keep its doors open. Ironically, cash is therefore not a liquid asset. Loans are considered illiquid even when current.

Funding volatility ratio

Calculating the funding volatility ratio for Mexico using the balance sheet data provided above shows a volatility ratio of 49.6 percent, suggesting that Mexican banks were relying on volatile sources of funds to finance almost half of their illiquid assets. This relatively high ratio suggests systemic vulnerability for the banking system. The ratio can also be calculated for the dollar sheet as well. In this case, Mexican banks in the aggregate fund 76.4 percent of their illiquid assets with volatile funding. As noted below, this ratio does not reveal the full exposure, particularly because off-balance sheet commitments are not reflected in this simplified account.[22]

Liquidity infrastructure

Table 4.8 provides information on the liquidity infrastructure prevailing in 1994. Mexico's liquidity infrastructure relied strongly on the safety net for banks and for their creditors through both deposit insurance and central bank facilities. By contrast, the infrastructure supporting day-to-day liquidity management by banks had weaknesses.

For example, before the crisis, Mexican banks prepared their quarterly financial statements under guidelines issued by the National Banking and Securities Commission (CNBV), many of which were considerably less rigorous than International Accounting Standards (IAS). The treatment of asset quality was particularly distorted, leading to an overstating of the value of assets (showing a more favorable volatility ratio). Loans were slow to be downgraded, and, even then, only the overdue payment themselves often needed to be classified as nonperforming. Interest

---

[22]For example, the impact of margin calls cannot be fully appreciated from the above balance sheet presentation.

Table 4.8. Mexico: Systemic Liquidity Infrastructure in 1994

Factor	Supportive of an Effective Liquidity Infrastructure?
Day-to-day liquidity management	
Disclosure	No
Prudential liquidity requirements	Yes
Creditor rights	No
Market depth, payments, monetary instruments	No
Foreign exchange liquidity	No
Safety net	
Credible deposit insurance	Yes
Lender of last resort	Yes

continued to accrue on the remainder of the loan balance, and accruals could not be reversed. Provisions, meanwhile, ran directly to capital, without passing through the income statement.[23]

A key prudential ratio (the "liquidity coefficient") required banks to maintain liquid foreign currency assets equal to 15 percent of their foreign currency liabilities. Mexico's general rules to protect creditors were known to be inefficient and ineffective. The 1943 law strongly favored the debtor, as well as the state and employees (Lubrano, 1996). Creditors found the process to be unworkable in the face of the many defaults of 1995. In retrospect, the authorities view the depth of financial markets as not satisfactory as evidenced by the experience that, during 1994, the government had to stop issuing one-year CETES and instead relied increasingly on dollar-indexed debt. But central bank instruments appeared to be broadly supportive of the infrastructure and banks were not subject to reserve requirements at the time.

Foreign exchange liquidity management was significantly flawed. In particular, assets lent to domestic borrowers were not secured sufficiently by the borrowers' ability to generate foreign exchange earnings. In the face of dwindling foreign currency reserves and suddenly changing exchange rates, the fungibility of peso and foreign currency assets and liabilities broke down, leaving banks vulnerable to defaults on outstanding obligations.

Safety net

Mexico's system of deposit insurance in 1994 centered on the FOBAPROA, the Bank Fund for Savings Protection, overseen by board members appointed by the central bank, ministry of finance, and the

---

[23]On December 29, 1995, CNBV issued Circular No. 1284 requiring that banks revise their accounting practices to conform more closely to IAS, beginning in 1997.

CNBV. It was created in 1990 and given the authority, but not the obligation, to "protect" bank creditors. The Fund could provide such protection by paying off creditors of defaulted banks or by extending preventive support, for instance, by lending to troubled institutions as part of a rescue plan (Karaoglan and Lubrano, 1995). Financing was provided by commercial bank contributions, supplemented by the FOBAPROA's ability to borrow from the central bank and government. The Fund's financial condition was not disclosed. Coverage was extended to virtually all instruments and all creditors, in any currency and without limit. Accrued interest was implicitly included.

FOBAPROA's guarantee seems to have been viewed differently within Mexico and abroad. Domestically, the widespread assumption was that the government would protect bank creditors. No one had lost money in a Mexican bank since the revolution. Bankers seemed to take confidence and, consequently, peso liquidity for granted, and they did little to protect themselves against the remote risk of depositor flight. Externally, creditors were more skeptical. The central bank attributed this, in part, to the previous experience in 1982 when dollar deposits were converted into pesos at a rate fixed by the authorities leading to significant losses by depositors.[24]

Crisis and response

Peso liquidity. Peso deposits decreased during 1994 and 1995. Overall bank accounts declined by 8 percent in real terms during 1995. Some peso depositors moved into dollars and banks sought to raise peso funds elsewhere. Furthermore, the decline in value of some assets pledged as guarantees to secure dollar borrowings forced Mexican banks to take action. Banks had to raise peso-denominated funds to purchase dollars to meet margin calls. However, this additional source of pressure on liquidity is not (or is insufficiently) reflected in the bank balance sheets, indicating an important shortcoming of available market data.

Dollar liquidity. Foreign holders of Mexican bank liabilities reacted to the turmoil culminating in the December 1994 devaluation. In January, exposures to Mexican banks were sharply reduced, by selling negotiable paper and by refusing to roll over maturing items.[25] One large bank found that it could roll over only 10 percent of its maturing dollar certificates of deposit (CDs). Foreign currency-denominated deposits

---

[24]The central bank had the authority and the willingness to act as a lender of last resort, as did the government-owned development banks, which had the ability to rediscount bank loans.

[25]Fourth quarter foreign exchange losses for the system as a whole were equal to 10 percent of total equity. See Karaoglan and Lubrano (1995).

dropped by $3.5 billion, or 23 percent of the total during the first quarter of 1995. The decline in dollar deposits was somewhat dampened by significant conversions from peso into dollar deposits.

The government produced a multipronged response. FOBAPROA established a special window in January to provide short-term dollar loans to banks. Maturities were limited to 28 days, and the loans had to be collateralized with government securities, securities of NAFIN (the state-owned development bank), or equity securities of the recipient bank. The interest rate was a punitive 25 percent, set in order to encourage banks to find substitute sources of funds quickly.

Banco de Mexico temporarily relaxed its 15 percent prudential liquidity coefficient, releasing banks to liquidate the dollar securities they had maintained against volatile dollar liabilities. Later, Banco de Mexico relaxed regulations that had limited bankers' ability to create a synthetic short dollar position with derivatives. This allowed the banks to substitute peso funding for dollar funding, using derivatives to cover the foreign exchange risk from their dollar loans. Seventeen banks took advantage of the FOBAPROA dollar window, accepting the punitive interest rate while searching for alternatives. On March 31, 1995, the banks had drawn down an aggregate of $3.3 billion. The facility peaked in April at about $3.9 billion. Banks also liquidated virtually all of the assets that had earlier fulfilled their liquidity coefficient requirement.

Argentina, 1994–95

From a liquidity perspective, an important aspect of Argentina's banking environment in 1994 was its fragmentation. The banking sector included a large number of weak players, especially public, provincial, and niche-oriented private banks, and a few strong domestic and foreign banks. Bank depositors and creditors had experienced confiscation of accounts in the 1980s and 1990s (through forced conversion into bonds), which weakened public confidence. Since 1991, Argentina had been committed to a rigorous monetary and fiscal regime, represented by a currency board. From a systemic liquidity perspective, this constrained the safety net because the Central Bank of the Republic of Argentina (BCRA) had only a limited ability to act as a lender of last resort. In addition, no deposit insurance scheme was in place until April 1995 when the government created a limited self-funded deposit insurance program.

Banking sector liquidity

Table 4.9 shows a breakdown of the banking sector balance sheet by currency and by liquidity of assets and volatility of liabilities, respectively,

Table 4.9. Argentina: Commercial Banks' Balance Sheets: December 31, 1994
(In percent of total assets)

	All Currencies			Foreign Currency Denominated Only		
	Total	Illiquid	Liquid	Total	Illiquid	Liquid
Assets:						
Cash and reserves	8	3	6	3	1	2
Securities	5	...	5	3	...	3
Loans	65	65	...	36	36	...
Other	22	22	...	3	3	...
Total assets	100	90	**11**	45	40	**5**
Liabilities:						
Deposits	50	28	22	24	12	12
Wholesale liabilities	11	1	10	11	1	10
Other	19	19	...	...	...	...
Total liabilities	80	48	**32**	35	13	**22**
Capital, subordinated debt	16	...	...	...	...	...

Source: Banco Central de la República Argentina, Boletín Estadístico.

as of 1994, shortly before the outbreak of the crisis in Mexico. For cash and reserves, Argentine reserve requirements were much higher than the need to cover intra day payments liquidity, and BCRA's willingness to release these funds during the emergency suggested (ex post) that, from a liquidity management standpoint, a significant portion of these balances could be considered liquid. Securities comprised short-maturity money market instruments and salable or pledgeable securities.

On the liabilities side, the lack of deposit insurance suggested that many depositors would be confidence sensitive. A significant portion of bank deposits (7 percent of total assets), however, came from the public sector. These are classified as stable. Wholesale liabilities are repurchase agreements, interbank liabilities, and bonds issued, which could largely be considered as volatile. Similarly, dollar assets and liabilities were classified using an optimistic assumption that dollar deposits were about as volatile as domestic deposits.

Funding volatility ratio

The funding volatility ratio for Argentina on September 30, 1994, allocating assets and liabilities as done above, was 24 percent, which indicates vulnerability to liquidity shocks. The dollar-only balance sheet at that time was also positive. It might be argued that in Argentina, foreign exchange deposits were relatively more stable than domestic ones given Argentina's demonstrated commitment to currency convertibility and exchange rate stability. Nevertheless, the

Table 4.10. Argentina: Systemic Liquidity Infrastructure in 1994

Factor	Supportive of an Effective Liquidity Infrastructure?
Day-to-day liquidity management	
Disclosure	Yes
Prudential liquidity requirements	No
Creditor's rights	Yes
Market depth, instruments, etc.	Yes
Foreign exchange liquidity	Neutral
Safety net	
Credible deposit insurance	No
Lender of last resort	No

volatility ratio would have remained positive for foreign currency balance sheet items, indicating net exposure to confidence-sensitive funds.

Liquidity infrastructure

Argentina's liquidity infrastructure, summarized in Table 4.10, shows a fundamentally different approach than that found in Mexico. Whereas Mexico provided a weak environment for early detection and remediation of bank health (day-to-day liquidity infrastructure), Argentina's was relatively strong. With respect to the safety net elements (deposit insurance and lender of last resort), the situation was reversed.

Regarding disclosure, Argentina complied broadly with international standards, although it was recognized that provisioning rules needed to be improved. Only two months before the impact of the Mexican crisis hit Argentina, BCRA had issued regulations that closed the gap, with implementation for periods ending December 31, 1994.[26] The rights of bank creditors appear to have been well established at the time of the crisis, in contrast to the situation a decade earlier. When a bank was liquidated, secured creditors and depositors were given priority over other creditors. Liquidation through court-supervised bankruptcy was a lengthy process, however, and in early 1995, it threatened to overwhelm the system. Part of the government's response was to put in place an enhanced set of laws allowing for a more streamlined liquidation process. A change in the charter of the central bank allowed for the separation between assets and liabilities of a bank, thus opening up the option to create "good bank–bad bank" type of restructuring plans.

Argentina did not have prudential liquidity requirements in place, although, as noted, relatively high reserve requirements compensated for this to some extent. As in Mexico, a major effort to upgrade the

---

[26]For a summary of recent reforms in the financial sector, see, for example, IMF (1998).

supervisory organization was under way when the crisis hit, although Argentina had progressed farther than Mexico. Nevertheless, fiscal constraints prevented the supervisors from acting as aggressively to close insolvent banks, which doubtless undermined the systemic confidence of institutional creditors.

Argentina had relatively well-developed financial markets in 1994, which may have cushioned the effects of the shock. Regarding central bank instruments, the BCRA imposed high reserve requirements on Argentine bank deposits—for example, 45 percent for dollar and peso demand deposit and savings accounts. This requirement constrained banks' liquidity management. However, it proved to be an important crisis-response tool for an otherwise financially restricted government.

On foreign exchange liquidity, about half of Argentina's bank assets and liabilities were dollar-denominated. The Convertibility Law of 1991 sought to provide assurance that foreign currency would be made available for repayment to creditors and that the dollar-peso parity would be maintained. Pre-crisis spreads of 2 percent to 3 percent between deposits denominated in the two currencies indicated that creditors had more confidence in the convertibility commitment than to the promise of continued exchange rate parity. These spreads widened to as much as 10 percent by March 1995, as depositors switched from pesos to dollars, while reducing their overall deposits at the same time. Eventually, the market regained confidence in the government's commitment, and the situation stabilized.

Safety net

Argentina had no deposit insurance at the time the Mexican crisis spread to Argentina. As a result, small depositors took flight along with institutional creditors. A limited, self-financed deposit insurance scheme (SEDESA) was established in April 1995, emphasizing small deposits. The currency board reduced the government's role in providing lender-of-last-resort support. BCRA's potential as a lender of last resort was similarly constrained (as well as by law), although it was able to marshal relatively significant resources for liquidity support using the available instruments

Crisis and response

In most respects, Argentina's liquidity infrastructure emphasized day-to-day liquidity management factors and early preventive action. The safety net was not formally in place. While this system was unbalanced, the emphasis on day-to-day management provided banks with strong incentives to create a robust system. In November 1994, Argentina's government bond market was weakened by the failure of a nonbank securities trading firm and by the subsequent tightening of credit to all securities dealers. A month later, the banking system was affected by the Mexican crisis. The one-branch wholesale banks, whose liquid assets fell in value just as their institutional sources of funds dried up, were the first to feel the impact. Within three months, there was a widespread withdrawal from the banking system—the total equivalent of $8 billion, or 16 percent of total deposits. The impact on the weaker wholesale, retail, and cooperative banks was much larger, however, since there was a shift of deposits to the larger domestic and foreign banks. Interest rates doubled for both peso and dollar deposits.

The government and BCRA responded to the crisis aggressively within the constraints of the 1991 Convertibility Law. BCRA decreased its high reserve requirements, releasing about $3 billion, plus another $2 billion through rediscounting and repo facilities, thus covering more than 60 percent of withdrawals. Emergency liquidity was assembled from public and private sources and made available to banks. In the aftermath of the crisis, the infrastructure was strengthened, including the establishment of a contingent liquidity facility adding to the resilience of Argentina's banking system today (IMF 1998, p. 61).

Lessons and Implications

The framework outlined for assessing the adequacy of arrangements for systemic liquidity is essentially that of auditing the infrastructural preconditions for deep and liquid money markets in the context of volatile funding arrangements by banks. The emphasis on a range of infrastructural preconditions makes the systemic approach presented in this chapter particularly suitable for a broad range of countries, including industrial and emerging economies. While detailed microstructural issues affecting actual liquidity operations and market design remain, the framework is sufficiently robust to be diagnostic. Moreover, the approach can assist in identifying prescriptive reforms toward increasing resilience in the financial system and, thus, serve as a basis for systemic liquidity policy.[27]

The benefits of deep and liquid money markets are multifaceted. Central banks have an interest because of their monetary policy responsibilities and their interest in financial sector stability. Deep markets

---

[27]The framework was used in the IMF's Financial Sector Assessment Program (FSAP) in Canada, London, and others. See the IMF's standards and codes webpage at www.imf.org.

facilitate the transmission of monetary policies; provide a basis for information and feedback indicators; and allow for intervention to achieve targets without undue price volatility. Public debt managers also have an interest in liquid markets. Robust primary and secondary markets in government securities allow for conditions to minimize public debt service costs. Moreover, resulting yields in these markets can serve as benchmarks against which private debt markets can develop. For commercial banks, the principal benefit lies in their ability to perform portfolio adjustments in response to shocks.

With these shared interests in systemic liquidity come responsibilities to forge a framework for resilience. Bank management capabilities are key to an environment fostering robust markets. In this regard, mere compliance with a liquid assets ratio does not indicate liquidity soundness. The maturity profile of assets and liabilities and reliance on particular types of markets for funding and resulting volatility are important considerations. An effective liquidity management policy should not only rely on having an adequate buffer of easily liquified assets, but also require active participation by bank management in monitoring and forecasting liquidity positions.

Thus, a volatility ratio can be used to assess individual banks' exposure to confidence-sensitive funds. Prudence would dictate that banks should have more liquid assets than confidence-sensitive liabilities using a substance over form analysis of balance sheets to identify truly liquid assets and volatile liabilities. Beyond providing a legal and regulatory framework for confidence, involving transparent creditor rights and information disclosure, monetary authorities need to invest in removing barriers to appropriate microstructures for market development. In this regard, issues of instrument design, prudential regulations, payment system design, and an appropriate balance between day-to-day and safety net arrangements are important.

The country reviews indicate mixed practices, suggesting a range on the scale of financial sector resilience to prospective liquidity shocks. Alternatively, where arrangements are inadequate not only is monetary management made less effective, but also banks could be forced into inefficiencies, holding large stocks of non- or low-yielding liquid assets as a hedge, leading to higher intermediation spreads.

This framework also raises implications for the conduct of monetary operations. Countries using a reserve operation framework often include excess reserves as an indicator to guide intervention. To the extent that the level of excess reserves depends on the opportunity costs of such reserves, central banks can influence these balances through operations to change market rates. Transmission can however be blunted, if owing to poor infrastructure the demand for excess reserves is sticky—as banks could risk illiquidity to invest outside of excess reserves. If intervention guides are set independent of an assessment of the robustness of the infrastructure, absorption could unnecessarily increase cost to the central bank for the same monetary effect. The state of infrastructure also impacts on interest rate operating frameworks through potential distortions to interbank markets. If banks are unsure of the conditions (due to rigidities or lack of information) for mobilizing funds, segmentation could occur, reducing the information content of the interbank rate as an operating target.

Finally, the framework provides an approach to an early warning indicator of potential stress and in this respect could be further developed toward a quantitative system of systemic liquidity analysis. Where financial systems overly rely on volatile funding sources to finance assets there is greater need for a robust infrastructure to fund potential shocks. Even where volatility ratios appear conservative, further analysis may be needed to ensure that markets really exist to realize the presumed liquidity.

References

Bank of England, 1981, *The Measurement of Liquidity* (London: Bank of England).

Bank for International Settlements, 1999, "Market Liquidity: Research Findings and Selected Policy Implications," report of a study group established by the Committee on the Global Financial Systems (CGFS) of the Group of Ten Countries (Basel: BIS).

Basel Committee on Banking Supervision, 1993, *A Framework for Measuring and Managing Liquidity* (Basel: Bank for International Settlements).

Borio, Claudio, 1997, *Monetary Policy Operation Procedures in Industrial Countries* (Basel: Bank for International Settlements).

Bundesbank, 1982, "Central Bank Money Requirements of Banks and Liquidity Policy Measures of the Bundesbank," *Monthly Bulletin* (Frankfurt: Deutsche Bundesbank).

Carstens, A., and M.J. Schwartz, 1998, "Capital Flows and the Financial Crisis in Mexico," *Journal of Asian Economies*, Vol. 9, No. 2, pp. 207–26.

Claessens, Stijn, S. Djankov, and Klapper Leora, 1999, *Resolution of Corporate Distress: Evidence from East Asia's Financial Crisis* (Washington: World Bank).

Dacey, John, and Jackie Bazel-Horowitz, 1990, *Liquidity Management: Recent Changes in Liquidity Management Practices at Commercial Banks* (New York: Federal Reserve Bank of New York).

Dattels, Peter, 1995, "Microstructure of Government Securities Markets," IMF Working Paper No. 95/117 (Washington: International Monetary Fund).

de Villiers, J.U., 1996, "The Liquidity of Financial Assets," *South African Journal of Economics*, Vol. 64, June, pp. 1–23.

Garcia, Gillian G.H., 1999, "Deposit Insurance: A Survey of Actual and Best Practices," IMF Working Paper No. 99/54 (Washington: International Monetary Fund).

Group of Twenty Two, 1998, *Report of the Working Group on Strengthening Financial Systems* (Washington: G-22, October).

Gulde, Anne-Marie, 1995, "Liquid Asset Ratios—An Effective Policy Tool? (unpublished; Washington: Monetary and Exchange Affairs Department, International Monetary Fund).

International Monetary Fund, 1998, *Staff Country Report—Argentina* No. 98/38, April (Washington).

Karaoglan, Roy A., and Mike Lubrano, 1995, "Mexico's Banks After the December 1994 Devaluation—A Chronology of the Government's Response," *Northwestern Journal of International Law and Business*, Vol. 16, No. 1, pp. 24–43.

Lamfalussy Report, 1990, *Report of the Committee on Interbank Netting Schemes of the Central Bank of the Group of Ten Countries*, November (Basel: Bank for International Settlements).

La Porta R., F. Lopez-De Silanes, A. Shleifer, and R. W. Vishny, 1997, "Legal Determinants of External Finance," *The Journal of Finance*, Vol. 52, July.

Lubrano, Mike, 1996, "Practical Difficulties in Mexican Workouts and Bankruptcy," *North American Corporate Lawyer*, Vol. III, No. 3.

Mendes, Antonio, 1995, "A Brief Incursion into Bankruptcy and the Enforcement of Creditor's Rights," *Northwestern Journal of International Law and Business*, Vol. 16, No. 1 (Fall), pp. 107–116.

O'Hara, Maureen, 1995, *Market Microstructure Theory* (Cambridge, Mass.: Blackwell Publishers).

Prestopino, Chris, 1994, *The Impact of Differential Reserve Requirements on Commercial Bank Liquidity and Portfolio Management* (Philadelphia: University of Pennsylvania).

U.S. Federal Reserve Bank of New York, 1990, *Funding and Liquidity: Recent Changes in Liquidity Management Practices at Commercial Banks and Securities Firms* (New York: Federal Reserve Bank of New York).

White, Michelle J., 1993, "The Costs of Corporate Bankruptcy: a U.S.-European Comparison," University of Michigan Institute of Public Policy Studies, Discussion Paper No. 346, August (Ann Arbor: University of Michigan).

5

Emergency Liquidity Support Facilities

Dong He

This chapter discusses the operational aspects of emergency liquidity support by central banks to individual institutions under stress.[1] Recent financial crises around the world have prompted renewed interest in lender-of-last-resort support as a key component of public financial safety nets. Although the basic principles of emergency lending, as developed by Thornton and Bagehot, have been known for more than a century, in practice their use has encountered considerable difficulties. The exercise of the emergency lending function, as contrasted with lending as part of standard money market practice, generally occurs when the solvency of the borrowing bank is in doubt. Typically, difficult decisions on whether to grant or deny credit to an institution seeking help have to be made rapidly and executed within a short period of time, and a delicate balance has to be struck between controlling moral hazard and avoiding systemic instability.

The study of emergency lending operations is hampered by a general lack of information on country practices in this area. There is a tradition among central banks of not saying much on the subject, both before and

---

The author would like to thank Huw Evans and Haizhou Huang for their detailed comments and suggestions. Comments from V. Sundararajan, Charles Enoch, Alain Ize, Barry Johnston, Marc Quintyn, Gillian Garcia, Claudia Dziobek, Barbara Baldwin, Greta Mitchell-Casselle, Peter Hayward, Luis Jacome Hidalgo, Matthew Jones, Arto Kovanen, and Jan Willem van der Vossen are also gratefully acknowledged.

[1]This chapter makes no attempt to provide a comprehensive survey of the literature on the theoretical aspects of the subject. For such a survey, see, for example, Freixas and others (1999).

after a rescue operation. Nevertheless, this chapter attempts to distill some common lessons from a variety of approaches to emergency support operations in different countries, based on the limited information available. It will aim to shed light on the following operational questions: Should emergency liquidity support facilities exist? If such facilities exist, should their existence be known to the public? Should the operational rules of such facilities be specified ahead of time? Should emergency lending be disclosed after the fact? What roles should the central bank, the supervisory agency, and the ministry of finance play in conducting emergency liquidity support? How can one ensure that monetary and exchange rate policy objectives are not vitiated by emergency liquidity support? What should be the terms and conditions for emergency liquidity support? What happens if preconditions of support are not met? What should be done in default situations? Should the modalities of emergency lending be different in times of systemic crisis from normal times?

This chapter argues that, although there may well be good reasons to maintain ambiguity over the conditions for lender-of-last-resort support and to avoid previous specification of the rules to follow in such operations, it is increasingly more attractive to follow a rule-based approach by setting out the necessary conditions for support, while maintaining that meeting such conditions is not sufficient for receiving support. This is particularly true for developing and transitional economies where central bank discretion itself is more likely to be subject to undue political pressure and regulatory forbearance and lead to the abuse of lender-of-last-resort support facilities. Whether the rules are spelled out in advance or not, it is essential to have properly designed lending procedures, clearly laid out authority and accountability, as well as rules for disclosure after the event, when such disclosure will not be disruptive to financial stability. This is all necessary so as to ensure accountability and to reduce the distortionary effect on incentives.

Another argument is that emergency liquidity support facilities are primarily for systemic purposes and should be used very infrequently. Decisions to lend to systemically important institutions, at the risk of insolvency or without sufficient quality collateral, should be made jointly by the monetary, the supervisory, and the fiscal authorities. Lending to nonsystemically important institutions, if any, should be made only to those that are deemed to be solvent and have sufficient acceptable collateral. When support has to be provided, it is essential that such support be made only on a short-term basis. Banks that receive such support should be subject to enhanced supervision and restrictions on activities, and a clear exit strategy should be designed so

> **Box 5.1. Key Considerations of Emergency Lending in Normal Times**
>
> - Have in place clearly laid out lending procedures, authority, and accountability.
> - Maintain close cooperation and exchange of information between the central bank, the supervisory authority (if it is separate from the central bank), the deposit insurance fund (if such a fund exists), and the ministry of finance.
> - Make decisions to lend to systemically important institutions at the risk of insolvency or without sufficient, acceptable collateral jointly by the monetary, supervisory, and the fiscal authorities.
> - Lend to nonsystemically important institutions only if those institutions are deemed to be solvent and with sufficient acceptable collateral.
> - Lend speedily.
> - Lend in domestic currency.
> - Lend at above average market rates.
> - Maintain monetary control by engaging effective sterilization.
> - Subject borrowing banks to enhanced supervisory surveillance and restrictions on activities.
> - Lend only for the short term, preferably not exceeding three to six months.
> - Have a clear exit strategy.
> - Disclose emergency support operations when such disclosure will not be disruptive to financial stability.

that the banks that prove to be nonviable will be closed or resolved in an orderly fashion (Box 5.1). In any case, the central bank should ensure that its monetary and exchange rate policy objectives are not weakened by its emergency lending.

In times of systemic crises, the modalities of lender-of-last-resort support will need to be adapted from good practices that are made in normal times. In a general environment of panic and instability, the existence and presence of an emergency lender should not be doubted by the market participants. The central bank should pronounce its willingness to lend readily and its support should be visible. Decisions to provide support should be part of a general crisis management strategy and should be made jointly by the monetary, the supervisory, and the fiscal authorities. The repayment terms may be relaxed to accommodate the implementation of the bank restructuring strategy. Emergency liquidity support in these circumstances should be explicitly guaranteed

> **Box 5.2. Key Considerations of Emergency Lending in Systemic Crises**
>
> - Have in place clearly laid out lending procedures, authority, and accountability.
> - Maintain close cooperation and exchange of information between the central bank, the supervisory authority (if it is separate from the central bank), the deposit insurance fund (if such a fund exists), and the ministry of finance.
> - Make public announcement of willingness to lend.
> - Decisions to provide support should be part of a general crisis management strategy and should be made jointly by the monetary, the supervisory, and the fiscal authorities.
> - Lend with speed.
> - Lend in domestic currency.
> - Lend at above average market rates.
> - Maintain monetary control by engaging effective sterilization.
> - Subject borrowing banks to intensive supervisory surveillance and restrictions on activities.
> - Relax repayment terms if necessary to accommodate the implementation of a systemic bank restructuring strategy.
> - Disclose emergency support operations when such disclosure will not be disruptive to financial stability.

by the government, and any loss thus incurred should be fully compensated by the budget (Box 5.2).

The remainder of the chapter is organized as follows. The following section discusses the nature and scope of emergency support operations. The third section discusses the issues that relate to the transparency and ambiguity in lender-of-last-resort support, whereas the fourth section discusses the modalities of emergency lending to specific banks in normal times. The final section discusses emergency lending in times of systemic crises. The Appendix lists selected texts of central bank laws that deal with emergency liquidity support in 20 countries.

The Nature and Scope of Emergency Liquidity Support

The term "lender of last resort" has been used to denote various lending functions that the central bank performs. In this paper we use the term in the sense of discretionary lending by the central bank, primarily out of concern for financial stability rather than as a tool of short-term monetary management.

Definition and Objectives of Lender-of-Last-Resort Support

Lender-of-last-resort support can be defined as "the discretionary provision of liquidity to a financial institution (or the market as a whole) by the central bank in reaction to an adverse shock, which causes an abnormal increase in demand for liquidity that cannot be met from an alternative source" (Freixas and others, 1999).[2] The relative importance of lending through the discount window to target aid to specific banks and to lend to the market through open market operations varies across countries and according to circumstances. One school of thought advocates that the lender of last resort rely solely on open market operations rather than on specific institutions, in order to counter the moral hazard often associated with discount window lending (Goodfriend and King, 1988). It is argued that liquidity assistance to banks through open market operations will filter through to the whole financial system through financial markets. However, such filtering may not occur in times of stress when confidence is low and the market becomes segmented. Indeed, Goodhart and Huang (1998) argue that adopting the view that the lender of last resort should lend only to the market is to reject the notion of the lender of last resort. In practice, many central banks combine use of the discount window with open market operations. This paper will focus on emergency support through discount window lending to specific banks.[3]

Discretionary emergency lending through the discount window typically has the following primary objectives: to prevent illiquidity at an individual bank from unnecessarily leading to its insolvency and to avoid runs that spill over from bank to bank. The first objective is related to the problem of fire sale induced insolvency. A distinguishing feature of banks is that their assets are largely illiquid term loans while their liabilities comprise predominantly unsecured short-term deposits. Moreover, deposits are paid out in full on a first-come-first-served basis. These features of banks' balance sheets make them susceptible to depositor runs. If a bank that experiences a significant deposit run cannot

---

[2]In this definition, lender-of-last-resort support or emergency lending does not include standing facilities, which are standard monetary policy instruments. Accordingly, this paper does not consider the operations of standing facilities.

[3]Lender-of-last-resort support could also take the form of off-balance sheet guarantees. The central bank as the crisis manager could orchestrate a rescue operation by providing an indemnity to a third party (for example, the peer group of the bank seeking liquidity support) that is willing to take part in the operation, rather than providing funds itself on-balance sheet. This practice is not recommended as a good practice since it is often done in a nontransparent manner. However, if it is used, it is important for the central bank's contingent liabilities to be properly and transparently recognized and recorded.

quickly attract sufficient replenishing funds to offset deposit loss, it may be required to sell at least some assets quickly at fire sale prices. To avoid selling assets at fire sale prices, troubled institutions require either a recycling of funds from deposit gaining institutions or access to credit from other parties, or both. If other private banks do not provide such assistance, then the central bank may have to be approached for liquidity support as the lender of last resort.

The second objective relates to contagion, a term used to describe the spillover of shocks from one or more banks to others. Bank contagion is of particular concern if adverse shocks, such as the failure or near failure of one or more banks, are transmitted in domino fashion not only to other banks and the banking system as a whole, but beyond to the entire financial system and the macroeconomy. Banking is subject to contagion for the following reasons. First, banks typically lend heavily to each other; when a particular bank is subject to runs, it will have to recall its interbank loans to other banks immediately, which may cause the other banks to become illiquid. Second, asymmetric information is typically a very serious problem with banking. Incomplete and costly information may make it difficult for depositors to distinguish sound from unsound banks.

Emergency support operations are risky. In providing support, the central bank takes credit risks that are unacceptable to all other lenders in the market. While such lending is meant to bridge a temporary period of illiquidity for institutions that prove to be viable after the lending has taken place, these same institutions that receive such loans may eventually turn out to be nonviable and have to be closed. In these cases, emergency lending could still serve a useful public purpose in providing time for the authorities to arrange for the orderly closure and resolution of failing institutions.

However, there are important costs associated with prolonged lending to troubled institutions. Such lending, for example, can allow uninsured depositors and other general creditors to exit a failing bank before its closure. When fully collateralized central bank loans replace funds that are not insured, the deposit insurance fund may face higher resolution costs. In addition, a perception that lender-of-last-resort assistance will be readily available to troubled institutions can weaken market discipline in the banking system and remove some of the pressure on bank regulators and supervisors to close troubled institutions promptly.

To minimize such costs, it is essential any lender-of-last-resort support must be primarily for systemic purposes. This means that in considering whether to provide support to an individual institution, the guiding principle must be whether the failure of that institution would, either by itself or through spreading contagion to other institutions, damage the stability of the financial system. Such a contagion effect could arise, for example, when other institutions are heavily exposed to the troubled institution or share similar characteristics, which could be interpreted as the origin of its problems. The vulnerability of other institutions to contagion will also depend on the general tone of sentiment at the time—for example, whether there is heightened uncertainty about the stability of the banking or the monetary systems (Yam, 1999). If lender-of-last-resort support is considered in any nonsystemic cases, it should be confined to institutions that are deemed to be solvent and, normally, with acceptable collateral.

The Meaning of "Last Resort"

In considering the use of emergency lending facilities, central banks typically require the borrower to demonstrate that the lender-of-last-resort support is genuinely being sought as a last resort, and the bank in question has made all reasonable efforts to raise the necessary liquidity. There are two approaches to ensuring that lender-of-last-resort support will be sought only as a means of last resort. First, the support is to be provided at a penalty interest rate. The difficulty with this approach is that it is often not easy to determine what is the right level of penalty and what interest rate should be charged, particularly when there is market segmentation or breakdown. In addition, adverse selection may imply that problem banks are not necessarily deterred by penalty interest rates (see further discussion in the fourth section, "Modalities of Emergency Liquidity Support"). The second approach is to impose harsh conditionality on the borrowing bank as an implicit price. This has been the typical approach of the Federal Reserve in the United States. Many central banks typically have resorted to both approaches to ensure that the assistance was sought genuinely as a last resort.

Regulation A of the Federal Reserve Board in the United States stipulates that banks must first exhaust market sources of funds before turning to the discount window. To ensure that this principle is met in practice, reserve banks regularly monitor the sources and uses of funds for institutions while they are borrowing (Clouse, 1994). In Hong Kong, as a precondition for support, Hong Kong Monetary Authority requires that "the institution has sought other reasonably available sources of funding before seeking LOLR (lender-of-last-resort) assistance," and "the shareholder controllers of the institution have made all reasonable efforts to provide liquidity and/or capital support as a demonstration of their own commitment" (Yam, 1999).

The Bank of England was traditionally as much a crisis manager as a crisis lender in dealing with banking problems by playing a managerial, facilitating, or coordinating role. Governor Eddie George (1993) pointed out that, as one of the operational principles, the Bank of England would explore every option for a commercial solution before committing the Bank of England's funds. Initially, the Bank of England would always look to major shareholders to provide support. Short of that, the Bank of England would encourage the troubled bank to try to find a buyer, for some or all of itself, even at reduced prices. Or a bank's major creditors may decide to provide support to protect their own positions. As an alternative, there may be a coherent group of other banks with a common interest in an orderly resolution. Only when these options have been exhausted would the Bank of England consider providing support itself—and even then it may decide against support, as it did in the case of British and Commonwealth Merchant Bank in 1990. Exploring these options does not necessarily imply it will take longer to decide whether to grant support or not. Speed is of the essence in handling liquidity problems. The Bank of England tried many of these options over the weekend in handling the failure of Barings in early 1995.

The Resource Constraint on Last Resort Operations

Central banks are often thought of as having unlimited access to resources since they can print money, but this is clearly simplistic (Giannini, 1998). Lending freely in a crisis may prove incompatible with the prevailing monetary regime. This is most clearly demonstrated by the constraints that a fixed exchange rate system places on the capacity for domestic money creation. Moreover, large loans to institutions at the risk of insolvency pose substantial credit risks to the central bank, which could complicate monetary management and contribute to inflation, since central banks typically have minimal capital and a small revenue base and tend to monetize their losses. Thus, when the scale of support is large, the fiscal authorities need to underwrite the credit risks taken on by the central bank. The ministry of finance will have to be involved in making decisions to lend to systemically important institutions at the risk of insolvency. As Goodhart and Schoenmaker (1995) point out, "he who pays the piper calls the tune."

Sterilization of the liquidity support provided through emergency lending facilities would enable central banks to recycle liquidity in the banking system and facilitate monetary control and exchange market stability. However, the extent of successful sterilization depends on the availability of necessary instruments and overall monetary and macroeconomic conditions. In the recent Asian crises, large amounts of liquidity support to problem financial institutions had to be sterilized; this occurred, to a large extent, in Korea and Thailand but not in Indonesia, which suffered a loss of monetary control. In Indonesia, the subsequent inflation and exchange rate depreciation led to more loss of confidence in the banks, making further liquidity support necessary. Until this vicious cycle was broken, the highly expansionary monetary policy resulted in high inflation, capital outflows, and a collapse of the rupiah.

Central banks need to have the necessary instruments to sterilize the additional liquidity. These include discretionary market-based instruments, such as reverse repos and foreign exchange swaps; semistanding facilities, such as a deposit facility; and higher reserve requirements. Given the difficulties in using higher reserve requirements in a time of banking crisis or distress, market-based instruments are preferable. This argues for developing deep and liquid money and securities markets as part of a sound banking system. Even with such markets, the inevitable market segmentation that emerges during a banking crisis will make volatility of interest rates unavoidable while sterilizing emergency liquidity support.

The resource constraint on the scope of emergency liquidity support is most apparent under a currency board arrangement. Under a currency board arrangement, the central bank can provide lender-of-last-resort support provided that it has sufficient excess coverage of foreign reserves or support from a common pool of bank resources—for example, interbank borrowing by the central bank. One solution, adopted in Bulgaria, is to set up a separate department (the banking department) within the central bank that is endowed with sufficient resources to lend in the event of a panic or a banking sector problem. Should the currency board arrangement permit,[4] the central bank may obtain automatic support from other central banks, as in Hong Kong, where a protocol of this kind was established with other Asian central banks in the wake of the Mexican crisis, or it may guarantee lines of credit with foreign banks on behalf of local commercial banks, as was done in Argentina.[5]

---

[4]International reserves required for backing in Argentina, Bulgaria, and Lithuania are calculated using the concept that it does not take into account the central bank's long-term external obligations (for example, to the IMF or the World Bank).

[5]Under this agreement, participating banks pay a premium to the central bank, which, in turn, pays a commission to the international banks to secure access to the funds. Local banks in need of funds will have to place certain securities with the central bank, which will enter into repurchase agreements with participating international banks.

The resources available to the central bank are critical, as are the legal and other limitations placed on the central bank in the exercise of its role as the lender of last resort. To avoid undermining the currency board arrangement, the central bank must be prudent in the use of the excess coverage.[6] The authority and conditions for accessing different sources of funds should be clearly laid out in the legislation or regulation governing emergency support operations.

While historically the central bank has usually been the lender of last resort, this role does not have to fall exclusively within the responsibility of the central bank. If a certain authority and access to resources are necessary for taking the leading role in managing a liquidity crisis, then a ministry of finance may be able to take on the responsibility as well as a central bank (Fischer, 1999). For instance, if the central bank is not in a position to play the role of the lender of last resort, a special fund for emergency lending purposes may be set up by the ministry of finance. In such cases, it would be essential to establish full transparency with regard to the operation of the fund and to seek the cooperation of the central bank and the supervisory authority in making decisions when the fund is to be drawn upon for emergency liquidity support.

Transparency and Ambiguity in Emergency Liquidity Support

There has been a strong tradition among central bankers to be deliberately ambiguous about their policies regarding emergency liquidity support. The economic rationale of this stance is, however, questionable under closer scrutiny.

Constructive Ambiguity

One possible way to avoid moral hazard in performing the function of emergency liquidity support is to make access to such facilities uncertain, something to be determined ad hoc in each situation. "A lender of last resort should exist, but his presence should be doubted" (Kindleberger, 1978). A tradition of constructive ambiguity has been practiced by some central banks. This is clearly illustrated by the following statement by Gerald Corrigan (1990), President of the Federal Reserve Bank of New York, before the United States Senate Committee on Banking, Housing, and Urban Affairs in May 1990:

---

[6]When the excess coverage becomes small, the currency board arrangement's credibility will come under serious scrutiny. Thus, if the excess coverage is limited, the case for not assuming the role of lender of last resort by the central bank under a currency board arrangement becomes strong.

> I believe that the workings of both the safety net and market discipline will be better served in a context in which the authorities maintain a policy of what I like to call "constructive ambiguity" as to what they will do, how they will do it, and when they will do it. . . . The circumstances associated with a particular case, the setting in which it occurs, and the assessment of the relative costs and benefits of alternative courses of action will always have to be looked at case by case. But in no case should it be prudent for market participants to take for granted what actions the authorities will take and certainly in no case should owners and managers of troubled institutions—large or small—conclude that they will be protected from loss or failure.

In a similar vein, the Governor of the Bank of England, Eddie George (1993), stated that,

> In reaching a decision on support, we take care not to be predictable. Central bankers have raised unpredictability to an art form, so that the phrase "constructive ambiguity" has become rather popular in our circles. But it is essential that no one—no one—should expect support as a matter of course. I often hear it said that some banks are "too big to fail," that some occupy such key positions that their failure is almost unthinkable. It is, indeed, true that size is an important factor in considering systemic effects. Even so, I have to say that there is nothing automatic about our acting as lender of last resort, and even if we did decide on support, no bank should assume that it would be immune from penalty.

Some policymakers, however, have moved toward transparency in policy for handling problem banks, particularly in setting out the necessary conditions for support, while maintaining that meeting such conditions is not sufficient for receiving support. From the rational expectations' perspective, economic agents will have some view of the likely extent of a financial safety net, so the possible existence of the safety net will have effects (both positive and negative) even if the central bank is not transparent in its intentions. Since managers, owners, creditors, and depositors must form some view as to the likelihood of the provision of a safety net, it is not obvious that ambiguity leads economic agents to believe the safety net will be less generous than what the central bank intends to provide (Enoch, Stella, and Khamis, 1997).

There are three reasons for a lender of last resort to spell out its rules to the extent possible (Fischer, 1999). First, by specifying a good set of rules, the central bank reduces the likelihood of unnecessary self-justifying crises. Second, by announcing and implementing a particular set of rules, the lender of last resort provides incentives for other stabilizing private sector behavior—for instance, in the holding of assets acceptable as collateral. Third, spelling out the rules in advance ties the hands of policymakers, reduces risks of politically motivated or spur-of-the-moment actions, and prevents any bias toward forbearance. The rules could be broken *in extremis*, but they still serve a useful purpose, since the lender of last resort would hesitate before incurring the cost of breaking them.

But others argue that a cookbook approach to problems in financial markets is likely to be inefficient (Quinn, 1996). It is impossible to determine in advance exactly in what form banking problems may emerge, and so it may not be possible to design effective operational rules to determine how the problems will be handled. Central banks will be reluctant to set out clear rules that they believe they may need to violate in order not to jeopardize their own credibility. Accordingly, ambiguous but credible rules are viewed to be superior to transparent rules that lack credibility (Enoch, Stella, and Khamis, 1997).

In practice, there are a number of approaches to ex ante specification of the operational rules of lender-of-last-resort operations.[7] At one end of the spectrum, there is no reference to emergency support functions in the treaties establishing the European Monetary Union or the statute of the European Central Bank (ECB). There is, thus, a great deal of uncertainty with regard to the ECB's role in maintaining financial stability.[8] In the middle of the spectrum, many central bank laws or banking laws have a fairly general stipulation that the central bank may perform the emergency support function when necessary without specifying how such a function should be performed. For example, Article 31 of the Reserve Bank of New Zealand Act stipulates that "the Bank shall, if the Bank considers it necessary for the purpose of maintaining the soundness of the financial system, act as lender of last resort for the financial system." Similarly, in Norway, Section 19 of the Norges Bank Act states, "when warranted by special circumstances, the Bank may grant credit on special terms." In addition to the general stipulation in central bank laws that the central bank has the power to make emergency loans, some central banks have detailed internal regulations governing the principles and procedures of emergency lending, but such regulations are not made public, which is the case in Japan.

At the other end of the spectrum, central bank laws or regulations specify in detail a rule-based approach to emergency support operations.

---

[7]The appendix at the end of this chapter lists selected text of provisions on emergency liquidity support from central bank laws in 20 countries.
[8]See also Padoa-Schioppa (1999), and Prati and Schinasi (1998).

Examples include Bulgaria, Hong Kong, and the United States. In the United States, the "Prompt Corrective Action" framework, the Federal Reserve Act, and Regulation A on "Extension of Credit by Federal Reserve Banks" specify in detail the solvency and collateral requirements, repayment terms, and interest rates to be charged on emergency loans by the Federal Reserve. In Hong Kong, the Hong Kong Monetary Authority has a policy statement on lender-of-last-resort support specifying in detail the preconditions of support, the instruments for support, as well as specifications of procedures to deal with cases that should be treated as exceptions to the rules. The National Bank of Bulgaria has a regulation with similar content.

Both theoretical arguments and country experiences lead to the conclusion that there is probably no single optimal approach to the question of whether there should be ex ante specification of the operational rules of lender-of-last-resort support. However, for developing and transition economies there is a good argument that a rule-based approach looks more attractive than total discretion. These economies typically do not yet have a mature governance structure with well-established checks and balances in the political system, and central banks are often under political pressure toward regulatory forbearance. A rule-based approach makes it easier to judge the appropriateness of the authorities' actions. In addition, in these economies, central banks, as well as market participants, have less experience in handling banking problems, and a rule-based approach is technically less challenging to implement.

The Preconditions for Last Resort Support

A rule-based approach would make clear to market participants through legislation or supporting regulations, circulars, or policy statements the requirements and parameters in setting out the mechanics for lender-of-last-resort support. The specification typically lays out the preconditions for support, the right to refuse to lend on the part of the central bank, and the decision process to deal with situations that need to be treated as exceptions to the rules.

As already discussed, the basic precondition for lender-of-last-resort support is the judgment of the central bank, the supervisory authority, and the ministry of finance that the failure of a troubled institution, if it is deprived of liquidity assistance, would damage the stability of the financial and monetary system. In addition, the following preconditions would typically apply:
- the institution is deemed to be solvent;
- the institution has sufficient collateral of acceptable quality; and

- the institution must be prepared to take appropriate remedial action to deal with its liquidity problems.

As a measure of whether an institution has a sufficient margin of solvency, the Hong Kong Monetary Authority generally requires the institution to demonstrate that it maintains a capital adequacy ratio of at least 6 percent after making adjustments for any additional provisions that might be necessary. In Bulgaria, upon receipt of the application for an emergency support loan, the Banking Supervision Department of the Bulgarian National Bank is required to present a written statement of opinion on the current solvency of the bank within 24 hours. In the United States, Regulation A of the Federal Reserve Board stipulates that before extending credit, a federal reserve bank should ascertain if an institution is undercapitalized or critically undercapitalized.[9] A federal reserve bank may make or have outstanding advances to, or discounts for, a depository institution that it knows to be an undercapitalized institution,[10] only:

(1) if, in any 120-day period, advances or discounts from any federal reserve bank to that institution are not outstanding for more than 60 days during which the institution is an undercapitalized institution; or

(2) during the 60 calendar days after the receipt of a written certification from the chairman of the board of governors or the head of the appropriate federal banking agency that the borrowing institution is viable;[11] or

(3) after consultation with the board of governors.

---

[9]Changes in capital categories for depository institutions are tied to dates associated with official actions, such as the required filing date for a Report of Condition and Income ("call report"), receipt of written notice from a primary regulator, or the delivery of a final report of examination.

[10]A bank is "undercapitalized" if the bank has (1) a total risk-based capital ratio that is less than 8 percent; (2) a Tier 1 risk-based capital ratio that is less than 4 percent; or (3) a leverage ratio that is less than 4 percent but not deemed as "adequately capitalized," or a leverage ratio that is less than 3 percent, if the bank is rated Composite 1 under the CAMELS rating system in the most recent examination of the bank, and is not experiencing or anticipating significant growth.

[11]A depository institution is deemed viable when the board of governors or the appropriate federal banking agency has determined, giving due regard to the economic conditions and circumstances in the market in which the institution operates, that the institution is not critically undercapitalized, or likely to become critically undercapitalized, or expected to be placed in conservatorship or receivership. The board of governors believes that ordinarily an undercapitalized institution is viable if the appropriate federal banking agency has accepted a capital restoration plan for the institution, and the institution is complying with that plan.

A federal reserve bank may make or have outstanding advances to or discounts for a depository institution that it knows to be a critically undercapitalized depository institution only:[12]
  (1) during the five-day period beginning on the date the institution became critically undercapitalized; or
  (2) after consultation with the board of governors.

If lending by the federal reserve exceeds these limits, and such lending causes losses to the Federal Deposit Insurance Corporation (FDIC), the federal reserve must reimburse the FDIC.

To determine the solvency of the potential borrower, the central bank must have access to relevant supervisory information, necessitating close and continuous contacts with the supervisory authority, if the central bank itself is not the supervisory authority. In the United Kingdom, when the supervision function was being transferred from the Bank of England to the newly established Financial Services Authority, the two agencies, together with the Treasury, signed a Memorandum of Understanding in October 1997 that set out the role of each institution and explained how they would work together toward the common objective of financial stability, including the gathering and sharing of information in the context of providing emergency support to financial institutions (Box 5.3). The Reserve Bank of Australia and the Australian Prudential Regulation Authority have a similar memorandum in place. In Canada, the Financial Institutions Steering Committee (FISC), which is chaired by the Superintendent of the Office of the Superintendent of Financial Institutions (OSFI) and includes the Governor of the Bank of Canada, the Deputy Minister of Finance, and the Chairman of Canada Deposit Insurance Corporation (CDIC), serves as an important channel of communication and sharing of information in relation to crisis management.

Exceptions

When the preconditions on which central banks will normally be prepared to provide lender-of-last-resort support are met, such support would be provided at the discretion of the central bank or the monetary authority. Where the criteria are not met, decisions to grant or deny support will have to be made at certain prespecified levels of authority to ensure a clear demarcation of responsibility and accountability, and to

---

[12]A bank is "critically undercapitalized" if the bank has a ratio of tangible equity to total assets that is equal to or less than 2 percent.

> **Box 5.3. United Kingdom: Memorandum of Understanding Between HM Treasury, the Bank of England, and the Financial Services Authority**
>
> In the United Kingdom, since the task of banking supervision has been transferred from the Bank of England to the Financial Services Authority (FSA), the Bank of England and the FSA have joint responsibility for organizing banking rescues.
>
> The memorandum of understanding establishes a framework for cooperation between Her Majesty's Treasury, the Bank of England, and the FSA in the field of financial stability.
>
> On emergency financial support, the memorandum states that:
>
>> In exceptional circumstances, there may be a need for an operation, which goes beyond the Bank's routine activity in the money market, to implement its interest rate objectives. Such a support operation is expected to happen very rarely and would normally only be undertaken in the case of a genuine threat to the stability of the financial system to avoid a serious disturbance in the UK economy. If the Bank or the Financial Services Authority identifies a problem where such a support operation might be necessary, they would immediately inform and consult with each other.
>>
>> Each institution would take the lead on all problems arising in its area of responsibility. The lead institution would manage the situation and coordinate the authorities' response (including support operations). The form of the response would depend on the nature of the event and would be determined at the time.
>>
>> In all cases, the Bank and the Financial Services Authority would need to work together very closely and they would immediately inform the Treasury in order to give the Chancellor of the Exchequer the option of refusing support action. Thereafter, they would keep it informed about the developing situation, as far as circumstances allowed.
>
> On information exchange, the memorandum states that:
>
>> The Financial Services Authority and the Bank will establish information sharing arrangements, to ensure that all information which is or may be relevant to the discharge of their respective responsibilities will be shared fully and freely. Each will seek to provide the other with relevant information as requested. The institution receiving this information will ensure that it is used only for discharging its responsibilities, and that it is not transmitted to third parties except where permitted by law.

ensure that any discretion and flexibility are matched by adequate checks and balances. Thus, if the institution is judged to be risking insolvency, or it does not have in its possession sufficient good quality collateral, but the institution still needs support, then the fiscal authority should be consulted and the decision to lend should be made jointly by the central bank, the supervisory agency (if it is separate from the central bank), the deposit insurance fund (if such a fund exists), and the ministry of finance.

In the United States, before the FDIC can provide open bank assistance, it must establish that the assistance is the least costly to the insurance fund of all possible methods for resolving the institution.[13] The FDIC may deviate from the least cost requirement only to avoid "serious adverse effects on economic conditions or financial stability" or "systemic risk" to the banking system. Only the Secretary of the Treasury has the power to grant this exception, after consulting with the President of the United States and with the recommendation by two-thirds of the boards of directors of the FDIC and the Federal Reserve.

In Argentina, the central bank law stipulates that "only when ordinary or extraordinary circumstances so warrant in the judgment of an absolute majority of the board of directors, shall it be possible to exceed the allotments of time or to maximum amounts per institution." In Hong Kong, if the potential borrower is unable to comply with the preconditions for lender-of-last-resort support, then funding support would only be provided with the specific prior approval of the Financial Secretary on its merits in light of the implications for systemic stability. In addition, the Hong Kong Monetary Authority would consider whether to appoint a manager to safeguard the assets of the institution and to protect the interests of depositors and other creditors.

Transparency After the Delivery of Last Resort Support

Any decision to grant emergency lending facilities to a bank always presents a risk of supporting a bad bank or of failing to support a good one.[14] One clearly would wish for a system that would minimize the risk of such mistakes. A transparent rule-based system would seek to achieve that objective. However, mere specification of rules is not likely to give an unequivocal guide to actual policy in any individual case. For instance, in assessing whether a particularly troubled bank should be supported, there may be questions as to whether the bank is insolvent or merely illiquid;[15] there may be issues as to whether the bank is systemically important; and perhaps whether the bank has operated badly or was driven by factors beyond its control. Hence, even the

---

[13]The term "open bank assistance" refers specifically to a resolution method where financial assistance is given to a troubled bank or thrift to prevent its failure.

[14]This section draws heavily on Enoch, Stella, and Khamis (1997).

[15]Goodhart (1999) argues that it is generally not possible to distinguish between illiquidity and insolvency, particularly in times of crisis.

prespecification of rules (i.e., ex ante transparency) will necessarily be consistent with substantial operational discretion.

If the authorities are left with such discretion, it will be important to balance this discretion with ex post transparency (i.e., firm rules for disclosure after the event) and specified standards of accounting and auditing so that disclosure will be substantive and meaningful.[16] Thus, the central bank should reveal—perhaps in a subsequent Annual Report—the amount of public funds that were provided to problem banks, and what the results were. As on monetary issues, central bank (or supervisory agency) operational autonomy must be matched by accountability, or the provision of detailed information after the event and the requirement to explain what has been done and to take responsibility for it. This is important not only to reassure the public that the authorities are operating competently and within the rules, but also to reassure the rest of the banking community, so that they can see what are the "rules of the game."

If a tradition of ex post public disclosure exists, it may isolate the central bank from undue political pressures, since the knowledge that lender-of-last-resort activities will eventually be disclosed may act as a restraint on improper use of the facility. Thus, it can act as a political shield for the central bank. It also raises the cost of using emergency support facilities for banks, since public revelation of their need for assistance is likely to impose a cost in terms of market discipline and, hence, reduce the moral hazard.

While there may well be reasons for not explaining immediately the full extent of financial support for a troubled bank, there must be an expectation that there will be full disclosure as soon as this is feasible without causing additional problems for the banking system. If this qualification implies that a very long delay in public disclosure would be required, there may be a strong argument that liquidity support was inappropriate in the first place. It is very unlikely that financial support to a bank can be justified if the existence of that support has to be kept secret for a long time.

Central banks are increasing their efforts to disclose emergency support operations. The Bank of Japan discloses regularly in its Annual Report details of emergency support, including the amount, maturity, collateral, and interest rate. The Bank of England discloses its financial support operations in footnotes to its financial accounts.[17] In the "subsidiaries in liquidation" section, the Bank discloses the conditions of

---

[16]This is consistent with the requirement of the IMF's Code of Good Practices on Transparency in Monetary and Financial Policies.

[17]The Bank of England reserves the right not to disclose its emergency lending to commercial banks, at least initially.

banks in financial difficulties that it has acquired. It discloses the name of the companies and total investments in them. The Bank also discloses its total provisions for bad loans to banks, which, in effect, provides an initial and partial public acknowledgment of the Bank's financial support operations. In Finland, the Bank of Finland granted FM1.9 billion to Skopbank in 1991 and another FM9.5 billion in 1992. Details of these loans were published in the Bank of Finland Bulletin (November 1992 and April 1993). Other financial agencies have also provided support to this bank. The nature and scope of this support was disclosed in the same editions of the Bank of Finland Bulletin.

Modalities of Emergency Liquidity Support

The determination of the terms and conditions of emergency assistance loans is controversial. There has also been a wide range of practices with regard to collateral requirements, interest rates, and repayment terms by central banks in various countries. In this section, we consider a set of operational guidelines for the design of the terms and conditions of emergency assistance loans consistent with the principles of transparency and prudence.

The Instruments of Support

Three basic instruments are typically used by central banks to provide lender-of-last-resort support to a troubled institution:
- discount of eligible paper (government securities, notes, drafts, and bills of exchange, etc.);
- advance with or without collateral; and
- repos of the institution's assets, which are acceptable to the central bank (securities and possibly other assets—for example, placements with other banks).

For the consideration that commercial banks should be responsible for foreign exchange risk management themselves, lender-of-last-resort support should be extended in domestic currency rather than in foreign exchange. This is consistent with best practices used in deposit insurance schemes that payments by the deposit insurance fund should be made in domestic currency, for deposits denominated in both domestic currency and foreign currency. In the latter case, the conversion should be made at the exchange rate prevailing on the day the payment is made.

In the United States, when obtaining credit in the form of a discount, the borrowing institution transfers eligible paper carrying its legal endorsement to the Federal Reserve Bank. In return, the borrower is credited in an amount equal to the discounted value of the eligible paper at the current discount rate. When the discount paper matures, it is returned to the borrower, and the borrower's reserve account is debited by the full amount of the paper. An advance is simply a loan by one of the 12 Federal Reserve banks to the borrowing institution on its note secured by adequate collateral. At one time, discounts were the predominant form of discount window credit. From an operational perspective, however, advances are more convenient and, thus, for many years all discount window credit has been in the form of advances. All discount window advances are demand loans and, hence, have no real maturity—they may be called at the discretion of the respective Federal Reserve bank. As a matter of convenience, discount officers may arrange to extend credit for a period of time without requiring the borrowing institution to make a formal request to renew the loan each day.

To mitigate the risk involved, central banks typically require that the value of the collateral used to secure lender-of-last-resort funding in the form of advances or repos would exceed the principal amount of the funding according to the haircuts and loan-to-valuation ratios. In Hong Kong, for example, the Hong Kong Monetary Authority would apply a 5 percent haircut to Exchange Fund Bills and Notes for repos, and require a loan-to-value ratio of 80 percent for a credit facility secured by residential mortgages.

The Collateral Requirement

Central banks traditionally protect themselves by demanding collateral when providing last-resort funding assistance to banks. By doing this, the lender of last resort avoids the need to form a judgment on the solvency of the institution applying for liquidity while retaining the capacity to operate at the speed necessary to halt a run. At the same time, by basing the decision to lend on the availability of acceptable collateral, the lender of last resort reduces the moral hazard that the potential borrower would take excessive risks in its portfolio by holding assets that would not be accepted as collateral (Fischer, 1999).

However, an insolvent bank with some acceptable collateral that obtains an emergency loan can still adopt a go-for-broke strategy. While the lender of last resort may be protected, the deposit insurance fund and the bank's other creditors (and society) are not. Conversely, a solvent bank with very large, immediate needs might have trouble providing enough collateral that is acceptable to the lender of last resort and might fail unnecessarily (Guttentag and Herring, 1983). Walter

Bagehot, in fact, recommended that the quality standards on collateral taken by the Bank of England during a crisis should be relaxed (Bagehot, 1873). If the lender of last resort, through its supervisory powers or those of another trusted agency, is reasonably assured of the solvency of the bank, it has little need for collateral.

In practice, country experiences vary greatly in terms of collateral requirement. The Hong Kong Monetary Authority's policy is to accept only high-quality paper (investment grade securities) and high-quality residential mortgages as collateral. In the United States, although collateral is required for extended facilities under the discount window, a wide range of financial instruments is accepted, including government securities, corporate bonds and money market instruments, collateralized mortgage obligations, residential mortgage notes, commercial, industrial, and agricultural notes.

In Korea, the Bank of Korea may provide emergency liquidity support "against the collateral of any assets which are *defined temporarily* (emphasis added) as acceptable security" with the agreement of at least four members of the Monetary Policy Committee. In Japan, the Bank of Japan law stipulates that the Bank of Japan "may provide *uncollateralized loans* (emphasis added) to financial institutions and other financial business entities prescribed by a Cabinet Order for a period within that prescribed by a Cabinet Order when they unexpectedly experience a temporary shortage of funds for payment due to accidental causes, including computer system problems, whereby the business operations of the financial institutions may be seriously hampered if the shortage is not recovered swiftly, provided that the advance is necessary to secure the smooth settlement of funds among financial institutions."

Any central bank should perform the good practice of announcing ex ante that it will normally provide lender-of-last-resort support only with collateral and to specify which assets are considered acceptable for such purposes, but also to make it clear that it may be willing to relax the requirements under exceptional circumstances. When the authorities decide to support a systemically important bank that does not have sufficient collateral of acceptable quality, there are two possible approaches. One is to take every asset on the balance sheet of the borrowing bank (for example, loans and fixed assets) as collateral. One potential problem with this approach is that the central bank is not usually in a position to judge within a short period of time whether the borrowing bank has a clean title on the asset or whether the asset has already been pledged. The central bank's claim will be subject to legal challenges if the assets are already pledged. A second approach is to request the government to provide a guarantee for the central bank.

The rationale for requesting such a guarantee is particularly strong if the central bank has serious doubts about the solvency of the bank.

Interest Rates and Supervisory Sanctions

Some have argued that a key element of the Bagehot rule of emergency lending is the prescription that the lender of last resort lend at "penalty" rates.[18] However, a careful reading of Bagehot (1873) would attribute his advocacy of a high lending rate to his view that internal and external drains typically accompany each other; the high rate was designed to stop the external drain (currency crisis), and lending freely would stop the internal drain (domestic bank runs) (Fischer, 1999). In an isolated case of funding difficulties in domestic currency, the effectiveness of charging a penalty interest rate would depend on the interest rate elasticity of demand for liquidity support. One can argue that when a bank cannot borrow from the interbank market and is in urgent need of short-term liquidity, its demand for lender-of-last-resort liquidity support would not be very elastic—thus, charging a penalty rate would not necessarily discourage the bank from approaching the central bank for support. In addition, if the bank is fundamentally insolvent, then its demand for lender-of-last-resort support would be inelastic, and in such cases, charging a penalty rate would not be effective. In other words, price signals would fail to act as a rationing device in the face of adverse selection.

But if restrictive limits on the quantities a bank may borrow exist, they may be interpreted as implicit prices (Benston and others, 1986). The larger the role of quantitative rationing and implicit prices, the less important the explicit pricing of the restricted lending becomes. In practice, this often means that banks that receive nonpenalty rate funding assistance from the central bank are subject to more intensive supervisory surveillance and are prohibited from engaging in certain activities, such as making new loans and paying out dividends.

In practice, interest rate policies on emergency liquidity support differ from country to country. In Japan, central bank loans to problem banks were often charged the official discount rate. In Hong Kong, the Hong Kong Monetary Authority's policy is to charge its lender-of-last-resort facilities "at the prevailing base rate plus a margin to be determined

---

[18]Goodhart (1999) argues that it is not accurate to interpret Bagehot's rule of lending at "high" rate as lending at "penalty" rate (i.e., at a rate higher than that available in the market place). Fischer (1999) argues that the penalty rate need not be defined relative to the rate at which institutions would lend to each other in the market during a crisis. Instead, the penalty should be relative to the interest rate during normal times.

taking into account current market conditions." In Canada, the interest rate the Bank of Canada charges on its emergency support loans is at least equal to the bank rate, which is typically 25 basis points above the average cost of overnight funds in the market. In the United States, the Federal Reserve policy is to charge the basic discount rate for the first 30 days of borrowing and a flexible rate that takes into account rates on market sources of funds, but in no case will the rate charged be less than the basic discount rate plus one-half percentage point. The flexible rate also could be applied sooner than 30 days at the discretion of the lending federal reserve bank. The policy of charging the basic discount rate has, in the past, meant subsidies to the borrower, since the basic discount rate was below the average interbank market rate.

Given that the underlying solvency position of the borrowing bank is not always obvious when lender-of-last-resort support is sought, a good practice is to have a combination of both explicit and implicit prices. The explicit price should be marginally above the average market interest rate, with perhaps a higher penalty attached to longer term borrowing. An excessively high penalty could make matters worse, not better, for the borrowing institution, which is typically in a fragile condition. As an implicit price, the borrowing bank would have to implement a liquidity restoration plan that is monitored frequently by the supervisory authority. The central bank or the supervisory authority should also have the power to take remedial actions against the bank when the lender-of-last-resort support loan is outstanding, such as changing the management or imposing a conservatorship, particularly when the loan has to be rolled over. The conditions attached should be more stringent if the underlying solvency of the borrowing bank is in serious doubt or if there is not sufficient collateral of acceptable quality. Such conditions may include restrictions on a bank's ability to take on new business and a moratorium on dividend payment.

In Israel, the law governing the Bank of Israel stipulates that "so long as the loan has not been repaid in full, the borrowing corporation shall not grant or extend any credit, or make any other investment without the prior approval of the Bank." The central bank laws in Korea and the Philippines have similar stipulations. In the Kyrgyz Republic, the law requires that "during the life of such a loan, the National Bank of the Kyrgyz Republic shall establish a special regime provided for in the regulations of the National Bank of the Kyrgyz Republic in respect of the borrower." In Hungary, the National Bank of Hungary can grant liquidity support "dependent on the emergency measure to be taken by the State Money and Capital Market Supervision, and on the compliance of the given credit institution with the measure initiated by the said authority." In the Philippines, if the amount of the first tranche of central bank support must exceed 25 percent of the bank's total deposit and deposit substitutes, "the principal stockholders of the borrowing institution must furnish an acceptable undertaking to indemnify and hold harmless from suit a conservator whose appointment the Monetary Board may find necessary at any time."

The Size Limit of Last Resort Support

Central banks may also impose a size limit on any lender-of-last-resort support they may provide to financial institutions to limit their own exposure to credit risks. In Argentina, the central bank law stipulates that liquidity support loans from the central bank should not exceed the net worth of the borrowing institution. In Hong Kong, the limit would normally be set between 100 percent and 200 percent of the capital base of the institution concerned, depending on the margin of solvency the institution can maintain, subject to a cap of HK$10 billion. It should be emphasized that the Hong Kong Monetary Authority retains the discretion to lend less than the maximum. In Turkey, the law requires that central bank emergency loans should not exceed twice the capital of the borrowing institution. In the Philippines, the amount of any emergency loan cannot exceed the sum of 50 percent of total deposits and deposit substitutes of the borrowing institution.

Whether to impose a size limit on lender-of-last-resort support is controversial. One can argue that central bank lending limits make sense when such support is for monetary purposes, but not for emergency lending where one should follow Bagehot and be prepared to lend without limit (lend freely). If the limit on lender-of-last-resort lending is too tight, it might encourage preventive runs on banks. On balance, the rationale for a size limit on emergency support facilities is not strong and, if it is introduced, the limit should not be too tight.

The Terms of Repayment

A key concept in lender-of-last-resort support is that any emergency lending should be only temporary and for the short term. Troubled banks seeking loans from the central bank may be likened to individuals seeking assistance from hospital emergency room personnel. Providers of either form of assistance perform simultaneously a first-aid function and a triage function. Central bank liquidity assistance should seek only to keep the bank going until a more authoritative examination can determine the institution's long-term viability

(Benston and others, 1986). Any institution that has to rely on central bank liquidity assistance for more than a few weeks is likely to be insolvent and the authorities should be ready to have it closed and resolved. Conversely, there should also be an incentive for the central bank to lend only for the short term. For example, the Federal Reserve Act stipulates that the Federal Reserve should be penalized by making a payment to the FDIC if it makes emergency loans for an extended period of time, as discussed earlier.

Central bank laws or regulations typically stipulate explicitly that liquidity support from the central bank is only for the short term. In Argentina, the central bank law requires that central bank advances to banks to relieve temporary illiquidity should not exceed 30 days. The approval of an absolute majority of the board of directors of the central bank is required to extend the maturity of the loan. In Chile, the central bank law stipulates that liquidity support to banks cannot be outstanding for more than 90 days, and the approval of a majority of the Board is required to extend the maturity of the loan; the Superintendency of Banks and Financial Institutions should also be notified in advance before extending the maturity of the loan. In Hong Kong, the Hong Kong Monetary Authority policy statement on lender of last resort states that liquidity support will be provided for an initial term not exceeding 30 days, although there will be provisions for it to be rolled over for a further 30 days on maturity.

Default Situations

Where lender-of-last-resort support is not repaid on maturity and the central bank is not prepared to roll over the funding, the central bank should take immediate actions in cooperation with the supervisory authority to have the borrowing bank resolved, including withdrawing its licenses, imposing receivership, and starting liquidation.

In practice, a particularly difficult situation is deciding how to resolve the default situation of those institutions that are considered "too big to fail." As Garcia (2000) points out, as long as the owners and managers of a failed bank are not bailed out and there is an operational and financial restructuring to restore viability to the bank, a too-big-to-fail policy means that the government saves the economic infrastructure of the bank, absorbs the losses, and often assumes ownership temporarily until reprivatization. If the initial restructuring measures do not make the bank viable, drastic measures should be taken. These measures could involve splitting up the bank, partially liquidating it, or engineering a major shrinkage of its balance sheet through structural and/or operational downsizing.

Confidentiality of Last Resort Support

Central banks tend to conduct lender-of-last-resort operations in private and to try to keep the fact that they are providing emergency support secret at the time. Since the health of a banking system depends in part on the confidence that the public has in the system, and since confidence may decline if it is known that a rescue has been mounted, there is an argument that the most efficient provision of lender-of-last-resort support is one that is not seen.[19] In addition, if the fact that an otherwise sound bank is seeking liquidity support from the central bank becomes known to the market, the borrowing bank is likely to suffer a reputational cost, which would drive up the borrowing cost. This is undesirable for the restoration to health by the bank. However, as argued previously, while immediate public disclosure may undermine efforts to support a particular institution or group of institutions, ex post disclosure with an appropriate delay is important to ensure the credibility and accountability of the central bank.

Emergency Liquidity Support in Times of Systemic Crises

During systemic crises the central bank, as lender of last resort, attempts to assure the public that it will act firmly and limit the scope of any financial disturbance. It may be necessary to provide support to all banks short of liquidity in the initial stage. In a widespread crisis situation, the criteria to judge whether an institution is systemically important may have to be relaxed as compared to normal times. In addition, emergency liquidity support is usually needed when a full guarantee of deposits is offered by the government. Initially, the full guarantee may well not be credible and the runs could continue unless central bank liquidity support is provided in large amounts. In such a situation, the modalities of lender-of-last-resort support may need to be adapted from those described in the preceding sections.

First, in a general environment of panic and instability, the existence and presence of an emergency lender should not be doubted by the market participants. Therefore, public announcements by central banks of their willingness to lend whatever is necessary to calm the situation becomes an important tool of crisis management.[20] Central bank support

---

[19]It is also possible to conceive circumstances where it might be useful for the central bank support to be known in the market (e.g., when the bank faces runs by retail depositors).

[20]Public pronouncements should be reassuring but minimal to avoid misinterpretation. The statement of the Federal Reserve Chairman at 8:15 a.m., before the markets opened on Terrible Tuesday in October 1987, during the stock market crash, met these specifications: "The Federal Reserve System, consistent with its responsibilities as the nation's central banker, affirmed today its readiness to serve as the source of liquidity to support the economic and financial system" (Garcia, 1989).

should be visible and should be provided rapidly. Interest rates should be somewhat above the average market rates to encourage banks to seek alternative sources before approaching the central bank for support, but the penalty should not be excessively high. More important, the borrowing institution should be subject to restrictions on activities and intensive supervisory monitoring, including, among other things, how the borrowed funds are being used.

Second, the usual preconditions of support such as solvency and collateral requirements may not be applied. This is because, in a systemic crisis, the solvency and soundness of collateral of financial institutions depend to a large extent on how the crisis is managed and whether the panic is stopped or not. In an environment of large volatility in asset prices, such as interest rates and exchange rates, it can be very difficult to differentiate mere illiquidity from insolvency. In addition, limits on repayment terms may have to be relaxed to accommodate the implementation of a systemic bank restructuring plan.

In general, emergency liquidity support in times of systemic crises should be an integral part of a comprehensive and well-designed crisis management strategy.[21] As such, decisions on whether to provide support and how much to lend should be made jointly by the relevant authorities, including the central bank, the supervisory agency, the deposit insurance fund, and the ministry of finance. There should be appropriate documentation of the decision process and ex post disclosure of the outcomes of major decisions in order to ensure public accountability.

In Sweden, during the banking crisis in the early 1990s, the banking system was free to obtain unlimited liquidity by drawing on its accounts with the central bank, and the Riksbank supplied liquidity on a relatively large scale at normal interest rates and repayment terms. Because the government issued a blanket guarantee, the Riksbank did not take on credit risks by making such loans.[22] The details of the authorities' support measures and their implications for depositors and investors were extensively reported both domestically and abroad to financial market participants.

When a major part of the banking system is insolvent, resources for solvency support should come from the government and private

---

[21]See Lindgren and others (1999), Garcia (2000), and Enoch (2000).

[22]In the face of a severe banking crisis, the Swedish parliament in 1992 passed a bill stating, among other things, that "the state guarantees that banks and certain other credit institutions can meet their commitments in a timely basis," that "the support system is to remain available for as long as it is needed" (subject to another act of parliament), and that "the support is constructed so that all the commitments of an institution can be met."

sector, not the central bank, and any public costs should be recognized explicitly. The government may decide that the central bank should provide support until a systemic restructuring strategy is in place, and perhaps thereafter; but such credit would normally be explicitly guaranteed by the government. Transparency would require that if such loans cannot be repaid by the institution (i.e., when it is necessary to call on the guarantee), the government should compensate the central bank for the losses.

One option is for the central bank not to transfer any profits to the government until all losses are covered. However, the central bank is not usually in a position to make any profits after making large nonperforming loans to insolvent banks. More typically, the claims by the central bank on the insolvent banks are converted into equity of the bank held by the government, and the government would, in exchange, issue securities to be held on the balance sheet of the central bank. It is very important that these securities be issued on market terms and be marketable for the central bank to be properly recapitalized.

Appendix: Provisions on Emergency Liquidity Support in Selected Central Bank Legislation

The following table excerpts parts of selected laws dealing with emergency liquidity support in 20 countries.

Country	Emergency Provision
Argentina	Article 17. The bank shall be authorized to carry out the following operations: (b) grant rediscounts to financial institutions for reasons of temporary illiquidity, not to exceed thirty (30) consecutive days, up to a maximum per institution equivalent to its net worth; (c) grant advances on account to financial institutions for reasons of temporary illiquidity, not to exceed thirty (30) consecutive days, that are guaranteed by public securities or other securities, or covered by a guarantee or special or general appropriation of certain assets, provided that the sum of the rediscounts or advances granted to one and the same institution does not exceed, under any circumstances, the limit established in the foregoing section. When necessary to provide adequate liquidity to the financial system, or when general or extraordinary circumstances make it advisable in the opinion of an absolute majority of the board of directors, the terms and ceilings per institution provided in (b) above and in the first paragraph of (c) may be exceeded, as long as the free reserves supporting the monetary base are not to this end compromised under any circumstances. When such extraordinary financing is granted, the shareholders shall, in addition to the guarantees constituted by the assets of the institution, pledge, as a minimum, the control share capital of the institution and shall agree to the possible later application of the procedure set out in Article 35 bis of the Law on Financial Institutions. Official banks may be exempted from this requirement.
Botswana	Article 37.3 Operations with account holders. The central bank may, on such terms and conditions as the board may from time to time determine, grant to account holders loans and advances for periods not exceeding 92 days—(b) unsecured or secured by such other assets, on such special terms and conditions as the board shall determine when, in its opinion, such a loan or advance is exceptionally necessary to meet the liquidity requirements of the borrower.

Country	Emergency Provision
Bulgaria	Article 33. (1) The Bulgarian National Bank may not extend credits to banks, except in the cases under para. 2. (2) Upon emergence of a liquidity risk that may affect the stability of the banking system, the Bulgarian National Bank may extend to a solvent bank lev-denominated credits with maturity no longer than three months, provided they are fully collateralized by gold, foreign currency or other such high-liquid assets. The terms and procedure for extension of such credits, as well as the criteria establishing the occurrence of a liquidity risk, shall be determined by a regulation of the Bulgarian National Bank. (3) Credits under para. 2 may be extended solely up to the amount of the excess of the lev equivalent of the gross international foreign exchange reserves over the total amount of monetary liabilities of the Bulgarian National Bank.
Chile	Article 36. The Authority to Safeguard the Stability of the Financial System. For the purpose of safeguarding the stability of the financial system, the bank shall be empowered to grant banking and financial institutions loans in case of emergency for a period not to exceed 90 days, when the problems stem from a temporary shortage of liquidity. To renew these loans, a Board decision adopted by a majority of the full membership, with a prior report to the Superintendency of Banks and Financial Institutions, shall be required. The bank may make the granting of loans contingent upon compliance by the borrower with particular rules of financial administration. In the situation foreseen in this numeral, the bank may, accordingly, acquire instruments from the placement or investment portfolios of the above-mentioned institutions.
Hungary	Article 17. Extraordinary Credit for Credit Institutions in Emergency Situations. The National Bank of Hungary may grant an extraordinary credit to a credit institution in case of emergency of the credit institution. The National Bank of Hungary may make the granting of such a loan dependent on the emergency measure to be taken by the state money and capital market supervision, and on the compliance of the given credit institution with the measure initiated by the said authority.
Israel	Part Eight: Credit Operations of the Bank 44. Emergency loans and advances. The governor, in circumstances

Country	Emergency Provision
	which, in his opinion, are emergency circumstances, may direct that loans are granted even to a banking corporation unable to fulfill the conditions prescribed under section 43 if such corporation has given security to his satisfaction, and may further direct that so long as the loan has not been repaid in full the borrowing corporation shall not grant or extend any credit, or make any other investment, without the prior approval of the bank.
Japan	Article 37.1. The Bank of Japan, irrespective of the provisions of Article 33, Paragraph 1, may provide uncollateralized loans to financial institutions (defined as those engaged in the business of taking bank deposits (deposits prescribed by Article 2, Paragraph 2 of the Deposit Insurance Law, Law No. 34 of 1971) as well as engaging in exchange transactions, the same definition shall apply hereinafter) and other financial business entities prescribed by a Cabinet Order (hereinafter referred to as "financial institutions" together) for a period within that prescribed by a Cabinet Order when they unexpectedly experience a temporary shortage of funds for payment due to accidental causes, including computer system problems, whereby the business operations of the financial institutions may be seriously hampered if the shortage is not recovered swiftly, provided that the advance is necessary to secure the smooth settlement of funds among financial institutions. Article 37.2. The Bank of Japan shall, when providing loans as prescribed by the preceding paragraph, report the fact to the minister of finance as well as inform the commissioner of the financial supervision agency of the fact without delay. Article 38.1. The minister of finance may request that the Bank of Japan conduct the business necessary to maintain an orderly financial system, including provision of loans, when it is believed to be especially necessary for the maintenance of an orderly financial system including the case where it is judged, after consultation with the prime minister pursuant to the provisions of Article 57-2 of the Banking Act (Law No. 59 of 1981) and other relevant laws and regulations that a serious problem in an orderly financial system may arise. Article 38.2. At the request of the minister of finance as prescribed by the preceding paragraph, the bank may conduct business necessary to maintain an orderly financial

Country	Emergency Provision
	system, including provision of loans under special conditions, in addition to the business prescribed by Article 33, Paragraph 1.
Jordan	Article 41 (C). The central bank may, in cases of emergency, or under extraordinary circumstances which, in the opinion of the central bank, constitute a threat to monetary or banking stability in the kingdom, extend special credit facilities to any licensed bank under such terms and conditions established by the board and approved by the council of ministers.
Korea	Article 65 (Emergency Credit to Banking Institutions) (1) The Bank of Korea may conduct credit operations against the collateral of any assets which are defined temporarily as acceptable security with at least four members concurring in any of following cases: 1. Conducting credit operations temporarily with banking institutions during a grave emergency that directly threatens monetary and banking stability; or 2. Conducting credit operations temporarily with banking institutions that are expected to experience pronounced difficulty in carrying out their operations due to temporary shortages of funds for payment caused by a breakdown of an electronic information processing system or other accidental mishap. (2) A banking institution in receipt of credit specified in the provisions of Clause 1 of paragraph (1) may not, while such debt is outstanding, increase the total volume of its loans and investments without prior authorization by the Monetary Policy Committee. (3) The Bank of Korea may, when it deems necessary, check and confirm the operations and status of the assets of a banking institution in connection with extension of credit as provided for in Paragraph (1).
Kyrgyz Republic	Article 4. Functions of the National Bank of the Kyrgyz Republic. The bank shall have the following functions: (4) acting as the lender of last resort to banks in accordance with the present Law; Article 28. Loans Granted to Other Banks. In emergency situations, in order to protect the integrity of the banking system, the National Bank of the Kyrgyz Republic may make unsecured loans or loans secured by other types of assets, on

Country	Emergency Provision
	terms established by the board of directors of the bank. An emergency loan may be granted for a term of not more than six months. This term may be extended by a decision of the board of directors of the bank. During the life of such a loan, the bank shall establish a special regime provided for in the regulations of the bank in respect of the borrower.
Madagascar	Article 34. Central Bank Assistance to Banks and Financial Institutions. In the event of temporary liquidity problems experienced by a bank or financial institution in connection with the implementation of a recovery plan acceptable to the Bank and Financial Institutions Control Commission and the central bank, the latter may grant such institutions a special advance on the conditions adopted by the board. Article 38. The central bank may make its assistance contingent on the submission of any documentation it deems necessary. It may, as appropriate, require that any real or personal guarantees be provided.
Mexico	Article 3. The bank shall perform the following functions: II. Operate as reserve bank and lender of last resort for credit institutions; Article 15. Provisions in Article 8 paragraph two and Article 14 will not apply to financing that the central bank may grant credit institutions in order to prevent disruptions in the payment systems, nor to operations effected by the bank as lender of last resort.
New Zealand	Article 31. Bank to Act as Lender of Last Resort—The bank shall, if the bank considers it necessary for the purpose of maintaining the soundness of the financial system, act as lender of last resort for the financial system.
Norway	Section 19. When warranted by special circumstances, the bank may grant credit on special terms.
Philippines	Section 83. Loans for Liquidity Purposes.—The Bangko Sentral may extend loans and advances to banking institutions for a period of not more than seven (7) days without any collateral for the purpose of providing liquidity to the banking system in times of need. Section 84. Emergency Loans and Advances.—In periods of national and/or local emergency or of imminent

Country	Emergency Provision
	financial panic, which directly threaten monetary and banking stability. The Monetary Board may, by a vote of at least five (5) of its members, authorize the Bangko Sentral to grant extraordinary loans or advances to banking institutions secured by assets as defined hereunder: Provided that while such loans or advances are outstanding, the debtor institution shall not, except upon prior authorization by the Monetary Board, expand the total volume of its loans or investments. The Monetary Board may, at its discretion, likewise authorize the Bangko Sentral to grant emergency loans or advances to banking institutions, even during normal periods, for the purpose of assisting a bank in a precarious financial condition or under serious financial pressures brought by unforeseen events, or events which, though foreseeable, could not be prevented by the bank concerned: Provided, however, that the Monetary Board has ascertained that the bank is not insolvent and has the assets defined hereunder to secure the advances: Provided, further, that a concurrent vote of at least five (5) members of the Monetary Board is obtained. The amount of any emergency loan or advance shall not exceed the sum of fifty percent (50 percent) of total deposits and deposit substitutes of the banking institution and shall be disbursed in two (2) or more tranches. The amount of the first tranche shall be limited to 25 percent of the total deposit and deposit substitutes of the institution and shall be secured by government securities to the extent of their applicable loan values and other unencumbered first class collaterals which the monetary board may approve: Provided, that as determined by the monetary board, the circumstances surrounding the emergency warrant a loan or advance greater than the amount provided herein above, the amount of the first tranche may exceed 25 percent of the bank's total deposit and deposit substitutes if the same is adequately secured by applicable loan values of government securities and unencumbered first class collaterals approved by the monetary board, and the principal stockholders of the institution furnish an acceptable undertaking to indemnify and hold harmless from suit a conservator whose appointment the Monetary Board may find necessary at any time. Prior to the release of the first tranche, the banking institution shall submit to the Bangko Sentral a resolution of

Country	Emergency Provision
	its board of directors authorizing the Bangko Sentral to evaluate other assets of the banking institution certified by its external auditor to be good and available for collateral purposes, and should be released if the subsequent tranche be thereafter applied for. The Monetary Board may, by a vote of at least five of its members, authorize the release of a subsequent tranche on condition that the principal stockholders of the institution: (a) furnish an acceptable undertaking to indemnify and hold harmless from suit a conservator whose appointment the monetary board may find necessary at any time; and (b) provide acceptable security, which, in the judgment of the monetary board, would be adequate to supplement, where necessary, the assets tendered by the banking institution to collateralize the subsequent tranche. In connection with the exercise of these powers, the prohibition in Section 128 of this Act shall not apply insofar as it refers to acceptance as collateral of shares and their acquisition as a result of foreclosure proceedings, including the exercise of voting rights pertaining to said shares: Provided, however, that should the Bangko Sentral acquire any of the shares it has accepted as collateral as a result of foreclosure proceedings, the Bangko Sentral shall dispose of said shares by public bidding within one (1) year from the date of consolidation of title by the Bangko Sentral.
Poland	Article 42. 3. The National Bank of Poland may also extend refinancing to banks for the implementation of a bank rehabilitation program. 4. Refinancing facilities may be granted: (1) up to a specified amount, as a line of credit; (2) against pledges of securities, up to an amount corresponding to a specified proportion of the face value of such securities (Lombard facilities), (3) in other forms, as specified by the National Bank of Poland Management Board.
Romania	Article 27. Protection against systemic risk. In order to mitigate systemic and payment risks, in exceptional circumstances and on a case-to-case basis, the National Bank of Romania may grant to banks loans that are either unsecured or secured with assets other than those provided for in Art. 20 hereof.
Sweden	Art. 8. In exceptional circumstances, the Riksbank may, with the end of supporting liquidity, grant credits

Country	Emergency Provision
	or provide guarantees on special terms to banking institutions and Swedish companies that are under the supervision of the Financial Supervisory Authority.
Turkey	Art. 40, II. (d) The Bank may, within the framework of sub-paragraph (b) of Article 36 of this Law, extend credits directly to banks within the scope of Article 64 of the Banking Law and to those that are the subject of uncertainty and lack of confidence due to the acceleration of the fund withdrawals or because of uncertainty and lack of confidence in the banking system, provided that the credits are extended against appropriate collateral and be limited to a maximum of one year maturity and twice the amount of the equity-capital.
United States	Section 10B—Advances to Individual Member Banks (a) Any federal reserve bank, under rules and regulations prescribed by the Board of Governors of the federal reserve system, may make advances to any member bank on its time or demand notes having maturities of not more than four months and which are secured to the satisfaction of such federal reserve bank. Notwithstanding the foregoing, any federal reserve bank, under rules and regulations prescribed by the Board of Governors of the federal reserve system, may make advances to any member bank on its time notes having such maturities as the Board may prescribe and which are secured by mortgage loans covering a one-to-four family residence. Such advances shall bear interest at a rate equal to the lowest discount rate in effect at such federal reserve bank on the date of such not. (b) Limitations on advances. (1) Except as provided in paragraph (2), no advance to any undercapitalized depository institution by any Federal Reserve bank under this section may be outstanding for more than 60 days in any 120-day period. (2) (A) If (i) the head of the appropriate Federal banking agency certifies in advance in writing to the Federal Reserve bank that any depository institution is viable, or (ii) the Board conducts an examination of any depository institution and the Chairman of the Board certifies in writing to the Federal Reserve bank that the institution is viable. The limitation contained in paragraph (1) shall not apply during the 60-day period beginning on the date such certification is received. (B) The 60-day period may

Country	Emergency Provision
	be extended for additional 60-day periods upon receipt by the Federal Reserve bank of additional written certification under sub-paragraph (A) with respect to each such additional period. (C) The authority of the head of any agency to issue a written certification of viability under this paragraph may not be delegated to any other person. (D) Notwithstanding paragraph (1), an undercapitalized depository institution which does not have a certificate of viability in effect under this paragraph may have advances outstanding for more than 60 days in any 120-day period if the Board elects to treat (i) such institution as critically undercapitalized under paragraph (3); and (ii) any such advance as an advance described in subparagraph (A)(i) of paragraph (3). (3) (A) Notwithstanding any other provision of this section, if (i) in the case of any critically undercapitalized depository institution (I) any advance under this section to such institution is outstanding without payment having been demanded as of the end of the five-day period beginning on the date the institution becomes a critically undercapitalized institution; or (II) any new advance is made to such institution under this section after the end of such period; and (ii) after the end of that five-day period, the Deposit Insurance Fund of the Federal Deposit Insurance Corporation incurs a loss exceeding the loss that the Corporation would have incurred if it had liquidated that institution as of the end of that period, the Board shall, subject to the limitations in subparagraph (B), be liable to the Federal Deposit Insurance Corporation for the excess loss, without regard to the terms of the advance or any collateral pledged to secure the advance. (B) The liability of the Board under subparagraph (A) shall not exceed the lesser of the following: (i) The amount of the loss the Board or any federal reserve bank would have incurred on the increases in the amount of advances made after the five-day period referred to in subparagraph (A) if those increased advances had been unsecured. (ii) The interest received on the increases in the amount of advances made after the five-day period referred to in subparagraph (A). (C) The Board shall pay the Federal Deposit Insurance Corporation the amount of any liability of the Board under subparagraph (A).

Country	Emergency Provision
	(D) The Board shall report to the Congress on any excess loss liability it incurs under subparagraph (A), as limited by subparagraph (B)(i), and the reasons therefore, not later than 6 months after incurring the liability. (4) A federal reserve bank shall have no obligation to make, increase, renew, or extend any advance or discount under this Act to any depository institution. Section 13 – Powers of federal reserve banks 3. Discounts for Individuals, Partnerships, and Corporations—In unusual and exigent circumstances, the Board of Governors of the federal reserve system, by the affirmative vote of not less than five members, may authorize any federal reserve bank, during such periods as the said Board may determine, at rates established in accordance with the provisions of section 14. Subdivision (d), of this Act, to discount for any individual, partnership, or corporation, notes, drafts, and bills of exchange when such notes, drafts, and bills of exchange are indorsed or otherwise secured to the satisfaction of the federal reserve bank: Provided, That before discounting any such note, draft, or bill of exchange for an individual, partnership, or corporation the federal reserve bank shall obtain evidence that such individual, partnership, or corporation is unable to secure adequate credit accommodations from other banking institutions. All such discounts for individuals, partnerships, or corporations shall be subject to such limitations, restrictions, and regulations as the Board of Governors of the federal reserve system may prescribe. 13. Advances to Individuals, Partnerships, and Corporations on Obligations of United States— Subject to such limitations, restrictions and regulations as the board of governors of the federal reserve system may prescribe, any federal reserve bank may make advances to any individual, partnership or corporation on the promissory notes of such individual, partnership or corporation secured by direct obligations of the United States or by any obligation which is a direct obligation of, or fully guaranteed as to principal and interest by, any agency of the United States. Such advances shall be made for periods not exceeding 90 days and shall bear interest at rates fixed from time to time by the federal reserve bank, subject to the review and determination of the Board of Governors of the federal reserve system.

References

Bagehot, Walter, 1873, *Lombard Street: A Description of the Money Market* (London: William Clowes and Sons).

Benston, George, Robert Eisenbeis, Paul Horvitz, Edward Kane, and George Kaufman, 1986, *Perspectives on Safe and Sound Banking: Past, Present, and Future* (Cambridge, Massachusetts: MIT Press).

Clouse, James, A., 1994, "Recent Developments in Discount Window Policy," *Federal Reserve Bulletin* (November).

Corrigan, Gerald, 1990, "Reforming the U.S. Financial System: An International Perspective," Federal Reserve Bank of New York *Quarterly Review* (Spring).

Enoch, Charles, 2000, "Bank Interventions in Banking Crises: The Experience of Indonesia," Policy Discussion Paper No. 00/2 (Washington: International Monetary Fund).

———, Peter Stella, and May Khamis, 1997, "Transparency and Ambiguity in Central Bank Safety Net Operations," IMF Working Paper No. 97/138 (Washington: International Monetary Fund).

Fischer, Stanley, 1999, "On the Need for an International Lender of Last Resort," *Journal of Economic Perspectives*, Vol. 13 (Fall), pp. 85–104.

Freixas, Xavier, Curzio Giannini, Glenn Hoggarth, and Farouk Soussa, 1999, "Lender of Last Resort: A Review of the Literature," *Financial Stability Review*, Bank of England, Vol. 7 (November).

Garcia, Gillian G.H., 1989, "The Lender of Last Resort in the Wake of the Crash," *American Economic Review*, Vol. 79 (May), pp. 151–55.

———, 2000, "Deposit Insurance and Crisis Management," IMF Working Paper No. 00/57 (Washington: International Monetary Fund).

George, Eddie, 1993, "The Pursuit of Financial Stability," *Central Banking*, Vol. 4 (Winter), pp. 22–35.

Giannini, Curzio, 1998, "Enemy of None But a Common Friend to All? An International Perspective on the Lender-of-Last-Resort Function," IMF Working Paper No. 99/10 (Washington: International Monetary Fund).

Goodfriend, Marvin, and Robert King, 1988, "Financial Deregulation, Monetary Policy, and Central Banking," in *Restructuring Banking and Financial Services in America*, ed. by W.S. Haraf and R.M. Kushmeider (Washington: American Enterprise Institute).

Goodhart, Charles, 1999, "Myths About the Lender of Last Resort," *International Finance*, Vol. 2 (November), pp. 339–360.

———, and Haizhou Huang, 1998, "A Model of the Lender of Last Resort," IMF Working Paper No. 99/39 (Washington: International Monetary Fund).

Goodhart, Charles, and Dirk Schoenmaker, 1995, "Institutional Separation Between Supervisory and Monetary Agencies," in *The Central Bank and the Financial System*, by C.A.E. Goodhart (Cambridge, Massachusetts: MIT Press).

Guttentag, Jack, and Richard Herring, 1983, "The Lender-of-Last-Resort Function in an International Context," Princeton University Essays in International Finance No. 151 (Princeton, New Jersey: Princeton University, May).

Kindleberger, Charles, 1978, *Manias, Panics, and Crashes: A History of Financial Crisis* (New York: Basic Books).

Lindgren, Carl-Johan, Tomas Baliño, Charles Enoch, Anne-Marie Gulde, Marc Quintyn, and Leslie Teo, 1999, *Financial Sector Crisis and Restructuring: Lessons from Asia*, IMF Occasional Paper No. 188 (Washington: International Monetary Fund).

Padoa-Schioppa, Tommaso, 1999, "EMU and Banking Supervision," available on the Internet at http://www.ecb.int/key/sp990224.htm.

Prati, Alessandro, and Garry Schinasi, 1998, *Financial Stability in EMU* (Washington: International Monetary Fund).

Quinn, Brian, 1996, "Rules vs. Discretion: The Case of Banking Supervision in the Light of the Debate on Monetary Policy," London School of Economics, Financial Markets Group Special Paper No. 85 (London: London School of Economics).

Yam, Joseph, 1999, "The Lender of Last Resort," *Quarterly Bulletin*, Hong Kong Monetary Authority, August, pp. 120–126.

6

Issues in the Unification of Financial Sector Supervision

RICHARD ABRAMS AND MICHAEL TAYLOR

Unified financial sector supervision—the regulation of the banking, insurance, and securities sectors by a single agency—remains relatively rare in the world today.[1] A number of countries have recently adopted this structure, however, sparking interest in the idea. The IMF has already provided technical assistance on the topic and is likely to provide further technical assistance in the future. The merits of a unified arrangement have also arisen as an issue in several recent Financial System Stability Assessments.[2] In providing such advice or an assessment, a fundamental concern is the suitability of this type of financial regulatory structure to the individual circumstances of particular countries. This chapter aims

---

The authors would like to thank the staff of the IMF's Monetary and Exchange Affairs Department for its comments and, in particular, Michael Andrews and Udaibir Das.

[1]Throughout this chapter "banks" and "banking" refer to any institution that performs the payment system and intermediation functions of a bank whether or not it uses the word in its name. For the time being, the issue of whether other parts of the financial sector (e.g., pension funds or finance houses) should also be included within the scope of a unified regulatory agency will be considered in the section entitled "The Scope and Functions of Limited Agency."

[2]Countries for which technical assistance has been provided on this issue include, among others, Estonia, the Republic of Korea, and Latvia. The issue has also arisen in the context of several countries participating in the IMF's Financial Sector Assessment Program, recently Hungary and Ireland.

to provide a broad framework within which the arguments for and against unification can be analyzed and examined.

Changing the structure of regulation cannot of itself guarantee effective supervision. Institutional structure is a second order issue to be considered once the various conditions for effective regulation, as discussed in the next section, are in place. Changing the structure of regulation might appear to answer to the desire to be seen to "do something"—especially in the aftermath of a financial crisis—but it will not necessarily address the root causes of the weaknesses of supervision that may have contributed to the crisis in the first place.[3] Hence, strengthening regulatory capacity needs to be given attention ahead of issues of the structure of regulation. Nevertheless, as will be discussed later in this chapter, unifying financial sector supervision can improve the efficiency and effectiveness of regulation in certain circumstances. For example, an integrated regulatory agency may be able to monitor the activities of integrated firms and markets more effectively than separate agencies, and thus may be an appropriate response—for example, to the formation of financial conglomerates. The chapter's central contention is that to be effective, the structure of the regulatory system needs to reflect the structure of the regulated markets. While appearing to provide a strong justification for unification in some circumstances, this factor is only one of several that needs to be taken into account; in some cases the balance of argument may tend to favor unification, whereas in others it will not.

Perhaps reflecting the diversity of financial systems, as well as other factors like history and governmental institutions, regulatory structures vary widely. Nonetheless, in approximately half the countries contained in a recent study by Llewellyn (1999), the revealed preference is for a regulatory structure based on specialist agencies, with the banking, insurance, and securities sectors, each supervised by a dedicated agency (Table 6.1).

In most cases where the specialist agency model prevailed, the banking supervisor was also the central bank. Nonetheless, this model is far from universal. In three countries (Chile, South Africa, and the Slovak Republic) the securities and insurance sectors have a common regulator, while banks are regulated by a specialist agency. In nine other countries, banks and securities companies have the same regulator, while insurance is regulated by a specialist agency. Both Germany and France have adopted a regulatory structure in which the

---

[3]It may, however, assist in the elimination of gaps in regulatory coverage that in some circumstances may have contributed to the financial crisis in the first place—for example, as the result of a systemically significant unsupervised group of financial institutions.

Table 6.1. The Regulatory Structures in Selected Countries

Separate agencies for each main sector	35
Combined securities and insurance regulators	3
Combined banking and securities regulators	9
Combined banking and insurance regulators	13
Unified supervision (in central bank)	3
Unified supervision (outside central bank)	10

Source: Courtis (1999).

prudential regulation of banks and securities firms is conducted by the same agency, while the oversight of securities markets is the responsibility of a specialist body; insurance companies are also supervised by a specialist regulator. In another 13 countries, banking and insurance regulation is combined while securities regulation is performed by a specialist agency.

As shown in Table 6.1, the unified model is not as common as the recent attention it has received might seem to suggest. The ten countries classified as having adopted this organizational form are Australia, Canada, Denmark, Iceland, Japan, Norway, the Republic of Korea, Singapore, Sweden, and the United Kingdom. However, in at least two cases—Australia and Canada—the regulatory structure is not fully unified, as securities regulation is conducted separately from banking and insurance regulation. Moreover, in Singapore's case, regulation has been unified within the central bank. This leaves only seven countries that have fully unified regulatory agencies separate from the central bank. Over half of these are in the Nordic countries. This observation may suggest that unified supervision has, to date, been a response to country-specific factors, and as such may not be universally applicable. One aim of this chapter is to consider this issue in some depth.

Prerequisites for Effective Supervision: A Summary

Maintaining and enhancing supervisory capacity and the effectiveness of supervision should be the primary goal of any proposed regulatory reform. As such, the development of regulatory capacity should be given prominence over the issue of regulatory structure, and the latter is only a matter of fundamental concern to the extent that it can assist in achieving this overarching objective. In general, there are a number of essential prerequisites that any regulatory structure should meet if it is to have a reasonable likelihood of success.[4] Furthermore, if these prerequisites are not met, policymakers should take steps to rectify these shortcomings before considering more complex forms of financial sector regulation, such as the development of a unified supervisory function. The following list does not aim to be exhaustive, but nonetheless attempts to provide an indicative set of key features that constitute an effective supervisory structure.

Clear Objectives

A regulatory agency must have clear objectives, preferably set forth in a statute. Clear objectives assist the agency's senior management in making decisions on the efficient allocation of resources and in determining the appropriate policy response to a given problem (see International Monetary Fund, 1999, Part V). Clear objectives can also help prevent regulation from expanding beyond the minimum necessary to correct the market failures that regulation is intended to correct (it should not become an unnecessary burden on the regulated institutions). Finally, they also provide a mechanism by which the regulatory agency can be held to account for its decisions and policies.

Independence and Accountability

A regulatory agency must be able to make decisions that belong to its sphere of competence without undue outside interference, whether they be from ministers, parliamentarians, industry leaders, or other government officials (including potentially central bankers). In this regard, it is especially important that senior management be protected from

---

[4]Basel Core Principle 1 states,

> An effective system of banking supervision will have clear responsibilities and objectives for each agency involved in the supervision of banking organizations. Each such agency should possess operational independence and adequate resources. A suitable legal framework for banking supervision is also necessary, including provisions relating to authorization of banking organizations and their ongoing supervision; powers to address compliance with laws as well as safety and soundness concerns; and legal protection for supervisors. Arrangements for sharing information between supervisors and protecting the confidentiality of such information should be in place.

While referring specifically to banking, the prerequisites identified in this Core Principle are equally applicable to the regulation of any financial institution or activity. The IMF's Code of Good Practices on Transparency of Monetary and Financial Policies ("transparency code") also contains a number of relevant principles.

arbitrary removal. The rules governing the dismissal of senior management must therefore be transparent and demanding, ideally set forth in an act of parliament. Budgetary autonomy, in the sense of the existence of an earmarked source of funding for the agency and its ability to allocate resources according to its own internal priorities, is equally important, for otherwise efforts to develop an aggressive and effective regulatory body can be prevented by cutting the agency's budget. Because of this, it is generally desirable that the regulatory agency be funded by a levy on regulated firms, rather than being dependent on allocations from the general government budget.

The need for regulatory independence should be balanced by a corresponding need to ensure that the agency can be held to account for its policies and actions (International Monetary Fund, 1999, Part VIII). Accountability as a first priority must be to government and to parliament, since these are the sources of the agency's powers. However, responsiveness to the regulated industry may also need to be taken into account. This might, for example, be accomplished by creating a mechanism of formal consultation with representatives of these various groups. The statutory industry panel established as part of the United Kingdom's new regulatory arrangements provide one possible way in which these might be achieved.[5] These types of accountability mechanism are especially important when the regulatory agency is funded by an industry levy, since it provides some means by which the industry can check and balance the regulator's power to raise funds and prevent the costs of regulation from becoming excessive. However, care needs to be taken that in introducing accountability to the industry the regulatory agency is not exposed to the risk of regulatory capture by the industry.

Adequate Resources

Allied to the funding issue is the consideration that the regulatory agency needs to have adequate resources to discharge its task effectively. Especially important is the ability to recruit, train, and retain a cadre of experienced, professional staff. Since the kinds of skills required to make

---

[5]The Practitioner Panel was also established in November 1998, and is now placed on a statutory basis by the Financial Services and Markets Act. Its membership comprises senior representatives of the businesses that are regulated by the Financial Services Authority (FSA). The panel may make representations to the FSA, and the act requires that the Authority "have regard" to such representations. By section II of the act, if the FSA disagrees with the view expressed or proposal made in the representation, it must give the panel a statement in writing of its reasons for disagreeing, and this statement may be made public.

an effective regulator are also likely to be in heavy demand in the private sector, it follows that the regulator must be able to offer a staff competitive remuneration. (This is a further argument in favor of funding by an industry levy because it gives the regulator greater flexibility in remunerating its staff.) Similarly, the regulator must also be able to command adequate resources to ensure timely and effective data collection and processing.

Effective Enforcement Powers

A regulatory agency must possess effective enforcement powers over the full range of the firms it is responsible for regulating. These powers should include, as a minimum, the ability to require information from regulated firms, to assess the competence and probity of senior management and the owners of the institution, and to take appropriate graduated sanctions against failure to comply with regulatory rules, including having the ultimate power to intervene in the institution's operations if necessary. Ideally, the regulatory authority should have the ability to revoke licenses to conduct financial services business. However, in some countries this may not be compatible with constitutional provisions that require a strict separation of executive and judicial functions. In the latter case, the authority should have the ability to make recommendations on the revocation of licenses, with the decision-taker required to give reasons in the event that the authority's recommendation is not acted on. Enforcement powers are likely to remain more effective if the regulator has the ability to amend them quickly. For this reason it is generally preferable to establish only the broad framework of the regulatory agency's powers in legislation, leaving the details to be filled in by directives and guidelines that can be issued and amended by the regulatory agency itself. To effectively carry out its responsibilities, the staff of the regulatory agency should also have immunity from any legal suit for actions taken in the discharge of their official duties.

Comprehensiveness of Regulation

Another essential feature of a regulatory system is that it should be comprehensive and free of regulatory gaps in that there should be no possibility of particular activities or types of intermediaries to escape effective regulation simply because there is doubt about which agency should be responsible for regulating these activities. A central component of comprehensiveness is that regulatory agencies should practice effective consolidated supervision of the institutions for which they are responsible. However, the case for comprehensiveness goes beyond this, such that all efforts should be made to eliminate gaps in the jurisdiction of the regulatory agencies, which could allow otherwise regulated activities or institutions to escape effective regulation. The regulators must also be in a position to respond quickly to market innovations to ensure that the regulatory framework remains up to date and does not become ineffective or act as a barrier to the legitimate evolution of the market.

Cost Efficient Regulation

Regulation imposes costs both directly and indirectly. The direct costs are those needed to sustain the activities of the regulatory agencies: they include staff salaries, administrative overheads (including accommodation costs), and the information technology budget. The indirect costs of regulation are more difficult to quantify, but are those incurred by the regulated industry as a result of the need to comply with regulatory requirements. These costs can take many different forms, ranging from the costs of employing specialist "compliance" staff to the costs of maintaining special systems for regulatory reporting that go beyond those necessary for an institution's own internal purposes. As a general principle, a regulatory arrangement with lower costs, both direct and indirect, is to be preferred to one that imposes higher costs.

The Effectiveness Criteria and Industry Structure

A key factor in a regulatory system's ability to meet the effectiveness criteria is that the institutional structure of regulation should reflect, at least to some degree, the structure of the industry it is called upon to regulate. Because industry structures vary markedly between countries, this implies that the regulatory structure will in turn need to exhibit a similar degree of variation. For this reason, no one type of regulatory structure will be optimal from the point of view of meeting the effectiveness criteria, and "one size fits all" solutions should be avoided.

For example, the case for combining banking and securities regulation is especially strong where the model of universal banking prevails. This is especially true in those countries that have derived their supervisory frameworks from EU law. In addition to providing for the universal banking model, this framework also establishes a set of uniform capital rules, in the form of the Capital Adequacy Directive, that apply to the securities activities of both bank and nonbank financial institutions. Application of these rules by a single agency reduces the possibility of competitive distortions and regulatory arbitrage opportunities. Moreover, a single agency is able to obtain oversight of all of a bank's activities, ensuring that risks arising from both its traditional banking activities and its activities in the securities markets are properly monitored and controlled. These considerations underlie the regulatory structures adopted in France and Germany, where the prudential regulation of banks and securities firms is conducted by the same agencies (the Commission Bancaire and the Bundesaufsichtsamt fur das Kreditwesen, respectively).

A further reason for combining banking and securities regulation is that risks tend to arise on the assets side of the balance sheet. However, the case of insurance companies is somewhat different, since here the main financial risks occur on the liabilities side of the balance sheet (i.e., the primary risk is unanticipated claims by policyholders). As a consequence, insurance supervision tends to be concerned with ensuring that the company maintains a sufficient stock of liquid assets (the "solvency margin") to meet claims that can be reasonably anticipated according to an actuarial assessment. Unlike credit or market risk, the scale of these risks tends to change relatively slowly over time. Because of these substantial differences between insurance and banking or securities regulation, the case for a combination of all three functions is less clear cut. Nonetheless, in a number of countries, the decision to unify their supervisory functions has been taken because of the growth of financial groups, which own both banking and insurance businesses.[6]

These considerations imply that in some circumstances a regulatory system might be better able to meet the effectiveness criteria if it is unified. It is possible that, where financial conglomerate groups form an important component of the financial system, a unified regulator might improve the comprehensiveness of regulation, as discussed in the following section. In addition, through achieving economies of scale it might also reduce regulatory costs and make more efficient use of resources. However, there are a number of the essential prerequisites of regulation that unification in and of itself will not enhance—for example, the effectiveness of regulatory powers and the independence and accountability of the agency. Much will depend on the way that unification is implemented and the way that the legislation is drafted; for every advantage that can be claimed for unification there is also a risk that needs to be balanced against it, as will be shown in the next section.

To Unify or Not?

The effectiveness criteria will now be used to examine the case for the unification of supervisory functions. The starting point is to consider the

---

[6]Sometimes referred to as "bancassurance" or "All-Finanz" groups.

appropriateness of merging the three core financial sector supervisory functions into a dedicated agency or commission. In doing so, it is not only necessary to consider the advantages and disadvantages of such a change, but also whether alternative approaches can achieve the same results in a more efficient, or possibly safer, manner. It is also important to consider the implications that the decision to unify will have for the role of the central bank, and in particular whether or not it would be appropriate to separate the monetary policy and banking supervision functions. Finally, it is necessary to consider those circumstances when unification may not be appropriate.

Arguments for Unification

A wide range of arguments have been advanced in favor of unification (see Briault, 1999, for a full discussion). Some of the most persuasive are based on efficiency gains, in particular the economies of scale, which seem to be offered by unification of supervisory agencies. However, some of the most prominent recent arguments are based on either the need to revise supervisory coverage in light of the rise of financial conglomerates or to ensure competitive neutrality in light of the blurring distinctions between the various classes of financial institutions.[7] These latter arguments, which have been advanced in the context of a number of industrial countries, may not be as universally applicable as those based on regulatory efficiency.

Supervision of financial conglomerates

The rise of financial conglomerates, which operate diverse groups of financial institutions domestically,[8] and often internationally as well, has led regulators to seek to identify ways to efficiently and effectively oversee their operations. Fragmented supervision may raise concerns about the ability of the financial sector supervisors to form an overall risk assessment of the institution on a consolidated basis, as well as their ability to ensure that supervision is seamless and free of gaps. There are also group-wide risks that may not be adequately addressed by specialist regulators, which have oversight jurisdiction over only part of a diversified conglomerate. Among these risks are whether the group as a whole has adequate capital and whether it has adequate systems and

---

[7]The literature on this subject is relatively extensive, given that the subject of regulatory structure has otherwise been underresearched. First to make this argument were Borio and Filosa (1994). Their work has been followed by Goodhart (1995), Taylor (1995), and Goodhart and others (1998).

[8]These groups combine at least two of the activities of banking, insurance, and securities.

controls for managing its risks. Financial sector supervisors must also be able to ensure that they are able to respond on an institution-wide basis should serious problems occur in any part of the conglomerate. Experience has shown that, while these firms generally claim to have financial firewalls between their various operations, they are often proven to be largely illusory when serious difficulties arise.

Ensuring effective supervision of diversified financial conglomerate groups places several requirements on the various financial supervisory bodies that are not usually present in more simple corporate structures. First, the supervisory bodies must have an effective and efficient system of rapidly sharing information with each other on each particular institution, while also ensuring the appropriate degree of confidentiality. Second, the supervisory bodies must have a close and ongoing working relationship to ensure that suspicions and findings are fully and promptly shared, and that regulatory gaps are identified and closed. Third, and most important, steps should be taken to ensure that, for each institution, one supervisory agency is given the power, authority, and responsibility to take the lead in both forming an overall risk assessment and to lead the regulatory response, should problems arise; this agency is generally referred to as the lead regulator.

Financial institutions also seek to minimize the burden of supervision by demanding that supervision of their operations be carried out as efficiently and with as little duplication as possible. For conglomerates, this requires that some attempt be made to address the additional burden associated with fragmented supervision. This can be done by minimizing overlap and duplication in reporting and oversight, and by simplifying the process of seeking decisions on the part of the regulator. Having a single contact point for all requests on regulatory issues may allow regulators to respond more rapidly and flexibly, while reducing the risk of regulatory gaps developing.

Although it might be possible for a series of specialist regulators to cooperate in the supervision of a diversified financial group—for example, by using the lead regulator arrangement—a unified approach seems nonetheless to offer a better prospect of coordination and the exchange of information than would occur between separate agencies.[9] One can argue that a unified supervisory function is best suited to deal with all of the above problems, for by placing all the financial sector supervisors for a given conglomerate under a single agency, one creates a single management structure that should be able to instruct—and, if need be,

---

[9]Achieving agreement on assigning a lead regulator has proved remarkably difficult in practice.

to enforce—the various operating divisions to closely cooperate and share information as it becomes available. Furthermore, cooperation in closing regulatory gaps and eliminating regulatory overlap can be more easily effected, as can binding decisions regarding the assignment of a lead regulator. Such an arrangement may also aid international cooperation, because foreign supervisors will be given a single contact point for all regulatory issues.

Competitive neutrality

A related argument is based on the blurring of the lines of demarcation between products and institutions as financial systems have evolved and matured. Thus, the situation may arise where financial institutions offering similar services or products are supervised by different authorities. In this case, there is a strong likelihood that there will be differences in their regulation and the associated costs of achieving compliance, which may, in turn, give certain institutions a competitive advantage in offering a particular service or product.

The existence of a range of supervisory authorities also poses the risk that financial firms will engage in some form of supervisory arbitrage. This can involve the placement of a particular financial service or product in that part of a given financial conglomerate where the supervisory costs are the lowest or where supervisory oversight is the least intrusive. It may also lead firms to design new financial institutions or redesign existing ones strictly to minimize or avoid supervisory oversight. If such attempts at regulatory arbitrage become widespread, these efforts may have second-round effects in that the various supervisory authorities "compete" to reduce the burden of their oversight in order to avoid a flight of their "clients" to other supervisory agencies. While some such competition is conceivably healthy, there is the risk that the authorities may allow prudential supervision to be weakened. A unified supervisory function is well-designed to deal with all of the above-noted problems, for a single supervisory body is better able to iron out differences and inconsistencies, whatever their source. Having a single management structure directly overseeing all supervisory bodies is also probably the most effective way to ensure that the various bodies do not compete for customers.

Complete regulatory neutrality should not be a primary objective of supervision, however. One of the main objectives of financial sector supervision is minimizing the risk of systemic difficulties. Thus, the potential social costs associated with financial difficulties in a participant in the payment system, whose failure might give rise to systemic problems, are very different from those associated with the failure of a mutual fund or a finance company. Accordingly, the optimal amount of oversight of a similar operation may vary markedly between different types of institutions. Thus, while supervisors may wish to closely examine a bank's activities in a potentially risky market—for example, stock market derivatives—their attitudes toward the same operations being carried out by a mutual fund would be very different. Given these differences, supervisors can argue that it is proper to supervise the same operation differently, depending on the nature of the institution that is carrying out the transaction. Thus, to a degree, supervisors should encourage a certain amount of regulatory arbitrage, insofar as it involves locating riskier operations in subsidiaries that are outside of the systemically important part of the conglomerate. Of course, if the conglomerate's firewalls are inadequate, this approach may be self-defeating.

Regulatory flexibility

A potential advantage of the unified approach to supervision is that it may allow for the development of regulatory arrangements that are more flexible than can be achieved with separate specialist agencies. Whereas the effectiveness of a system of separate agencies can be impeded by "turf wars" or a desire to "pass the buck," these problems can be more easily limited and controlled in a unified regulatory organization. Specialist agencies can also be impeded from operating effectively where their respective enabling statutes leave doubts about their jurisdiction or locus for dealing with a particular matter, especially when a new type of financial product or institution emerges, which was not covered by the original legislation. As a result, a unified agency may offer a more effective way of responding to market developments or innovations.

While flexibility is useful in the context of the developed financial markets, where the rapid pace of financial innovation rapidly leads to the obsolescence of regulations and rules, it is also desirable in emerging and transition economies as well. This is so because countries that have recently liberalized their financial systems often experience rapid change in the financial industry, which may include the growth of certain types of nonbank financial intermediaries that can pose a significant threat to financial sector soundness.[10] Thus, having a regulatory agency with the scope and capacity to respond rapidly to these changes by extending its regulatory jurisdiction is a major benefit of a properly constituted unified agency. However, achieving this objective requires

---

[10]This can happen, particularly, when they are formed to evade effective supervision.

that the enabling statute for the unified agency be drafted with sufficient flexibility to permit it to rapidly respond to market innovations. If the range of products and institutions subject to regulation is too narrowly defined in the legislation, or if the legislation cannot be amended quickly, then the benefits of a unified approach versus a set of separate agencies will be more limited.

Regulatory efficiency

Although scale economies are difficult to measure in a regulatory organization, as a matter of general principle, a larger organization permits finer specialization of labor and a more intensive utilization of inputs. In a regulatory context, unification may allow cost savings on the basis of shared infrastructure, administration, and support systems. The existence of multiple, specialized regulatory bodies has generally resulted in the duplication of support infrastructures—for example, in data collection and processing and personnel administration. These are areas where there would appear to have been significant opportunity for cost savings and economies of scale from unification. Unification may also permit the acquisition of information technologies, which become cost-effective only beyond a certain scale of operations and can avoid wasteful duplication of research and information-gathering efforts. A more unified approach to data collection may also set forth the basis for a more efficient reporting system, which could result in significant cost savings for the regulated enterprises, particularly financial conglomerates. But, as discussed below, there are also important synergies between the data necessary for banking supervision and for monetary policy purposes that may outweigh the synergies between the data required for banking supervision and for the regulation of other financial intermediaries. Which factor should be given greatest weight to a large extent will depend on the structure of the financial system; one in which financial conglomerates form a significant element will probably benefit to a greater extent from combining the data collection effort for all types of financial institutions.

The absence of hard data makes it difficult to assess the strength of the economies of scale argument, although it is worth noting that in all of the Scandinavian countries—which were the first to establish this type of regulatory agency—it is believed that the approach has made it possible to realize significant economies (Taylor and Fleming, 1999). Britain's Financial Services Authority (FSA) has also reported substantial savings from the unification of support services. In most cases, the supervised institutions also seem to take the view that unification has eliminated unnecessary duplication and overlap (Briault, 1999).

The arguments for economies of scale are most applicable in countries where supervisory agencies tend to be not as large and well developed as in industrial countries, notably in smaller countries or those with less sophisticated financial systems. In these countries, the benefits of merging the administrative and data processing functions of the various supervisory functions are difficult to dismiss. Such overheads can constitute a heavy cost for such functions, and the economies of scale in sharing these services can be great, particularly if the supervisory functions do not share these functions with some other larger institutions, such as the central bank or the finance ministry. In fact, one former head of a unified supervision function viewed this as the strongest argument for unification. However, similar benefits may be gained by having the supervisory functions share such services individually or as a group, even though they remain independent from one another in their management and all of their other operations. This approach may be taken a step further by having the supervision function(s) effectively subcontract administrative and electronic data processing services from a larger body, such as the central bank. This option is discussed in more detail in the following section.

Developing a body of professional staff

An essential requirement of effective regulation is that a regulatory agency should be able to attract, retain, and develop skilled professional staff. Unification can assist in this process, especially in those countries where regulatory capacity is still being developed. As the single largest employer of financial regulators, a unified agency might be better placed to formulate a coherent human resources policy, including a career planning strategy for its personnel. It would be able to offer its staff a more varied and challenging career than they would enjoy in a specialist regulator, and might be sufficiently large to develop its own tailored, in-house training programs.

Unification also makes it easier for supervisors to share specialized knowledge. First, it could allow supervisors for one group of financial institutions to borrow a specialist from another group, or even to hire a single specialist to support several different supervisory functions. Second, it may lay the basis for efficiency gains by having supervisors work together on issues of mutual interest, either with respect to particular financial conglomerates or on regulatory and reporting issues in general. Third, this arrangement may also help preserve scarce management skills, for in many countries finding a sufficient number of capable managers to lead their supervisory functions is problematic.

The shortage of supervisory resources is a serious problem in a number of countries, notably in the Baltic states, Russia, and the other countries of the former Soviet Union. But while most are clearly applicable in small countries or smaller financial systems, this argument also applies in larger financial markets as well, especially in those areas where developments in regulatory techniques have required regulators to recruit and retain human resources with highly marketable skills. Given that the public sector always has difficulties in competing with the private sector for these skills, one of the attractions of unification is that it enables these scarce human resources to be deployed to their greatest effect.

Improved accountability

A final argument in favor of unification is that it improves the accountability of regulation. Under a system of multiple regulatory agencies, it may be more difficult to hold regulators to account for their performance against their statutory objectives, for the costs of regulation, for their disciplinary policies, and for regulatory failures. The existence of multiple agencies, perhaps with overlapping responsibilities and areas of jurisdiction, makes possible a disbursement strategy of culpability among the regulators, thus making it difficult to hold any of several agencies accountable. One advantage of a unified agency is that by creating a single management structure, it should be clear to politicians, the industry, and the public who should be held to account for particular regulatory actions or failures.

But the relationship between unification and improved accountability is essentially second-order. A unified agency might still be difficult to hold to account if its objectives are ill-defined, while multiple specialist agencies might be more easily held to account if their objectives are clearly specified. Hence, the fundamental consideration should be the clarity of regulatory objectives rather than the number of agencies involved in regulation.

Arguments Against Unification

Not surprisingly, the list of arguments against unification is almost as long as the list for unification. These include claims that unification will result in unclear objectives for the regulatory agency; economies of scope will prove hard to achieve as long as the banking, securities, and insurance businesses are subject to different regulations; the agency will suffer from diseconomies of scale; and that it will extend moral hazard concerns across the entire financial services sector. There is also the concern that the change process itself may be poorly managed or become politicized. As a result, it will be subject to unpredictable and possibly undesirable outcomes (Box 6.1).

Unclear objectives

One of the most powerful arguments advanced against unified regulatory agencies is that it will be difficult for them to strike an appropriate balance between the different objectives of regulation. Given the diversity of these objectives—ranging from guarding against systemic risk to protecting the individual consumer from fraud—it is possible that a single regulator might not have a clear focus on the objectives and rationale of regulation, and might not be able to adequately differentiate between different types of institutions. Indeed, rather than improving accountability, the creation of a unified regulator might diminish it because of the difficulty of designing a single set of objectives for it. As a result, its statutory responsibilities may be vague and ill-defined, which in turn can give rise to problems of holding the regulatory agency to account for its activities. Vague objectives may also provide little guidance for the regulator when (as inevitably will be the case) its different objectives come into conflict. Specialist agencies with a clear focus on a specific regulatory objective are arguably both more easily held to account for their actions and less likely to extend regulation inappropriately (see Taylor, 1995, for elaboration of this point).

Diseconomies of scale

Despite the strength of the economies of scale argument, a single unified regulator may also suffer from some diseconomies of scale. One source of inefficiency could arise because a unified agency is effectively a regulatory monopoly, which may give rise to problems typically associated with monopolies. A particular concern about a monopoly regulator is that the new function could be more rigid and bureaucratic than separate specialist agencies. This view is based on the premise that larger organizations tend to be more bureaucratic, particularly if their operations become so broad that the line managers are unable to fully understand the range of operations of the organization. However, this issue is more likely to hinge on the organization and management of the function than on its size. If the supervisory body is poorly managed, staffed, or organized, it is likely to be inflexible and bureaucratic whether it is large or small. It must not be forgotten that a unified function in a small country may still be smaller than each of the main supervisory bodies in a large country, and that many large countries have efficient and flexible financial sector supervisors.

> **Box 6.1. Unification Risks**
>
> A serious disadvantage of a decision to create a unified supervisory agency can be the unpredictability of the change process itself. This risk has a number of different dimensions.
>
> The first risk is that opening the issue for discussion will set in place a chain of events that will lead to the creation of a unified agency, whether or not it is appropriate to create one. The problem is one of political power. Powerful actors within the government and the public sector may see such a proposal as an opportunity to increase their influence within government by taking on important additional powers. Furthermore, the individuals that see themselves best placed to lead the unified agency will tend to push the issue aggressively and seek to rush the proposal through parliament quickly, before the internal balance of power shifts against them. In such circumstances, there is clearly a risk that mistakes will be made in the design of the agency, and that the plan may be pushed forward even if it appears likely that the unified authority will be sufficiently flawed as to make its creation inadvisable. If the process of creation becomes tied to an internal battle for power, it would also increase the risk that the unified agency will have insufficient autonomy, or worse be highly politicized.
>
> The second risk is legislative. The creation of a unified agency will generally require new legislation, but this creates the possibility that the process will be captured by special interests. As a result, issues, which had previously been thought settled under existing financial services legislation—for example, decisions on the scope of activities subject to regulation or the appropriateness of exemptions from regulation—may be reopened. Thus, depending on the balance of parliamentary powers, the legislative outcome may be weaker than the original legislation under which the separate regulatory agencies had been established. One way to minimize this risk is to limit the need for legislation to a simple enabling act. This would establish the unified agency and effect a transfer of powers to it from the existing regulatory bodies, while leaving existing statutes otherwise unaffected. However, this minimalist approach has its disadvantages. One is that it does not permit the harmonization of legislation across the different financial services sectors, which is one of the primary advantages of regulatory unification. Another is that it may also fail to

Another source of diseconomies of scale is the tendency for unified agencies to be assigned an ever-increasing range of functions, sometimes called the "Christmas-tree effect." This may arise because the formation of a unified agency may tempt politicians and policymakers to require it to perform tasks that may be only tangentially connected to its core functions. For example, in some Scandinavian countries, unified agencies address the issue of regulatory gaps. A final problem is that it does nothing to reduce the risks that the reorganization will result in a power grab that will undermine the autonomy of the individual agencies.

The third risk created by the change process is a possible reduction in regulatory capacity through the loss of key personnel. Many of the staff will view the unification process change with concern, while others may see this as a difficult and trying period, which they would prefer to avoid. Thus, many staff members who would be important or valuable additions to the new organization may view this as a time to test the job market or retire. This has been a serious problem during the formation of a number of unified agencies, with staff turnover in some cases reaching unsustainable levels. It is likely to be compounded in the event that the change involves extraction of banking supervision from the central bank. Many of the best bank supervisors may prefer either to remain with the central bank or to move into the private sector, rather than risk the perceived reduction in pay and/or status, which joining a specialist regulatory body would involve. Thus, there is a real risk that many seasoned workers and highly qualified professionals may be lost—a very serious consideration if the supervisory function is not particularly strong or well-staffed. On the positive side, this is also a time when it may be particularly easy to weed out the weaker, less skilled staff within the old function.

The fourth risk is that the change management process itself will go off track. The process of creating a unified regulatory agency places heavy demands on management resources, often in environments where such resources are already in short supply. The management challenge of putting together a number of disparate regulatory agencies should not be underestimated, and there will be a need for a well-conceived and carefully monitored change management program to make it effective. During the transition process itself, this risk may be addressed by ensuring that the new supervisor body has—or hires—experts with the skills to bring about such a reorganization in an efficient, cost-effective manner. However, the management issues, which will arise in the early years of the unified agency, cannot be dealt with in a similar way and are for the agency's own management itself to address.

have been required to take on the regulation of real estate brokers, although this arguably detracts from their primary function. Similarly, the United Kingdom's FSA has already been the subject of several attempts to assign it new responsibilities beyond its already broad scope. These include the regulation of mortgages (on consumer protection grounds) and encouraging competition in the financial services industry.

Limited synergies

Some critics of unification argue that the synergy gains from unification will not be very large; in other words, economies of scope are likely to be much less significant than economies of scale. In this regard, it is true that the cultures, focus, and skills of the various supervisors vary markedly. For example, it has been noted that the sources of risks at banks are on the asset side, while most of the risks at insurance companies are on the liability side. Furthermore, the behavior of the various types of supervisors vary markedly, with some describing banking supervisors as being more like doctors examining the health of the patient, while securities supervisors are more like policemen trying to catch the miscreant securities dealers.[11] The evidence of unified authorities to date tends to suggest that even within a single organization these differences of style and culture will remain, and trying to create a single agency culture has been one of the most difficult tasks for management. To some extent the difficulty has been compounded—or at least not assuaged—by the fact that the internal organization of these agencies has tended to mirror traditional institutional lines—that is, most have been established with separate departments for banking, securities, and insurance regulation. However, this is now changing, as some authorities are beginning to experiment more with matrix-based organizations—for example, the Complex Groups division of the United Kingdom's FSA, which specializes in the supervision of financial conglomerates. However, while there is a consensus that efficiency gains from unification can be substantial, the evidence to date that the unified agencies can achieve significant synergies among their different functions is mixed and difficult to quantify.

Moral hazard

Perhaps the most worrisome of all the criticisms of unified regulation is the "moral hazard" argument. This argument is based on the premise that the public will tend to assume that all creditors of institutions supervised by a given supervisor will receive equal protection. Hence, if depositors, and perhaps other creditors, are protected from loss in the event of bank failure, then the customers and creditors of all other financial institutions supervised by the same regulatory authority may

---

[11]It may also be significant that international cooperation also tends to occur along institutional lines, and in this respect the work of the Joint Forum (the Joint Forum of the Basel Committee on Banking Supervision, the International Organization of Securities Commissions, and the International Association of Insurance Supervisors was originally called the "Joint Forum on Financial Conglomerates," but changed its name to the "Joint Forum" in 1999) is the exception rather than the rule.

expect to be treated in an equivalent manner. Clearly this is an informational problem, and in the event of unification, the new supervisory body will need to clarify the rules of the game regarding the treatment of the various financial institutions.[12] Furthermore, it may be necessary for the supervisor to reinforce its position by treating any nonbank institutions that get into trouble strictly according to the preannounced rules of the game.

The Role of the Central Bank

A further dimension to the arguments for and against unification is the extent to which the central bank is, or should be, directly involved in banking supervision. The earliest examples of unified supervision—in Denmark, Norway, and Sweden—were established in systems where the central bank had not been the banking supervisor. This state of affairs does not occur in most of the rest of the world. Thus, in many countries, the decision to create a unified supervisory agency will probably necessitate the extraction of banking supervision from the central bank, as has happened recently in Australia and the United Kingdom. Although an alternative possibility would be to combine all supervision within the central bank, as practiced in Singapore, moral hazard considerations may weigh heavily against this structure. (This option is discussed in more depth later in this section.) For the purposes of the present discussion, it will be assumed that the unification of supervision will involve the separation of the banking supervision and monetary policy functions. This requires some consideration of the arguments for and against the combination and separation of monetary policy and banking supervision within the central bank.

The arguments for and against the separation between supervision and monetary policy have been well examined (Goodhart and Schoenmaker, 1995). The arguments against separation are strong. In particular, since banks are the conduit through which changes in short-term interest rates are transmitted to the wider economy, the central bank needs to be concerned about their financial soundness as a precondition for an effective monetary policy. This argument is reinforced by a number of others, including the synergies between the information required for the conduct of monetary policy on the one hand and the supervision of the banking sector on the other; the central bank's need to assess the creditworthiness of participants in the payment system, which will inevitably involve it in forming judgments about the

---

[12] In such circumstances, constructive ambiguity may not be that constructive.

solvency and prudent conduct of banks; and the central bank's need to have access to information on the solvency and liquidity of individual banks in order to exercise its lender-of-last-resort functions. These arguments have traditionally been seen as making a powerful case for combining the banking supervision and monetary policy functions, and their strength is attested to by the fact that the practice in many countries remains for the central bank to be responsible for banking supervision.

In addition to these arguments, it is also possible to cite a number of operational considerations in favor of combination. First, the economies of scale obtained from the combination of monetary policy and banking supervision may be as substantial as those that arise from combining the regulation of the different financial sectors. The commonalties in the information requirements for these respective functions have already been mentioned. In addition, to the extent that there is an overlap in the knowledge and skills required for these different functions, then a central bank may enjoy a comparative advantage in recruiting and retaining the best staff. This argument is particularly strong in countries where the absolute level of human capital with this skill is very small.

Another important consideration, notably in the Baltics, Russia, and other countries of the former Soviet Union, is that many central banks now have a strong guarantee of their independence, sometimes even written into constitutional law. This degree of independence, established primarily for the purposes of ensuring a credible monetary policy, can also help to shield banking supervision from undue parliamentary or ministerial influence. Thus, in transitional or emerging market economies there may be a case for retaining banking supervision within the central bank not only on the traditional grounds cited above, but also out of a concern to avoid the politicization of bank regulation.

It may, however, be possible to develop governance and funding arrangements for the unified regulator that give it adequate political autonomy. Moreover, it should be borne in mind that there are several general arguments for the separation of banking supervision and monetary policy, irrespective of whether or not the separation arises out of the unification of supervision. First, a central bank, which is also responsible for supervision, may err on the side of laxity if it fears that tight monetary conditions may lead to bank failures.[13] Second, bank failures inevitably will occur and when they do they will be blamed on

---

[13]However, as Goodhart and Schoenmaker (1995) argue, the validity of this argument is to a large degree dependent on the structure of the banking and financial system; the greater that the system involves intermediaries financing maturity mismatch positions through the wholesale markets, the greater the potential for conflict between monetary and financial stability goals.

the supervisor. If the supervisor is the central bank its credibility will be undermined, and with it its credibility in the conduct of monetary policy. In addition, it has also been argued that changes in payment system technology, most notably the move to real-time gross settlement (RTGS), changes the nature of the oversight that the central bank needs to exercise over participants in the system.[14] Finally, as the financial system centers less on banks and becomes more dominated by financial conglomerate groups that offer other financial services in addition to banking, the moral hazard issues discussed above gain increased significance, and these may point to the need for a regulatory structure with comparative distance between the central bank—as provider of lender-of-last-resort assistance—and the agency responsible for routine supervision and regulation.

So far the discussion has concerned only the combination of banking supervision with monetary policy within the central bank. However, another option in structuring regulation would be to combine a wider range of regulatory functions within the central bank. Thus, the central bank might be responsible for supervising the securities markets, as well as banks, and possibly even insurance companies as well. This arrangement is likely to seem particularly attractive in some quite specific circumstances: first, when the financial sector, and especially the nonbank financial sector, is relatively small, making it difficult to establish viable regulatory agencies outside the central bank; second, where banking is the main form of financial intermediation, and other financial sectors are dominated by groups with a bank at their head; third, where the central bank has a strong competitive advantage in attracting staff with the right skills and credentials—for example—where central bank salaries are significantly above those available for other public officials; and, finally, where the central bank has strong guarantees of its independence, thus providing a defense against the politicization of regulation. In circumstances where all, or most, of these conditions prevail, the option of centralizing all regulatory functions within the central bank may seem to have much to commend it.

However, this option also suffers from a number of serious disadvantages. Clearly, the moral hazard problem will be even more pronounced if the unified supervisory function is conducted by the central bank itself. It may be difficult for a central bank, which also supervises a wide range of financial intermediaries, to make sufficiently clear the

---

[14]While the RTGS system and other institutional arrangements to control risk may act to decrease systemic risks, issues relating to the increased complexity and opacity of settlement arrangements pose a new set of concerns for the supervisor (Commonwealth of Australia, 1997).

differentiation between them. Thus, it may give rise to a perception in the public mind that all types of financial contract will receive the same degree of protection in the event of firm failures. While it may be possible for the authorities, through a campaign of public education, to explain the different levels of protection available to the holders of different types of financial claims, their attempts to do so may be undermined by the perception that holders of all financial claims will enjoy the prospect of central bank support.

A second difficulty is that this approach might be perceived as granting the central bank excessive powers. Combining all regulatory functions within the central bank will result in the central bank having responsibility for the conduct of monetary policy and the regulation of all financial intermediaries, both banks and nonbanks. A related problem is the risk that particular regulatory failures may tarnish its reputation and credibility, especially in its conduct of monetary policy. Both of these objections might be minimized in the event that the supervisory function remains a legally independent agency, albeit one located within the central bank. But if this is done, it will be important to ensure that the supervisory agency is able to establish a distinct identity of its own in the public mind.

Alternatives to Full Unification

If the balance of the argument seems to favor a unified approach to financial sector supervision, but the necessary preconditions for successful unification are not in place, it may be worth considering whether other institutional arrangements might be more practical, at least as an interim solution, and possibly as a long-term alternative to unification as well. This might avoid the need for wholesale reform of the financial regulatory structure, and thus avoid some of the risks identified in Box 6.1 while still achieving some of the advantages of a unified authority. There are a number of possible variations on this minimalist approach, which include the use of an oversight board, and sharing facilities either on a stand-alone basis or with the central bank.

A Unified Oversight Board

The most limited option would be to leave the existing regulatory structure in place, but to overlay it with a newly established oversight board. The board could be formed from the heads of the various regulatory agencies, or it could be broadened to include third parties, such as representatives of the ministry of finance and the central bank. Depending on its terms of reference, the board might provide either a forum for expediting communication and information sharing between the agencies or it could be charged with executive decision making, including the setting of policy. An important function of this body could be to coordinate regulatory efforts—for example, by arranging joint inspection visits. (A possible model is represented by the board created in South Africa as an alternative to regulatory unification.)

An oversight board provides a more formalized basis for coordinating the supervision of financial conglomerates than a lead regulator arrangement, but it does not eliminate problems that can occur from differences in regulations, rulebooks, and enforcement powers. It may also provide an opportunity for the regulatory agencies to gain some experience working together with a view to facilitating their unification at some point in the future. Since it leaves in place all of the existing regulatory system, it does not require major new legislation or a far-reaching change management process. However, the modest ambitions of this approach may also be its greatest weaknesses. The chairmanship of the oversight board, depending on its functions, could be a key position, which will therefore generate rivalry among the heads of the regulatory agencies, and if the board is broadened to allow for an outside leader, political disputes and power plays could easily emerge. Furthermore, this approach is not appropriate when significant economies of scale may be possible. In view of these considerations, the oversight board approach is most appropriate for comparatively large financial markets in which conglomerates are an important component of the financial system, but where the overall market size is sufficient to support a number of specialist regulators.

Unification of Support Services

One way to achieve economies of scale without unification would be to keep the agencies as separate legal entities, but to locate them in the same building with shared infrastructure and support services. An oversight board structure could also be included to give overall direction to the separate agencies and to ensure that they coordinate their efforts; alternatively, a centralized management structure could be developed as an administrative rather than legislative matter. The physical proximity of regulatory staff may also encourage greater informal information sharing and coordination.

Such an arrangement could be continued indefinitely or used as a prelude to eventual formal unification.[15] It could be relatively quick

---

[15] A similar arrangement was adopted by the United Kingdom's FSA, albeit as an interim measure pending new legislation.

and easy to implement, although finding an appropriate building to house all of the regulatory agencies might take time.[16] However, it appears to offer many of the advantages of unification without some of the associated costs, and it avoids the risk that new legislation might result in a suboptimal outcome. Its primary disadvantage is that the absence of a strong central management authority might lead to rivalries and unresolved tensions between the senior staff of the different agencies.[17] This arrangement may also not be designed to deal well with financial conglomerates. For though administratively unified, the different agencies would continue to operate under different statutes and rulebooks and would exercise different powers. Hence, consistent treatment of diversified financial groups might be hard to achieve.

This approach would therefore seem best suited to countries with small financial sectors in which financial conglomerates are not a significant presence. In such cases, this approach would allow them to achieve the economies of scale without running the risks associated with more fundamental change. However, in those cases where banking supervision is currently conducted by the central bank, this may not be a feasible option, since, as noted earlier, removing the banking supervision function from the central bank—in fact if not in law—would be likely to result in the problems of staff retention and a reduction of regulatory capacity.

Share Facilities with the Central Bank

The above-noted problem might be avoided if the regulatory agencies were to share the central bank's facilities. One option, discussed in the previous section, would be to make the central bank responsible for the supervision of all financial intermediaries. However, an alternative approach would be to establish the supervisory agency as a separate legal entity, but one that shares the support services of the central bank, as was done in Finland.[18]

The Finnish approach has two main attractions. First, it allows for the realization of significant economies of scale, comparable—or

---

[16]This was a problem in Latvia, for example, where locating suitable accommodation for the unified agency contributed to delays in implementation.

[17]This outcome was avoided in the United Kingdom because a new centralized management structure was implemented in advance of the new legislation.

[18]The Finnish Financial Supervisory Authority is responsible for the supervision of banks and securities companies. Insurance company regulation is combined with the regulation of private sector pension funds in a separate authority. This arrangement reflects the relative unimportance of financial conglomerates in Finland compared with other Nordic countries. See Taylor and Fleming (1999) for further discussion.

perhaps greater—than those that might be expected from a stand-alone unified supervisory agency. Second, this arrangement may actually prove superior to a stand-alone agency for crisis management. If the supervisory agency shares the same premises and information technology systems as the central bank, and its staff are also employees of the central bank (as is the case in Finland), then information flows and coordinated action in the event of a crisis should be facilitated. This was a major factor behind Finland's decision to adopt this approach.

The primary disadvantage of this approach is moral hazard. As noted previously, one of the most serious objections to unification within the central bank is that it might extend the perceived central bank guarantee of support to all financial institutions, including nonbanks. Hence, if a unified supervisory agency is located within the central bank, even while remaining legally distinct, there is a risk that the public and industry perception will be that the two institutions are in fact the same, which may, in turn, encourage the view that central bank support will be available to all supervised institutions.

The Scope and Functions of a Unified Agency

A further issue to examine when considering a unified authority is its precise scope and functions.

Issues of Agency Scope

A fundamental concern is whether the unified agency should be responsible for both prudential (safety and soundness) and consumer protection (business conduct) regulation. Most integrated agencies are concerned only with ensuring the prudential soundness of financial intermediaries. The United Kingdom's FSA is practically unique among unified authorities in being responsible for both prudential and business conduct matters.

There are arguments both for and against the separation of prudential and business conduct objectives. Arguments in favor of separation are that the skill sets required of prudential and of conduct of business regulators are different.[19] Moreover, separation also allows the agency charged with prudential oversight to focus more explicitly on the detection and management of risks to the financial system. The ability to

---

[19]This argument was influential with the Australian Wallis inquiry, which decided against establishing a single regulator for the financial sector. See Commonwealth of Australia (1997).

adopt a narrow focus is especially important in countries that are prone to financial instability. Furthermore, consumer protection regulation tends to be relatively resource intensive. As a result, taking on the broader mandate may actually undercut a supervisory authority's efforts to establish a system of effective prudential regulation, particularly in smaller and developing countries.

But defenders of a combined function argue that there are several regulatory judgments—especially relating to the adequacy of systems and controls and the fitness and probity of management—that overlap in the two functions (Briault, 1999). The degree of overlap may not be extensive, however, and in most countries it has not been regarded as a sufficiently strong reason to bring consumer protection within the unified agency's scope. Prudential matters and conduct of business regulation are most frequently combined in securities regulation, whereas in banking and insurance regulation it has been the general practice to keep the two functions clearly separate. If a unified regulator is to focus only on prudential regulation, this raises the issue of where responsibility for the securities regulator's business conduct functions is to be assigned.

This consideration also led to the further question of whether the unified agency should be responsible for regulating markets—for example, the stock market or futures exchange—as well as intermediaries. One solution might be to combine the business conduct and market oversight functions within a specialist agency, leaving the unified regulator to focus only on prudential matters.[20] The skills required to ensure that a market meets standards for transparency and trade reporting, and that it is not subject to manipulation, are similar to those required for business conduct regulation, while in turn being somewhat different from those that are normally needed for effective prudential regulation. However, the activities of securities and investment firms might be difficult to monitor without access to the type of information that the market oversight function would normally provide, although close cooperation and coordination between the relevant agencies should minimize this problem.

---

[20]This arrangement has not been widely adopted, although the regulatory structures in France, Germany, and Italy reflect it to some degree (prudential regulation in those countries not being fully unified). Thus, in France, the Commission Bancaire is the prudential supervisor of banks and securities firms, but the Commission des Operations de Bourse (COB) is the market surveillance regulator. Australia deals with the issue in a different way, by combining prudential regulation with respect to banks and insurance companies in the Australian Prudential Regulatory Authority (APRA). The Australian Securities and Investments Commission (ASIC) is responsible for all aspects of securities regulation: prudential matters, business conduct, market integrity, and disclosure by listed companies.

A final set of issues relates to the type of nonbank financial intermediaries that should come within the integrated agency's scope. One issue that frequently arises is whether the unified agency should regulate pension funds. Defined contribution schemes are usually provided by investment management companies, and therefore it might be a natural extension of the agency's functions to bring them within its scope. By contrast, defined benefit schemes raise issues similar to those that arise in assessing the solvency of insurance companies and, indeed, are often provided by those companies. Actuarial assumptions are the most important factor in the assessment of the balance sheets of both insurance companies and defined benefit pension funds, which also share in common the need for a long-term asset structure combined with short-term liquidity requirements. Hence there is a strong case for combining the regulation of defined benefit pension funds with that of insurance companies.

Other nonbank financial intermediaries that might potentially come within the scope of a unified agency include finance houses and leasing companies. In many jurisdictions these companies are not subject to regulation. However, their role in initiating a number of financial crises raises the question whether the unified authority should at least have the power to require them to provide it with information on request. When considering which nonbank financial intermediaries to include within a unified agency's scope, however, it is worth bearing in mind that overextending the scope of the supervisory authority may blur its focus and seriously erode its effectiveness. Moreover, the case for explicitly including these institutions within the agency's scope only arises if they are not covered by the consolidated supervision of banks and other regulated entities. Provided that the regulatory agency conducts effective consolidated supervision, many of the systemic risks arising from this sector will be contained.

Ancillary Functions

In addition to the above array of functions, unified agencies may also be asked to take on a number of functions that are either ancillary to their primary functions or do not directly relate to the regulation of financial markets and institutions. One such function concerns the setting of accounting standards, or at least the oversight of the professional body that sets them. In some jurisdictions—for example, in the United States—the capital markets regulator, the Securities and Exchange Commission (SEC), is responsible for overseeing accounting standards that apply to publicly listed companies. Consequently, in countries where the capital markets authority has been modeled on the SEC, one result of unification may be that the new agency will acquire this role from its predecessor agency. While it can be helpful for the regulatory agency to have responsibility for the accounting standards that apply to regulated institutions (especially banks), there is no necessary connection between prudential soundness regulation and oversight of accounting and auditing firms. Hence, it would appear generally preferable for this function to be transferred elsewhere. Similarly, the extent to which the unified agency becomes involved in the implementation of Stock Exchange listing requirements will depend partly on the preexisting scope of the capital markets regulator.

Competition policy is another function that is peripheral to the primary responsibilities of a financial regulator. In most jurisdictions, it is normal for competition in the financial sector to be subject to the general rules on industrial competition and, hence, to be under the jurisdiction of a specialist competition authority. However, in some countries, an argument has been advanced that the financial sector regulator should also have an obligation to promote competition within its sector. This point of view has been urged in particular in the United Kingdom, where some have argued that the FSA should have this obligation incorporated in its statutory duties. However, this argument is made largely on consumer protection grounds, since competition is seen as a partial substitute for sales practice regulation. Where the unified regulator has a specifically prudential scope, this question is unlikely to arise.

Conclusion

The main conclusion of this review of the issues raised by the unification of financial sector supervision is that no one model of regulatory structure will be appropriate for all countries. While fully unified supervisory agencies—those regulating banking, insurance, and securities—do offer certain advantages over separate agencies, the advantages appear to vary sharply between countries. Moreover, they must also be weighed against the disadvantages, the strength of which will also vary considerably from case to case. The same points apply to the other regulatory structures considered in this chapter. Hence, in each case, it is essential to first perform a full assessment of the advantages and disadvantages of applying a particular model developed in one country to the conditions of another.[21]

---

[21]A checklist of issues to review in this context is included as an Appendix to this chapter.

The assessment of advantages and disadvantages should take into account two overarching factors. The first is that any change involves risks, and the greater the proposed structural change, the greater will be the risks. Many of these risks are examined in Box 6.1, but perhaps the most important single factor is that the change process may result in a serious reduction in existing regulatory capacity unless it is well managed.[22] This concern is particularly great with respect to banking supervision, which is the key supervisory function in many developing and transition economies given the centrality of banks to their financial systems. In these countries, great care will need to be exercised to ensure that banking supervisory capacity is not compromised by unification. Another important factor is the need to preserve (or enhance) the independence of the regulatory agency. If a proposal to create a unified authority threatens either agency capacity or independence, then it is probably not worth undertaking. In any case, the benefits of change should be relatively clear and unambiguous before embarking on a proposed unification. Where the evidence of the benefits of unification is more ambiguous, or the costs of change may be high, more modest institutional innovations should be considered, ranging from the formation of a unified oversight board to shared facilities with the central bank.

The second overarching factor is that the institutional structure of regulation should reflect the institutional structure of the industry it is designed to regulate. For example, the combination of banking and securities regulation is most clearly appropriate where the system comprises universal banks. In countries where banks are not significant players in the securities markets, the case for a combination of functions is much less strong. Similarly, the combination of banking and insurance regulation is most appropriate where linkages between banks and insurance companies are particularly significant. Combining the regulation of all three sectors within a single agency will, therefore, be most appropriate when the financial services industry of the country comprises a number of diversified, multiactivity groups or where the distinctions between different types of financial intermediaries have become blurred. In the latter case, a strictly institutional approach to regulation may no longer adequately reflect the distribution of risk in the financial system.

These various factors suggest that policymakers will need to differentiate according to the stage of development of the financial market and its degree of complexity. Moreover, the question of regulatory struc-

---

[22]This is likely to be a particular concern in transition or developing economies where regulatory capacity may already be relatively weak.

ture should be seen not as an end in itself—regulatory structure by itself is not the primary issue—but as a possible means, together with other measures, to achieve the primary objective: the provision of effective supervision, by a well-staffed, adequately funded, and independent regulatory agency. A well-designed regulatory structure that is appropriate for the conditions of a particular country's financial sector can deliver many benefits.

Appendix: Unification of Supervision—Checklist of Issues to Review

The following are prerequisites for effective supervision. (If not in place, unification may not be a priority.)
- Are supervisory objectives clear and preferably set out in statute?
- Do supervisory authorities have adequate political independence?
- Do supervisory authorities have adequate budgetary independence, including access to sufficient human resources?
- Are supervisory authorities subject to sufficient degree of accountability?
- Is the regulatory framework comprehensive?
- Do supervisory authorities have an appropriate range of enforcement powers (graduated corrective action)?
- Can and do the supervisory authorities make appropriate use of their enforcement powers?

Regulatory Framework

- Are there serious regulatory gaps or excessive areas of regulatory overlap?
- If financial conglomerates are important:
  a) Is supervision conducted on a consolidated basis?
  b) Is regulatory arbitrage a problem or likely to become one?
  c) Are there clear lines of accountability for and between the supervisory authorities?
  d) Is coordination and cooperation between supervisory agencies a problem?
  e) Are there agreements regarding the "lead" regulator in the event of financial difficulties in a conglomerate?
- Is the system able to quickly respond to financial innovations?

Structure of Financial System

- Is banking sector dominant?
- Is a universal banking model used?
- Do financial conglomerates play a major role in the system?
- Has there been or is there likely to be a blurring of distinctions between the classes of financial institutions (notably the financial products offered)?
- Are capital markets well developed?
- Is the financial sector being liberalized or rapidly transformed?

Issues Relating to the Central Bank

- Is the banking supervision function located in the central bank?
- If so, is the central bank credible and does it have stature?
- If banking supervision is moved out of the central bank, is there a serious risk that the supervisor's political or budgetary autonomy will be compromised?

Regulatory Efficiency

- Is it likely that significant economies of scale can be achieved through unification (particularly avoiding wasteful duplication of functions and resources)?
- Do there appear to be significant synergies to having multiple supervisory agencies under a single roof (such as sharing expensive and specialized experts or making better use of scarce resources)?
- Is the regulation cost-effective?

Likelihood of Unpredictable or Undesirable Outcome (Unification Risks)

- Will opening this issue result in pressures to create a unified agency whether or not such an agency is found useful?
    a) Will the unified agency be created as more of a tool to enhance some individual(s) political power than an agency whose formation is really appropriate?
    b) Might the above-noted pressures result in legislation being rushed through the Parliament even if it is not well thought out and designed?
- Could political pressures undermine the budgetary or financial independence of the new agency or in some other way cause it to be weaker than the ones it replaces?

- Is there a risk that the formation of the new agency could result in a sufficiently large loss of key staff that regulatory capacity might be undermined? Is there a real risk that poor management of the change would aggravate these problems?

Scope and Function of Agency

- Which types of financial institutions share a common ownership? (Also see the section on the structure of the financial system.)
- Are other nonbank financial institutions important in the financial sector?
  a) Are most of the major nonbank institutions part of financial conglomerates and (effectively) supervised on a consolidated basis?
  b) Would the unified supervisory authority have the resources to effectively supervise these institutions?

References

Briault, Clive, 1999, "The Rationale for a Single National Financial Services Regulator," FSA Occasional Paper, Series 2, FSA/PN/048 (London: The Financial Services Authority).

Borio, Claudio E.V., and Renato Filosa, 1994, "The Changing Border of Banking: Trends and Implications," BIS Economic Paper No. 43 (Basel: Bank for International Settlements).

Commonwealth of Australia, 1997, *Financial System Inquiry: Final Report*, p. 377 (Canberra: Australia).

Courtis, Neil, 1999, *How Countries Supervise Their Banks, Insurers, and Securities Markets*, (London: Central Banking Publications).

Goodhart, Charles, 1995, "Some Regulatory Concerns," London School of Economics, Financial Markets Group Special Paper No. 79 (London: London School of Economics, December).

———, David Llewellyn, Philipp Hartmann, Liliana Rojas-Suárez, and Steve Weisbrod, 1998, *Financial Regulation: Why, How and Where Now?* (London and New York: Routledge).

Goodhart, Charles, and Dirk Schoenmaker, 1995, "Institutional Separation Between Supervisory and Monetary Agencies," in *The Central Bank and the Financial System*, ed. by C.A.E. Goodhart (Cambridge, Massachusetts: MIT Press).

International Monetary Fund, 1999, "Code of Good Practices on Transparency in Monetary and Financial Policies: Declaration of Principles" (Washington: International Monetary Fund). Available via the Internet: http://www.imf.org/external/np/mae/mft/code/index.htm.

Llewellyn, David, 1999, "Introduction: The Institutional Structure of Regulatory Agencies," in *How Countries Supervise Their Banks, Insurers and Securities Markets*, ed. by Neil Courtis (London: Central Banking Publications).

Taylor, Michael, 1995, *Twin Peaks: A Regulatory Structure for the New Century* (London: Centre for the Study of Financial Innovation, December).

———, and Alexander Fleming, 1999, "Integrated Financial Supervision: Lessons of Northern European Experience," World Bank Policy Research Working Paper No. 2223 (Washington: World Bank).

7

The Financial Sector—
The Responsibilities of the Public Agencies

PETER HAYWARD

In most countries, a number of public agencies play an influential role in the life of financial institutions, affecting the interests of their shareholders and customers as well as the general public. The extent to which these agencies are allocated clearly defined responsibilities and how they coordinate their activities can have important implications for the soundness of the financial system as a whole. The purpose of this chapter is to examine the respective roles of specific public policy organizations that together constitute the framework within which financial institutions operate. While institutional differences between countries abound, and many variations work adequately, those systems that work best define and explain relative responsibilities so that they are clearly understood, and provide for effective coordination between the various parties, particularly in times of stress. Temporary crisis-management functions are touched on only briefly.

The organizations responsible for the financial system in virtually all countries include:
- A *minister of finance*, responsible for the legal framework and the provision of public funds where necessary;
- A *central bank*, responsible for stable financial markets, the provision of "last-resort" liquidity, and the safety of the payment system;
- One or more *supervisory authorities*, responsible for issuing and enforcing detailed prudential rules, the issue and revocation of

---

The author is grateful to Michael Andrews, Huw Evans, Jan Willem van der Vossen, and participants in a seminar hosted by the IMF's Monetary and Exchange Affairs Department for their helpful comments.

licenses, and for all supervisory relationships with individual financial institutions;
- In an increasing number of countries, a *deposit insurance agency*, ideally financed by the financial institutions whose liabilities are insured, designed to protect small depositors; and
- Where a systemic threat exists, a *crisis management capability*.

The respective roles of these agencies need to be clearly defined so that the agencies' powers can be effectively enforced and they can be held accountable for their performance. By so doing, conflict can be minimized and gaps avoided. The following principles should guide these relationships:

- The *minister of finance* should be responsible for the legal framework but should be protected from the need to take responsibility for decisions that affect specific institutions;
- The *government's involvement with individual institutions* should be limited to cases where a commitment to use public funds might be involved. Even in such cases, the supervisory authority, rather than the government, should be in a position to insist, whatever mechanism is used to allow the institution to remain in business following the injection of public funds, that it continues to meet supervisory requirements;
- The *central bank*, if not itself responsible for supervision, needs to have access to information that will enable it to discharge its responsibility as the *lender of last resort*. It may also provide information gathered in its monetary operations and in carrying out its responsibilities for payment and settlement systems;
- The *supervisory authorities need to have adequate legal powers and discretion to make their own rules*, so that the regulatory framework can be kept up to date and so that the supervisors can act with speed and flexibility. Specifically, they should have sufficient power to sanction and intervene in problem banks;
- The *supervisory authorities should have full powers over licensed financial institutions from the cradle to the grave*. Only a supervisory authority can make the complex judgments about the suitability of an applicant and its continuing satisfaction of the licensing requirements. The possibility that the supervisory authority may not be in full control of the revocation process can erode its ability to compel action by a problem institution;
- There should be *no gaps in the supervisory framework*. All financial institutions that take funds from the general public, or hold themselves out as providing financial services to the public, should be subject to a supervisory agency's authority;

- *Remedies against poor administration* should be clearly established and administered in a way that gives confidence in their impartiality;
- Where a system of *deposit insurance* exists, the administration and funding must be autonomous to maintain the scheme's credibility with its beneficiaries. Such a scheme will help allow small institutions to exit the system without triggering contagion or requiring any claim on public funds;
- *Crisis management arrangements* should facilitate both rapid decision making and a high degree of transparency and accountability so as to restore and strengthen confidence; and
- A workable system of *coordination*, which respects the autonomy of the various agencies, needs to be able to cope with systemic crises as well as isolated problems.

Role of the Institutions

First, it is necessary to describe the responsibilities of the various organizations participating in the financial framework, namely the central government agency, usually the minister of finance, the central bank, the financial supervisory agency or agencies, the deposit insurer, and where applicable, a crisis management agency.[1]

Central Government

The minister of finance is normally the government official responsible for proposing legislation to the legislature, as well as amendments to existing legislation, on financial sector issues.[2] Such legislation includes

---

[1] In many countries the central bank is itself a supervisory agency. The principles in this chapter still apply in such cases, although some of the relationships will be internalized. The issue of whether the supervision of financial intermediaries should be conducted within the central bank or by one or more specialized agencies is not explored. For material on this subject, see Tuya and Zamalloa (1994) and also Chapter 6 in this volume by Abrams and Taylor (2002) on the recent approach to bring all supervisory responsibilities under one roof.

[2] A partial exception is the United States, where the Secretary of the Treasury has only limited responsibilities for the well-being of the financial system, with the Congress—to whom regulatory bodies and the central bank are accountable—holding the major role. Primary responsibility for the drafting of legislation lies, therefore, with the relevant committees within the Congress. Nonetheless, insofar as the executive branch of the U.S. government has a role, the Secretary of the Treasury is clearly in the lead. This chapter makes reference to the minister rather than the ministry. In most countries, legislation specifies the minister as the holder of authority, although his responsibilities may be delegated to others. The extent of such delegation is normally governed by legislation dealing with the machinery of government, or, occasionally, in legislation specific to the subject delegated.

that establishing the central bank, the organizations responsible for the supervision of financial institutions, and, in some cases, that upholding competition policy.[3] Ministers of finance may also be responsible for legislation relating to the process of supervision and to the conduct of business, where these are specific to the financial sector. Such legislation should nevertheless be prepared in close consultation with the supervisory authority, who should be available to the legislators when they consider proposed legislation. Equally important, the legislative framework should be drawn in broad terms only. The supervisory authority should be empowered, by the law, to make the necessary detailed implementing rules.[4] Accounting and auditing standards may often be the responsibility of other ministers, although in some cases specific legislation relating to financial institutions may be the preserve of the ministry of finance. The minister of finance may also be responsible for "consumer protection" in the financial sector, which may include providing protection for depositors, regulating the behavior of financial institutions toward their customers, and carrying out laws relating to the taking and enforcing of security and to insolvency and the power of creditors. Again, to the extent that these are not specific to the financial sector, responsibility for such consumer protection elements may lie elsewhere.

Ministers of finance sometimes assume a role in the promotion of the financial sector, particularly where institutions compete across national boundaries. In such cases, ministers have to reconcile interests that may conflict, although in the long run the best form of promotion is usually a reputation for soundness.

As noted above, the legislation should deal with the broad parameters. The making of prudential rules and the setting of accounting standards should be left to supervisory and independent accounting standard setting bodies respectively. Of course, ministers can only propose legislation. It is up to the legislative bodies to examine critically such proposals and to enact those that pass scrutiny. Increasingly, legislatures delegate this role to specialist committees, who may well contribute to the preparation of legislative proposals; ministers often, therefore, consult such committees before making formal proposals, and are held to account by them.

The minister's second major role is the provision and safeguarding of public funds that may be required from time to time to maintain an

---

[3]Normally, competition law will apply to all businesses and will be the responsibility of the minister of justice or commerce and trade. See Andrews (2002).

[4]In practice, wide differences exist between countries, based on constitutional practice, as to what is contained in primary legislation, and what can be reserved for secondary regulation, made by the minister (often subject to approval, before or after the event, by the legislature), and what may be delegated to the central bank or supervisory agencies referred to below.

orderly financial system. In healthy financial systems, this will be a very rare occurrence in that most bank failures should not require the commitment of taxpayers' funds, but nonetheless many countries have established procedures, not always formalized in legislation, to discharge this responsibility. In some countries, even where it exceeds the traditional function of the lender of last resort, this has been carried out by central banks from their own resources. But it is now conventional in almost all OECD countries that a commitment to provide such finance, other than for temporary liquidity purposes where the risk is believed to be low, needs to be met ultimately from government resources.[5] The process normally allows the supervisory authority freedom to deal with individual institutions, including, as a last resort, their closure, but requires prior notification by the supervisory authority to the minister in cases where the failure of the institution concerned could have systemic consequences, possibly involving the use of public funds. Ministers will be involved only to the extent that they conclude that the use of public funds to keep an institution open is desirable.[6] In a well-ordered system, public funds should not be needed when an institution fails; uninsured creditors can be allowed to suffer loss. But in most countries there have been exceptional cases of such importance that governments have felt obliged to intervene. The more robust the financial system, of course, the rarer such cases are likely to be.

While the minister should not have primary responsibility for dealing with individual institutions, as discussed below, he may play a quasi-judicial role in cases where an affected institution may appeal against a decision by a supervisory organization. This appeal function may extend to appeals against decisions on the licensing and delicensing of financial institutions. In such circumstances, procedures are usually established to ensure that the minister can be seen to be acting in such cases in a disinterested fashion. In countries such as the United States, appeals against decisions of this type are sent directly to the courts to avoid any suspicion of conflict of interest. Ministers, and indeed other public agencies, including supervisory authorities, should

---

[5]In some cases the procedure may well involve a loan by the central bank, backed with an indemnity or guarantee from the government. In other cases, the government may guarantee another lender. See He (2000).

[6]In the case of the failure of Barings Bank, in the United Kingdom in 1995, for example, the supervisory authority (then the Bank of England) concluded that in its view there were no grounds for using public funds to keep the institution open. The minister was informed and given the opportunity to take a different view. He declined to do so and the bank was therefore referred to the insolvency courts. See Bank of England (1995).

strive to distance themselves from the management of financial institutions, so that such conflicts of interest can be avoided.

A minister may also play a role as the controlling shareholder in a state-owned financial institution. Such institutions may be specialized bodies set up by statute to carry out a specific public policy purpose—for example, development banks or export/import banks. In some, but not all cases, such institutions may be supervised by the supervisory authority responsible for commercial institutions. This is desirable where the institution competes with private sector financial institutions (e.g., if it has deposit-taking powers), but less necessary where the specialized body is confined to specialist activities. More problematic are purely commercial institutions, directly competing with privately owned institutions, that may be owned or controlled by the state. In such cases, the minister may well have the power to appoint directors and management, and cases of conflict with the supervisory authority could arise. For example, budgetary constraints could make it difficult for the government to respond to calls by the supervisory authority to increase the capital of the institution. It is important in such a case that the point of view of the supervisory authority be allowed to prevail.

The Central Bank

In many countries—for instance, China, France, India, Italy, and the United States—the central bank also supervises deposit-taking institutions. But even when it does not have a formal supervisory role, (e.g., in Canada, Germany, Japan, Switzerland, and the United Kingdom) the central bank normally has a responsibility to protect the stability of the financial system as a whole. In many old legislative arrangements, this responsibility was implicit, or at least not referred to in the legislation establishing the central bank, but more modern legislation often makes this responsibility quite explicit. It is, however, hard to define financial stability, and it would be normal for the minister and the supervisory authority to be consulted, particularly if the central bank perceives a threat to financial stability. Such a threat could affect the central bank's ability to implement monetary policy, or indeed the government's ability to implement exchange rate policy, as well as the activities of the supervisory authority. In such circumstances early exchange of information between the three parties is particularly important.

The central bank's responsibility may well include the supervision of markets, particularly the money and foreign exchange markets in which the central bank operates for monetary and exchange rate policy purposes, as well as the clearing system on which financial institutions rely. In a number of cases, the central bank itself provides clearing services, but in nearly all countries, it still provides the ultimate mechanism for settling imbalances between financial institutions over accounts with itself. The adoption by many countries of real-time gross settlement procedures has meant that the central bank's involvement in the settlement of payments has become more explicit, even if the risks have been reduced. This responsibility sometimes extends to the settlement of securities transactions, especially where delivery versus payments procedures are adopted.

To carry out these functions a central bank needs to have information about the conduct of business in financial markets and about the standing of the major players. In some countries—for example, Japan and, to some extent, Germany—the central bank will examine its counterparties in the financial markets in which it operates, or at least gather prudential information from them directly; in most other countries, the central bank relies on information provided by the supervisory agencies. Because banks are at the center of the financial system, a central bank is usually concerned with the ability of major banks to settle transactions with each other. This may be a remote risk, but it is increasingly regarded as potentially large. It is for this reason that many central banks have fostered the development of gross settlement arrangements, and require collateral to cover any credit risk on participating banks. (See the Committee on Payment and Settlement Systems, 2000).

While such arrangements are often confined to banks, in some countries other financial institutions have access to central bank settlement procedures. For example, for many years, the Bank of Japan has supervised those securities houses with accounts at the Bank and with which it undertook open market transactions. Similarly, nonbank securities dealers in New York have been subject to supervision by the Federal Reserve, even though open market transactions are normally conducted on a fully collateralized basis. The failure of Drexel, Burnham, Lambert, and the prospective failure of Long-Term Capital Management have also shown that nonbank institutions can contribute to systemic problems that merit the attention of a central bank.

Central banks may also assume, or be mandated with, responsibility for promoting the use of their financial markets. Such a responsibility may go beyond a responsibility for ensuring that the system is sound, and therefore attractive, and imply a role more akin to "marketing." This may happen, for example, where a financial center is being promoted as an "offshore" or "international" center to institutions incorporated or run from other countries. It is important that any such "marketing" activities be organized separately from any supervisory functions exercised by the central bank.

Supervisory Authorities

In all countries, one or more agencies have been established by law to supervise financial institutions. In many cases, for banks, this is the central bank, while in others it is a separate organization. In respect of nonbanks it is typically a supervisory authority outside of the central bank. In a still small, but growing number of countries, combined agencies have been set up to supervise a number of different categories of financial intermediary.[7] This development has been mainly in response to the breakdown of institutional barriers and cross sector competition. These developments have meant that regulatory arbitrage has become potentially more damaging and has made coordination among different supervisors of one financial conglomerate more difficult. Among the OECD countries, the Scandinavian countries were the first to take that step, but, to a partial extent, Canada, and more recently, Australia, the United Kingdom, Japan, Korea, and Mexico, have all followed.[8] The principle in these cases is that all financial intermediaries, or at least those with liabilities to the public, should be subject to comparable rules administered by a single supervisory agency. The financial linkages between different types of institution, which deregulation is strengthening, and the need to avoid regulatory arbitrage, which distorts competition, are key reasons for observing that principle. In some cases, detailed responsibility may be delegated to a self-regulating organization (SRO), for example a stock exchange, a federation of cooperatives, a financial futures exchange, a clearing house, etc. Normally the authority of an SRO is established by law, although it may derive from the members of the SRO whose authority is then recognized by the supervisory agency.

Supervision begins before licensing with an assessment of a firm's integrity, skills, and financial strength, to ensure the safety and soundness of all authorized financial institutions.[9] Once licensed, supervision involves a continuous assessment to ensure that the firm always

---

[7]See Abrams and Taylor (2002) for an account of the advantages and disadvantages of establishing single regulatory bodies charged with the supervision of all, or most, financial institutions.

[8]Securities companies in Canada are subject to supervision by provincial authorities while banks and insurance companies are supervised by an agency, the Office of the Superintendent of Financial Institutions (OSFI), established by the federal government. Many securities companies are now owned by banking groups, however, and the consolidated supervision of such groups falls to the OSFI.

[9]Core Principle 3 of the Basel Committee on Banking Supervision states, "the licensing process, at a minimum, should consist of an assessment of the banking organization's ownership structure, directors and senior management, its operating plan and internal controls, and its projected financial condition, including its capital base." See Basel Committee on Banking Supervision (1997).

meets licensing conditions. This involves a determination of the adequacy of capital, the effectiveness of accounting procedures and internal systems and controls, and the competence of management in handling the risks of the business, so as to minimize the chances of failure and consequent loss to creditors and customers. This process not only includes periodic examination on the premises, but also a continuous assessment, on the basis of prudential reports provided regularly by the institution, and subsequent discussion with, and questioning of management. Supervisors also need to be able to impose sanctions on firms that fall out of compliance to ensure that their recommendations are carried out effectively. Such formal actions should be graduated and progressive, dependent upon the seriousness of the failing. The ultimate sanction is revocation of the license; possession of this sanction gives the supervisory authority a powerful enforcement tool with which to deal with a serious violation of prudential requirements. But it also adds credibility to informal requests by the supervisor that are not made under specific statutory powers. Many supervisory authorities are, therefore, able to exert considerable influence on the management of financial institutions to ensure prudent behavior. Consequently, in virtually all OECD countries the effective power to license and revoke a licence lies with the supervisory authority. In some countries the formal authority lies elsewhere, but in others there is a growing tendency to transfer that authority to the supervisor so as to remove any suspicion that licensing decisions can be influenced through political and other pressures.[10] Ensuring that the supervisory authority has the licensing power also makes the authority more clearly accountable for the soundness of the system. While it is not the supervisory authority's responsibility to ensure that no bank ever fails, it is responsible for ensuring that any failure does not have contagious effects on the system as a whole.

In general, while the minister is responsible for the overall framework, often after consultation or at the proposal of the supervisory agency, the agency is responsible for the execution of that authority in individual cases, within the legislative framework. Thus the minister is protected from carrying the responsibility of authorizing, restricting, and ultimately closing individual institutions, decisions that are then taken outside the political arena. In the interest of efficiency and speed of response, the supervisory agency is also normally empowered in the legislation to make detailed rules and decisions on the application of the law, usually after consultation with affected institutions. This

---

[10]For example, Sweden amended its banking law to transfer this power to the Supervisory Authority effective May 1, 1999.

process is at an early stage in some emerging markets, where the tradition of regulation by central government is still strong. There are, therefore, dangers that prudential rules may not adequately reflect the needs of effective supervision. Given fast moving financial markets, this process needs to be flexible and quick. Agencies need to account for the exercise of such delegated powers, as discussed below. However, the extent of this delegated authority can vary considerably. For example, in many countries, capital ratios and large exposure rules are specified in the law in some detail in order to ensure consistent application of such rules. In other countries, the legislation prescribes broad principles, giving the supervisory authority some latitude to apply the rules in a flexible manner according to the risk appetite of the institution and its managerial capacity.[11]

To command credibility, the agency needs to have enough operational autonomy to be seen to be a disinterested party. Such autonomy is particularly necessary given the nature of supervision. Whereas regulation deals with what an institution may or may not do, and sometimes even the terms on which it does it, and compliance is readily verified, supervision is concerned with the manner in which the business is carried out and the adequacy of the management to carry the risks without exposing creditors and customers unnecessarily. Difficult judgments are involved, often concerning individuals who carry positions of trust, requiring decisions to be above reproach.

Moreover, supervisory agencies need to be close to the market they supervise, as their decisions often need to be made rapidly; it is possible for the fortunes of a financial institution to deteriorate very quickly and speed of response is of the essence. Supervisors need specialized staff who understand the risks involved in the activities of supervised institutions. The management structure of the agency and the remuneration need to be flexible enough so as to attract and retain the requisite skills.

The identification of liquidity risks may well involve close contact with the central bank, where that institutions does not have supervisory responsibilities. Liquidity problems may well become apparent to the central bank during the course of its activities in the financial markets. If such problems reach the point at which lender-of-last-resort facilities become an issue, then a more formal dialogue would normally ensue. This aspect is considered further under "Coordination and Cooperation" below.

---

[11]Within the European Union, pressure has been exerted to ensure greater uniformity so that there is a more consistent basis on which to apply the so-called "passport" procedures whereby a bank licensed by one supervisory authority is permitted to undertake business throughout the Union.

Deposit Insurance

Most OECD countries, and an increasing number of other countries, now also have a system of deposit insurance. (Similar arrangements exist to protect customers of other financial institutions.) Such schemes work best if limited to those depositors who cannot assess the risks in lending to any one institution, normally small retail depositors, and if they are financed by the institutions themselves (see Garcia, 1999). Often, however, such financing is supplemented by a line of credit from the central bank or the government for use in emergencies in order to enhance the credibility of such schemes. Limiting the reliance on public funds minimizes the moral hazard (i.e., that expectations of a bailout promote unwise or reckless behavior among investors and financial institutions) always attendant on deposit insurance. The existence of such a scheme also makes it easier for the political implications of closing an institution to be accepted. Governments, and indeed supervisors, normally feel able to accept a closure more readily if the more vulnerable depositors are protected. However, where the threat is systemic, as has been the case in a number of countries experiencing banking crises, a more pervasive safety net, inevitably financed by the government, has been necessary. While a blanket guarantee raises considerable moral hazard, it does provide some stability to the system. Such a blanket guarantee, which tends to favor weak institutions more than strong ones, should not continue longer than necessary. The duration of such a guarantee will depend on how long it takes to restore both the strength of the financial system and the public's confidence in the system. Ideally, a system should reach the point where the failure of a single institution will not cause contagion and panic leading to problems in otherwise sound institutions.[12]

The location of deposit insurance schemes varies. Sometimes it is the responsibility of a separate organization established by law, but in many countries the supervisory agency provides the service, although normally separately accounted for. In yet others, the banking industry itself may manage it. In the majority of cases, a fund is built up in advance of claims, as in the United States, but in some others, such as the United Kingdom, assessments are made on the relevant institutions at the time the scheme is activated. The tendency in recent years is to adopt more formal structures. The main requirement is that the capacity of the scheme to protect beneficiaries should inspire confidence among the potential beneficiaries. In many countries, and particularly

---

[12]Experience to date is largely limited to that of the Nordic countries, which have removed blanket guarantees imposed during the crises of the early 1990s without significant problems. The Korean authorities removed their blanket guarantee, beginning in January 2001, and the Japanese in the following year.

in the early stages, this argues for a fund financed out of prior contributions directed by an independent board, publicly accountable (see Garcia, 1999, for a fuller discussion).

Crisis Management Arrangements

In most countries, issues affecting the restructuring of financial sectors, that is mergers, acquisitions, closures etc., can be left to the market to sort out, with the government's role restricted to ensuring adequate competition by limiting excessive concentration. However, when the situation becomes such that several, or the majority of, institutions become distressed, special arrangements, often involving the provision of public funds, will be needed. Institutional arrangements differ in such cases, but a model that has been used in several cases—for example, in Sweden, to a limited extent in the United States,[13] more recently in Japan, and in some southeast Asian countries, such as Indonesia—is the establishment of a separate authority, or at least a high-level committee, with a senior but independent figure as chairman who can command authority, assisted by representatives from the supervisory authority, the central bank, and the ministry of finance. Because confidence building is crucial at the outset of a financial crisis, the choice of arrangement may need to depend on the personal standing of the leaders of the various agencies at the time.

Independence is needed to avoid, or at least to manage in a disinterested way, the conflicts of interest between those responsible for the custody of public money, the protection of bank creditors, and the stability of the financial system. But in a crisis, decisions have to be taken fast and effectively, and also have to be justified and explained. In some countries such as Thailand and Korea, this model has not been followed, and the crisis management and restructuring function has been situated in the central bank or the supervisory agency itself, although separated to some degree from those agencies' ongoing functions.[14] This arrangement clearly exposes the central bank or the supervisory agency

---

[13]In the United States, the Resolution Trust Corporation (RTC) was established to handle the insolvencies of savings and loan associations, but problems in the banking sector were handled through existing institutional arrangements.

[14]In Korea, the staff of the financial and corporate restructuring units is not regarded as part of the Financial Supervisory Service that is responsible for the ongoing supervision of financial institutions. Staff members of these units are expected to return to the agencies from which they have been seconded, principally the ministry of finance and economy, once their task is complete. In Thailand, much of the work has been done in the Bank of Thailand itself, through its subsidiary, the Financial Institutions Development Fund.

to potential conflicts of interest. Provided the need for such a function does not extend for a long period, these conflicts are capable of being managed, and there may be efficiency gains from using established machinery at a point where time and resources are short.

Accountability

The need for arrangements for accountability, whether formal or informal, is more necessary the more autonomy a public body possesses. The arrangements are well established and clear for ministers in a democratic system, as they must be accountable to the legislature and ultimately to their electorate. But for the other agencies discussed in this chapter it is necessary for specific arrangements to be made, preferably by statute. Many countries have now followed the U.S. model and set up procedures for specialized committees of the legislature to conduct these processes. The mechanisms for nonelected officials heading the agencies need also to be clear if the bodies are to command public support and be effective in the long run. One aspect that is helpful is for such bodies to be headed by a board comprising nonexecutive members as well as the agency's management. This is true of most such agencies, including central banks. (The Comptroller of the Currency in the United States and the Financial Services Agency in Japan are, however, exceptions with a single head, personally accountable.) Such nonexecutive members must not be beholden to any vested interest. A board structure ensures that decisions are made in a collegiate manner, ensuring adequate discussion and record keeping.[15] For an institution to be properly accountable, it must have a clearly defined mandate. The institution can then be entrusted with the powers and resources necessary to carry out that function and held responsible for discharging it. Strong accountability can also work in favor of the agencies. Because they can be held to account for the exercise of their powers, they can also appeal for the support of those to whom they are accountable if attempts are made to subvert the proper discharge of their responsibilities. It thus may be easier in such circumstances for the agencies to exercise their powers in a responsible manner.

---

[15]Following criticism of the Bank of England's role as supervisory authority in the 1970s and 1980s, an advisory board was established in the 1984 Banking Act with outside members in the majority, who had an obligation to report to the minister of finance if they considered the Bank was not acting appropriately to discharge its supervisory functions. The board's functions have been replaced by more comprehensive accountability provisions under the new Financial Services and Markets Act, 2000, under which all financial institutions are supervised by an independent regulatory agency, the Financial Services Authority.

There are four main interest groups to whom a financial sector public body needs to be accountable. First, the legislature should require any body that it establishes to report to it. Thus, the governor of the central bank or the head of any supervisory agency, and its board members, should be required to furnish written reports on the agency's activities and appear periodically before the legislature.[16] There may be cases where it is appropriate not to require full disclosure about specific institutions—for example, where to do so could erode confidence in an institution and cause loss to its creditors—but these should be narrowly defined, and, in general, the agency's work fully disclosed.[17] Second, it is now common practice for a supervisory agency to be financed by the institutions it regulates, and thus be accountable to those who finance it.[18] In the case of an SRO, such accountability can be formal; for a statutory agency, there is less scope for formal accountability. But such an agency should consult frequently with supervised institutions on policy issues, as well as with the interested parties in individual cases. The agency should be able to demonstrate that its decisions and actions have been taken in accordance with announced procedures, that those affected have had an opportunity to be heard, and that the agency can

---

[16]In most cases, heads of such agencies are required to appear before specialized committees rather than the legislature itself.

[17]An example of limited nondisclosure can be found in the statement of accounting principles in the Bank of England's annual financial statements where the notes to the accounts state,

> In exceptional circumstances, as part of its central banking functions, the Bank may act as "lender of last resort" to financial institutions in difficulty in order to prevent a loss of confidence spreading through the financial system as a whole. In some cases, confidence can best be sustained if the Bank's support is disclosed only when conditions giving rise to potentially systemic disturbance have improved. Accordingly, although the financial effects of such operations will be included in the Banking Department's financial statements in the year in which they occur, these financial statements may not explicitly identify the existence of such support. However, the existence of such support will be disclosed in the annual report when the need for secrecy or confidentiality has ceased.

See Bank of England (2000), p. 63.

[18]Most independent supervisory agencies are financed by fees levied on supervised institutions. (The Financial Services Agency in Japan is an exception and is financed by budgetary allocation by central government; to be reliant on fees is regarded as exposing the agency to a conflict of interest that could reduce public support for the agency.) Central banks normally recover the cost of supervision through income generated by the employment of required reserves. This is one reason why central banks rarely supervise nonbank financial institutions that are not normally required to hold reserves at the central bank. Where the ministry of finance is responsible for supervision, budgetary allocation is the norm; the Office of the Comptroller of the Currency in the United States is, however, financed by fees levied on supervised banks. Deposit insurance corporations are normally financed through premia levied on insured institutions.

do its job not only effectively but economically. In some senses this form of accountability may be more passive than that of a minister. Supervised institutions will accept the authority of the supervisor, particularly in cases where legal sanctions are not being invoked, more readily if they respect the agency's efficiency and fairness. There is, of course, a danger in central banks or supervisory agencies having too close a relationship with the institutions over which they have authority. This aspect of accountability therefore needs careful handling if "regulatory capture" (i.e., that the regulator becomes unacceptably close to the institution being regulated) is to be avoided. Nonetheless, a central bank or supervisory agency that is not close enough to financial institutions to understand their behavior is unlikely to be effective.

Third, a supervisory agency, like a central bank, must be accountable to the public at large—for example, by publishing information about its activities—and demonstrate that it has the interests of financial stability in general, and depositors in financial institutions in particular, as its foremost objectives. The IMF's *Code of Good Practices and Transparency in Monetary and Financial Policy* lays out in considerable detail best practice for disclosure to the public of the activities of central banks and financial supervisory agencies (see International Monetary Fund, 1999). Finally, a supervisory agency must be accountable to those who are affected by its decisions. They should have some right of redress in cases of maladministration, and, if any such right is invoked, the appellant should have the right to be heard by an impartial and disinterested party and ultimately have the right of legal redress in the courts. In view of this capacity, the staff of the supervisory agency must have some legal protection in cases where it is neither negligent nor acting contrary to the agency's rules. In addition, the agency needs to have powers to manage, and, if necessary, to intervene in an institution while such an appeal is being heard so as to deter frivolous or mischievous appeals.

Balancing these various interests can be difficult. For example, the use of SROs has become less acceptable in many countries because these agencies were felt to be more accountable to their members' interests than to those of the public at large. In other cases, the financing of a supervisory agency can affect the reputation of that agency and its ability to account to the general public.[19] In other cases, the suggestion that supervisory authorities should be directly accountable to legislatures is resisted, and ministers of finance have required that immediate accountability should be to them. Independence from the minister is now widely accepted for a central bank's discharge of its monetary policy responsibilities; it is less well established with regard to supervision,

---

[19]See the point about the Japanese Financial Services Agency referred to in footnote 18.

although there is a strong case for arguing that operational autonomy is just as important in this area.

Accountability can vary in extent from time to time, depending upon public confidence in the agency concerned. A well-regarded agency may be endowed with considerably more operational latitude and discretion than one whose record is perceived as questionable. Finally, in small countries, arm's length relationships between public agencies, and indeed between private financial institutions and public agencies, may be difficult to ensure.

Practice varies in relation to cases where banks are accused of treating their customers unfairly. Many supervisory authorities would regard such activity as beyond their responsibility. In some countries, government departments charged with consumer protection issues generally are responsible. But in a growing number of cases, supervisory authorities have been given the responsibility, and not just in cases where the complaint is so significant as to damage the reputation of the institution, and, therefore, its potential financial soundness.[20] A particular example is the growing involvement of supervisory agencies in the fight against the abuse of financial institutions by those seeking to launder assets acquired by criminal and other illegal means. But more generally there has been a growth in the desire of legislators to encumber supervisors with consumer protection functions. Probably the United States is in the lead, with the long standing "Truth in Lending" legislation expanded to include the provisions of the Community Reinvestment Act.

Coordination and Cooperation

Although all countries recognize the need for the various public agencies involved in the governance of the financial sector to cooperate, the means by which they do so vary extensively. In normal circumstances, it may well help to deal with potential conflicts of interest for each party to act independently. It is now accepted, for example, that a supervisory agency should be free to take what action it thinks fit with regard to individual entities, including action that may lead to closure—all in the interest of protecting the interest of depositors, even though the agency must also concern itself with the impact of a closure on other banks. The central bank will be motivated by the need to protect the soundness of the markets in which it operates and the integrity of the payment system. Most supervisory authorities have the power to close an institution as a last resort, although in

---

[20]Under recent legislation, the British Financial Supervisory Authority is given four objectives, two of which are to protect and educate consumers of financial services.

significant cases they may have an obligation to inform central banks and governments of problems in individual institutions so that they may have an opportunity to intervene. Intervention may include providing financial assistance so as to enable the institution to continue to meet supervisory requirements. Moreover, possession of the power to revoke a license considerably strengthens the hand of a supervisory authority when it is dealing with a problem, or uncooperative, bank. Where the supervisory authority does not have formal powers, in most OECD countries it nonetheless effectively makes the decision. As noted earlier, a growing number of countries are transferring the formal power as well. Other bodies, including ministries of finance and central banks, find it convenient not to be associated with such decisions. However, in a number of countries, traditions of patronage are still an important factor motivating ministers to retain control over the destiny of individual financial institutions. In either case, ministers can expect to be criticized if the agency responsible is perceived, by the legislature or by the press, to have executed its authority incorrectly, or without sufficient diligence.

Similarly, central banks will reach their own view as to the creditworthiness of counterparties in the markets, without consulting supervisors who might feel inhibited in disclosing information on which the central bank might act. The existence of deposit insurance also makes it less necessary for other parties to be involved as deposit payout will act to defuse the political ramifications of banking problems, and will not normally involve the use of public funds. Where, however, the use of public funds does become a matter for consideration, and particularly where that might result from systemic problems, then additional coordination is clearly necessary. This may be quite informal unless an overt crisis emerges when some form of crisis resolution machinery, such as that described above, becomes necessary. However, where, as is increasingly the case, the responsibilities of central banks and other agencies are more precisely defined by statute, a formal understanding between the relevant agencies becomes more necessary.[21] However, formal machinery, particularly if rarely used, may turn out to be of limited value and could even, in some circumstances, impede crisis coordination, especially where action has to be taken fast. Coordination

---

[21]See, for example, the Memorandum of Understanding between the U.K. Treasury, the Bank of England, and the Financial Services Authority. Apart from laying down procedures for coordination in an emergency, the agreement provides for a tripartite committee of officials from the three agencies that meets regularly on policy and specific supervisory cases. In a sense, this committee also provides for some mutual accountability between the respective agencies.

machinery therefore needs to be "tested" from time to time to ensure that it helps rather than hinders the crisis resolution process.

To recapitulate, this chapter has dealt mainly with the behavior and relationships of the various public agencies in normal times. In financial crises, different arrangements may well be necessary. The use of public funds in such circumstances may have to be more extensive, giving rise to a more prominent role for the minister of finance. However, as argued above, experience suggests that in such cases a separate and temporary authority, endowed with considerable political as well as financial powers and resources, may well need to be created.[22]

This chapter has attempted to set forth the respective roles of the various public bodies involved in the governance of the financial system. It is important that these individual organizations have clearly defined responsibilities, and that overlapping functions, as well as any gaps are minimized. If that is done, the respective agencies can be entrusted with a greater degree of operational autonomy. Such autonomy, which should include responsibilities for their own costs, should be conditional on adequate procedures for accountability on the lines described above.

There are a number of areas where current practice in many countries does not accord with best practices in most OECD countries:

- The supervisory authority needs to have adequate legal powers and discretion under the basic laws, to make its own rules, so that the legal framework does not hinder the speed and modality of supervisory action, and, in particular, sanctions against, and intervention in problem banks;
- The supervisory authority should have full powers over licensed financial institutions from the cradle to the grave. Only the supervisory authority can make the complex judgments about the suitability of an applicant and its continuing satisfaction of the licensing requirements. The same considerations apply to approvals for specific lines of business that authorized institutions may carry out. The possibility that the supervisory authority may not be in full control of the revocation process can erode its ability to compel action by a problem institution;
- There should be no gaps in the supervisory framework. All financial institutions that take funds from the general public, or hold themselves out as providing financial services to the public, should be subject to the supervisory agency's authority;
- The government's involvement with individual institutions should be limited to cases where a commitment to use public funds might

---

[22]See, for example, Lindgren and others (1999), which gives a useful account of experience in this area in the recent Asian financial crisis period.

be involved. Even in such cases, the supervisory authority should be in a position to dictate the timetable and modalities of supervisory action. Such action should only be halted to allow the provision of public funds to enable an institution to stay open on the basis of clear criteria announced in advance; and
- The provision of remedies against maladministration should be clearly established and administered in a way that instills confidence in the supervisor's impartiality and in the impartiality of the rules.

References

Abrams, Richard, and Michael Taylor, 2002, "Issues in the Unification of Financial Sector Supervision," Chapter 6 in this volume, *Building Strong Banks Through Surveillance and Resolution* (Washington: International Monetary Fund).

Andrews, Michael, 2002, "Addressing the Prudential and Antitrust Aspects of Financial Sector Mergers and Acquisitions," Chapter 8 in this volume, *Building Strong Banks Through Surveillance and Resolution* (Washington: International Monetary Fund).

Bank of England, 1995, "Inquiry Into the Circumstances of the Collapse of Barings," report by the Board of Banking Supervision (London: United Kingdom).

———, 2000, *Annual Report*, (London: United Kingdom).

Basel Committee on Banking Supervision, 1997, *Core Principles for Effective Banking Supervision* (Basel: Bank for International Settlements).

Committee on Payment and Settlement Systems, 2000, *Core Principles for Systematically Important Payment Systems* (Basel: Bank for International Settlements).

Garcia, Gillian G.H., 1999, "Deposit Insurance: A Survey of Actual and Best Practices," IMF Working Paper No. 99/54 (Washington: International Monetary Fund).

He, Dong, 2000, "Emergency Liquidity Support Facilities," IMF Working Paper No. 00/79 (Washington: International Monetary Fund).

International Monetary Fund, 1999, "Code of Good Practices on Transparency in Monetary and Financial Policies: Declaration of Principles" (Washington: IMF)

Lindgren, Car-Johan, Tomás Baliño, Charles Enoch, Anne-Marie Gulde, Marc Quintyn, and Leslie Teo, 1999, *Financial Sector Crisis and Restructuring: Lessons from Asia*, IMF Occasional Paper No. 188 (Washington: International Monetary Fund).

Tuya, José, and Lorena Zamalloa, 1994, "Issues on Placing Banking Supervision in the Central Bank," in *Framework for Monetary Stability*, ed. by Tomás Baliño and Carlo Cotarelli (Washington: International Monetary Fund).

Part II
Resolution Strategies

8

Addressing the Prudential and Antitrust Aspects of Financial Sector Mergers and Acquisitions

MICHAEL ANDREWS

Mergers and acquisitions involving regulated financial institutions have a prudential dimension that differentiates them from such transactions in other sectors of the economy. While an ill-conceived merger of a manufacturing company may have many undesirable consequences if the merged firm subsequently fails, an unsuccessful financial sector merger is far more significant because of the potential to disrupt key elements of the system upon which all transactions in the real economy are dependent. Further, there is the systemic concern that one failure might destabilize the entire financial sector by triggering subsequent failures of other financial institutions. Thus, a well-defined process is needed to deal with the prudential dimensions of financial sector mergers and acquisitions, in addition to antitrust and other public policy concerns, which are as applicable to the financial sector as to any other merger transaction.[1]

The author is grateful for helpful comments and suggestions from Claudia Dziobek, Charles Enoch, Huw Evans, Gillian Garcia, Sami Geadah, Garry Goddard, Michael Grant, Peter Hayward, Cem Karacadag, Marina Moretti, Brent Sutton, Jan Willem van der Vossen, Hugh Williams, Delisle Worrell, and the participants in two seminars who discussed earlier drafts of the paper.

[1]This chapter focuses on banks, but the principles are equally applicable to other regulated financial institutions that play key roles in the economy. Accordingly, the terms bank and regulated financial institution are used interchangeably throughout this chapter. Many of the points would also apply to other regulated industries.

The generic process for reviewing a financial sector merger presented in Figure 8.1 clearly indicates the primacy of prudential concerns because the entire process will come to an abrupt end if the prudential supervisor objects. In reviewing a merger, the supervisory authority would use an approach similar to that used when considering an application for a new license, because the transaction in effect creates a new institution. The antitrust review would apply the merger enforcement rules that would be applicable to other transactions in the economy. Other public policy issues will undoubtedly influence the decision-making process, and in many countries they are explicitly incorporated into the merger review. A key point illustrated by Figure 8.1 is that there is no provision for these other considerations to lead to completion of transactions where either the prudential or the antitrust authority objects.

While the need for a clearly defined process is evident, the intersection of competition law and banking law may create a number of gaps or uncertainties. In some industrial countries, the process for considering banking mergers and acquisitions has developed over time, and while it is understood by market participants, it may not be formally defined. Developing countries may not have a competition law of general application, so there may not be an established process for considering the antitrust dimensions of a merger.[2] In the case of both industrial and developing countries, where there is a competition law, it may not be clear how it interacts with the banking law.[3] These issues are of increasing importance given the upward trend in both number and value of financial sector mergers (Figure 8.2), and increasing financial sector concentration levels in countries throughout the world.

---

[2]This is increasingly less common, however. Since 1990, more than 35 developing and transition economies have enacted or substantially revised competition laws. See Khemani (1997, pp. 23–27).

[3]A recent example of the difficulties that can arise from such a lack of clarity is the attempted hostile takeover of Standard Bank Investment Corporation by South Africa's Nedcor. In November 1999, Nedcor applied to the prudential authority, the South African Reserve Bank, for approval to acquire control of Standard Bank. The initial view was that only the approval of the prudential regulator was required, but as part of its defense against a hostile takeover, Standard Bank successfully challenged this position in court. This challenge led to the negotiation of a memorandum of understanding between the prudential authority and the Competition Commission on how to consider competition issues as well as concerns over financial stability in the review of bank mergers. On June 21, 2000, the Finance Minister rejected the transaction, citing concerns over systemic risks if the merged entity failed, increased concentration and diminished competition, and job losses.

Figure 8.1. Reviewing a Financial Sector Merger or Acquisition

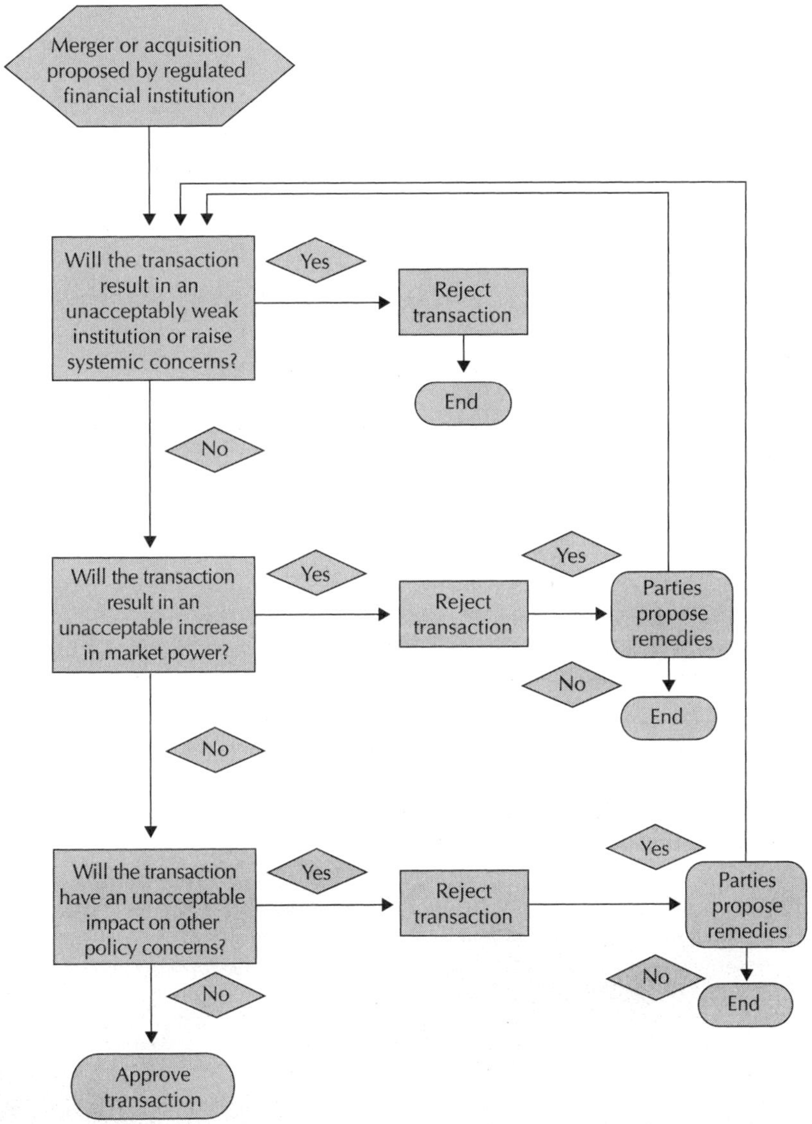

Figure 8.2. Worldwide Financial Sector Mergers and Acquisitions

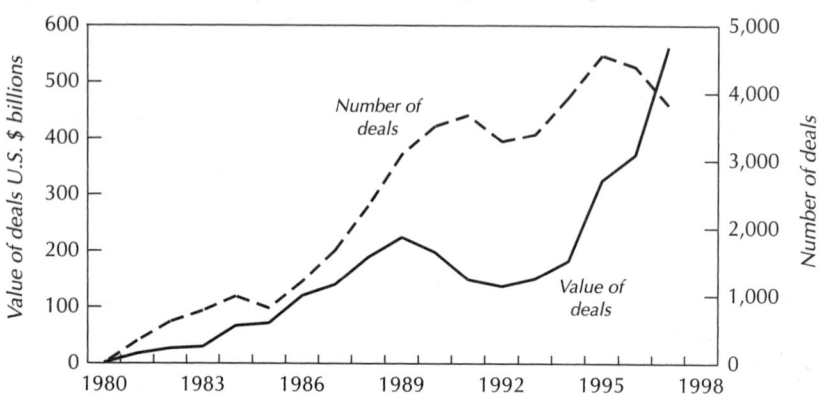

Source: McKinsey and Company (1998).
Note: Includes commercial banks, savings institutions, credit unions, personal and business credit institutions, mortgage brokers, securities dealers and brokers, life insurance companies, and bank holding companies.

The link between prudential issues and macroeconomic stability is well understood; a weak banking system is unable to intermediate savings efficiently, and fragility in the banking system is generally detrimental to economic growth.[4] While the antitrust dimension does not immediately affect the macroeconomic framework, it is an important longer-term consideration. A banking industry characterized by a lack of competition will tend to maintain high spreads and fees, and thus will not provide the efficient intermediation of savings necessary for strong growth.[5] Thus, failure to consider the potential antitrust implications of a banking merger or to seek alternatives to highly concentrated financial sectors will be detrimental in the long run. Other public policy concerns, such as foreign ownership and the impact on employment, arise from any large merger, but often take on particular significance in the case of financial sector transactions. Consideration of these issues is important, but because of the broader macroeconomic implications their status is eclipsed by the weighting first of prudential concerns, and then by antitrust issues.

Despite a large body of research and practical experience in both prudential regulation and competition law, very little published material

---

[4]See Lindgren, Garcia, and Saal (1996).

[5]While the literature contains no conclusive view, empirical evidence supports the widely held position that there is a strong positive link between the functioning of the financial system and long-run economic growth. See Levine (1997, pp. 688–726).

addresses the intersection of these two topics.[6] In most countries, mergers and acquisitions "fall under the jurisdiction of both the banking regulators and the competition authority, giving rise to a need for some mechanism for resolving possibly conflicting regulatory decisions."[7] This chapter is intended to provide an overview of the principles and best practices that apply in reviewing financial sector mergers and acquisitions, thus ensuring that there are not conflicting regulatory views.[8] This guidance will typically be required in one of three instances. The first arises when reviewing or providing drafting assistance for either financial institution legislation or a competition law of general application. A second instance occurs when advising on reviews of mergers or acquisitions involving large financial institutions, which may include privatization transactions. A third instance may arise when dealing with a systemic crisis.

The Policy Approach

This section outlines the policy considerations that apply in financial sector mergers and acquisitions and suggests the key elements for an effective, clear, and transparent review process. Developing an effective, clear, and transparent process for the review of financial sector mergers and acquisitions can involve many kinds of approaches. An effective process provides for due consideration of the relevant public policy issues. Clarity is provided if an enumeration of the role of the various official agencies involved and procedural steps to be followed is readily accessible in the public domain. In a transparent process, the public policy concerns that will be evaluated in reaching a decision and the criteria that will be considered for each relevant issue are publicly identified in advance, and the reasoning for a particular decision is publicized.

---

[6]Among the very few publications on the subject are *Enhancing the Role of Competition in the Regulation of Banks* (OECD, 1998a) and *Competition and Related Regulation Issues in the Insurance Industry* (OECD, 1998b). While they identify the lack of clarity in many countries over how competition law should be applied to financial sector mergers and acquisitions, neither offers any guidance on principles that might be used to address the issue.

[7]See OECD (1998a, p. 11).

[8]This chapter does not address other key elements of competition law such as collusion, abuse of dominance, and consumer protection. Unlike mergers and acquisitions, there is no prudential dimension to the application of these aspects of competition law to the financial sector. In many countries, though, activities seen to have general benefits, such as the maintenance of a single industry-owned agency for health data to facilitate life underwriting or clearinghouses owned by a consortium of competitors, have been exempted from prohibitions on collusion that normally would preclude such activities.

Effectiveness

Multiple public policy considerations are part of the review of a financial sector merger. The key to an effective process is that lower-order issues cannot take precedence over issues of greater public policy importance. Thus, the most essential element of an effective process for dealing with financial sector mergers and acquisitions is that the prudential supervisory authority has the ability to prohibit a transaction. Otherwise, the entire rationale for prudential supervision would be undermined because a transaction likely to raise systemic concerns could proceed despite the objections of the supervisor. It is not necessary that the prudential authority be the final decision-making body, only that a decision to approve a transaction cannot be made over the objections of the supervisor.

The second most important element of an effective process for dealing with financial sector mergers is an explicit consideration of potential antitrust implications. The reason antitrust issues rank immediately behind prudential concerns is the importance of a competitive market to the development of a vibrant financial sector that will be able to meet the intermediation and transaction needs of the economy. Thus, it is quite possible that a merger, while acceptable from a prudential perspective, should not be allowed because of the long-term detrimental effects that would arise from a significant reduction of competition in the market. Given the prudential regulator's vested interest in stability, there may be a readiness to tacitly accept less than vigorous competition and thus approve a merger that might lead to oligopolistic behavior. This possibility suggests that there are benefits to an antitrust review that is independent of the prudential review.

Issues beyond prudential and antitrust concerns also have a legitimate place in the public policy debate. In the United States, for example, the banking regulator is explicitly charged with the consideration of the broader needs of the communities served by merging banks. In France, India, the United Kingdom, and a number of countries in Central and Eastern Europe, competition law explicitly addresses issues such as employment, regional development, or other social or political considerations.[9] In a number of countries including Australia, Austria, Canada, Ireland, and Norway, the minister responsible for the financial sector has "reserve powers" that might be used to disallow for broad public policy reasons a merger that might be acceptable on both prudential and antitrust grounds.

While it can be argued that prudential and antitrust issues should be the only factors taken into consideration in the merger review process,[10]

---

[9]Khemani (1997, p. 25).
[10]See Commonwealth of Australia (1997, pp. 417–478).

other public policy concerns such as the impact on employment or regional development will inevitably influence the decision-making process. There may be legitimate policy reasons not to permit a merger that is acceptable from a prudential and antitrust perspective. But in an effective merger review process other policy considerations will not result in the approval of a merger or acquisition that is objectionable from a prudential or antitrust perspective. For example, a transaction viewed as desirable to maintain domestic ownership of a large financial institution would not be approved if there were concerns about the soundness of the merged institution, or if there were concerns that the transaction would lead to a significant lessening of competition.

Clarity and Transparency

Ideally, every country should have a well-defined process specifying the sequence of events and the role of each participant involved in the review of a financial sector merger. As a practical matter, though, the intersection of the various policy concerns and the multiple regulatory agencies that may be involved may mean it is not immediately clear how the review should proceed. A clear process could be defined in several ways, including explicit references in banking and competition law. With a well-drafted bank statute and competition law of general application, however, specific legislative provisions dealing with financial sector mergers are not required. A bank statute that meets international best practices will provide supervisors with "the authority to review and reject any proposals to transfer significant ownership or controlling interests in existing banks to other parties."[11] As long as there is no possibility that the competition law could be construed as empowering the antitrust authority to approve a financial sector transaction without the consent of the prudential regulator, the more generally applicable antitrust review of a merger can be applied to a financial sector transaction.

A merger, like an application for a license, results in the creation of a new institution.[12] Thus, as discussed in more detail in the next section, the supervisory authority can use a methodology similar to that used to consider the application for a new license to review the prudential aspects of a merger. Provided that licensing criteria are well documented in legislation, regulations, or policy statements, the supervisory authority has only to indicate publicly that it will be guided by its licensing criteria in evaluating a merger proposal. If the criteria are not already well defined in

---

[11]Basel Committee on Banking Supervision (1997), Principle 4.

[12]The differences between a start-up and a merged entity are clear, though. Also, rejection of a merger proposal does not deny the economy of a new competitor, but in fact prevents a reduction in the number of competitors.

legislation or regulations, it is probably better to address this shortcoming in the context of licensing requirements, rather than through a statement on the process that will be used to evaluate mergers and acquisitions.

An explicit policy statement or administrative guidance on the process for consideration of financial sector mergers is relatively rare, although this step arguably provides the greatest clarity and certainty for market participants. Australia and Canada are among the few countries to have outlined the process clearly, probably because in both countries the highly concentrated financial sector makes the prospect of financial sector mergers even more highly politically charged than is frequently the case in other industrial countries. In Australia and Canada it has been clearly established that a merger would move to the final stage of consideration, where other policy considerations might still prohibit a transaction, only if there were no prudential or antitrust objections.

In the United States, the Bank Merger Act of 1960 establishes the primacy of the bank regulatory agencies in approving a merger, although the antitrust authority may still seek a court order within 30 days of approval to overturn a transaction approved by the relevant banking agency (Box 8.1). The Department of Justice cannot seek approval of a transaction denied by the banking agencies, which are also charged with consideration of a range of nonprudential issues, but these issues do not take precedence over the prudential or antitrust considerations. For example, the Community Reinvestment Act, which requires consideration of the merger proponent's record of compliance with the act's provisions, provides only that a merger may be denied. It does not provide that a bank with a strong record in community reinvestment would be permitted to consummate a merger that raised prudential or antitrust concerns.

The increasing number of financial sector mergers in Europe has recently led to increased focus on both the prudential and the antitrust aspects of these transactions. Within the European Union, a merger is subject to specific country requirements, which may pertain to both prudential and competition issues, and also to antitrust review by the Directorate General IV (Competition) of the European Commission. As a practical matter, financial sector transactions have generally led to declarations of "nonopposition" from the European Commission. While in many cases there have been high levels of national concentration, the Commission has generally found either that the relevant geographic market is large, or that even with a narrow geographic market definition there are enough alternatives to ensure no likelihood of a significant lessening of competition. Even the most problematic of the large European bank mergers, the 1997 merger of two of the three

> **Box 8.1. Bank Merger Review in the United States**
>
> Until the mid-1960s, the United States had a long history of not applying antitrust legislation to the banking sector. The Bank Merger Act 1960 considered that the banking agencies would receive but not be bound by the views of the Department of Justice, which enforced antitrust provisions.[1] However, the landmark Supreme Court *Philadelphia* decision in 1963,[2] and a series of follow-up cases[3] established that bank mergers were subject to the Clayton and Sherman antitrust acts. This raised the possibility that the Justice Department might obtain court orders to unwind consummated mergers that had already been approved by the banking regulators. Amendments to the Bank Merger Act in 1966 addressed this uncertainty by immunizing previous transactions and limiting the time period for a challenge by the Justice Department to 30 days after approval by the relevant banking agency.
>
> The Bank Merger Act provides that the regulatory authority (the Federal Reserve, the Office of the Comptroller of the Currency, or the Federal Deposit Insurance Corporation) that would have responsibility for the resulting institution is the agency empowered to provide final regulatory approval of a merger. The responsible agency is required to consider advisory opinions from the other federal banking authorities and the Department of Justice as part of the review process. The criteria to be considered by the responsible agency are:
> - the effect of the transaction on competition;
> - the financial and managerial resources of the existing and proposed institutions;
> - the future prospects of the existing and proposed institutions; and
> - the convenience and needs of the community to be served.
>
> The first point explicitly deals with antitrust concerns, while the second and third deal with prudential concerns. The fourth point takes into account a range of other public policy concerns. The responsible banking agency is not bound by the opinion of the Department of Justice, but clearly would be subject to legal challenge if it approved a merger in spite of objections on antitrust grounds.
>
> ---
> [1] Bernard Shull (1996, p. 257).
> [2] U.S. v. Philadelphia National Bank et al., 374 U.S. 321 (1963).
> [3] Most notably U.S. v. First National Bank and Trust Company of Lexington, 376 U.S. 665 (1964); and U.S. v. Manufacturers Hanover Trust Co., 240 F. Supp. 867 (S.D.N.Y. 1965).

largest Swiss banks, was quickly approved with minimal conditions imposed. The Competition Commission had identified as its primary concern the small business loan market, because of the potentially dominant position of the merged Union Bank of Switzerland and Swiss

Bank Corporation. These concerns were mitigated by the parties' agreement to divest a number of branches and subsidiaries, with all the agreed divestitures completed in March 1999.[13]

In most European countries, "the objective of 'stability' of the banking sector is placed alongside the objective of enhancing competition."[14] In some countries such as Switzerland, the antitrust law provides that the competition authority makes the final decision and that the input of the banking regulator is simply part of the process. While the primacy of prudential concerns may not be established in law, it is generally clearly understood by market participants that in practice a merger would not be approved over the objections of the prudential regulator. Typically, merger proponents would make an informal approach to the prudential regulator before proposing such a transaction.

Public disclosure is an important element of transparency,[15] but public knowledge that a proposed merger had been rejected on prudential grounds might lead to a loss of confidence in the merger proponents. For this reason, merger advocates frequently seek a favorable indication from the supervisor before making a public announcement of their intentions. It would be unusual for a bank to proceed with an attempted acquisition or merger in the face of an unfavorable advance indication from the prudential regulator. But this did take place in 1982 when Hong Kong and Shanghai Banking Corporation proceeded with a bid for Royal Bank of Scotland. The transaction was subsequently denied by the Monopolies and Mergers Commission.

If merger advocates have publicly announced their intention, the prudential supervisor might find it advisable to provide the proponents with an unofficial indication of an unfavorable decision to allow them an opportunity for a face-saving "voluntary" termination of the merger discussions. Should there be an "official" denial of the merger, transparency would dictate that the prudential authority publicize the rationale for its decision. If one or more of the merger entities are publicly traded, an unfavorable decision by the supervisor would be a material event under securities law in many countries, and thus subject to public disclosure by the parties, notwithstanding any decision by the supervisor not to release its decision to the public.

Antitrust authorities frequently have sought to bring greater transparency to the merger review process by providing published guidelines,

---

[13]Swiss Competition Commission, *Competition in Practice*, Case RPW 1998/2.

[14]See OECD (1998a, p. 11).

[15]See, for example, the emphasis on open processes and public availability of information in the "Code of Good Practices on Transparency in Monetary and Financial Policies," available at www.imf.org/external/np/mae/mft/code/index.

and in rarer instances specific guidelines have been published for the antitrust analysis of bank mergers. The guidelines provide greater certainty in dealing with financial services products and markets, which differ in a number of aspects from the real sector transactions that constitute the bulk of transactions likely to be subject to antitrust review. As detailed in a later section, though, the issues of financial services product and market definition have become well-enough defined through the merger review process in a number of countries that specific bank merger guidelines are not necessarily required to ensure a well-understood and transparent analytical process. Ensuring that the decisions of antitrust authorities are made public, along with supporting analysis, is an important element of transparency, and thus it is a best practice for countries with a competition law of general application.

Other considerations that might lead to disapproval of a merger or acquisition transaction frequently relate to industrial or regional economic policies. While good practices in transparency dictate that such reasons should be clearly enunciated and disclosed as the basis for a decision, the considerations outlined later in this chapter in the section "Other Considerations" may lead to contravention of multilateral trade agreements. These transgressions should not occur, but in reality they frequently carry great political weight, and it is naïve to advocate that they be dealt with transparently.

A recent example of the difficulty in separating true prudential concerns from other issues is the denial of the June 1999 bid by Spain's Banco Santander Central Hispano for control of Portugal's Mundial Confiança. The European Union found that Portugal's refusal to approve the transaction appeared to cloak national protectionism in the guise of prudential concerns, and the issue was referred to the European Court of Justice.[16] From a practical perspective, the objective to be achieved in reviewing mergers and acquisitions is to ensure that other policy considerations do not compromise prudential and antitrust concerns.

The section that follows contains a detailed discussion of the relevant prudential, antitrust, and other policy considerations, and makes observations on how these issues can be taken into account during the review process.

Prudential Considerations

The guiding principle of dealing with a merger or acquisition is the same as that applied to any other material change in a regulated financial

---

[16]European Union, 1999, *Competition Policy Newsletter* (October), pp. 48–49.

institution: The resulting regulated entity must comply with all prudential standards. Compliance includes ensuring that the owners have met "fit and proper" standards, that management is qualified and suitable, that all capital requirements are met, and that the entity has a reasonable business plan that provides for continuing compliance with prudential standards. Much as with bank licensing, the onus is on the transaction proponents to provide the supervisory authority with full and complete information to enable completion of a detailed assessment. Information required includes a pro forma balance sheet and income statement, a business plan, and full details on the proposed management team and ownership. In addition to applying analysis similar to that used in considering a new license application, the supervisory authority will focus on prudential issues arising specifically from the merger transaction.

Transactions involving only regulated financial institutions are simplified by the fact that the owners involved should already have been vetted by the supervisory authority and been deemed fit and proper. Also, the quality of management and the financial strength of the institutions should be made known to the regulators. This leads to a presupposition that mergers and acquisitions among regulated institutions would normally not be prohibited on prudential grounds. If the supervisor objects to a proposed merger, the objection indicates either concern over the current risk profile of the merger proponents or concern that the proposed transaction would create an institution with an unacceptable risk profile.

Because activities outside the regulated financial institutions but within a corporate group can affect safety and soundness, a good banking statute will provide a mechanism to ensure prudential review of significant transactions involving the owners or subsidiaries of financial institutions.[17] While the issue does not arise in the case of a widely held institution, in the case of majority or significant shareholdings the supervisor will require assurance that after a merger or acquisition, the shareholders would continue to be fit and proper. This is a particular concern if the transaction would result in a major shareholder of a bank also having a major shareholding in a commercial group, because it raises the issue of related party transactions. If the owners of one bank are to become owners of another bank or financial institution, the bank supervisor must be satisfied with the availability of financial information to provide a complete picture of all the institutions having common ownership links.

---

[17]Core Principle 5 of *The Basel Core Principles for Effective Banking Supervision* requires that supervisors have the ability to judge acquisitions or investments by banks. Core Principle 4 requires that supervisors be able to review and reject proposals to transfer significant ownership or controlling interests in banks.

The prudential risks of subsidiaries of financial institutions are dealt with in several ways. Provided that the banking law contains appropriate provisions, which may include deducting the investment in a subsidiary from the regulatory capital base, limiting the total capital that may be invested in single and all subsidiaries, and establishing a list of permitted subsidiaries, specific prudential provisions to deal with mergers and acquisitions of a financial institution's subsidiaries are not required. The general banking law will determine whether the specific approval of the prudential supervisor is required for a given transaction, and a competition law of general application will generally provide guidelines to determine readily when a transaction is of enough significance to warrant antitrust review.

Transactional Issues

Mergers and acquisitions are proposed in the expectation of economic gain, which is typically expected to arise from one or more of the following sources:
- accessing information and proprietary technologies in the target firm;
- increasing market power to permit widening of margins or acquiring the ability to carry out large transactions that would otherwise require participation by other firms;
- reducing unit costs and increasing operating efficiency by eliminating redundant facilities and personnel, as well as improving the quality of management;
- achieving economies of scale or scope;
- reducing risk through greater diversification; and
- achieving tax benefits.[18]

The expectation is that the financial results of the merged firm will exceed the sum of the premerger firms' results. However, there are many costs associated with completing a merger or acquisition that have to be recouped before any net gain is recorded. In all mergers, there is uncertainty at the outset about the ability of management to complete the merger transaction itself effectively and then

---

[18]Smith and Walter (1996, pp. 14–15). Another possible reason for mergers is that the interests of the management of a financial institution may not be compatible with those of the shareholders. Management may derive higher compensation from managing larger institutions and may seek personal gain. Management thus may manage as a large institution. Hence mergers and acquisitions are desirable despite empirical evidence that, beyond a relatively small critical mass, there are no economies of scale and scope in financial services. For a summary of the literature on economies of scale and scope in financial institutions, see Berger, Hunter, and Timme (1993, pp. 221–49).

to implement the measures required to realize the expected gains. This uncertainty over the attainability of financial projections takes on an additional dimension in the financial sector, and there are also a number of specific regulatory concerns inherent to transactions within the financial sector.

Demands on management

A large merger or acquisition places a major demand on management and staff at all levels in an institution. It is important that both the management proposing a merger and the prudential supervisor recognize that there is an inevitable disruption through the transition period. Significant senior management time will be required for a successful integration of the merging entities. This of course can be a cause of prudential concern if the supervisor has any reservations about the depth and quality of the management team. These concerns will be exacerbated if one or more of the merging institutions have preexisting problems such as a weak loan portfolio, lax internal controls, or poor operational systems. A merger or acquisition is one way in which shareholders of a weak institution can institute a change in management designed to address weaknesses, even when these weaknesses have not yet come to the attention of the regulator.[19] The complications of completing the merger transaction itself introduce additional risk elements, though, and these risks increase with the relative size of the weak bank to the strong bank.

The evaluation of the general competence and depth of the management team proposing the merger is a key element in assessing the potential impact of other transactional issues on the strength and soundness of an institution. Greater reliance can be placed on the projections prepared by a team that is favorably viewed and demonstrates an awareness that the probability of achieving all the targets in a merger plan is something less than one. Most of the transaction-related issues that a regulator will have to consider require substantial subjective judgment even though they involve many quantifiable aspects.

Financial projections

The key to most financial sector mergers is anticipated cost-cutting arising from staff reductions, elimination of duplication in headquarters and back-office functions, particularly data processing, and the closure of overlapping branch office locations. Despite numerous empirical studies focusing on bank mergers, and a broader literature addressing mergers in general, there is no certain way to determine in advance which mergers

---

[19]Macey and Miller (1996).

will meet financial projections.[20] Although a strong commitment to cutting costs and acquiring firms that are more efficient than (or as efficient as) the target may be important, they apparently are not sufficient to ensure efficiency gains.[21] Diseconomies of scale in the management of a larger institution, delays in the realization of expected savings, and unexpectedly large transaction-related issues such as difficulty in integrating computer systems or corporate cultures are among the factors that might result in lower than expected financial performance in a merger.

While historically less important in financial sector mergers, the search for economies of scope by using an existing distribution channel for additional financial products and services has recently become more of a driver for mergers (Table 8.1). Economies of scope are even more elusive than the search for economies of scale, because the melding of diverse cultures and operations is even more difficult than the merging of similar institutions in search of economies of scale.

The prudential regulator is not likely to be able to arrive at better estimates of the financial results than the management team planning the merger. The supervisor should be satisfied, though, that even without achieving all the expected gains, and even considering the costs of the transaction exceed projections, profitability will be maintained and capital will not be impaired. The supervisor necessarily must rely on management, but should carefully question the underlying assumptions and also conduct sensitivity analysis using less favorable assumptions.

Goodwill

One of the most important quantifiable issues is the creation of goodwill, an intangible asset arising from the payment of a premium over book value for an acquisition. Required accounting practices differ among jurisdictions,[22] but from a regulatory perspective, the creation of goodwill or

---

[20]A succinct summary of the banking merger efficiency studies is found in Berger, Demsetz, and Strahan (1999, pp. 135–94).
[21]Rhoades (1998).
[22]Since June 30, 2001 the U.S. approach has required use of the purchase method to account for business combinations rather than the pooling method that previously had been generally applicable. The purchase method results in the creation of goodwill in the amount that the purchase price exceeds the fair value of assets at the date of the acquisition transaction. Due to a concurrent change in the accounting treatment of intangibles, goodwill is no longer amortized but instead is subject to an ongoing impairment test. Goodwill created in an acquisition will only be written down if it becomes evident that there is impairment in its value. In 2001 Canada, which already required use of the purchase method to account for most acquisitions, replaced the requirement to amortize goodwill with an impairment test approach similar to that adopted in the United States. In the United Kingdom and much of the rest of Europe, the write-off of goodwill created in an acquisition is taken immediately as an extraordinary item.

Table 8.1. Recent Bank-Insurance Acquisitions

Acquirer/Country	Target/Country	Year
ING (Netherlands)	BHF-Bank (Germany)	1999
Unibank (Denmark)	Tryg-Baltical (Denmark)	1999
Storebrand ASA (Norway)	Finansbanken (Norway)	1999
Citibank (United States)	Travelers Group (United States)	1998
ING (Netherlands)	Banque Brussels Lambert (Belgium)	1998
Credit Suisse (Switzerland)	Winterthur Group (Switzerland)	1998

Sources: U.S. Office of the Comptroller of the Currency (1999); Shutt and Williams (1999).

revaluation of assets needs to be dealt with conservatively. From a theoretical perspective, the accounting treatment of a transaction should be immaterial because the market would efficiently use whatever accounting information is provided to determine the underlying economics of the transaction. But the basis of prudential requirements is generally "book" or accounting values, and regulatory practice and economic theory deal differently with the element of uncertainty, so the accounting treatment of a merger or acquisition transaction is a material consideration.

The regulatory treatment of the difference between a bank's book value and its market value provides a useful parallel when considering how to account for an acquisition premium. Market value is a reflection of the present value of expected future cash flows, which may well be more than the amount by which the book value of assets exceeds the book value of liabilities. Some portion of this difference reflects assets with book values substantially lower than their market values. The real estate holdings of a bank, for example, may have been acquired many years previously and carried at a book value well below current market value. These real assets typically make up a small proportion of the total assets of a financial services firm, but they may account for a significant portion of capital. Financial assets and liabilities are more likely than real assets to have accounting values that closely approximate their market values. Nevertheless, banks and other financial services firms may be valued at a multiple of their book value, reflecting the net present value of anticipated future cash flows. The multiple of book value captures intangibles such as established customer relationships, the value of branch networks as distribution channels for additional products, and the intellectual resources of the firm.

Market value represents the best current estimate of the expected future cash flows that will be generated by a financial services firm. For publicly traded firms, market value changes constantly, reflecting continually changing views on likely future performance.[23] Thus, the premium of market value over book value lacks one of the key elements of

---

[23]For privately held or state-controlled firms, market value can be difficult to determine because this information is not available on an ongoing basis.

capital: It is not permanent. Regulators can take comfort in a high multiple of market value to book value as an indication of positive market sentiment about the likely future performance of the bank, but they continue to rely on book values for the purposes of determining compliance with capital requirements. Similarly, because there is no guarantee that any premium paid for an acquisition will actually be realized in the form of increased future cash flows, for regulatory purposes the goodwill that might arise in an acquisition has no value.

A premium beyond the premerger market value of the target firm introduces a further element of uncertainty. The premium will largely reflect an estimate of the present value of cost savings and revenue increases, net of the costs of the merger, which can be generated by the merged firm relative to the two premerger firms.[24] These projections may not be achievable, and the empirical evidence indicates that the majority of mergers fall short of achieving the results projected by the merger proponents.[25] Expenses to complete the merger and the time required to achieve cost savings are frequently underestimated, while efficiency gains are frequently overstated. Thus, the valuation arrived at by allowing for increased revenues and reduced costs in the merged firm frequently proves to have been overly optimistic.

The prudent regulatory approach would be to use an accounting method for the business combination that does not write up the value of assets or create goodwill, but generally accepted accounting principles (GAAP) in a given country may mandate another treatment. Executives of a bank involved in an acquisition will generally share the regulator's preferences for avoiding goodwill if at all permissible under GAAP, although for a different reason. If goodwill is created and has to be subsequently amortized, this has the effect of reducing earnings in future periods. While this is a noncash expense and in theory analysts should see through reported earnings to the underlying economics, executives generally believe that the amortization of goodwill does have a negative impact on analysts' perception of the value of a stock. If GAAP in a given country does require the creation and amortization of goodwill to account for an acquisition, the goodwill should be deducted from Tier 1 capital for regulatory purposes.

---

[24]A contributor to a premium may also be the writing up of the book value of assets to reflect their current market value. As noted above, however, the excess of the market value of individual real assets over their book value is likely to be small, relative to the total assets and liabilities of a financial services firm.

[25]For further detail on the literature evaluating the efficiency gains from bank mergers, see Boyd and Graham (1996); and Rhoades (1994). The literature is largely based on U.S. data, but the findings seem likely to be more widely applicable.

Operational risks

Operational risks are an issue for any merger, but they take on a special significance in financial sector mergers because of the potential threat to both the solvency of the merged firm and the possibility of disruption of the financial system more generally. Accurate and complete information on the assets and liabilities of a financial institution is necessary for risk management. Merging institutions requires dealing with multiple data systems, raising the possibility that vital information such as maturity and yield may be lost or corrupted, with the result that inaccurate or incomplete data are used to manage the liquidity, interest rate, and maturity risk of the institution. Other functions with the potential for high operational risks are the maintenance of customer account data, particularly with regard to assets under management or held in trust. Similar opportunities for confusion and system failure arise in dealing with the links to clearinghouses, depositories, payment systems, and settlement accounts. While the possibility of insolvency of an institution or a systemic threat to the payments system is remote, these are far from academic concerns. The most frequent and serious problem in banking mergers is the unexpected difficulty in integrating data processing and operations.[26] Concern over Y2K issues led to the decision in many 1998 and 1999 mergers to run parallel systems until 2000, despite the additional expense.

In addition to ensuring that the merger proponents have appropriately planned to deal with institution-specific operational risks, the prudential supervisor will want to examine the plans for managing the merged institutions' links to the rest of the financial system. Ensuring uninterrupted transactions processing requires that measures, including contingency plans to deal with possible disruption, be jointly implemented by the merging institutions and the relevant clearinghouses and payment systems.

Hostile bids

Some prudential supervisors discourage or prohibit transactions where an acquirer is attempting to act against the wishes of the management and directors of the target institution. In March 1999, the Italian prudential supervisor blocked proposed acquisitions involving four of the largest Italian banks: a takeover of Banca di Roma by San Paolo IMI and the acquisition of Banca Commerciale Italiana by UniCredito. In both cases, the central bank opposed the hostile bids on the grounds that such takeovers present greater transactional risks than mergers or

---

[26]Rhoades (1998, p. 11).

acquisitions where all parties are willing participants. Regulators in France and Germany have also discouraged hostile takeovers in the financial sector; in North America they do not often take this position. No empirical evidence actually provides a conclusive view, but it is certainly plausible that the difficulties of successfully completing a transaction will be increased by efforts by the target institution to resist a transaction, by the reduced ability to plan the integration in advance of the closing date, and by the likelihood of less than full cooperation from the target's management team. When considering a hostile takeover, it would be appropriate for the prudential supervisor to take a very conservative view of transactions costs and potential difficulties in successfully integrating the business of the acquired institution.

Mergers to resolve problem banks

Prudential supervisors use mergers as a resolution technique to deal with problem banks, both in the case of individual weak banks in an otherwise healthy system, and to deal with systemic crises. There is no empirical evidence on the general success of such orchestrated mergers, but it is possible to draw some conclusions from the available evidence on mergers generally and the studies of systemic crises.

In resolving a problem bank addressing the underlying weaknesses is essential. This can be achieved through a merger, because the stronger management and better systems of the sound partner can improve the performance of the weak bank. Thus, while it may be necessary for a transaction to be publicly presented as a merger, it should be internally clear that the management of the strong bank is actually taking over the weak bank. It is arithmetically evident that the capital and loan portfolio of a stronger bank will deteriorate, simply because of the negative effect of the weak bank. This impact obviously decreases as the size of the stronger partner relative to the weaker partner increases. Similarly, the ability of management to deal with the transactional risks of the merger will be a function of both the size of the problem bank and the depth of the problems. Thus, the larger the size of the weak bank relative to the strong bank, the more wary a supervisor should be of orchestrating a merger for fear of dragging down the strong bank and ultimately creating a larger problem.

The risks of arranging a merger to resolve a weak bank can be mitigated through provision of financial assistance to the acquiring bank, thus ensuring that it does not have to absorb the capital deficiency. While use of public funds for bank resolution is generally not appropriate in a noncrisis situation, a deposit insurance fund charged with seeking least-cost solutions may determine that an assisted merger is preferable to other possible resolution techniques.[27] Even where financial assistance is provided, though, the key to a successful resolution is that the underlying causes of the problem bank have to be addressed. This is highlighted in the study of systemic banking crises, where progress toward successful restructuring is found to be correlated with addressing the management deficiencies that contributed to the systemic crisis.[28]

As a rule of thumb, the supervisory authority will want to avoid mergers as a resolution technique unless it is satisfied that management will be able to address the underlying causes of the problem banks' difficulties. Supervisors will further want to be satisfied that the resulting merged entity will be able to maintain acceptable prudential ratios, either because of the relatively small size of the capital deficiencies assumed or through the provision of financial assistance.

Conglomerate Mergers

A transaction involving different types of financial institutions subject to the authority of different prudential authorities, or a regulated institution and a commercial firm, highlights the need for effective consolidated supervision of financial conglomerates. The divergence of regulatory structures throughout the world has hampered the development of an international consensus on anything but the most general principles of supervision of conglomerates.[29] Some country authorities such as Australia and the United Kingdom have attempted to deal with the issues of consolidated supervision, at least within their own borders, by creating a single regulatory authority covering multiple sectors of the financial services industry. Notwithstanding the difficulties in achieving international agreement, where there are multiple authorities responsible for regulation of the various parts of the financial sector within a given country, formal agreements are generally viewed as a prerequisite for effective consolidated supervision. At a minimum, such agreements provide for information sharing, ensure that there is groupwide assessment of risks and capital adequacy of a financial conglomerate, and establish a means to coordinate the supervisory activities of the various authorities. Having such agreements in place means that it is not necessary to develop ad hoc procedures to examine the prudential aspects of proposed mergers among different types of financial institutions. To

---

[27]The FDIC provided financial assistance to allow healthy banks to purchase more than 1,000 insolvent U.S. banks between 1984 and 1999. See Berger, Demsetz, and Strahan (1999, p. 148).

[28]Claudia Dziobek and Ceyla Pazarbaşıoğlu, "Lesson and Elements of Best Practice," in Alexander and others (1997).

[29]See Joint Forum on Financial Conglomerates (1999), available at www.bis.org.

eliminate any uncertainty, these agreements can clearly specify that the regulatory authority having lead responsibility for the merged firm will coordinate the merger review process. Consistent with the Basel Core Principles, the supervisor should be able to prohibit a transaction that would create a structure that would impair effective supervision.

Cross-Border Transactions

The proposed acquisition of a financial institution in another jurisdiction creates the need for a formal relationship between the home- and host-country regulators. For the host-country regulator, the process parallels the one that would be followed if the foreign financial institution had sought to enter the host country by obtaining a new license. At a minimum, the host country would ensure that the foreign institution is supervised by a home-country authority that capably performs consolidated supervision, and would contact the home country to ensure that it consented to the proposed transaction. But the current state of agreement on international best practices on cross-border supervision is at a level of such generality that supervisors will have to rely on bilateral agreements and understandings to ensure that all cross-border operations are, in fact, subject to effective home and host supervision.[30] Ideally, the home and host regulators would have a formal agreement on information sharing, ensuring among themselves that there is consolidated or group-wide assessment of capital adequacy and risk, and that regulated activities do not escape the purview of the supervisors, while avoiding duplication. In practice, this ideal will be difficult to attain.

Potentially, a financial sector merger also has a significant cross-border antitrust dimension. Internationally active financial institutions will be subject to merger review in multiple jurisdictions, because most countries will have jurisdiction to deal with competition issues based on the potential domestic effects of a transaction.[31] This could conceivably lead to different decisions on the same transaction. An example would be a proposed merger of two internationally active banks that did not raise antitrust concerns in their home countries but did raise concerns in a third country where both happened to have subsidiaries with large shares of the local market. The result could be that the antitrust authority in the third country might require divestitures to address potentially significant lessening of competition, despite the lack of concern on the part of the antitrust authorities in both home countries. A hypothetical example is readily found in New Zealand. A merger between Lloyds TSB and

---

[30]See the Basel Committee on Banking Supervision (1992 and 1996).
[31]Baker (1998). See also Davies (1998); and Baker and Rowley (1996).

National Australia Bank would not raise competition concerns in either the U.K. or Australia. But because subsidiaries of Lloyds TSB and National Australia Bank are two of the three largest banks in New Zealand, such a hypothetical transaction could raise serious antitrust concerns in New Zealand. Thus, the intended merger of subsidiaries of international institutions will generally be subject to the same competition review as a merger of domestic firms, and remedies such as divestiture in the local market may be required to address antitrust concerns.

Too Big to Fail

A proposed merger or acquisition involving very large institutions raises the possibility of creating an institution that is "too big to fail," or one that may reduce the options that would be available to deal with the failure of a large institution. Institutions have been viewed as too big to fail when the costs of closure would exceed the costs of extraordinary measures such as the use of public funds to prevent failure. The potential for one failure to trigger other failures, disruption of the payment system, immediate creation of a liquidity crunch, and the longer-term creation of a credit crunch are all arguments used to suggest that particular institutions are so important to an economy that they cannot be allowed to fail. Although never explicitly stated, a possible rationale for owners to propose a merger of large banks is to gain the benefit of an implicit government guarantee. If the market perceives that an institution is too big to fail, its valuation will be somewhat higher than otherwise warranted.[32]

These will be very difficult issues to address, both because of the reluctance of regulators to officially acknowledge that a bank might be too big to fail and because of the subjective judgments required and their potential implications.[33] In considering the possibility of mergers among large

---

[32] Analysts' reports on banks in developing and transition economies illustrate this market perception. See, for example, Thomson Bank Watch's August 1, 2000, rating of Bank Turan-Alem (Kazakhstan), which explicitly notes that the bank, a product of a merger of two smaller banks, is large enough "that it is highly likely that the government would support the bank in extremis."

[33] If there were certainty that some institutions would not be allowed to fail, market incentives to manage those institutions in a prudent manner would be removed. In the event of a crisis, though, regulators would want to preserve the option of taking extraordinary steps to deal with large institutions to preserve systemic integrity. The result is that regulators are generally reluctant to officially discuss or document criteria that might determine whether an institution was "too big to fail" or the measures that might be adopted as an alternative to the failure of such an institution. This so-called doctrine of constructive ambiguity, whereby regulators avoid acknowledging that some institutions are too big to fail by virtue of their systemic importance, serves to reduce moral hazard. It is widely acknowledged, though, that the notion of "too big to fail" is an implicit part of many regulatory regimes. See Hanweck and Shull (1999, pp. 251–284).

Canadian banks, the prudential supervisor noted that "if the mergers were approved and one of the merged banks experienced serious problems, these options [recapitalization, sale of individual businesses, various forms of restructuring, liquidation and piecemeal or en bloc sales of individual assets and business lines, and an outright sale of the bank to another financial institution] would probably remain, but, given the relative size of the institution in relation to potential buyers and investors, some would be more difficult and more time consuming to implement and a 'least-cost' resolution could be more difficult to achieve."[34]

While the "too-big-to-fail" issue will have to be considered in the case of large mergers, the prudential regulator may be reluctant to cite creation of an institution that would be too big to fail as a reason for objecting to a proposed transaction. Fortunately, such a large transaction is likely to involve antitrust and other public policy considerations that can be taken collectively with the prudential concerns to form a body of evidence to support a decision to reject a very large merger.

Competition Law Issues

The principal objective of competition law is to maintain and encourage competition as a means of promoting economic efficiency and consumer welfare. The primary competition or antitrust concern regarding a proposed merger or acquisition transaction is that it might lead to a lessening of competition in a market (Box 8.2). A reduction of competition in this context does not refer to a diminution in the number of competitors, but rather to a situation where one or more competitors may be able to exercise market power. Market power arises when, in the absence of reasonable alternatives, a purchaser chooses a product or service that permits the seller to earn "extraordinary profits." Extraordinary profits usually are evident in higher prices than could be sustained in a competitive market, but they may also arise from a lessening of service, quality, variety, or innovation. While market power is a theoretically simple concept, defining and measuring it in practice is fraught with difficulty.

Market Definition

Financial services have traditionally been defined on an institutional basis—the banking market, the insurance market, and securities markets. This approach is not very useful for antitrust analysis, where the appropriate market has both a product and a geographic

---

[34] Office of the Superintendent of Financial Institutions (1998, p. 3).

> **Box 8.2. Antitrust Review of Mergers**
>
> "Merger review is an unusual activity because it requires *ex ante* judgments on often imponderable questions concerning the medium- or long-term future of markets and enterprises."[1] While the process outlined below varies somewhat from country to country, competition law generally contains these provisions and procedures for the evaluation of mergers. The practice of reducing these theories and principles to numbers that can form the basis of a decision is inevitably open to debate and discussion because of the assumptions and conclusions that have to be made about likely future events and behavior.
>
> 1. Pre-notification.
>
>   There is generally a size threshold, defined in sales or assets, above which the proponents of a merger must notify the competition authority in advance of consummating a merger. The competition authority typically undertakes a quick preliminary review, and if it is immediately clear that there are no antitrust concerns, permission (or non-objection) is provided, permitting the merger to proceed. In other cases, a more detailed review of the likely impact of the merger is undertaken.
>
> 2. The Anticompetitive Threshold.
>
>   A merger will generally be found to lessen or prevent competition if the merged entity would be able to exercise greater market power in all or a substantial part of the market for a significant period after the merger. The focus of determining whether market power can be exercised is usually on the ability to impose and maintain a price increase, but consideration will generally also be given to the possibility of lessening of competition with respect to service, quality, variety, or innovation.
>
> 3. Market Definition.
>
>   Market definition is central to determining if a merger is likely to lessen or prevent competition. A relevant market is generally defined as the smallest group of products and the smallest geo-
>
> ---
> [1]Baker (1998).

dimension. Consideration of possible alternative providers of similar products illustrates the pitfalls in an institutional-based market definition. A consumer seeking a basic account to provide transactions services and household savings might, depending on the particular country, be able to turn to cooperative or other nonbank institutions, mutual funds, securities brokers, or insurance companies. Thus, the size of the market would be significantly understated and hence the

> graphic area in which sellers could impose and maintain price increases above those that would likely exist if the merger did not take place (the "hypothetical monopolist test"). Conclusions have to be reached as to the likelihood of buyers switching to a substitute product or the same product sold in a different area, and a determination made of the probability of entry by new competitors and supply response by existing competitors.
>
> 4. Estimating Market Power.
>
>   Market share (percentage) or concentration measured by the Hirschman-Herfindahl Index (HHI) is generally used as an indicator of the likely effect of competition on a market. There are usually threshold levels below which the presumption is that there will not be competition concerns. For example, the U.S. Bank Merger Screens indicate that a transaction resulting in a post merger HHI of 1800 or less, and an increase in the HHI of 200 or less is unlikely to require further review. This is a rule of thumb, and does not preclude greater examination if circumstances warrant. Even when concentration exceeds the "safe-harbor" levels, the merger may be approved if there is evidence of low barriers to entry, probable future entry of new competitors, or other mitigating factors.
>
> 5. Efficiency exemptions.
>
>   An anti-competitive merger may still result in a net gain to the economy as a whole if there are economies of scale or scope that outweigh the likely losses from decreased competition.
>
> 6. Appeal of decisions.
>
>   Decisions of the antitrust authority are frequently negotiated with the parties, but where agreement cannot be reached there is usually recourse to the courts. In some cases the first recourse is to a special judicial or quasi-judicial body. Decisions of this special competition authority are generally subject to appeal and judicial review.

concentration significantly overstated if only banks were included in the antitrust analysis of a banking merger.[35]

Market definition has a geographic dimension in addition to the product aspect. A market physically consists of the geographic area within

---

[35] For fuller discussion of market definition issues, see Kwast, Starr-McCluer, and Wolken (1997); and Andrews (1993).

which a purchaser will seek alternative suppliers. Empirical evidence supports the theory that a purchaser will travel further to get a better price on a relatively expensive and infrequently purchased product, with the implication for antitrust analysis in financial services that the geographic size of a market varies significantly for different products.[36] This means that the antitrust analysis of a proposed merger of financial sector firms involves potentially hundreds of products in thousands of local markets.

In practice, this potentially overwhelming analytical challenge is dealt with in practice in two ways. First, the number of geographic markets that require analysis can be reduced by use of an initial screening mechanism. In the United States, a somewhat arbitrary market definition and approach to measurement,[37] using deposits as a proxy for a cluster of banking services,[38] is used as an initial screening mechanism to identify mergers that are not likely to raise competitive concerns. The process has been codified through literally thousands of bank mergers, to the extent that merger proponents typically have already identified likely competition concerns and they propose remedies concurrently with making their application to the regulator for merger approval.[39] Despite recent consolidation, the U.S. banking market is still characterized by a significant number of competitors in most local markets, so the use of the bank merger screens serves to immediately eliminate most geographic markets from further antitrust analysis, even in mergers involving the largest banks.[40] This results in rel-

---

[36]See Berger and Hannon (1989); Cole, Wolken, and Woodburn (1996); and Rhoades (1996a and b).

[37]Markets are geographically defined as either Federal Reserve markets, Ranally Metropolitan Areas, or, for nonmetropolitan areas, counties. See the joint Department of Justice and banking agencies "Bank Merger Screens" (U.S. Office of the Comptroller of the Currency, 1995). To date, the agencies have not accepted arguments that geographic boundaries on the market are becoming irrelevant, or at least are much larger because of both the increasing prevalence of regional banking networks and the increased use of electronic distribution such as ATMs, telephone, and PC banking. The arguments to consider larger geographic markets are well presented in Radecki (1998); and Smith and Ryan (1997).

[38]The U.S. Federal Reserve uses deposits as a proxy for the cluster of banking services that are viewed as the relevant product market. The European Competition Commission divides the services provided by a bank into three products: retail banking, corporate banking, and financial market services. Merger analysis in Canada and Australia has used narrower product definitions.

[39]Burke (1998).

[40]For example, in the merger of NationsBank and BankAmerica in 1998 to create the largest bank in the country, the merger screens identified only 11 local markets with antitrust concerns. This permitted the focus of analytical efforts on these markets, much reducing the time that otherwise would have been required to consider the application. Further, because the U.S. process has been so well established over time, the merger proponents were able to propose remedies at the time of their application with the reasonable expectation that these would be acceptable to the banking agencies. See Federal Reserve Board (1998).

atively quick consideration of even the largest mergers because the analytical resources can be concentrated in the markets of most concern.

A variation on this approach is, either arbitrarily or as a result of detailed market analysis, to determine that the relevant geographic market is national. This determination facilitates the collection and analysis of market share data and builds on work done in a number of European countries that have opted to use national markets in the analysis of bank mergers. Finland, France, the Netherlands, Norway, Sweden, and Switzerland[41] are among the countries that have relied on a national or even a European geographic market definition in the antitrust analysis of bank mergers. The European Competition Commission has consistently held that banking markets are either national or international.[42] Arguments in favor of national markets have included the relative ease of a current competitor expanding its geographic scope, the increasing ease and prevalence of electronic transactions, and the existence of overlapping market areas that effectively discipline all competitors even if all competitors are not active in every sub-market.

These findings from Europe are contrary to recent evidence from Australia, Canada, and the United States indicating that despite innovations in electronic delivery of financial services, individual consumers remain reliant on nearby financial services firms.[43] While consumers will shop a wider geographic area for larger purchases such as mortgages and investment products, the majority of consumers still tend to choose a checking account provider in proximity to either their home or work. The need to have a convenient location to deposit cash receipts makes small businesses even more dependent on having a nearby provider of a transactions account. Further, because lenders frequently tie the provision of operating credit (working capital or overdraft facilities) to the provision of a transactions account to monitor account activity, small businesses wishing to borrow are generally limited to choosing from nearby financial services providers.

It is quite plausible, though, that the smaller geographic size of Finland, the Netherlands, Norway, Sweden, and Switzerland relative to Australia, Canada, and the United States makes the national market definition more appropriate. For developing and transition economies, even if there is evidence to suggest that smaller geographic markets

---

[41]OECD (1998a).

[42]See any of the Commission decisions related to the financial sector, for example, Case No IV/M.1172, Fortis AG/Generale Bank.

[43]Board of Governors of the Federal Reserve System (1995); Ekos Research Associates Inc. (1998); Commonwealth of Australia (1997, Chapter 10).

than national are appropriate, it may ultimately be necessary to measure concentration on a national basis because of the lack of available data. Reliable market share data on a regional or local basis is seldom readily available, and cost and time considerations may preclude obtaining it as part of the merger review process.

A second approach to reducing the number of markets is to eliminate from further consideration those where a broad range of alternative suppliers and substitute products, or wide geographic markets, exist. This approach draws on available evidence from developed countries and concludes that multinational and large national businesses have many financing alternatives and thus are not likely to be adversely affected by increasing financial sector concentration. More generally, it also finds that there are a range of alternatives, increasing market size, and relative freedom of entry in some consumer products.[44] This elimination of some products generally leaves basic consumer transactions and savings accounts, along with financing and transactions accounts for small and medium-sized businesses, as the areas of major concern in bank mergers in developed countries. These same products are likely to be a concern in developing countries as well, especially because well-developed capital markets to meet business-financing needs are less likely to be present.

Estimating Market Power

Having defined the markets of concern in terms of both product and geographic scope, the antitrust analysis turns to the measurement of the likely impact of a merger transaction on market power. Concentration levels are generally used as a proxy for market power, based on empirical evidence of links between concentration and price.[45]

Increases in concentration

Even though concentration is a less than ideal measure of market power, and other mitigating and exacerbating factors will be included in the analysis, the level of and increase in concentration in the product markets of key concern will be a focal point in antitrust analysis. Two methods are used to measure concentration, one being a simple summation of market shares, and the other being a summation of the square of the market shares. The second approach, the Hirschman-Herfindahl Index (HHI),[46] provides greater weighting to larger firms,

---

[44]Radecki (1998); OECD (1998a); McKinsey & Company (1998); and Commonwealth of Australia (1997).

[45]Weiss (1989).

[46]The HHI is the sum of the squared market share of all of the firms selling in a particular market, and will equal 10,000 (100^2) when one firm has 100 percent market share.

and thus at least in theory makes greater provision for the potential for collusion and oligopolistic behavior in an industry dominated by a few large competitors. The two differing approaches do not yield remarkably different results in practice. For example, in comparing the "safe-harbor" provisions of the Canadian *Merger Enforcement Guidelines*, which are based on market share, and the HHI approach in the U.S. Bank Merger Screens, it is virtually impossible to construct a theoretical market structure that would fall within one safe-harbor provision and not another, despite the differing approach.

There are no absolute definitions of the level of concentration that is likely to lead to an unacceptable ability to exercise market power. As a rule of thumb, U.S. banking regulators will not normally have antitrust concerns about a transaction resulting in a post-merger HHI of 1,800 or less and an increase in the HHI of 200 or less. But in nonbanking mergers in the United States, the safe-harbor threshold is an HHI of 1,600. The Canadian safe harbor is a resulting industry structure where the merged firm would have less than 35 percent of the market, or the merged entity would have a market share of less than 10 percent and the four largest firms combined have less than 65 percent of the market. The Australia Competition and Consumer Commission uses a slightly more liberal safe-harbor threshold; the presumption is that transactions resulting in the merged firm having less than 40 percent of the market, or less than 15 percent of the market when the four largest firms have less than 75 percent market share, generally will not result in a significant lessening of competition.

An important consideration, however, is that concentration is only an indicator of the likely ability to exercise market power. Should a transaction not fall within the safe-harbor provisions, it still might not have a detrimental effect on competition if there were mitigating factors such as likely new entrants to the market. Conversely, even if the transaction fell within the safe harbor it might be subject to further review, if for instance the industry had a history of collusion or conscious parallelism. It can be argued that the tendency for all competitors to adjust interest rates at the same time, and the unique nature of lending as a "product,"[47] mean that a level of concentration acceptable in other industries should not be accepted in banking. An alternative argument is that nonbanks compete with banks, but this competition is not captured in the usual market definition and analysis, so a higher

---

[47]A loan is probably the only product where a seller would not provide as much of the product as desired by a buyer willing to pay a given price. Normally in banking this behavior is evidence of appropriate assessment of default risk by the lender, but it could also be used by banks acting in collusion to ration supply and thus artificially increase the price of credit.

level of concentration might be acceptable in banking than in other industries.[48]

New entrants

It is at least theoretically possible that even a market dominated by a single seller might still be competitive. If a market is contestable, that is, it has the potential to be entered by vigorous new competitors, the existing players cannot engage in uncompetitive pricing because the excessive profits earned will attract new competitors and drive the prices down. Contestable markets typically have few barriers to entry, while most financial services markets have traditionally been characterized by high barriers to new entrants. Minimum capital requirements, the sunk cost investment in physical infrastructure such as a branch network, and the significant informational advantage of incumbents over new entrants are all significant barriers to entry.[49] While the relevance of these barriers is declining as electronic delivery of financial services becomes more prevalent, probable future entry is still generally not viewed as a significant mitigating factor when considering financial sector mergers.

In addressing merger transactions in developing or transition economies, the "doctrine of probable future entry" can be considered as a means of fostering a greater number of competitors. This doctrine, used in merger analysis in the United States, maintains that a merger should be disallowed if there is likelihood of the acquiring party entering the market by way of a start-up rather than by acquisition.[50] In the case of a market characterized by a number of weak institutions, however, the authorities might consider a moratorium on new licenses as a means of encouraging stronger foreign competitors to enter the market by acquiring weaker domestic firms. The intent in either case is to bring innovation and financial strength to the market through the entry of new competitors rather than just reforming existing banks on a stand-alone basis.

Empirical evidence indicates that financial sector capacity develops more quickly when a new or parallel private banking system is allowed to emerge than it does when the government tries simply to reform existing state-owned banks.[51] One reason is that the new entrants bring new competitive forces to previously stagnant markets. Thus, from a competition perspective it is preferable for foreign banks to enter a

---

[48]Tangible support for this argument is found in the United States, where the Bank Merger Screens have higher HHI safe harbors than the more broadly applicable *Horizontal Merger Guidelines*.

[49]For a good discussion of barriers to entry in financial services, see Rhoades (1997).

[50]For a review of the literature, see Amel (1989, pp. 29–68).

[51]Claessens (1996).

country through start-ups or small acquisitions rather than through acquisition of large domestic banks. In many cases, though, the large domestic banks need to obtain the management expertise and financial strength that a foreign parent could provide, making entry by acquisition more attractive from the prudential perspective.

Efficiencies Gains

In considering the impact of concentration on competition, it is important to remember that competition is a means of creating an efficient market rather than an end in itself. This gives rise to the efficiencies defense, whereby transactions likely to result in a significant reduction of competition may still be approved if the benefits such as economies of scale and scope outweigh the detrimental impact.[52] The theoretical argument is that the economy as a whole is better off, because consumers would benefit from the lower prices made possible by scale or scope economies. Even if the resulting loss of competition means that the full amount of the efficiencies is not passed on to consumers and that firms earn somewhat higher profits than would be possible in a competitive market, there is still a net efficiency gain from the merger for the economy as a whole.

The efficiencies defense is difficult to substantiate, because it is difficult to show conclusively that economies of scale and scope actually exist, and if they exist that they cannot be realized in some manner that is more conducive to maintaining competition. For example, a consortium of banks might invest in a joint venture to provide a shared automated teller network as an alternative to mergers leading to only one or two retail bank competitors. The empirical evidence in developed countries on the extent to which efficiency benefits are passed on to the public is mixed.[53] In developing and transition economies, a number of considerations make it at least as likely that any efficiency gains from an anticompetitive merger would be more than offset by the exercise of market power and actually result in a dead-weight loss to the economy. These economies typically have less mature capital markets and fewer vigorous nonbank competitors, making longer-run emergence of substitute products and new competitors less likely. There may also be weaker institutional structures or corruption, making it less likely that a vigilant competition authority would intervene in the event of collusion

---

[52]Efficiencies considerations are explicitly addressed in merger review in Australia, Canada, New Zealand, the United Kingdom, and the United States. In other jurisdictions, efficiencies considerations enter merger evaluation less directly. See McFetridge (1998, pp. 91–103).

[53]Avkiran (1999, pp. 991–1013).

and abuse of dominance. Thus, close scrutiny of the efficiencies defense is warranted, particularly in developing and transition economies.

Other Considerations

While many would argue that prudential and antitrust considerations should be the only factors to consider when determining whether to permit financial sector mergers, a number of other broad public interest factors related to the structure of the financial services industry will also influence the decision-making process. Many of these factors involve trade-offs among various policy objectives and may well result in decisions that are suboptimal from an economic efficiency perspective. But industrial policy considerations will no doubt have some effect on the merger review process.[54]

National Champions and Domestic Control

A desire for "national champions" and maintaining domestic control of the largest financial institutions are two related public policy objectives that frequently come up in discussions of mergers. One of the motivations for both objectives is an element of pride or nationalism associated with having strong domestically owned companies. There are also economic arguments, although they could not be supported in a world of perfect information, complete freedom of movement and fungibility of capital, and frictionless transactions. Because these theoretical conditions are seldom seen in real economies, though, the arguments in favor of national champions and domestic control cannot be dismissed.

The economic argument for national champions is that a national economy will be diminished in the long run if it becomes merely a "branch plant" without the benefits of the headquarters functions of international firms. Investment in research and development, tax revenues, high-quality employment opportunities, and the potential for development of clusters of excellence around successful firms are all viewed as accruing asymmetrically to countries in which international firms are headquartered.[55] For the financial sector, an additional argument in support of national champions is that a country's financial services firms, building on domestic relationships, will provide more favorable and consistent trade financing to the nation's exporters and

---

[54]Industrial policy is shorthand for any economic or social concern, other than competition policy and efficiency, that influences antitrust law enforcement. For a discussion of some of the industrial policy considerations that have influenced recent major merger decisions, see Snyder (1997).

[55]See Porter (1998).

importers than will foreign firms.⁵⁶ Thus, having a strong international financial sector can contribute to the development of other sectors.

Domestic ownership of some of the largest institutions is a necessary condition for national champions. Even without the explicit objective of fostering national champions, benefits are believed to stem from domestic control. In a country without a strong domestically owned financial sector, availability of financial services may be affected by external events. Empirical evidence suggests that a bank facing capital constraints will choose to curtail its activities outside its home country first.⁵⁷ Domestically owned banks are arguably less likely to favor foreign business over domestic customers if faced with capital constraints, and they are more susceptible to the exercise of moral suasion by government. Similarly, domestic banks cannot withdraw from a market in the same way that a foreign-owned subsidiary might curtail certain activities or even withdraw completely from a country as a result of a change in the strategic focus of the parent bank.

Creation of institutions that will be significant players within the broader market of the EU has been one of the driving forces behind the long-term trend of consolidation evident in many European countries. The trend has intensified over the last few years, with an increasing number of domestic mergers "which can be seen as an effort to increase market power at the domestic level, thus increasing their size from an EU perspective and creating the necessary conditions for future cross-border expansion."⁵⁸ Most notably, concentration has continued to increase, even among countries with already highly concentrated financial sectors.

The Netherlands is frequently cited as an example of a country that has facilitated, if not actively encouraged, the emergence of large firms to compete in international markets. In the financial sector, this was reflected in rapid domestic consolidation through mergers among the largest banks and insurance companies between 1989 and 1991. While the Netherlands has one of the world's highest levels of concentration in its domestic markets, ING, ABM-Amro, and Rabobank are financial conglomerates that provide the Netherlands with a much greater international presence than would be expected based on the relatively small size of the domestic economy. Acceptance of high domestic concentration, despite the potential for a reduction in competition in products generally not subject to international competition such as consumer and

---

⁵⁶See Aliber (1984).

⁵⁷See Peek and Rosengren (1997), who find that Japanese banks facing capital constraints in the late 1980s significantly reduced their loan portfolios in the United States while their domestic portfolios were protected from shrinkage. The observed effect was attributed to a decision to maintain close lending relationships in Japan.

⁵⁸European Central Bank (1999, p. 15).

Table 8.2. Assets of the Five Largest Credit Institutions as a Percentage of the Total Assets of Domestic Credit Institutions

	1985	1990	1995	1997
Sweden	60.2	70.0	85.6	89.7
Netherlands	69.3	73.4	76.1	79.4
Finland	51.7	53.5	68.6	77.8
Denmark	61.0	76.0	74.0	76.0
Portugal	61.0	58.0	74.0	76.0
Belgium	48.0	48.0	54.0	57.0
Austria	35.9	34.6	39.2	48.3
Spain	38.1	34.9	45.6	43.6
Ireland	47.5	44.2	44.4	40.7
France	46.0	42.5	41.3	40.3
United Kingdom	...	...	27.0	27.0
Italy	20.9	19.1	26.1	24.6
Luxembourg	...	...	21.2	22.4
Germany	...	13.9	16.7	16.7

Source: European Central Bank (1999).

small business banking, was a conscious policy decision because the Netherlands viewed home market consolidation as a means of strengthening the position of Netherlands' banks internationally.

Other countries have implicitly accepted similarly high levels of domestic concentration as a cost of fostering national champions (Table 8.2). Portugal, which already has banking sector five-firm concentration in excess of 75 percent, is now considering two proposed mergers that would reduce the banking sector to two large private sector groups and the state-owned savings bank. Similarly, Finland has permitted mergers and increased domestic concentration as a cost of having banks able to compete against other regional and international banks. Although France's financial sector is much less highly concentrated than those of some other European countries, competition concerns have been considered in recent bank merger discussions involving three large banks, Banque Nationale de Paris (BNP), Paribas, and Societé Générale, which resulted in the acquisition of Paribas by BNP. The competition concerns were not viewed as serious obstacles, however, because the relevant markets were defined as European, thus eliminating from the analysis concerns about domestic concentration.

Few major countries have explicit restrictions on foreign ownership of major financial institutions, but it is notable that most large institutions in developed countries are either by law or simply in practice widely held and domestically headquartered.[59] Approval of the regulator

---

[59]Background Paper No. 2, *Organizational Flexibility for Financial Institutions: A Framework to Enhance Competition* (Ottawa: Task Force on the Future of the Canadian Financial Services Sector, 1998), pp. 19–20.

is generally required for acquisition of more than 5 or 10 percent of the shares in a major institution, and while these issues tend to be dealt with in a nontransparent manner, it is generally understood that a foreign shareholder would have more difficulty in meeting the "fit-and-proper" test. For example, the proposed 1982 acquisition of the Royal Bank of Scotland by the Hong Kong and Shanghai Banking Corporation was rejected on "national interest grounds," while the corporation's acquisition of a larger U.K. bank, Midland, was approved in 1992. A key difference in the two cases is that in 1990 Hong Kong and Shanghai Banking Corporation had established a U.K.-based holding company. Thus, the actual acquirer of Midland was the U.K.-based holding company, parent of Hong Kong and Shanghai Banking Corporation. Not only did this provide the U.K. regulator with the ability to supervise the banking group effectively, acquisition of a large clearing bank by a U.K.-based holding company was seen as more consistent with the national interest than acquisition by a large foreign bank. A further consideration was that Midland was viewed as being in a financially weak condition, and thus acquisition by a stronger bank was viewed favorably.

A desire for national champions and maintenance of domestic ownership of major financial institutions is frequently a factor in efforts to privatize former state-owned banks throughout the developing world, and it can also be a concern of national authorities when dealing with restructuring in the wake of a systemic crisis. Fiscal considerations, with the government understandably wanting to maximize privatization proceeds, may also come into conflict with competition concerns. The issue could arise because obtaining the best price for the monopoly state savings banks may well come from divesting to a single private owner, resulting in the effective replacement of the state savings banking monopoly with a private savings bank monopoly.[60] If alternatives such as divesting different parts of the business to different investors are not readily available, then ease of entry for qualified foreign banks or provisions for the establishment of sound new domestic banks can be important aspects of mitigating the dominance of the privatized bank.

The cases of New Zealand and Poland are interesting counterpoints to the national champions argument. In the case of New Zealand, permitting foreign takeover of the largest banks was viewed as a preferable alternative to the option of taxpayer-financed restructuring, with the result that the New Zealand banking industry is dominated by large foreign-owned banks. Poland has a banking sector that is two-thirds (as

---

[60]Baker (1999, p. 517). This conundrum applies in the privatization of any state-owned monopoly.

measured by capital) controlled by foreign-owned banks. Despite a certain amount of political unpopularity, the need to increase capital and gain management expertise so that the banking system can properly contribute to economic growth has taken precedence over nationalism concerns in the privatization of a number of Polish banks.

Essential Services and Employment

The desire to maintain banking services and employment in remote regions will frequently be an issue in the privatization of state-owned institutions as well as in mergers and acquisitions. Pressure to approve a financially questionable transaction if the acquirer is prepared to commit to maintain services and employment can create prudential concerns. Even if a more financially viable and thus prudentially more attractive option exists, there can be strong political pressure to reject such a transaction because of the unpalatable rationalization of branches and employment. If the commitment made by an acquirer to the maintenance of services and employment will foreseeably create losses of a magnitude that would threaten solvency, the prudential supervisor clearly would prohibit such a transaction. In practice, however, the question of whether such commitments render the institution not practicable will not be clear-cut. Even when locations and operations are generating institution-threatening losses, an acquirer will generally have plans for restructuring and rationalization that are intended to improve financial performance while adhering to service and employment commitments. Without conclusive evidence and analysis, the prudential supervisor would not supplant the projections of the management of the financial institution, but would certainly require strong assurances as to the feasibility of turning around loss-making operations. Should solvency subsequently be threatened by ongoing losses, decisive supervisory action would be required, including forcing the closure of unprofitable locations and business lines. If public policy concerns make such closures unacceptable, it is preferable that government explicitly acknowledge the policy objective and appropriately provide for the necessary expenditure to maintain financial services in remote areas.

Antitrust Issues in a Systemic Crisis

Dealing with antitrust issues in two different kinds of systemic crises brings different responses. In one case, a quick decision must be made to deal with the imminent failure of one or a small number of systemically important banks within an otherwise healthy financial sector. In the other case, an entire financial sector must be restructured with significant involvement of public funds following macroeconomic shocks.

In the first instance, competition issues will be a concern because systemically important banks, by definition, will have large shares of various financial services markets. But when faced with the imminent failure of a systemically large bank, merger with another large bank may be the preferable public policy option, even considering the potential decrease in competition. Most competition laws contain a "failing-firm" provision, which would permit an otherwise objectionable transaction as a means of dealing with a firm on the verge of failure. Generally the firm is required to demonstrate that there is no other alternative that results in less reduction in competition. This would require the shopping of the assets to a wide market. Because financial difficulties can develop and reach crisis proportions suddenly, and the act of seeking buyers for the business of a large bank might itself trigger a crisis, it may not be possible to meet the failing-firm provision of a competition law.

This possibility is explicitly contemplated in the competition law of a number of countries including Canada, Italy, and Switzerland. To preserve the stability of the financial system, the competition law contains a provision allowing for dispensing with the usual requirement for approval of a merger or acquisition by the competition authority. In each case, the circumstances where such a provision may be used are limited to dealing with a crisis, and the provision has not yet been used in any of the three countries. This type of provision is not common in competition law, and one of the arguments against such an approach is that it inclines the decision-making process in favor of an arranged merger among large institutions. With the ability to conclude a large merger, despite existing antitrust concerns, prudential regulators and policymakers may not actively pursue solutions that would be less likely to result in a significant reduction in competition such as the sale of various parts of the business of a failing large institution. A further argument against such a provision is that despite the clear intent that it only be used to deal with a crisis, its availability could be misused, leading to political interference. The alternative to such a provision in the competition law is the use of emergency legislation to amend the statute or provide a specific exemption in a time of crisis. While this avoids the pitfalls of having explicit exemptions in the competition law, the need for special legislative measures will certainly complicate dealing with a crisis in a timely manner.

In the second case of broad financial sector restructuring as a result of a systemic crisis, it is desirable to address antitrust issues and the maintenance of competition at the same time as long-term solutions are sought. While it may be necessary, as in the case of Indonesia, for a bank-restructuring agency to assume temporary control of a percentage of the banking sector that would normally give rise to concerns about a decrease in competition, this is clearly an extraordinary situation that should not raise antitrust concerns. But the desirability of ensuring a healthy level of competition can be taken into account in implementing resolution plans for the banks under the control of the restructuring agency. While the prudential objective of ensuring that the market is ultimately made up of sound institutions will take precedence, the emergence of one or two large banks with a majority of the market is less preferable than a sector characterized by a larger number of vital competitors. Entry of well-regarded foreign institutions through new incorporations or small acquisitions is particularly desirable as a means of providing a larger number of vigorous competitors in the marketplace. Thus, it is important that the banking and other laws, and the exercise of discretion and judgment by the authorities, does not create greater barriers to entry for foreign firms than for domestic firms. Development of one or more shared ATM networks may be valuable in encouraging competition in retail banking markets, and liquid capital markets reduce the dependency of businesses on bank financing, limiting the possibility of exertion of market power.

Fostering competition may be an especially difficult challenge in markets historically dominated by a single state-owned bank. The state savings bank typically has the bulk of retail business in the former Soviet countries, and relatively large state-owned banks are common in many other developing and transition economies. Creation of additional retail networks is not likely to be an attractive business, at least in the short run, and the track record of regional institutions that collectively might provide competition for the national network is, at best, uneven. It can be a difficult matter to strike the middle ground between encouraging competition and new entrants and guarding against the possible detrimental effects on the safety and soundness of the system. The objective from a prudential perspective is the maximum amount of competition that is consistent with a sound and stable financial system.

Conclusion

Both the prudential and the antitrust dimensions of financial sector mergers and acquisitions need to be explicitly addressed in a merger review process. In many countries today it is not clear how the events in a merger review process should be sequenced, or how the interaction should take place among the prudential and antitrust authorities and other parties such as government officials. In many cases, a clear understanding has developed over time among market participants, but the greatest clarity is provided by an explicit policy statement that outlines the process and, most important, establishes the ability of the prudential supervisor to prohibit a transaction if soundness and stability are concerns.

In reviewing a merger, the prudential authority will use a methodology similar to that used in reviewing the application for a new license, because a merger or a large acquisition in effect creates a new institution. In addition, the prudential authority will focus on specific transactional issues, primarily by checking that all material transactional risks have been identified and addressed and by performing a sensitivity analysis using less favorable assumptions than those used by the merger proponents.

The antitrust review, which to speed the process can be undertaken concurrently with the prudential review, will apply the merger enforcement rules that would be applicable to other transactions in the economy. Evidence from other jurisdictions can be used to assist in market definition and analysis, enabling more resources to be devoted to those products and markets that are likely to be of greatest competitive concern—for instance, consumer and small business banking.

When dealing with weak financial institutions, the prudential regulator may actively encourage mergers as part of a resolution strategy. It may be desirable to complete such transactions, even at the risk of reducing competition, to maintain stability in the financial system. However, the decision to proceed in spite of antitrust concerns must be taken cautiously in light of the longer-term detrimental impact of reduced competition in the financial sector.

Public policy concerns beyond financial sector stability and antitrust issues will undoubtedly influence the merger review process, and they may even be specifically accommodated in countries where the prudential or antitrust regulator is charged with considering other issues, or where a final governmental approval is required. While arguments of economic efficiency would dictate that these other issues not be considered, they have a practical importance in any country. An appropriate review process ensures that these other issues cannot force completion of a transaction where there is either prudential or antitrust concern, regardless of the other perceived benefits.

When dealing with a systemic crisis, it may be desirable and necessary, for the sake of making immediate decisions, to dispense with the detailed antitrust scrutiny that a large financial sector transaction would ordinarily entail. But because of the importance of competition in fostering a long-term, healthy, and efficient financial sector, even when dealing with a crisis it is desirable to consider alternatives to the creation of one or a few large institutions that dominate the market.

References

Alexander, William E., Jeffrey M. Davis, Liam P. Ebrill, and Carl-Johan Lindgren, eds., 1997, *Systemic Bank Restructuring and Macroeconomic Policy* (Washington: International Monetary Fund).

Aliber, Robert Z., 1984, "International Banking: A Survey," *Journal of Money, Credit, and Banking*, Vol. 16 (November), pp. 661–95.

Amel, Dean F., 1989, "An Empirical Investigation of Potential Competition: Evidence From the Banking Industry" in *Bank Mergers: Current Issues and Perspectives*, ed. by Benton E. Gup (Boston: Kluwer Academic Publishers).

Andrews, Michael, 1993, *Size, Competition and Concentration in Canadian Financial Services* (Ottawa: The Conference Board of Canada).

Avkiran, Necmi Kemal, 1999, "The Evidence of Efficiency Gains: The Role of Mergers and the Benefits to the Public," *Journal of Banking and Finance*, Vol. 23 (July), pp. 991–1013.

Baker, Donald I., 1998, "Antitrust Merger Review in an Era of Escalating Cross-Border Transactions and Effects," paper presented at the International Bar Association, Second Annual Competition Seminar, Florence, Italy, October.

———, 1999, "Protecting Consumers in the Privatization Process: A Critical Task for the Competition Agency," *International Business Lawyer*, Vol. 27 (December), pp. 517–18.

Baker, Donald I., and J. William Rowley, eds., 1996, *International Mergers: The Antitrust Process* (London: Sweet and Maxwell).

Basel Committee on Banking Supervision, Bank for International Settlements, 1992, *Minimum Standards for the Supervision of International Banking Groups and Their Cross-Border Establishments* (Basle).

———, 1996, *The Supervision of Cross-Border Banking* (Basle).

———, 1997, *Core Principles for Effective Banking Supervision: Consultative Paper* (Basle).

Berger, Allen N., and Timothy H. Hannon, 1989, "The Price-Concentration Relationship in Banking," *The Review of Economics and Statistics*, Vol. 71 (May), pp. 291–99.

Berger, Allen N., William C. Hunter, and Stephen G. Timme, 1993, "The Efficiency of Financial Institutions: A Review and Preview of Research Past, Present and Future," *Journal of Banking and Finance*, Vol. 17 (April), pp. 221–49.

Berger, Allen N., Rebecca S. Demsetz, and Philip E. Strahan, 1999, "The Consolidation of the Financial Services Industry: Causes, Consequences, and Implications for the Future," *Journal of Banking and Finance*, Vol. 23 (February), pp. 135–94.

Board of Governors of the Federal Reserve System, 1995, *Survey of Consumer Finances* (Washington).

Boyd, John, and Stanley L. Graham, 1996, "Consolidation in U.S. Banking: Implications for Efficiency and Risk," Working Paper 572 (Minneapolis: Federal Reserve Bank of Minneapolis).

Burke, Jim, 1998, "Divestiture as an Antitrust Remedy in Bank Mergers," Finance and Economics Discussion Series No. 14 (Washington: Federal Reserve Board).

Claessens, Stijn, 1996, "Banking Reform in Transition Economies," Policy Research Working Paper No. 1642 (Washington: World Bank).

Cole, Rebel A., John D. Wolken, and Louise R. Woodburn, 1996, "Bank and Nonbank Competition for Small Business Credit: Evidence from the 1987 and 1993 National Surveys of Small Business Finances," *Federal Reserve Bulletin*, Vol. 82 (November), pp. 983–95.

Commonwealth of Australia, 1997, *Financial System Inquiry: Final Report* (Canberra).

Davies, John, ed., 1998, *Merger Control: The International Regulation of Mergers and Joint Ventures* (London: Law Business Publishing Ltd.).

Ekos Research Associates Inc., 1998, *Public Opinion Research Relating to the Financial Services Sector* (Ottawa: Task Force on the Future of the Canadian Financial Services Sector).

European Central Bank, 1999, *Possible Effects of EMU on the EU Banking System in the Medium to Long Term* (Frankfurt am Main: European Central Bank).

European Union, 1999, *Competition Policy Newsletter* (October), pp. 48–49.

Federal Reserve Board, 1998, *Order Approving the Merger of Bank Holding Companies*, August 17, available online at www.federalreserve.gov/regnsup.htm.

Hanweck, Gerald A., and Bernard Shull, 1999, "The Bank Merger Movement: Efficiency, Stability and Competitive Policy Concerns," *The Antitrust Bulletin*, Vol. 44 (Summer), pp. 251–84.

Joint Forum on Financial Conglomerates, 1999, *Supervision of Financial Conglomerates*. Available via the Internet: http://www/bis.org/publ/bcb547.pdf

Khemani, R. Shyam, 1997, "Competition Policy and Economic Development," *Policy Options*, Vol. 18 (October), pp. 23–7.

Kwast, Myron L., Martha Starr-McCluer, and John D. Wolken, 1997, "Market Definition and the Analysis of Antitrust in Banking," *The Antitrust Bulletin*, Vol. 42 (Winter), pp. 973–95.

Levine, Ross, 1997, "Financial Development and Economic Growth: Views and Agenda," *Journal of Economic Literature*, Vol. 35 (June), pp. 688–726.

Lindgren, Carl-Johan, Gillian Garcia, and Matthew I. Saal, 1996, *Bank Soundness and Macroeconomic Policy* (Washington: International Monetary Fund).

Macey, Jonathan R., and Geoffrey P. Miller, 1996, *Bank Mergers and American Bank Competitiveness*, paper presented at a Conference on Mergers of Financial Institutions, Stern School of Business, New York University, New York, October.

McFetridge, Donald G., 1998, *Competition Policy Issues* (Ottawa: Task Force on the Future of the Canadian Financial Services Sector).

McKinsey & Company, 1998, *The Changing Landscape for Canadian Financial Services: New Forces, New Competitors, New Choices* (Ottawa: Task Force on the Future of the Canadian Financial Services Sector).

OECD, 1998a, *Enhancing the Role of Competition in the Regulation of Banks* (Paris).

———, 1998b, *Competition and Related Regulation Issues in the Insurance Industry* (Paris).

Office of the Superintendent of Financial Institutions, 1998, *Report to the Minister of Finance on proposed mergers between the Royal Bank of Canada and the Bank of Montreal, and the Canadian Imperial Bank of Commerce and the Toronto-Dominion Bank* (Ottawa).

Peek, Joe, and Eric S. Rosengren, 1997, "The International Transmission of Financial Shocks: The Case of Japan," *American Economic Review*, Vol. 87 (September), pp. 495–505.

Porter, Michael E., 1998, *On Competition* (Boston: Harvard Business School Publishing).

Radecki, Lawrence J., 1998, "The Expanding Geographic Reach of Retail Banking Markets," *Federal Reserve Bank of New York Economic Policy Review*, Vol. 4 (June), pp. 15–34.

Rhoades, Stephen A., 1994, "A Summary of Merger Performance Studies in Banking 1980-93, and an Assessment of the 'Operating Performance' and 'Event Study' Methodologies," *Staff Study 167* (Washington: Board of Governors of the Federal Reserve System).

———, 1996a, "Bank Mergers and Industrywide Structure, 1980–94," *Staff Study 169* (Washington: Board of Governors of the Federal Reserve System).

———, 1996b, "Competition and Bank Mergers: Direction for Analysis from Available Evidence," *The Antitrust Bulletin* (Summer).

———, 1997, "Have Barriers to Entry in Retail Commercial Banking Disappeared?" *The Antitrust Bulletin*, Vol. 42 (Winter), pp. 973–995.

———, 1998, "The Efficiency Effects of Bank Mergers: An Overview of Case Studies of Nine Mergers," *Journal of Banking and Finance*, Vol. 22 (March), pp. 273–91.

Shull, Bernard, 1996, "The Origins of Antitrust in Banking: An Historical Perspective," *The Year in Review* (Ottawa: The Conference Board of Canada).

Shutt, Theresa, and Hugh Williams, 1999, *The Canadian Financial Services Industry: The Year in Review* (Ottawa: The Conference Board of Canada).

Smith, Brian W., and Mark W. Ryan, 1997, "The Challenges Electronic Distribution of Financial Products and Services Will Present for the Assessment of Competition Among Providers of Those Services," paper presented to the Federal Reserve of Chicago Annual Conference on Bank Structure and Competition, Chicago, May.

Smith, Roy C., and Ingo Walter, 1996, "Global Patterns of Mergers and Acquisition Activity in the Financial Services Industry," Working Paper S-96-48 (New York: New York University Salomon Center).

Snyder, David, 1997, "Mergers and Acquisitions in the European Community and the United States: A Movement Toward a Uniform Enforcement Body," *Law and Policy in International Business*, Vol. 28 (Fall), pp. 135–37.

United States, Office of the Comptroller of the Currency, 1995, "Bank Merger Screens," *Advisory Letter 94-4* (Washington).

Weiss, Leonard W., ed., 1989, *Concentration and Price* (Cambridge, Massachusetts: MIT Press).

9

Guidelines for Bank Resolution

DAVID S. HOELSCHER

A sound banking system is composed of solvent banks, run in a safe and proper manner. Banks that become insolvent and that cannot be rehabilitated or sold should be closed and liquidated as quickly and efficiently as possible so as to minimize disruption to bank customers and to prevent contagion of banking distress to other financial institutions.

The procedures for bank liquidation must be clearly described in the national laws. Because laws differ among countries, universally applicable procedures for bank liquidation cannot be developed. But a number of issues must be addressed irrespective of the legal environment, including the treatment of shareholders, the respective responsibilities of the central bank and the supervisory agency, and the role and responsibilities of the bank liquidator. The necessary steps in the liquidation process can be described even though the legal framework will lay out specific procedures at each stage of the liquidation process. These steps include the initial control and stocktaking of the failed bank, the verification of claims and assets, the valuation and sale of assets, and the distribution of proceeds.

Since 1980, three-fourths of IMF member countries have experienced significant banking sector problems. Banking crises arise because of external factors or from excessive risk-taking by the banking sector itself. These crises jeopardize the overall economic health of a country, distorting resource allocation and impeding financial intermediation.

The author is grateful for helpful comments and assistance from Warren Coats, Carl-Johan Lindgren, Greta Mitchell, Jan Willem van der Vossen, and Henry Schiffman.

The supervisory authorities must be in a position to respond to the emergency. They must be authorized to require corrective measures from bank management. If unsuccessful, the authorities must have the authority to close and liquidate the bank.

Bankruptcy laws and practices differ significantly among countries. Areas of difference revolve around whether financial institutions are governed by the general bankruptcy legislation or by special statutes covering the bankruptcy and liquidation of financial entities. Similarly, a country may not have a sufficiently well-developed bankruptcy law. The law may not be precise enough or it may not address issues critical to financial institution liquidation, such as defining the role of owners or limiting the ability of the institution to continue to function after bankruptcy.[1]

The scope of this chapter is limited in a number of ways. First, the chapter does not seek to propose specific procedures for bank liquidation. Procedural recommendations that are appropriate in one environment may be inappropriate or unworkable in others. Rather, this chapter has two principal objectives: to outline the issues that must be considered when faced with an insolvent bank and to identify practices that are generally considered appropriate in any legal jurisdiction. Second, the chapter does not address bank resolution issues under conditions of systemic banking crises. Resolution techniques may differ in important areas when the entire banking system is facing a financial crisis. Such techniques are outside the scope of this chapter.

Overview of Bank Resolution

A bank is considered insolvent when the value of its assets is less than its liabilities.[2] At that point, the agency responsible for the safe and sound conduct of the financial system (usually the supervisor) may take control of the bank to ensure the safe and sound functioning of the financial system.[3] Under some circumstances (discussed below) the supervisor may wish to continue working with the existing shareowners and managers to implement a restructuring program. More often, though, the agency closes the bank, withdraws the bank's

---

[1]For a discussion of these issues, see Schiffman (1997).

[2]For a detailed discussion, see Frécaut, Sullivan, and van der Vossen, "Bank Equity and Its Measurement," forthcoming Working Paper.

[3]The agency responsible for intervention varies among countries and may include the bank supervisor, the deposit insurer, or some other agency that has adequate legal authority.

license, and disenfranchises the bank's shareholders.[4] When the bank is closed, the shareholders lose their investments. But bank closure does not necessarily mean that bank clients lose access to banking services or that depositors and other creditors necessarily lose their investments. The impact on bank clients and bank creditors depends on a variety of factors, including the financial state of the bank and the resolution technique adopted by the supervisors. Bank closures result in losses to the shareholders but not necessarily losses to others associated with the bank.

A liquidator or receiver must then be appointed to resolve the failed institution.[5] The liquidator has a number of options to resolve the now closed bank. The whole bank may be sold to qualified investors or merged with a sound financial institution to be restructured and run as a going concern. Alternatively, the liquidator may seek to split the bank into parts, selling the viable parts to sound financial institutions and liquidating the remaining parts. Failing these alternatives, the supervisors may move to pay off the secured depositors and liquidate the bank's remaining assets.

Sometimes, the choice between rehabilitation and liquidation is relatively easy. Some banks may not engage in true banking business, may play no role in financial intermediation, or may be so deeply insolvent that rehabilitation is not a viable option. Examples are numerous and could include the "pocket banks" of the former Soviet Union, which were more like treasuries of enterprises than banks. More frequently, it is impossible to tell immediately if a bank can be rehabilitated or not. As a result, the decisions to rehabilitate or liquidate can be made sequentially. The liquidator will first attempt rehabilitation and, if that fails, will liquidate the bank. In this process, there cannot be the presumption that all banks will be rehabilitated, just as there cannot be the presumption that all banks will be liquidated.

Taking control of a bank, either for its restructuring or for its liquidation, requires the introduction of a new authority in the bank. Typically, the supervisory authorities will introduce a receiver or liquidator to evaluate the bank's condition and decide on a resolution strategy. The functions and the responsibilities of the new authority, as well as its relations with management, shareowners, and creditors, will differ depending on whether the supervisory authorities intend to rehabilitate or liquidate the bank.

---

[4]In civil law countries, the shareholders frequently cannot be disenfranchised. Accordingly, the supervisors must have the authority to write down the value of the original shareholders' equity to a nominal sum (such as US$1).

[5]The terminology used in bank rehabilitation varies among jurisdictions. Liquidators may be referred to as bank receivers.

The role of the shareholders merits particular attention. The law must identify when shareholder rights are suspended and when such rights may be returned to shareholders or are terminated. In some jurisdictions, for example, shareholders retain important authority throughout the liquidation process, and as a result the liquidation process can be slow and inefficient. Under such circumstances, either the supervisor of an ongoing but failed bank or the liquidator of the failed bank may be forced to work with the shareholders. For that reason, the bank resolution techniques may be differentiated by the role and authority retained by shareholders.

Resolution Options Preserving Bank Shareholders

Supervisors may be reluctant or unable to withdraw a bank's license and disenfranchise the bank's shareholders. Supervisors may consider that the deterioration in the bank's financial conditions was outside the control of the shareholders and the managers, that the bank's profitability can be quickly reestablished, and therefore that there is no need to take control of the bank. Supervisors may be faced with a systemic crisis affecting all banks in the system, and may be unable or unwilling to close all banks. Alternatively, supervisors may be unable to evaluate fully the true financial conditions of the bank and may wish to examine the bank for a period of time. Under such conditions, supervisors may (1) adopt a policy of forbearance, allowing the bank to continue operations, (2) impose restrictions on the activities of the bank, including limited operations and forced recapitalization, or (3) place a conservator in the bank to evaluate the true financial condition of the bank and determine the appropriate resolution strategy.

Forbearance

If the supervisors believe that a bank in financial distress will be able to resolve its financial difficulties in time (either because of a reversal in external conditions or because of a restructuring program), they may allow the bank's management time to formulate and implement both financial and operational restructuring without interference by the regulators. During this period of adjustment, the enforcement of existing prudential regulations (primarily capital adequacy but maybe also provisioning and other regulations) is temporarily relaxed. Forbearance is frequently exercised in a nontransparent way, with banks allowed to function without adequate safeguards against risk taking or with time limits imposed on the exercise of forbearance.

Where forbearance has been implicit and unmonitored, success has been rare. Banks have rarely outgrown their financial distress, and the eventual costs of bank resolution have been increased. Assumptions about bank performance are frequently overoptimistic, and measures needed to achieve improvements in bank performance often are not implemented. Where successful, forbearance programs have been explicit and have included careful and continual monitoring of the bank. If the shareholders and managers are unable to fully implement agreed measures, supervisors should move quickly to close the bank and implement resolution programs. A distinction is sometimes made between forbearance and gradualism. Whereas forbearance is exercised by the supervisors without enhanced oversight of the problem banks, gradualism allows banks time to meet all prudential requirements within a program containing safeguards against risk taking. In particular, banks must agree to implement a clear and demanding timetable of reforms.

There are strong arguments against forbearance. It creates the opportunity for continued deterioration of the bank and for contagion to healthy banks, and it may result in increased resolution costs. Concerns about contagion are of particular importance as otherwise sound banks come to believe that they will not be held accountable for unsafe and unsound banking practices. One example of the costs of forbearance is the U.S. savings and loan crisis of 1980–94.[6]

Monitored Restructuring

Supervisors may opt to establish an explicit monitoring program with existing shareholders. The plans would be a combination of financial restructuring—including recapitalization—and operational restructuring—including strengthening of internal risk controls and concentration of activities to core businesses. The plans agreed on with the supervisor would include a formal memorandum of understanding that lays out the restructuring measures to be adopted and a timetable for their implementation. The memorandum of understanding might also include a statement that failure to implement the restructuring program will result in the withdrawal of the banking license and the liquidation of the bank.

Under very special circumstances, the government may agree to allow the original shareholders to keep their investment in the bank and even to participate in the recapitalization program.[7] This option may be more frequently used in a systemic crisis, where the deterioration in the financial conditions of the banks is generalized and is caused in large part by factors outside their control. In this case, the government may consider that participation with the private sector in the

---
[6]FDIC (1998, p. 25).
[7]For more details, see Enoch, Garcia, and Sundararajan (2001).

recapitalization of the banking system is less costly than taking over and running all banks in the system.

Conservator

The supervisor may consider that it does not have sufficient information to make a judgment about the true financial conditions of a bank or its future viability. Under these circumstances, the supervisor may suspend bank shareholders and take temporary control of the bank. The objective of a conservator is to preserve the bank as a going concern while reviewing the bank's financial conditions and implementing rehabilitation measures. Under a conservator, the bank continues to operate. The conservator takes over bank management and is responsible for the day-to-day operations of the bank, as well as for the in-depth analysis of the bank's financial conditions. Typically, though, the powers of a conservator do not exceed those of management.

Under conservatorship, the rights of the shareholders are suspended and those of the conservator prevail. The consent of shareholders is needed for any action that would normally require their concurrence. For example, conservators do not usually have the authority to restructure the bank, require additional capitalization from shareholders, or sell significant parts of the bank to other financial institutions. A key responsibility of the conservator is to evaluate the prospects of the bank and, if warranted, prepare a rehabilitation plan. This plan should analyze the current financial situation, identify the source of future earnings of the bank, and indicate the bank's key client base. In addition, measures for operational restructuring should be described. These might include identifying and proposing appropriate reforms. This plan should be developed in conjunction with the shareholders of the bank (to ensure full agreement with the measures proposed) and approved by the supervisory authorities. The plan should have time-bound performance criteria so that the supervisory authorities can monitor progress in rehabilitating the bank.

The rehabilitation plan should include measures for the financial restructuring of the bank, including how the bank will be recapitalized and how it will remain liquid. Shareholders should be expected to invest additional funds. In recapitalizing, debt-to-equity swaps should be considered, to possibly strengthen the capital position of the bank. Not all creditors are likely to agree with recapitalization, however, raising the possibility that a small minority of creditors could prevent bank rehabilitation. Some countries therefore permit the majority of creditors (which must be defined in the law but may be two-thirds or three-fourths of the creditors) to make the recapitalization plan binding on all creditors (a cram-down provision).

The costs of a conservatorship can be substantial. Depositor confidence may erode in the face of a conservatorship, and interbank markets may disappear. Accordingly, conservatorship is generally imposed only for a short period of time. Once an appropriate rehabilitation strategy is agreed among the conservator, the supervisory authorities, and the shareholders, responsibility for managing the bank should be returned to the shareholders.

Resolution Options for a Closed Bank

If the existing shareholders and the managers of a bank are unable to reverse the bank's financial deterioration, the supervisors should withdraw the bank's license, write down or eliminate the shareholders' equity holdings in the bank, begin resolution proceedings, and appoint a liquidator or receiver. While the closure of the bank means that the shareholders lose their investment, it does not necessarily mean that the clients of the bank or the creditors (including the depositors) lose. The liquidator has a variety of resolution techniques available. The distribution of the costs depends on the underlying condition of the bank and the resolution technique adopted by the agency responsible for the resolution of failed banks.

Role of the Liquidator

The first step in the resolution of a closed bank is the appointment of a liquidator or receiver of the failed institution. The objective of the liquidator is not to manage the bank but to ensure the greatest return to creditors, including the depositors. The liquidator has full control of the bank, with the authority to sell and transfer some assets to another institution, to sell fixed assets, and to negotiate settlement with the creditors. The law may grant the liquidator special authority to repudiate some contracts considered burdensome and to temporarily halt litigation.[8]

Once the liquidator takes control of the bank, the rights of the shareholders are terminated and the liquidator is given the freedom to restructure the bank and transfer the bank's business to other financial institutions. At the same time, the shareholders often have the right to contest the actions of the supervisory authorities in courts. The issue that must be clarified in the law is whether the shareholders can reverse the actions of the supervisor. If supervisory actions can be reversed, shareholders can often severely impede the restructuring process.

---

[8]Such authority must be specified in the laws governing the liquidator because the liquidator may be liable for damages.

The liquidator may also be given the authority to halt legal action by creditors. Creditors acting independently can jeopardize the maximization of overall return by seeking to gain immediate advantages through the exercise of their individual legal rights. Equally important, creditors may move too rapidly to allow the liquidator a chance to sell the bank as a going concern. A liquidator, therefore, must be able to place a "stay" on the exercise of creditors' legal rights. This authority must be clarified in the law and must be time-bound. The one exception could be treatment of creditors with secured collateral. Requiring such creditors to wait until all or a large portion of bank assets are sold before they are reimbursed would nullify the benefits of being a secured creditor. That said, a short but reasonable stay of secured creditors (e.g., 30 or 60 days) may be appropriate to allow the liquidator to determine the best way to maximize the value of the bank's assets.

In carrying out these early phases of bank liquidation, the liquidator requires extensive banking skills, such as experience in organizing bank mergers or developing purchase and assumption agreements (see next section). In the final stages of the liquidation, however, the liquidator must have relatively more expertise in the legal and accounting aspects of bank liquidation, including the disposition of both nonperforming and fixed assets. It is perhaps for this reason that, in some jurisdictions, the liquidator process is divided into several stages, the first governed by someone with banking skills and the last governed by someone with a stronger legal background.

Resolution Techniques

Broadly, three techniques for bank resolution can be identified as (1) whole bank resolution, (2) purchase and assumption agreements, and (3) liquidation and deposit payouts. The impacts on bank clients and creditors differ in each case, as do the costs of the bank resolution.

Whole bank resolution

Once the shareholders are removed, one option liquidators often consider is the sale of the bank as a going concern to a third party or the merger of the bank to another financial institution. This option preserves the bank's franchise value and ensures that the banking services to the community are maintained. If a merger is contemplated, the acquiring institution must be sufficiently strong to absorb the failed institution. Both the sale of a whole institution and a merger may require enhancements of the balance sheet of the failed institution. This might entail the separation of the bad assets from the bank's portfolio (see below).

In cases of large complex banks that have failed, some jurisdictions permit the establishment of a de novo institution or bridge bank as part of the resolution process. Bridge banks are temporary banking structures designed to take over the operations of the failing institution and maintain banking services for customers. Bridge banks provide the authorities with time to get control over the failed bank's business, stabilize the situation, and determine the appropriate resolution. Operational costs of the bridge bank are often high, in part because new management may be required. In addition, if the bank's problems are not quickly solved or, alternatively, if the bank is not quickly closed and resolved, the authorities become responsible for the bank's subsequent deterioration.

Establishment of a good-bank–bad-bank arrangement is another resolution technique. This allows the supervisors to increase the attractiveness of a bank by transferring the bank's nonperforming assets to a shell bank or to an asset management company and prepare a clean bank for sale to private investors or for merger with another financial institution. Under these arrangements, the good bank has greater franchise value and is able to operate more profitably than if the nonperforming loans remained on its books.

The structure of the bad bank will depend on the institutional structuring of the financial sector, the extent of the nonperforming loans in the system, and the profitability of the banking system. A bad bank can be established as a subsidiary of the parent bank, a separate bank with its own license, or part of a publicly owned asset management company.[9]

In marketing a failed institution, the liquidator must develop an information package including financial data on the institution, legal documents, and other requisite documents describing the assets being offered. Bidders must then be invited to participate. The liquidator has the responsibility of ensuring that the bidders have the appropriate skills and the financial capacity to manage the assets. The liquidator also must permit due diligence visits by potential bidders to assess the value of the assets. All bidders receiving information packets or conducting due diligence visits must sign confidentiality agreements stating that they will not disclose or use information obtained from the bidding process for purposes other than evaluating the assets being sold.

Purchase and assumption agreements

If attempts to sell the whole bank or merge the bank with another financial institution are considered unfeasible or fail, a variety of tools

---

[9]The good-bank-bad-bank split may also be used by open banks, either as part of their own restructuring efforts or as part of the public sector's efforts to deal with a systemic crisis.

are available. The liquidator can bundle performing assets and liabilities for sale in purchase and assumption transactions (P&As). In its most general form, a P&A is a transaction where a healthy bank purchases some or all of the assets of a failed bank; the liabilities transferred include some or all of the deposits and secured liabilities. A P&A transaction can be more attractive to the purchasing bank because the assets and liabilities are clearly defined and the purchaser runs relatively low risk of facing unexpected liabilities. As a result, the demand for such transactions can be higher than for the purchase of a whole bank or a merger with the failed institution. P&As are less disruptive than liquidating the bank and paying off the creditors because customers suffer no break in service and lose no accumulated interest.

Best practices usually require the transfer of as many of the assets as possible, thus returning assets to the market as quickly as possible. A modified form of a P&A is to package homogeneous loans in the expectation that such loans may be easier to market.[10] Some categories of assets, such as claims against former directors and officers, are rarely, if ever, included in a P&A; they remain with the liquidator.

A P&A transaction must ensure that depositors are treated appropriately. There is no difficulty if all deposits can be shifted to a new institution or if full deposit insurance exists. When depositors are not fully insured, the authorities can package performing assets and sufficient government securities to match the full amount of insured deposits in the failed bank. The uninsured deposits, then, remain in the failed institution to be paid out using the proceeds from the liquidation of the bank's assets. If the asset liquidation is insufficient to cover all uninsured creditors, proceeds are distributed on a pro rata basis.

Some P&A agreements allow the purchasing bank to sell selected assets back to the government, commonly referred to as "put-back transactions." Under some jurisdictions, it would be possible for the bank to "put back" any number of poor or nonperforming loans, thus insuring itself against unexpected or unanticipated reductions in the value of an asset. The bank would remove the nonperforming loan from its portfolio and receive an offsetting cash injection. Such practices would have to be clearly delineated in the bankruptcy legislation and could have a variety of restrictions, including a time limit for implantation and limitations on the size of putback transactions. Any time limit must be long enough for the acquiring bank to fully evaluate its assets, although not so long as to provide an explicit guarantee against bad management on the part of the purchaser.

---

[10]P&A transactions can become quite specific. Distinctions can be made among total P&As, small loan P&As, P&As involving only guaranteed deposits, and other arrangements. The objective is to design a package that maximizes the probability of sale.

Experience with put options has been mixed. The U.S. Federal Deposit Insurance Corporation (FDIC) used such options to increase the attractiveness of failed savings and loans in the late 1980s. It found, though, that significant problems developed.[11] First, the acquiring banks were able to "cherry pick" the assets, choosing to keep only those with market values above book values. Second, assets tended to be neglected by the acquirer during the put period, adversely affecting their value. As a result, the full risk of managing the assets remained with the government agency responsible for the resolution rather than with the new owners. The FDIC discontinued the use of put options as a liquidation tool in 1991.

An alternative to the put option is the development of loss-sharing agreements. In these transactions, the supervisor covers the majority of the loss on certain pools of assets but receives the majority of the recovery. The acquiring bank agrees to take the loss on a smaller portion of the assets.

Liquidation and deposit payout

When no acquirer is found for a bank, the liquidator must opt for a general depositor payoff and liquidation of the bank's assets. In this case, the supervisor closes the bank. No liabilities are assumed and no assets purchased by other banks. The supervisor or the deposit insurer then calculates the deposit balances at the end of the day of business closure. The supervisor or the deposit insurer then pays all insured deposits except those associated with illegal activities, or, if permitted by law, those retained in order to net against delinquent loans. Depositors with uninsured funds and other general creditors may be given liquidator certificates, entitling them to a share of the net proceeds from the liquidation of the failed bank's assets.

The payout can be made either directly by the deposit insurer or through an agent bank. Paying off depositors directly has some disadvantages. Depositors must go to the authorities in charge to receive their check. Long lines and pressures on available staff may result. Reliance on an ongoing financial institution to act as the payout agent for the authorities may address these disadvantages.

Liquidation procedures can take considerable time, and the uninsured creditors may have to wait before they receive any payout. Some jurisdictions respond by making available a portion of the estimated liquidation value of the assets, allowing creditors to receive something immediately rather than after the liquidation is complete (which can take a number of years).

---

[11] FDIC (1998, p. 15).

Options for Managing Assets

As the size and number of failed banks increase, it becomes important to develop adequate arrangements to effectively identify such institutions and then liquidate their assets. Agencies may attempt to rely on their own staff for sale of each asset case by case. As the number and value of the assets increase, though, agencies have sought to bundle the assets in a variety of ways. A question that must be addressed is whether the agency can manage to dispose of the acquired assets or whether it is wise to establish a separate asset management company, an institution that specializes in the disposition of assets, by selling them, recovering value by foreclosing on collateral, or restructuring them through negotiations with the creditors.[12]

Asset management has several objectives. Agencies may seek a prompt resolution of assets in the expectation that swift resolution is essential for restoring access of financial institutions to the market and for enabling the market to assess counterparty risk. Alternatively, the agency may seek to maximize the recovery of assets. A high recovery rate will benefit the creditors of the failed institution and may benefit new borrowers by lowering risk premiums. Maximum recovery may take some time, however. Selling a large portion of the assets at one time may depress market prices. The agency may prefer to wait for a recovery of economic activity before it begins asset sales. The authorities will need to determine the public policy objectives and establish the objectives of the asset disposition process accordingly.

Once the broad parameters for the asset disposal are agreed on, there are several methods for disposing of assets. The authorities themselves can take charge of the valuation and marketing process. They would then conduct some combination of negotiations with individual buyers, negotiations with a group of selected bidders, and public auctions. Each of these three alternatives has advantages and disadvantages. Negotiated sales with individual buyers may be implemented rapidly. Negotiations could even take place with the original borrower, where the liquidator forgives all obligations of a borrower in exchange for some amount of cash, perhaps substantially less than the full amount legally due. Whereas this approach may save time and may result in repayment of both performing and nonperforming loans, it entails substantial risks of fraud. The liquidator would have to ensure that it received an adequate return for any asset sold in this fashion. A requirement, for example, that the central bank board, as the oversight body for the liquidation, approve such agreements would help reduce the risks.

---

[12]For recent discussion of asset management companies, see Woo (2000).

Competitive bidding for assets by a group of bidders selected by the liquidator reduces the risk of fraud and provides protection for the liquidator by precluding subsequent questions about the fairness of the sale process. A private competitive bidding process typically is less expensive and quicker to organize than a public bidding process, but it may not expose the loan to as wide a range of bidders, and thus it may not ensure maximum recovery. A public auction is usually the most time-consuming and costly to organize and conduct, but it attracts the maximum number of potential bidders (bidders should be screened to exclude those not "fit and proper" to own banks or those without sufficient financial resources). The choice among these sale processes depends on a variety of factors, including location and economic conditions.

Rather than deal directly with potential purchasers, the liquidator can contract a third party to liquidate the assets. Three broad types of arrangements have been used. First, the liquidator can hire a private firm to evaluate and market the assets, agreeing to pay cost plus a fixed fee or a percentage of the final sale price. A second alternative is for the liquidator to sell all assets to a third party at a deep discount. This alternative limits government involvement in the liquidation process and gets the assets off the government books quickly; however, the deep discount may well represent a substantial cost. A third alternative may be an agreement to form a joint public/private entity. The assets would be sold to this entity, but the supervisory agency would retain some influence over the process. The final arrangement depends on the structure of the market, the availability of such third parties, and the objectives of the supervisory agency.

Steps in Resolution of a Failed Bank

Intervention in a failed or failing bank requires careful planning. The specific steps must be developed in line with the laws and regulations of each country. But a generalized description of issues to be addressed can be developed.

After the supervisory authorities have decided to close a bank, they should follow certain procedures that are outlined below. A step-by-step list for the first few days of liquidating a bank is shown in the Appendix.

Preparatory Steps

When a bank is suspected of failing or being insolvent, a team of supervisors may be placed in the institution to monitor and evaluate the situation. The team should evaluate the assets and liabilities of the bank, monitor bank operations, and prepare updated financial statements. It should also monitor the use of the physical and liquid assets of the bank, because asset stripping often becomes a serious concern once a bank is suspected of insolvency. Physical assets can be removed and liquid assets can be transferred. If the inspectors identify unusual activity, especially in foreign accounts, the central bank or supervisory authority should be notified immediately so that actions to freeze the assets and to close the bank can be accelerated.

If the owners or the management of the bank are not cooperative, the supervisory authorities should be given the responsibility to appoint a conservator to take over the bank's operations until a final disposition of the bank is decided. If efforts to resolve the bank's financial problems are unsuccessful, the bank should be closed and its operations taken over by a liquidator. At that point, the owners should lose their equity investment in the bank.

The interveners, be they conservators or liquidators, must be accountable to the central bank or the agency that appointed them or to the court. Some estimate of the length of time required for the bank's resolution should be established and progress in implementing the resolution monitored. Significant slippage must be addressed, either by changing the phasing envisioned in the bank intervener's contract or by changing intervener. The intervener should be required to submit reports at least every three months to the central bank board or the supervisory agency's board and, if also required, to a court.

First Step in Liquidation: Physical Control and Stocktaking

If these efforts fail and a decision is made to close the bank, the liquidator must immediately take physical control of the bank's assets.[13] This action involves securing the bank's premises and equipment using security guards, police, or whatever other means are available. Physical possession must also be taken of valuable items such as cash and securities, automobiles, and artwork. Door locks to the bank premises should be changed and new guards posted so that the liquidator can control access to bank assets and records.

Once the bank is closed, ownership and control over its financial assets shift from the original shareholders, managers, and directors to the liquidator. Shareholders no longer have any control over the disposition of the bank's assets or liabilities. No new loans can be undertaken, and all resources should be placed in a special liquidation account in the central bank clearly labeled as "Bank [X] in Liquidation." The liquidator should have the exclusive authority to use the

---

[13]If the bank is already under the control of a conservator, the liquidator will take over responsibility for the bank from the conservator.

account; the previous shareholders of the bank should not have access to the account.

Special care must be taken with the bank's correspondent accounts, especially with accounts held in foreign banks, because of their size, liquidity, and vulnerability to unauthorized access. It is therefore critical to notify immediately all financial institutions, domestic and foreign, holding funds in the bank that those funds have been placed in the liquidation account and that withdrawals or transfers can be authorized only by the liquidator. This notification should be made by the most expeditious means possible, such as by fax, telex, or hand-delivery by representatives of the liquidator. It may also be appropriate initially to communicate through a telephone call, notifying that the written communication is forthcoming. If accounts are held in correspondent banks, or if balances are held in foreign accounts, ownership of the assets should be transferred to the central bank. Foreign currency–denominated balances should be held in separate liquidation accounts for foreign currencies.

An additional immediate step in liquidation should be the announcement to the press of the closure of the bank. Generally, a banking crisis is a matter of considerable concern and media attention. Either the central bank or the supervisory agency should take the initiative in such circumstances, announcing the closure and explaining the implications for the banking system. The objective of the announcement should be to create an atmosphere of calm professionalism and to minimize any systemic effect by maintaining confidence in the banking system.

Second Step: Verification of Claims and Assets

Because the liquidator may not be able to rely on existing records, or available information may be out of date, a bank's creditors should be invited to confirm their claims on the bank. The liquidator must validate these claims, clarifying any inconsistencies. The liquidator should revise the balance sheet, verifying and reconciling correspondent account statements, currency holdings, and equipment lists. Notes receivable must also be verified against balance sheet and subsidiary records.

A bank in liquidation must halt activities, so must not accept any new deposits. All work in the bank, including unprocessed deposits and incoming loan payments, should be posted to the general ledger and subsidiary accounts. A final statement and balance sheets should be prepared. Loan payments received after the bank closure should be recorded in the loan documentation and the payments deposited in the liquidation account in the central bank. At the same time, the liquidator should recognize that the clients of the bank must continue to operate. For example, a small business loan may be secured by furniture and plant equipment, and the business itself may be making its loan repayments on schedule from ongoing business activity. Under such circumstances, it would be imprudent to recall the loan or foreclose on the furniture and equipment because this action would put the firm out of business and eliminate further sources of loan repayment. As a result, there may be value in not calling in performing loans while the liquidator seeks to sell the bank's loans to another financial institution.

One issue that must be clarified is the continued accrual of interest on deposits held by the bank. Such interest payments may be justified, particularly under conditions of high inflation, which reduces the deposit value. Interest paid, however, would increase the cost of the bank's resolution. The liquidator, perhaps subject to central bank approval, should have the right to determine an appropriate interest rate under such circumstances.

A clear distinction must be made among branches, affiliates, and subsidiaries. There is no legal distinction between ownership of the assets by the head offices and branches. All branches of a failed bank are part of the bank itself, and the assets of all branches (including the main branch or the head office) should be consolidated in the liquidation account opening statement. The liquidator's responsibilities are the same for the branch and head office assets. Affiliates are separate legal entities such as companies or banks that are related in some way (normally through share ownership) but that, in legal terms, are not directly affected by the liquidation of a bank.[14] If the affiliates are banks, however, they could be indirectly affected by the liquidation of the bank, particularly if the creditors and the depositors are aware of the relationship between the affiliate and the failed bank. In such an instance, affiliated banks could be confronted with large withdrawals and could become illiquid.[15] Conversely, if an affiliated bank is closed or encounters difficulties, the parent bank may feel strong pressure to provide financial support.

Subsidiaries are companies in which the bank owns a majority of shares. In this case, the bank's asset is the stock in the subsidiary company, not that company's underlying assets. Generally, a liquidator will maximize recovery by allowing the subsidiary to continue as a going concern and to sell its stock.

Third Step: Valuation and Sale of Assets

Valuation of liquid financial assets poses few problems. Notes, coins, and correspondent bank accounts denominated in domestic and foreign

---

[14]Of course the closed bank's assets held by the affiliate must normally be liquidated.

[15]When confronting the closure of a bank with one or more affiliates, it is wise in the preparation phase to plan for the contingency that affiliated banks also may fail.

currencies have set values. Similarly, items such as stocks and bonds for which there is an established and active market can be rapidly disposed of for a fair value. The liquidator must be aware, though, that if the market for those instruments is thin, the market price of those assets can fall sharply as liquidation begins. Under these circumstances, there may be a trade-off between the speed of liquidation and the resources generated from the asset sale. The mix chosen will depend on a variety of factors, including the state of the banking system, the risks of contagion, the number of unsecured creditors, and the general economic environment.

The most time-consuming and difficult category of financial assets to liquidate is the loan portfolio. Often it is not profitable to spend the time and the effort to identify, assess, and sell every loan. Accordingly, the liquidator may undertake a statistical sampling of the portfolio. Loans can be divided into categories such as real estate or commercial loans. Each loan in each category can then be classified as either performing or nonperforming. To estimate the liquidation value of the portfolio, a sample of loans is then selected from each category for in-depth analysis and evaluation. The estimate of the value for the sample is then applied to the broad subcategory of loans.

If the loan is not classified, it is highly probable that the value of the loan should approximate its principal balance plus interest due (at the time the loan is sold). For these loans, a liquidator can usually find potential buyers (banks or other financial companies) and sell the loans without significant difficulties. Problem credits typically pose significant difficulties, in which case the liquidator may resort to negotiated sales with potential buyers.

The valuation of nonfinancial assets can be more difficult than the valuation of financial assets. Efforts to establish a market value may be complicated, particularly in turbulent or thin markets, and the use of professional appraisers may serve to protect the liquidator in case the sale decisions are questioned. Following the evaluation of nonfinancial assets, the liquidator should make the proposed sale of the assets known to potential buyers. If an asset is sold for substantially less than the estimated value after consideration of all relevant factors, it is recommended that the reasons for such a decision be documented in writing, because the liquidator could later be held accountable.

Fourth Step: Distribution of Proceeds

All creditors, including foreign banks, should be informed when a bank enters liquidation. Creditors could be asked to submit evidence of their claims against the failed bank, or the liquidator could notify them of the amount in the bank's records. In either case, a cutoff date for the identification and presentation of claims should be established, with claims submitted after that date not honored.

Netting of claims

There must be rules for the netting of the claims of a creditor on a liquidated bank against the claims of the liquidated bank on that creditor. While civil law on netting differs from country to country, some basic elements are as follows: Netting is normally allowed only between claims that have fallen due. Otherwise, proceeds from asset sales may be reduced, thus limiting the ability of the liquidator to repay creditors. The netting of unmatured claims at full value could result in unequal treatment of other creditors, because netted claims are settled in full, while other claims may be settled only on a pro rata basis with resources from the asset liquidation. Also, the claims should be uncontested. Netting of claims does not automatically take place; a declaration of one of the parties addressed to the other is required. Both parties should be authorized to collect and pay the claim.

The claims do not have to be of equal size. The remainder of the larger of the two claims after netting continues to exist as a claim. Netting of bearer claims is also possible. In such cases the bearer paper could, for instance, be signed by the creditor as "paid" and returned to the issuer of the paper. When netting claims are in different currencies, the exchange rate of the day of netting can be used.

Interbank contracts may contain so-called cross-default clauses, implying that default on a loan to one party leads automatically to a repayment obligation with regard to a loan from another party. This could lead to a situation where a loan that would not have been "nettable" becomes subject to netting. Under such conditions, the loan is repaid earlier than originally intended because of the cross-default effect.

The relationship between a bank in liquidation and parties that are closely connected to the bank—such as managers, directors, and shareholders—can be complicated. In general, the deposits of, and loans to, managers, directors, shareholders, and their relatives should not be treated differently from deposits or loans to other parties. If any loan to managers, directors, shareholders, or their relatives is delinquent, the normal collection policies applied to other loans should be followed. But shareholders should not be allowed to net any claims for repayment of their capital contributions with claims of the bank on themselves resulting from a loan agreement or other claim. Repayments of capital contributions are to be considered only if the liquidation shows a surplus (i.e., after all creditors' claims have been satisfied). It is also conceivable that the bank may still have a claim on the shareholder. This claim should not be netted against capital contributions already paid in or any other claim of the shareholder the bank.

Ranking of creditors

If resources generated by asset liquidation are insufficient to reimburse all creditors, creditors must be ranked in order of priority. The establishment of creditor priorities, in principle, is a matter for national legislation. All fully secured claims are paid first, up to their full value or the value of the security, whichever is lower. Then all liquidation costs are paid. For that reason, the liquidator must have a reasonably accurate estimate of total costs and must ensure that sufficient resources from the proceeds of the sales of remaining assets are preserved. In principle, all unsecured creditors are reimbursed last. If the proceeds from the sales of the bank's assets do not cover all unsecured creditors (including uninsured depositors), such creditors should be reimbursed on a pro rata basis, and creditors would each receive a percentage of their total claim. The liquidator must be certain to ensure that the claims of each class of creditor are fully met before proceeding to the next category of creditor.

Notwithstanding the above, legislation in some countries provides for preferential treatment of all depositors, or of certain categories of depositors such as households or small depositors, over other unsecured creditors. Under these schemes, depositors are reimbursed up to a certain amount before other unsecured creditors such as holders of bearer instruments or interbank credits. One benefit of such preferential treatment of depositors is that the potential for runs on the banking system is reduced. The decision on deposit preferences is a public policy choice to be reflected specifically in legislation.

If a deposit insurance scheme exists, eligible qualified depositors will be reimbursed immediately upon closure of the bank from the resources of the insurance fund. As the bank is liquidated, the insurance fund may be given preferential treatment and reimbursed up to the amount it paid to depositors. This treatment would help prevent decapitalization of the fund. Under these conditions, other uninsured creditors will be reimbursed next. As noted, shareholders should be reimbursed for their capital investment only after all other creditors have been satisfied.

Bank liquidations can take considerable time.[16] Because of this possibility, the central bank may ensure that unsecured creditors periodically receive partial payment, rather than having to wait until the entire liquidation process is completed. Partial payments should be

---

[16]Some bank liquidations have taken in excess of 10 years because of complex legal issues involved with the closure of a bank.

based on the estimated recovery value of the assets under liquidation. In most cases, for example, a significant portion of the assets of the bank can be liquidated and distributed to creditors within the first year following the bank's closure.

The role of the central bank must be carefully considered. One option is to treat the central bank like any other creditor. If its claims are collateralized, it would be immediately reimbursed. For noncollateralized claims, it would stand with all other nonsecured creditors. Alternatively, the central bank could hold a privileged position, receiving full reimbursement before other unsecured creditors. Although the second alternative may strengthen the financial position of the central bank, this procedure increases the costs to other creditors and could be viewed as unfair by other nonsecured creditors.

The use of reserves held in the central bank as collateral raises similar issues. Typically, there is no contractual or legal basis for treating reserves as loan collateral. Reserve requirements are not generally imposed to serve as a source for collateral, but rather as a monetary or prudential tool. Moreover, reserves are not related to a particular central bank loan, but are related to the deposit base of the bank. Beyond this, the prudential function of reserves would be illusory if reserves cannot be used to meet the needs of the creditors of the bank in case of liquidation. Because the use of reserves to offset central bank claims on the liquidated bank reduces proceeds for other creditors, it breaches the principle of "equality of creditors." For these reasons, central banks should not net reserves against claims of a failed bank, but rather should require other forms of collateral when lending to commercial banks.

Finally, the law should state that the central bank will not assume any responsibility in case the proceeds from the sale of assets are insufficient to meet the claims of some or all creditors. The law should also make clear whether the government will assume any such responsibility. The lowest-cost option is for the government not to be involved and to return to the creditors only the realized value of a bank's assets.

These procedures for bank liquidation—the initial stocktaking, the verification of claims and assets, asset sales, and the distribution of proceeds—must be fully supported by the legal status of the country. The status covering such steps is often found in several laws, including the law on banks, the law on the central bank, the civil code, and the bankruptcy laws. Not only must the individual laws be clear and unambiguous, they must be consistent among themselves. While the specifics of the bank resolution may differ among countries, the issues covered above need to be addressed if the resolution process is to be efficient and complete.

Appendix: Initial Steps upon Closing a Bank

The first hours of a bank closure are of particular importance. Steps must be taken immediately to secure the bank, prevent employees or shareholders from gaining unsupervised access to bank assets, and protect credit interests. The following checklist provides a guide for activities in the first day of bank liquidation:

- Take physical control over bank premises.
- Pick up keys from all employees.
- Ensure that all doors are locked.
- Count cash and cash items and then seal.
- Count travelers' checks and any liquid securities and seal.
- Seal the bank's insurance policies, board minutes, and audit accounts.
- Do not allow employees to put the vault under a time lock.
- Seal collateral, trust accounts, credit files, notes, and charged-off loans.
- Keep one person controlling access to the vault until security guards are in place or until locks and combinations have been changed.
- Call a locksmith and security guards.
- Notify the post office and change combinations and address.
- Notify utility companies.
- Notify correspondent bank accounts and follow up with a fax or telegram.
- Notify courier services.
- Check on bank property not on the premises, including cars and credit cards.
- Notify the bank's attorney. If the attorney has any documents or notes belonging to the bank, these should be returned.
- Post notices of closure on the entrance door.

References

Enoch, Charles, Gillian Garcia, and V. Sundararajan, 2001, "Recapitalizing Banks with Public Funds: Selected Issues," *IMF Staff Papers*, Vol. 48, No. 1, pp. 58–110.

Federal Deposit Insurance Corporation, 1998, *Managing the Crisis: The FDIC and RTC Experience 1980–1994* (Washington: FDIC).

Frécaut, Olivier, Kenneth Sullivan, and J.W. van der Vossen, forthcoming, "Bank Equity and Its Measurement," IMF Working Paper (Washington: International Monetary Fund).

Schiffman, Henry, 1997, "Legal Measures to Manage Bank Insolvency in Economies in Transition," paper presented at the EBRD conference on Bank Failures and Bank Insolvency in Economies in Transition, London, October.

Woo, David, 2000, Two Approaches to Resolving Nonperforming Assets During Financial Crises, IMF Working Paper No. 00/33 (Washington: International Monetary Fund).

10

Two Approaches to Resolving Nonperforming Assets During Financial Crises

DAVID WOO

The unprecedented rise in nonperforming financial assets during the recent Asian financial crisis severely tested the limit and the capacity of the existing asset management infrastructure, leading policymakers to consider new approaches to resolve them. This chapter examines two such approaches—the creation of asset management companies and the development of out-of-court centralized corporate debt workout frameworks—that came to define the core asset management setting in countries most seriously affected by the crisis. In addition to investigating their respective roles, and evaluating their strengths and weaknesses, this chapter seeks to establish some best practices as benchmarks in the design of these two approaches.

What are nonperforming financial assets? For the purposes of this discussion, nonperforming assets are defined as debt instruments whose obligors are unable to discharge their liabilities as they become due. The term debt instruments refers to both loans and bonds.

Nonperforming financial assets are typical by-products of financial crises. Rising interest rates (raising the burden of debt service), eco-

---

The author is grateful to Michael Andrews, Barbara Baldwin, Charles Enoch, Edward Frydl, Anne-Marie Gulde, Peter Hayward, Seng Chee Ho, Alain Ize, Mats Josefsson, Barry Johnston, Daniela Klingebiel, Bernard Laurens, Carl-Johan Lindgren, Elizabeth Milne, Jun Nagayasu, Charles Siegman, Mark Stone, Jan Willem van der Vossen, and Delisle Worrell for helpful comments.

nomic slowdowns (eroding the viability of borrowers), and exchange rate depreciation (increasing the liabilities of borrowers with unhedged positions in their foreign currency borrowing) can all severely undermine the capacity and sometimes the willingness of borrowers to continue servicing and to repay their debt. The financial crises of 1997 to 1999 witnessed a more than threefold increase in nonperforming assets in most Asian crisis countries. By the end of 1998, nonperforming loans as a percentage of GDP had reached 14, 27, 32, and 51 percent for Korea, Indonesia, Malaysia, and Thailand, respectively.[1]

If left unresolved, nonperforming assets can deepen the severity and the duration of financial crises and complicate macroeconomic management. They can do so by tying up resources and impeding the resource allocation process, thereby prolonging the economic stagnation accompanying financial crises.[2] In addition, they can thwart economic recovery by weakening the financial system, whose dynamic financial intermediary role is critical for the resumption of economic activities.[3] Therefore, it is imperative that effective asset management policies, designed both to contain any further deterioration of asset quality and to resolve nonperforming assets, be an integral part of financial crisis stabilization.

Two key questions confronting policymakers in the formulation of asset management policies are: (1) *where* should nonperforming assets be managed (physical depository of the assets) and (2) *how* can these assets be best resolved (i.e., the means through which the assets are dealt with)? Experience shows that answers to these questions depend on the characteristics of the assets in question, the attendant legal environment, the capacity of the market to absorb these assets, and the financial strength of the obligors and the holders of these assets.

Against the backdrop of an unprecedented rise in nonperforming assets, widespread failures in both the corporate and the financial

---

[1] To some extent the discrepancy in these numbers is likely to result from different loan classification rules in the four countries mentioned.

[2] An example would be a nonperforming loan of which the lender can eventually recover at least a portion of the value by liquidating its underlying collateral. Until liquidation is completed, the lender's funds are tied up by the loan, whereas they could be put to use by a viable borrower in the form of a new credit. The same may also be true for the collateral of a nonperforming loan (a factory, or other commercial or residential properties) which, until it is sold and reemployed in the economy, may be left idle, thus performing no useful function even as depreciation sets in.

[3] Many countries require banks facing a rise in their nonperforming assets to increase their loan-loss provision. Such provision can result in a reduction in bank capital, which in turn can limit the ability of banks to make new loans. This phenomenon (which is often exacerbated by flights to quality over concerns about the solvency of the banks in question) is sometimes referred to as a "credit crunch" (Bernanke and Lown, 1991; Woo, 1999).

sectors, and the largely underdeveloped asset markets and often inefficient legal systems, the countries most affected by the Asian crisis (Indonesia, Korea, Malaysia, and Thailand) introduced two emergency measures to address the two questions above. In many respects, these measures—the creation of asset management companies and the development of out-of-court centralized corporate debt workout frameworks—have come to define the crisis asset management setting in these countries.

Asset management companies, which are public or private entities whose main function is to take over the nonperforming assets of distressed financial institutions, are generally founded on the supposition that they can help facilitate financial restructuring and maximize the recovery of nonperforming assets at the same time. The Asian crisis saw an expansion of the traditional mandates of asset management companies, particularly with respect to the types and the number of institutions they were designed to deal with. By April 1999, government-owned asset management companies in Indonesia, Malaysia, Korea, and Thailand had taken over assets whose face value was equivalent to 20, 17, 10, and 17.5 percent of the GDP of these respective countries (Lindgren, and others, 1999). This chapter explores a survey of the roles of asset management companies in different countries (with emphasis on Asian crisis countries) and, drawing on the experience of a wide range of countries, establishes some basic guidelines in their optimal design.

The social and political repercussions of large-scale liquidations of nonperforming assets during financial crises are often of such magnitude that policymakers are reluctant to resort to them. On the other hand, rehabilitation of nonperforming assets may not only be beneficial to obligors and holders of the assets (if the latter indeed recover more than they would otherwise under liquidation),[4] it may also produce welfare gains on a wider social scale. For these reasons, policymakers in Asian crisis countries have increasingly focused their attention on debt restructuring, and to facilitate the process they have implemented out-of-court centralized debt workout frameworks. This chapter, in addition to laying out the common operational characteristics of these frameworks, will identify some practical considerations affecting their smooth functioning.

---

[4]This may be the case when debtors fall into arrears over their debt repayment mainly because of the weakness of the general economic environment rather than any inherent problem in their viability.

Definitions, Objectives, and Prerequisites

This section defines asset management policies, states their main objectives, and sets out some prerequisites for their successful implementation.

What Is Asset Management?

Broadly defined, asset management is the process whereby nonperforming assets are first identified and organized into one of four categories of action (selling, recovering, restructuring, and writing off according to their individual characteristics), and then resolved. Asset management policies are any institutional arrangements or techniques that facilitate this process.

- To *sell* a nonperforming asset, the market for such an asset must exist, and if no such market exists it must be organized. The sale of nonperforming assets facilitates diversification of risks and reallocation of resources.
- To *recover* a nonperforming asset, the holder of the asset initiates a process, often legal, by which a part or the whole of the value of the asset can be recouped through the seizure and the liquidation of its collateral or through the sale of other assets in the possession of the asset's obligor. The effective functioning of this process largely depends on the existing legal framework and procedures, the perceived working of which often will have a significant influence on market valuation of the asset and assets in general.
- To *restructure* a nonperforming asset, the holder of the asset enters into negotiation with the asset's obligor with the aim of strengthening the ability of the obligor to service and eventually to repay the principal. This usually involves redefining the terms of the original contract, a process that often entails some concessions on the part of both the holder and the obligor. Successful debt restructuring can benefit both creditors and debtors. But the process should be initiated only if the economic return from the rehabilitation of the asset exceeds that of its liquidation.
- To *write off* a nonperforming asset, the holder of the asset takes a loss equivalent to its book value[5] and removes it from the balance sheet. The holder will normally do so only when the prospect of recovery is very low and when the cost of recovery or maintenance of the asset exceeds its value.

---

[5]When the holder is a financial institution, this amounts to 100 percent provisioning.

Objectives of Asset Management Policies

Successful asset management policies are guided by well-defined objectives. The following are the most important of these objectives.

Facilitation of financial restructuring

Deterioration in the quality of financial assets can severely weaken the soundness of financial institutions (e.g., by raising questions about their solvency) and distract them from their primary function as financial intermediaries. Asset management policies should aim at restoring liquidity and solvency to financial institutions, restoring confidence in their valuation, enhancing credit discipline (by discouraging opportunistic defaults), and allowing them to resume their normal functions.

High rate of recovery

A high rate of recovery is primarily an equity objective, restoring to asset holders what is owed to them. In addition, a high rate of recovery performs a signaling function, reassuring lenders at large as to the prospects of any outstanding and new credits. A high recovery rate can thus benefit new borrowers by reducing the risk premium on the interest rates of their borrowing. Finally, where the government is committed to assume the liabilities of intervened financial institutions (e.g., under existing deposit insurance schemes), a high recovery rate of assets reduces the burden on taxpayers.

Prompt resolution

The prompt resolution of nonperforming assets, mainly an efficiency objective, accelerates the resource reallocation process vital to economic recovery. Moreover, to the extent that nonperforming assets create uncertainties over the net worth and the creditworthiness of both the holders and the obligors of these assets, a swift resolution is essential for restoring the market's ability to assess counterparty risk.

Normalization of asset markets

A large overhang of nonperforming assets can paralyze asset markets by exerting downward price pressure on all assets and by crowding out good assets from the market (adverse selection).[6] Effective asset management policies can help create market benchmarks for previously overvalued

---

[6]For example, a substantial increase in nonperforming loans may cause lending rates to rise for all borrowers if risk-averse banks do not have proper credit assessment capabilities. Worse still, asymmetric information is likely to lead to unsound and risky borrowers (who are willing to pay higher interest rates) forcing good borrowers to withdraw from the credit market (Stiglitz and Weiss, 1981).

assets (such as real estate) and at the same time prevent excessive downward pressure on assets prices (overshooting resulting from "fire sales").

Conflicts may arise among the competing objectives of asset management. For example, a high rate of recovery and swift resolution are sometimes incompatible.[7] This can also be the case between prompt resolution and normalization of asset markets. Good asset management policies should therefore recognize the trade-off between these objectives and be able to set priorities for them to preserve their effectiveness.

Some Prerequisites for Effective Asset Management Policies

Critical to the success of asset management policies is the supporting environment, whose design should be aimed at strengthening the ability of the market to carry the asset resolution process and reducing dependence on government-led initiatives. The following is an overview of what constitutes such an environment.

An effective legal system

An effective legal system should clearly define the rights of ownership as well as the legal obligations between debtors and creditors and provide for the orderly resolution of disputed claims, including debt recovery and realization of collateral for unpaid debt. This system should also balance the protection of creditors with that of debtors. Overprotection of debtors can lead to protracted resolution and breakdown in credit discipline, while overprotection of creditors can cause social strife and weaken the political support for the resolution process. An orderly and effective insolvency system, by providing a framework for efficient resolution of nonperforming assets, can help enhance credit discipline by reducing the incentive for obligors of assets to default deliberately in order to avoid repayment.

A sound financial regulatory and supervisory framework

Such a framework can help facilitate and rationalize decisionmaking in the management of nonperforming assets. For example, a good loan classification system, which allows policymakers to assess the extent of impaired assets and monitor their migration over time, is important when financial institutions' own credit assessment is unreliable and when it is in the interest of these institutions to hide the true magnitude of their impaired assets. Appropriate provisioning rules, correctly reflecting the underlying value of nonperforming assets, are necessary to prevent financial institutions, often

---

[7]On the other hand, it is also true that the quality, and thus the value, of some assets can deteriorate rapidly once they become nonperforming.

the largest holders of nonperforming assets, from holding on to these assets indefinitely, causing the market for these assets to stagnate.[8]

A neutral tax framework

A neutral tax framework can help promote both financial transactions and restructuring. For example, to facilitate the sale of nonperforming assets, financial transaction taxes[9] should be removed and, if necessary, replaced by taxes based on income generated by financial transactions (capital gains taxes). Tax deductibility of specific loan-loss provision, by inducing financial institutions to recognize voluntarily the true value of their nonperforming assets (Dziobek, 1996), can increase their willingness to resolve them more aggressively. Other tax issues are discussed in other relevant sections of this chapter.

A stable macroeconomic environment

Such an environment can restore the viability of nonperforming assets and increase their attractiveness by reducing the uncertainties associated with the investment environment. For example, exchange rate stability is often a condition for the entry of foreign buyers in domestic asset markets. Another important factor is the interest rates, which can have a crucial impact on the timing of asset resolution. High interest rates, by increasing the cost of funds, can discourage potential buyers of assets and depress asset prices (which may, in turn, increase the reluctance of sellers to part with them).[10] Low interest rates, on the other hand, by reducing the carrying cost of holding on to nonperforming assets, increase the likelihood that the holders of these assets will sit on these assets indefinitely.[11]

Asset Management Companies

This section examines the roles of asset management companies in financial restructuring and evaluates their strengths and weaknesses for

---

[8]An example could be the case of a bank that, because of weak provisioning requirements that allow it to overstate the value of its loans or collateral, appears to be in compliance with the prevailing capital adequacy requirement. Because selling its loans would force it to recognize the market value of its portfolio and thus the true value of its capital, the bank may prefer to hold on to the loans.

[9]These taxes are charged—usually irrespective of whether the transaction represents a loss or a gain for the sellers of the transaction—either on a fixed rate basis or as a percentage of the value of the transaction.

[10]At the same time, high interest rates can further erode the quality of these assets by increasing the interest burden on the obligors.

[11]Market observers have suggested that the near zero interest rates in Japan were one of the main factors for the stagnation of the Japanese real estate market in the 1990s.

the management of nonperforming assets. The section will also investigate issues pertaining to the optimal design of asset management companies, drawing lessons from—in addition to the Asian crisis countries (Indonesia, Korea, Malaysia, Thailand)—France, Mexico, Sweden, and the United States, where asset management companies have been an important feature in the context of financial restructuring.

Why Asset Management Companies?

To minimize the fiscal and perhaps the private cost associated with the restructuring of distressed financial institutions, financial restructuring programs should be aimed at maximizing the value of restructured financial institutions and that of the assets of closed financial institutions over time. To achieve these objectives, some analysts suggest that good assets of distressed financial institutions should be separated from their bad assets and that asset management companies should be set up as receptacle vehicles to take over the latter.

The typical arguments in favor of separating nonperforming from performing assets of distressed financial institutions are listed below.

Division of labor

The separation of nonperforming loans from distressed banks enables the managers of the banks to focus on rebuilding the banks and new lending, and allows managers of the asset management companies to concentrate on the recovery of the nonperforming assets of the banks. This separation can be particularly useful when the magnitude of nonperforming assets is sizable relative to the total assets of the banks.

Facilitation of valuation

Separating bad assets from distressed banks may help the market to assess more correctly the value of the banks. This could be an important consideration when the banks need to raise capital in the market.

Strengthening of credit discipline

Separating bad loans from their original credit officers may lead to more objective (and sometimes more drastic) steps in the management of these loans. By breaking any unhealthy ties between banks and their corporate borrowers, asset management companies may be better able to collect on delinquent loans (such as connected loans).

Economies of scale

When there is a scarcity of asset management expertise, centralization of assets from several financial institutions at a single or few asset management companies may increase the efficiency of asset recovery and enhance the marketability of assets for sale. Because they are able to offer relatively larger quantities of assets for sale, centralized asset management companies may attract bigger potential buyers, especially investors who prefer to deal with one seller rather than many sellers in the market. Centralization may also facilitate the securitization of assets.

Enhanced bargaining power

Centralized asset management companies, by collecting multiple claims on individual debtors, may be better positioned than single claim holders when negotiating with the debtors. This can be a particularly important consideration when credits are scattered in the system, collateral is pledged to multiple creditors, and the size and the clout of the debtors are large relative to the banks.

There are also several sets of counterarguments against the separation of good and bad assets and specifically against asset management companies.

Loss in institutional knowledge

Separating nonperforming loans from their originating banks, by weakening the knowledge base about these loans, reduces the probability of their recovery. Furthermore, lessons learned by credit officers from loan recovery and collection can strengthen their credit assessment skills and reduce the probability of recurrence of bad and lax lending.[12]

Weakening of credit discipline

Transferring loans out of banks may increase the difficulty of recovery. Borrowers are less likely to repay asset management companies; they have no ongoing relationship with these companies and they cannot rely on them for new funding.

Difficulty in pricing transferred assets

It is difficult to price nonperforming assets correctly, especially during financial crises. In the absence of market benchmarks for asset prices, sellers may transfer too many of their assets to the asset management companies which in turn may pay excessive prices for them.

---

[12]The proponents of this view often favor in-house asset management departments, which retain direct access to the existing institutional knowledge base about the assets under their management.

Political interference

It would be difficult to insulate the management of government-owned asset management companies from political interference and pressure from borrowers.

Lack of competency

Government-owned asset management companies may lack comparative advantage and expertise in the recovery of nonperforming assets. It would be faster and more efficient to build such expertise and infrastructure in banks than in these new institutions.

This list shows that while asset management companies have their advantages, they are not without drawbacks. The challenge for policymakers, therefore, is to balance the pros and cons when considering setting them up, and once a decision has been made to adopt them, to design them so as to exploit their strengths while curtailing their weaknesses. It is equally important to recognize their limitations. Empirical assessment of their effectiveness has demonstrated that the most successful ones have been those with more narrowly defined mandates (Klingebiel, 1999). In this connection, using asset management companies to recapitalize financial institutions (by purchasing nonperforming loans from these institutions at above market value)[13] is inferior to direct recapitalization, which is more transparent and provides the government with more leverage in the recapitalized institutions (IMF, 1999a).

Before the chapter turns to the issue of the optimal design of asset management companies, the following three subsections will briefly review their three principal roles in practice (Table 10.1). These roles are the facilitation of (1) the resolution of insolvent and nonviable financial institutions, (2) the restructuring of distressed but viable financial institutions, and (3) the privatization of government-owned banks and government-intervened banks.

---

[13]An example of this is the Mexican portfolio purchase program during 1995–96. The program involved the Fondo Bancario de Protección al Ahorro purchasing nonperforming loans in an amount equal to twice the private contribution to capital, including subordinated debt, made by existing and new shareholders. It purchased the loans at book value (net of provisions) with ten-year zero-coupon bonds. Although the responsibility for administering the loan portfolios remained with the selling financial institutions and there was a limited government-bank loss-sharing arrangement, the government was exposed, and still is, to potential losses arising from a further deterioration in the quality of the loans. By purchasing the nonperforming loans from banks at book value, Fondo Bancario was essentially offering the banks free capital or a subsidy. In contrast, in Indonesia assets were bought from banks at zero price with a provision that the seller could share in any upside.

Facilitate the Resolution of Insolvent and Nonviable Financial Institutions

This role is the most narrowly defined of the three principal roles of asset management companies. Their task with this role is to manage and liquidate assets of insolvent financial institutions that have been determined to be nonviable and therefore should be or have been closed. For example, the U.S. Federal Deposit Insurance Corporation (FDIC) is obliged by law to take over the assets (in addition to the liabilities) of failed banks. In its role as the "receiver," the FDIC undertakes the liquidation of the assets of these banks and issues receivership certificates to depositors with uninsured funds and to other creditors of failed institutions, entitling them to a share of the net proceeds from the liquidation.

In some cases, the liquidation of failed institutions is undertaken either by an appointed private liquidator or by a government-funded asset management company. An example of the latter is the **U.S. Resolution Trust Corporation** (RTC), which was established by the Financial Institutions Reforms, Recovery, and Enforcement Act of 1989 to resolve the U.S. savings and loans crisis. The RTC took over the assets of insolvent institutions from the FDIC, which had acted in the place of the Federal Saving and Loan Insurance Corporation (FSLIC) as conservator for these institutions. The RTC's main objective was to maximize the return and minimize the loss of the assets it took over from the failed thrifts.[14]

In East Asia, an example of a government-funded asset management company involved in the liquidation of assets of closed banks is the **Korea Asset Management Corporation** (KAMCO).[15] In 1998, the Financial Supervisory Commission of Korea engineered the takeover of five insolvent banks by five healthy banks[16] under purchase and assumption arrangements. The acquiring banks assumed selected assets and liabilities to the exclusion of nonperforming assets of the acquired banks. The deal required that KAMCO take over the nonperforming assets of the acquired banks and, as an additional incentive to the acquiring banks, the nonperforming loans of the latter.

---

[14]The RTC's other missions were to: (1) minimize the impact of its activities on local real estate and financial markets, and (2) maximize the preservation of the availability and affordability of residential property for low- and moderate-income individuals.

[15]As will be discussed later, KAMCO's mandate is wider than that of a liquidator of closed banks.

[16]The five insolvent banks are Dongnam, Ching Chong, Dong Hwa, Kyungki, and Dae Dong, and the five healthy banks are Kookminm, Shinhan, Koram, Housing and Commercial, and Hana Bank.

Table 10.1. Main Characteristics of Representative Asset Management Companies (AMCs) in Asian Crisis Countries

AMC	Type	Purchase or Take Over Assets From	Funding
Korea Asset Management Corporation (KAMCO)	Centralized AMC	Banks and nonbank financial institutions.	Contribution from financial institutions; borrowing from Korea Development Bank and KAMCO's government guaranteed bond issues.
Danaharta, Malaysia	Centralized AMC	Bank, finance companies, and merchant banks, according to relative strength of institutions.	Government contribution; loans from Khazanah; zero coupon government guaranteed Danaharta bonds. For Sime Banking Group, separate government funding.
Indonesia Bank Restructuring Agency (IBRA)	Centralized AMC	Recapitalized banks and closed banks. Took over assets from former shareholders of failed banks.	Most of its funding comes from liquidation of its holdings of assets.
Thai Asset Management Corp. (TAMC)	Centralized AMC	Purchased assets from auctions of closed finance companies.	Initial capital from government. Borrowing from domestic and international sources not exceeding 12 time of the capital fund.
Radanasin	Decentralized AMC	Radanasin Bank	Financial Institution Development Fund (FIDF).
Nakornthon	Covered asset pool	Nakornthon Bank	FIDF.

Sources: KAMCO, Danaharta, TAMC, IMF staff.
[1]Recovery proceeds net of Danaharta's commission accrue to the government.

Criteria for Asset Purchase or Transfer	Purchase or Transfer Price	Pays With	Asset Disposition
Ordinary NPL: loans in default for 3 months or longer. Special NPL: loans that have obtained court approval for restructuring as part of corporate reorganization.	Ordinary NPL: 45 percent of appraisal value of collateral minus senior lien amount; Special NPL: present value of discounted projected cash flows. Unsecured loans: 3 percent of face value.	70 percent in KAMCO bonds and 30 percent in cash.	Foreclosure auctions; public sale; outright sale; equity partnership securitization.
NPLs over RM 5 million at market value. For Sime Banking Group and BBMB Group, NPLs over RM 1 million.	Secured loans: value of collateral; unsecured loans: 10 percent of principal. Surplus on recovery shared with sellers on a 20/80 basis. Acquired NPLs of Sime Banking Group at book value.[1]	Zero coupon Danaharta bonds.	Private auctions; public tenders; securitization.
Loss loans of recapitalized banks and assets of closed banks.	Buys at zero value.		Cash collection; Initial public offerings; auction.
All assets that fail to sell in the second round of auction of assets of closed finance companies. Bad assets from institutions taken over by FIDF.	Market value calculated based on collateral appraisal, and evaluation of the financial conditions of the debtors and guarantors.		
Assets rejected by United Overseas Bank.	Transfer at book value.	Note issued by the AMC (backed by the FIDF).	
Assets rejected by Standard Chartered.	Transfer at book value.	Assets stay on the balance sheet of the new bank. They are, however, guaranteed by FIDC.	

The terms of agreement between the government and the acquiring banks also allowed the acquiring banks to sell back to KAMCO any loan from acquired banks' portfolios that became nonperforming within six months of acquisition, and required the Korean Deposit Insurance Corporation to cover the loss.[17]

The **Thai Financial Sector Restructuring Agency** (FRA), a de facto asset management company, was set up in 1997 to deal with suspended finance companies. After the closure of 56 finance companies, the FRA took over their assets with the aim of preserving their value before their disposition. The FRA subsequently organized and held public auctions of these assets.

Sometimes the scope of this type of asset management company goes beyond liquidating closed financial institutions. The government may have reasons to choose to keep a financial institution open even after it has been decided the institution will eventually be closed. In such situations, these asset management companies may take on the role of "conservator." For example, the RTC was given conservatorship power when there were delays in obtaining funding to close the failed thrifts in the1980s. As conservator, the RTC took control of the failed thrifts and operated them according to specified guidelines, with the goal of preserving their value and preparing them for resolution.

Facilitate the Restructuring of Distressed But Viable Financial Institutions

The handling of nonperforming assets sometimes requires skills that distressed banks lack (Berggren, 1996). When this is the case, it may be optimal to separate a distressed bank from the management of its nonperforming loans by creating a "bad bank"—either a division, or a subsidiary of the bank, or an independent entity outside the bank—to which the nonperforming assets of the bank are transferred. To maximize the operational gains from this separation, usually the bad bank is operationally, financially, and legally isolated from the bank. When the bad bank, or asset management company, is an independent entity outside the bank, it can be designed to manage exclusively the nonperforming assets of the bank, or to manage those of several banks.

An example of an asset management company designed to take over nonperforming assets of a single bank is the **Swedish Securum**. In 1992, suffering from severe capital deficiency following substantial

---

[17]This put option is useful when the government wants to sell more of the borderline loans of an insolvent financial institution or when the uncertainties of the economy obscure the prospect of the quality of the bank loan portfolio.

credit losses, Nordbanken, a major Swedish commercial bank, was bought out by the Swedish government.[18] In addition to its equity contribution to the bank, the government extended a guarantee to Securum, which was at the time an asset management subsidiary of Nordbanken. Later, with additional funding from the state, Securum took over from Nordbanken about 3,000 loans (most of which were collateralized by real estate). The equity invested in Securum allowed it to cover the cost of further write-downs of assets taken over from Nordbanken and to manage the divestment of the loans. At the end of 1992, Securum was formally separated from Nordbanken and became an independent company owned by the state.

Examples of centralized asset management companies designed to take over nonperforming assets from more than one financial institution include KAMCO and the **Malaysian Danaharta**. Danaharta was created in 1998 in part to allow financial institutions to "focus on their core business of lending" to "assist in revitalizing the real economy." In principle, all financial institutions are eligible to sell nonperforming assets to Danaharta, although Danaharta focuses its loan purchase program on those institutions with the highest level of nonperforming assets and loans to priority sectors, such as manufacturing and construction. Another important difference between Securum, Danaharta, and KAMCO is that the latter two, in addition to taking over nonperforming loans from government-owned banks, also bought nonperforming loans from operating private banks.

Like Danaharta and KAMCO, the Asset Management Unit of the **Indonesian Bank Restructuring Agency** (IBRA) is designed to facilitate both the resolution of closed financial institutions and the restructuring of ongoing ones. In this capacity, the unit took over the entire loan portfolio of closed banks, as well as loss loans from state-owned banks and banks the government helped recapitalize. These loans were transferred to the unit at zero value. In addition, the Asset Management Investment Division of IBRA took over the assets of the former shareholders of closed banks,[19] which it controls through a holding company structure.

Private banks can also set up their own asset management companies to help facilitate their restructuring. A number of Thai private banks established asset management company subsidiaries to take over some of their nonperforming assets. For instance, **Thai Farmers Bank** has created an asset management company for the management of the

---

[18]About 70 percent of Nordbanken was already owned by the government when the problems surfaced.

[19]A shareholder settlement agreement was reached in 1998 that requires former owners of failed banks to repay the government Rp 110 trillion.

assets from its failed finance company, Phatra Thanakit, and established one for the management of selected nonperforming loans from the bank itself (contracts have been signed with GE Capital and Goldman Sachs to manage the company).

Cinda Asset Management Company was established in April 1999 by the Chinese authorities to take over the nonperforming assets of China Construction Bank, one of four distressed state-owned banks whose main activity was and is the financing of state-owned enterprises. Cinda and three more asset management companies that are being set up for the four state-owned banks are expected to take the leading role in the restructuring of distressed state-owned enterprises.

Facilitate the Privatization of Government-Owned Banks and Government-Intervened Banks

Asset management companies have been used to facilitate the privatization of government-owned banks and intervened banks whose liabilities are guaranteed by the government. One example of the former is the **French Consortium de Realization**, created as a subsidiary of Credit Lyonnais in 1995 to take over nonperforming assets from the bank before its privatization in 1999.

It has been often argued that the most suitable manager for the nonperforming assets of a government-owned or -intervened bank is the eventual buyer of the bank. This is because, on the one hand, the new owner will inherit the institutional knowledge about these assets in the former bank and, on the other, the government often lacks expertise to manage these assets. In a recent agreement between the United Overseas Bank (UOB) of Singapore and the Financial Institutions Development Fund (FIDF) of Thailand for the sale of **Radanasin Bank** to UOB, it was agreed that the impaired assets of Radanasin were to be transferred into an asset management company owned by the FIDF but managed under contract by UOB. The removal of the nonperforming assets from Radanasin was financed by a note issued by the asset management company (backed by the FIDF) to Radanasin paying 1 percent less than the prevailing weighted average six-month deposit rate at the four largest banks. The gain/loss-sharing arrangement was designed in such a way that 5 percent of any excess recovery over the estimated fair market value of the assets and 15 percent of any loss went to Radanasin and the remainder to FIDF.

A similar transaction was the sale of the **Thai Nakornthon Bank** to Standard Chartered. Although the impaired assets of Nakornthon were to remain on the bank's balance sheet, these assets were guaranteed by the FIDF so that the bank did not need to set aside any capital against them.

Standard Chartered managed the "covered asset pool" under a gain/loss-sharing arrangement similar to that in the Radanasin deal,[20] which sought to create incentives for the bank to expedite asset resolution.

To stabilize the price floor at public auctions of assets seized from closed finance companies (and thus minimize the cost to the government for assuming partial liabilities of these companies), the **Thai Asset Management Corporation** (TAMC) was created to assume the role of "bidder of last resort." Although it did not participate in the first round of bidding, it behaved like a "sweeper" in the second round. Thereafter, the TAMC managed the assets with the view to maximize the recovery rate of these assets.

Optimal Design of Asset Management Companies

This section discusses the optimal design of asset management companies—the focus being on the most critical aspects of their institutional and operational features.

Legal basis

The legal basis of an asset management company is critical to its success. One issue of particular importance concerns the transfer of assets. The legal basis should provide for clear transfers of titles and priority in the transactions of assets. For example, the Danaharta Act allows Danaharta and the selling bank to effect the acquisition by way of statutory vesting that allows the transfer of priority from the selling bank to Danaharta.[21]

Similarly, legal obstacles for the transfers of assets, such as the requirement that the permission of the debtors be obtained before the transfer of loans can be effected, should be removed. Asset disposition by state-owned asset management companies may be retarded by perceived potential political and legal liabilities to their management (who could be accused, for example, of selling the assets too cheaply). When this is a problem, legal protection for the employees of the asset management companies in the execution of their responsibility in good faith should be considered.

---

[20]The difference is that instead of the asymmetric gain/loss-sharing arrangement of the Radanasin sale, a symmetric arrangement was agreed upon. Specifically, Nakornthon received 15 percent of any upside and has been responsible for 15 percent of any downside from asset recovery relative to the agreed-upon estimated market value of the assets.

[21]On completion of the acquisition, Danaharta issued vesting certificates to evidence the acquisition. The vesting certificates will then be accepted for the purpose of registration. For example, upon producing the vesting certificate, the Registrar of Land will record Danaharta's interest as the new chargee in place of the selling bank.

Regulatory framework

Consolidated supervision is necessary to prevent private financial institutions from using their asset management company subsidiaries as a means to boost their capital positions artificially by transferring their assets to the management company at too high a price. For this purpose, the Bank of Thailand issued a regulation requiring any financial institution holding a 50 percent or more equity interest in an asset management company, either directly or indirectly, to include the assets and liabilities of its asset management company subsidiaries in the calculation of its capital-to-risk-weighted-assets ratio. The regulation also requires these institutions to prepare consolidated financial statements for each calendar quarter and at the end of each accounting period.

Centralized versus decentralized approach

The Asian crisis saw two distinct approaches to the structure of asset management companies. In Indonesia, Korea, and Malaysia, centralized asset management companies were set up to serve all or some distressed financial institutions, while China established separate companies for individual distressed financial institutions; Thailand used both approaches. Although there are no clear-cut rules as to the superiority of the centralized versus the decentralized approach and it is too early to evaluate the relative effectiveness of these two approaches, each has its advantages and disadvantages. While the economies of scale and enhanced bargaining power arguments favor the centralized approach, the decentralized approach allows asset management companies to tap into the knowledge base associated with the loans and assets transferred to them from the originating institutions. Moreover, the decentralized approach, by allowing more tailoring of the management companies to the specific characteristics of assets from different financial institutions, may provide more flexibility in the management of the assets. There may even be some rationale to group assets by types and to transfer them accordingly to asset management companies specializing in the management of a particular type or types of assets.

Governance

Good governance is necessary to safeguard the effective operation of asset management companies, especially when they are government-owned. For this purpose, an asset management company should have a board of directors, with at least most of its members appointed from outside the organization. Because often the principal characteristics of government-funded asset management companies are that they are themselves under liquidation (many such companies have a termination point), and since the more successful they are, the sooner the employees will lose their jobs, their boards need to counterbalance whatever incentives the employees may have to prolong the life of the companies unnecessarily (Berggren, 1996). These boards should be also sufficiently independent so as to resist political interference and pressure from borrowers.

Especially because of the often large sums of public money involved, the operations of government-owned asset management companies should be transparent. Transparency promotes accountability of the managers and the boards vis-à-vis the public and reduces the possibility for corruption. In particular, the companies should be audited regularly to ensure that the prices at which they purchase assets reflect market prices (auditors can focus on the process used to approximate the value of these assets). The audits should be undertaken by independent auditors. The companies should also be required to publish regular reports describing their performance in pursuing their objectives. The reports should contain their balance sheets, income statements, and records of their transactions.

Selection of asset transferred

When government-owned asset management companies have some discretion in the choice of assets to purchase or take over, they should apply strict criteria in the selection of the assets. In principle, they should take on only those assets they are likely to manage more effectively. Good candidates for such transfers to them might include fixed assets, such as foreclosed properties, and loans that require foreclosure or settlement with debtors. On the other hand, loans with potential for restructuring and those whose obligors are customers with which the banks would like to maintain long-term relationships should be kept within the banks. Small credits, whose recovery can be undertaken more efficiently by the bank branches where the credit originated, should also be left with the banks. If possible, asset management companies should transfer all the assets that are linked to each other (such as loans to the same debtors or loans linked to the same collateral) to achieve economies of scale.

Asset transfer pricing

The transfer of assets to the asset management companies, regardless of the methods of transfer, should be executed at fair market value. There are a number of reasons for doing so. First, as pointed out earlier, private asset management companies set up as subsidiaries of banks should not serve as a means by which the banks boost their capital by transferring their nonperforming assets at above market value to the management companies. This consideration can be especially important when the companies are established as limited liability companies and are allowed to borrow directly from the market. At least in theory, such companies can go bankrupt with the banks losing only their initial equity investment in them.

Second, asset management companies should not serve as a means by which the government bails out private financial institutions by buying their nonperforming assets at above market value. When that happens, financial institutions may end up selling to asset management companies an overly large number of their nonperforming assets.

Third, transferring assets to government-owned asset management companies at fair market value provides asset managers of the companies with a clear opportunity to realize the goal of returning some of the original equity capital to the government (Ingves and Lind, 1997). Thus, even in the case of a government takeover of nonperforming assets from failed banks or distressed state-owned banks, the transfer of assets to management companies should be at market value, with the government absorbing losses up-front. This is because the value of financial restructuring should be reflected as soon as possible, and asset management companies should not be allowed to become a window dressing operation for the cost of this restructuring.

While it is often difficult to price nonperforming assets (especially in the midst of financial crises), an approximation of their value, based on the probability of recovery, cash flow projection (with appropriate discount rate applied), and appraisal of collateral, should be carried out and used for the purpose of the transfer. When timing is an issue and a great number of assets are involved, the transfer can take place at an initial price, with the explicit agreement that the final price of the transaction be established after the value of the assets has been estimated or the assets have been sold. The drawback of this approach is that it may reduce the willingness of the sellers to part with the assets because they will still maintain their exposure to the final price of the assets. In this situation, some form of profit/loss-sharing arrangement can help to overcome some of this problem.

The task of having to price a large number of assets has sometimes led to attempts to simplify and standardize the pricing process. Excess simplification can result in adverse selection. For example, a system in which a uniform price is applied to unsecured loans in the same loan classification categories could cause the sellers to select for sale only the most inferior loans in each class.

Other aspects of the transfer process

When the purchase of assets by asset management companies is designed to support distressed but operating banks, it should be made clear that the purchase is a one-time deal, not to be repeated. An open-ended transfer arrangement could create moral hazard problems, undermining the credit discipline of the banks.

A crucial aspect of the transfer process relates to the relocation of asset files, especially when the number of assets taken over by the asset management company is large. When management companies have some discretion in the selection of assets they take over, they should reject any assets that are not accompanied by proper documentation. Documentation, including specific details about loans and borrowers, internal evaluation of loans, business plans, and collateral, is essential to the recovery process. The development of an internal information inventory system that will allow asset managers to manage the assets in their possession effectively is a critical part of the initial stages of the transfer process.

Finally, to effect successful sales of the assets, buyers need to be assured that nobody else has a claim on the assets. Asset management companies therefore should undertake due diligence before the transfer of assets to determine any prior claims and contingent claims.

Funding

It is important that public asset management companies be sufficiently funded to perform their intended functions. They should also be subject to hard budget constraints. Striking the right balance is a key consideration of the funding process. To achieve transparency, the operating budget of the company should be separate from its funding for asset takeover.

Funding for government-owned asset management companies, especially when it involves a very large sum of money, often cannot come directly from the budget. In these cases, funding could either come from the proceeds of government bond issues or be raised by the company's own bond issues backed by the government, with the proviso that whenever the company realizes losses, the losses will be directly absorbed by the budget. Although the latter expedient is sometimes preferred because it is more transparent, in countries where the government bond market is small, it is important that the bonds issued by the management companies do not lead to a segmentation in the secondary markets for government and government-backed bonds. To avoid that situation, bonds issued by the management companies should carry the same characteristics as existing government bonds, and any issues should be closely coordinated with other government bond issues. When the financing needs of the management companies are large, representatives of the company could usefully take part in the government debt management committee.

To facilitate the purchase of foreign exchange–denominated assets, government-funded asset management companies should be given access to the foreign exchange market. But to minimize their exposure to foreign exchange risk, the companies ideally should finance the purchase of foreign exchange–denominated assets by issuing foreign currency-denominated bonds (or domestic currency-denominated bonds and a currency swap) rather than by purchasing foreign exchange in the market.

Asset management and disposition

Concerning operations once asset management companies have taken over the transferred assets, the assets should be sorted into different groupings to facilitate resolution. Two teams (an asset team and a credit team) should be set up to specialize in the management of physical assets and credits. The credit team should then determine whether to maintain the credits. Once a decision has been made to do so, the team will determine whether to reschedule payments, undertake debt/equity swaps, restructure the loan and sell it back to banks, or repackage the loan for sale. Otherwise, the credit team will recommend seizing the collateral attached to the credit and turning over the case to the asset team.

Effective asset management requires a well-defined strategy for asset disposition. To maximize the rate of recovery, the decision by the asset management company to dispose of an asset generally should be based on market conditions, as well as the funding cost of the companies. Sometimes it might be in the interest of the company to invest in the improvement of the physical assets in its holdings (e.g., finishing an uncompleted building project or securing income for its holdings of fixed assets) to maximize the sale price of the assets. The general rule of thumb is to dispose of the assets as soon as they can no longer be improved upon, taking into account the carrying cost of the assets. This would suggest that the first assets to be disposed of should be those with the highest rate of depreciation.

At times the value maximization strategy of government-owned asset management companies may be constrained by the need to help stabilize asset markets. For example, to prevent disposition from causing a substantial decline in asset prices that are already depressed (because, for example, the volume of assets is above the capacity of markets to absorb even in normal times) a company may delay disposing of its holdings of assets. At least in theory, however, the warehousing of assets (to avoid "fire sale") may not prevent prices from tumbling, because the future supply of assets will likely be discounted in current prices.

At other times, the need to catalyze activities in stagnant markets may lead government-owned asset management companies to dispose of some assets quickly, even though by postponing the disposition they might obtain better prices. By ensuring an ample supply of assets in the market, setting a price floor, and stabilizing market expectation, these companies can actually set the tone for an orderly sale of assets.[22]

There are many techniques for the disposition of assets (auctions, bulk sale, securitization of assets, and so on). Some are more suitable for the disposition of certain types of assets than others. For example, bulk sale is effective for bundling less attractive assets with attractive ones; securitization is useful to dispose of a large group of assets with similar characteristics where markets for such securities exist. The Appendix examines various techniques for the disposition of large groups of assets.

Another issue is whether asset management companies should sell their holdings of nonperforming assets to the obligors of the assets. The advantage in this type of transaction is that generally debtors are willing to pay more to buy back their loans and the underlying collateral than anyone else (when, for example, the collateral is employed by the debtors). The disadvantage is that it may undermine credit discipline and cause obligors of performing assets to default deliberately in order to negotiate better deals with their creditors. In any case, the sale of nonperforming loans to the obligors of the loans often cannot be avoided, even when obligors are not allowed to buy these loans directly from the sellers. In Thailand, for example, several U.S. investment banks bought assets at auctions of the assets of closed finance companies with the intention of reselling these assets to the obligors. To curtail the shortcomings of selling assets to their original owners, transparency to ensure equity and fairness, and mechanisms for creditors to establish all the resources at the disposal of the debtors (e.g., credit bureaus), can be very important elements.

Incentive structure

A proper incentive system is critical for asset management companies (especially government-owned ones) to maximize the recovery of the assets under their management. The system may involve bonuses directly tied to the performance of the management or another

---

[22]Asset markets are vulnerable to failure during financial crises because of market participants' uncertainties about the future and the perceived lack of information in asset prices. The uncertainties may arise from the belief that prices do not reflect the fundamental value of assets but that they may reflect, for example, only the liquidity condition of the sellers.

acquiring institution in the recovery of assets based on an established benchmark. The gain/loss-sharing schemes of both the Radanasin and Nakorthon Bank deals are good examples of how incentive schemes can be designed. The Appendix discusses the incentive structure of an equity partnership arrangement.

Legal power

Sometimes asset management companies can be vested with extraordinary legal power to facilitate the asset resolution process. This can occur either when the existing legal system is not equipped to deal with the magnitude of the nonperforming assets and endeavors to reform the system would be overly time-consuming, or when the authorities want to restrict certain legal powers of creditors to just the management companies. For example, in Malaysia, the Pengurusan Danaharta National Nerhad Act of 1998 confers on Danaharta the power to appoint special administrators to manage the affairs of distressed companies. More precisely, when a corporate borrower is unable to service its debt, Danaharta has the right to appoint a special administrator (with the approval of an oversight committee) to take over the control and management of the assets and affairs of the borrower. The administrator's role is to prepare a workout proposal that will be implemented after it is approved by the oversight committee and has obtained the support of the majority of creditors.[23] This legal power allows Danaharta to take the initiative as a catalyzer for the corporate debt restructuring process. It was judged that if the process were left entirely up to negotiations between creditors and debtors, it would be very time-consuming, in part because of their lack of expertise in debt restructuring.

Lending capabilities

Given that the separation of nonperforming assets from their originating banks is often intended to achieve a division of labor, asset management companies—which are not banks—should not engage in normal banking operations, especially in making new loans. In fact, prohibiting management company subsidiaries of banks from extending new credits will likely lead parent banks to retain those nonperforming assets that they themselves can most effectively manage (e.g., restructurable loans whose obligors are inherently viable).

---

[23]To preserve the assets of the borrowers, a 12-month moratorium takes effect with the appointment of the special administrator. During this time, creditors are not allowed to take actions against the borrower.

Tax issues

Tax neutrality should be in place so as not to create any disincentive for financial institutions to transfer their assets to their asset management company subsidiaries. For example, there should be no taxation on the sale or transfer of assets between different management companies or for assets sold back to the parent financial institutions. Also, any tax deductibility for loan-loss provisioning should be extended from the parent institutions to the management companies. Gains and losses on asset sales between the parents and the subsidiaries should be consolidated for tax purpose.

Out-of-Court Centralized Corporate Debt Restructuring

This section outlines the corporate debt workout process and identifies important practical considerations. In most countries, when a debtor has failed to meet its liabilities as they become due, the insolvency system provides the creditors (and sometimes the debtor) with the option to initiate either liquidation or rehabilitation procedures. Creditors often opt for rehabilitation when the restructuring of the operations (company reorganization, downsizing, and so on) or of the balance sheets of the debtor will enable them to recover more than they would expect through liquidation. Rehabilitation may also serve a broader social interest, by, for example, granting the debtor a second chance as well as protecting the jobs of the employees of the debtor (IMF, 1999a). Table 10.2 summarizes design aspects of effective asset management companies.

There are generally three different approaches to the rehabilitation of corporate debt: (1) court-supervised company reorganization or liquidation,[24] (2) restructuring based on out-of-court negotiation between individual creditors and debtors, and (3) restructuring based on out-of-court negotiation in a centralized framework with established procedures and principles (Kawai, 1998). The last two approaches are also often called "voluntary workout." Given that the first approach is generally considered too time-consuming during financial crises (especially when the legal infrastructure is poor and there are large numbers of cases), the last two approaches are often preferred by both creditors and debtors under these circumstances.

For the second approach to be effective, lead creditors, usually the banks with the largest outstanding credit to the debtors, must be willing and able to play pivotal roles in leading negotiations and monitoring the

---

[24]For example, Chapter 11 in the United States.

Table 10.2. Summary of Design Aspects of Effective Asset Management Companies

Legal basis	Provide for clear transfer of titles and priority in the transactions of assets; remove requirement of permission from debtors before asset transfers. Provide legal protection to employees and management of public asset management companies in the exercise of their responsibilities in good faith.
Regulatory framework	Consolidated supervision prevents financial institutions from using their asset management company subsidiaries as a means to artificially boost their capital positions.
Governance	Asset management company's board needs to counterbalance the incentives of its employees to unnecessarily prolong the life of the company, and to resist political interference and pressure from borrowers. Transparency is important to promote accountability.
Selection of assets transferred	Large assets, fixed assets, and loans requiring foreclosure are good candidates for transfer to asset management company. Restructurable loans and loans whose obligors banks would like to maintain a long-term relationship should be kept with the bank.
Asset transfer pricing	Transfer of assets should reflect market prices. Pricing of assets should be based on probability of recovery, cash flow analysis, and appraisal of underlying collateral.
Funding	Sufficient funding but hard budget constraint are required. The operating budget should be separated from takeover funding.
Incentive structure	An incentive structure, including gain/loss-sharing arrangements and bonuses tied to the recovery rate, rationalizes management of nonperforming assets and maximizes recovery.
Asset disposition	A decision on asset disposition should be based on market conditions as well as the funding cost of the asset management company, consistent with the objective of achieving maximum recovery rate.
Legal power	Asset management companies vested with extraordinary legal power can help facilitate the asset resolution process, especially in the corporate debt restructuring process.
Lending	Asset management companies should not be allowed to engage in lending. Such restriction can help optimize the division of assets between financial institutions and management companies.
Tax issue	Tax neutrality is important for not creating disincentive for banks to transfer assets to their asset management company subsidiaries.

agreed restructuring. In Japan, the "main bank" system lends itself to this type of arrangement. This may not be the case elsewhere, especially in systems where there are many creditors with competing interests and the larger creditors lack clout with other creditors. In these systems, the third approach, notwithstanding the problems associated with it, may be appropriate—and sometimes may be unavoidable in a full-blown financial crisis with a substantial increase in delinquent debt. The starting point of this approach is a more active involvement of a disinterested third party, an "honest broker," a function that can be assumed by the government or the central bank, whose role is to coordinate among the creditors to help reach a solution beneficial for all parties. The remainder of this section focuses on the design of the centralized debt workout framework.

The Workout Intermediary

The most famous of the centralized out-of-court workout methodologies is the "London Approach," named after an informal framework[25] developed by the Bank of England during the recession in the early 1990s to help steer corporate workouts in the United Kingdom. This framework has been the basis for the development of similar frameworks in Korea, in Thailand (also called the Bangkok Approach), in Indonesia (the Jakarta Initiative), and in Malaysia, despite very important departures in each of these new frameworks from the original London Approach.

The London Approach is a framework that is "flexible and adaptable and rests entirely on a voluntary acceptance by the banking community" (Kent, 1997). This means that the workout intermediary (the Bank of England) tries to keep its intervention to a minimum and restricts its role to one of "suasion." For example, the Bank of England does not comment on its role in individual cases, and it expresses its views on the developments of the workout process through speeches rather than formal policy documents.

In East Asia, where the London Approach has been adapted, the role of the government intermediary is more active than in the United Kingdom. The framework is also more formalized. In Korea, under the Corporate Restructuring Accord (CRA),[26] a steering committee, consisting of representatives from participating financial institutions, is responsible for

---

[25]Because of the objection of foreign banks involved in workouts in the United Kingdom that formalizing such a framework would invite legal challenges, and perhaps scrutiny from their national supervisors, the Bank of England decided against formalizing the workout framework in a written document (Kent, 1997).

[26]The steering committee is backed by the Financial Supervisory Commission, which is in charge of financial restructuring and supervision.

implementing, amending, and terminating the CRA. The steering committee appointed the Corporate Restructuring Committee, an arbitration committee responsible for assessing the viability of corporate candidates for restructuring, arbitrating differences among creditors, enforcing the CRA's decisions, and modifying workout plans proposed by participating creditors if necessary (Liberman and Mako, 1999). In Indonesia, the Jakarta Initiative Task Force (JITF) is involved in the design of restructuring plans and negotiations between creditors and debtors. The JITF is also authorized to recommend that the Public Prosecutor file bankruptcy proceedings against recalcitrant debtors (IMF, 1999b). Similar bodies were set up in Thailand (Corporate Debt Restructuring Advisory Committee) and in Malaysia (Corporate Debt Restructuring Committee) to oversee the voluntary corporate debt workout.

There are no clear-cut rules as to which government agencies should take on the role of the workout intermediary. Often the central bank comes across as being a more disinterested party and therefore commands more credibility in the market. Potential conflicts of interest may arise if the central bank (or other workout intermediary) is also the bank supervisor. For this reason, the department of the Bank of England involved in the corporate workout was set up to be completely separate from the banking supervision department.

General Principles of Government-Led Workout

The main elements of the London Approach (Kent, 1997) are:
- Banks should remain supportive on hearing that a company with which they have a lending arrangement is in financial difficulty. In practice, this means that banks keep their facilities in place and do not appoint receivers.
- Decisions about a company's longer-term future should be made only on the basis of comprehensive information, which is shared among all the banks and other parties to a workout.
- Banks should work together to reach a collective view on whether and on what terms a company should be given a financial lifeline.
- The seniority of claims continues to be recognized, but there has to be an element of "shared-pain"—equal treatment for all creditors of a single category.

Design of the Framework

Stage 1: Consensus on rules and procedures

A successful workout requires endorsement of the basic rules and procedures from all creditors, because the actions of creditors who refuse to participate in the workout can derail the entire workout process. For example, the workout of distressed firms typically requires creditors of the firms to suspend temporarily their demand for repayment—a so-called debt "standstill"—but if some creditors refuse to abide by the decision of the workout group and initiate foreclosure procedures, this will greatly undermine the willingness of the other creditors to continue the workout. Once consensus on the rules and procedures has been reached, compliance with the agreed-upon system becomes important. Because workouts generally do not have a legal basis, the enforcement of compliance with the rules of the workout will require clout and moral suasion on the part of the intermediary and the lead banks.

The most important workout rule is the voting power of minority creditors. While a unanimity requirement for decisions protects their interests, it allots them disproportionate power. Country experience on this practice differs widely. In the United Kingdom, for example, unanimity is the prevailing practice—allowing all creditors equal voting rights—while in Indonesia and Korea workout decisions require approval by financial institution creditors holding at least 75 percent of the credits of the debtors. In Korea, penalties regarding compliance are also explicitly built into the workout rules. For example, if a CRA signatory fails to comply with an approved workout agreement or a Corporate Restructuring Committee arbitration decision, the committee may fine this signatory up to 30 percent of the credit amount in question or up to 50 percent of the cost of noncompliance (Liberman and Mako, 1999).

Stage 2: Identification of workout candidates and appointment of lead banks

Stage 2 begins with the identification of workout candidates by the banks. This requires the banks to perform an evaluation of the viability of their distressed debtors, at which point they rank these debtors according to their conditions and their ability to return to profitability. The banks then select the workout candidates from these debtors. Ideal candidates should be companies whose difficulties are temporary in nature and whose problems are related to liquidity rather than solvency. In fact, the banks should be discouraged from going into workout with companies that are insolvent.

Once the workout candidates have been identified and agreed upon by the banks, a lead bank for each candidate, which is usually the largest creditor for the candidate, needs to be identified and appointed. This bank (or another large nonbank creditor) will assume responsibility to actively manage and coordinate the workout process according to the objectives and deadlines set out by the workout committee.

The lead bank will also take a leading role in negotiating with the debtors. Once the choice of workout candidates has been agreed upon by all parties concerned, the debt standstill will go into effect. It is important that new credit extended to the debtors during the standstill (to allow continuing operations of the debtors) receive senior status.

Stage 3: Negotiations

The next stage of the workout process involves negotiations among the creditors and subsequently between the creditors and the debtors. The object of these negotiations is to arrive at an agreed upon workout plan (a memorandum of understanding) that specifies the terms of the workout. Generally speaking, the terms that directly affect the creditors may include a debt/equity swap, the reduction of loan principal or interest, an extension of the term of the loan, or the provision of new credits. Terms that require actions on the part of the debtors may include sales of noncore business, new equity issues, downsizing/layoffs, and other restructuring steps.

At this stage of the process, the role of the workout intermediary should be more passive than active—allowing the ground rules established at the outset (stage 1) to guide the negotiations and acting only in an advisory capacity. The workout intermediary should encourage the creditors and the debtors to reach mutually beneficial solutions, and only when required should it arbitrate over their differences—and in a fair manner. The object of the workout is *not* financial engineering or an effort designed to bail out the debtors.

The time it takes to reach a debt restructuring settlement can vary from case to case. To accelerate the process, countries may provide tax relief for settlements completed by a certain deadline. Alternatively, penalties can be imposed on creditors and debtors for failing to reach settlement by the deadline. Another way to accelerate the process is by imposing an deadline for individual cases. For example, in Thailand, creditors and debtors are required to complete their negotiation in 90 days. Precautions should be taken, though, to ensure that the deadline is not too tight. When it is, it can backfire and lead to sub-optimal decisions.

Stage 4: Implementation

The fourth stage of the workout process involves creditors and the debtors implementing their agreements. An important aspect of this stage is the monitoring of the implementation of the plans, especially the progress in company restructuring. For this purpose, the banks may choose to install their own staff at the firms subject to restructuring, because the concessions made by the banks are contingent on the firms' reaching the benchmarks set forth in memorandums of understanding. If these benchmarks are missed, the banks need to reevaluate their options. The results of the revaluation may cause them to suspend the workout process and initiate liquidation, or to return to the negotiation stage.

Practical Considerations

Bank restructuring

To reach meaningful and credible corporate debt restructuring settlements, creditors must be able to negotiate from a position of strength. When banks are undercapitalized and weak (and therefore do not want to recognize the true value of their nonperforming loans), they are generally reluctant to go into restructuring negotiations, especially when the final settlement agreement might require them to absorb losses for which they do not have the capacity. Even when weak banks do take part in workouts, they may do so only to buy time, often with the results that the restructuring is mostly cosmetic (such as rescheduling of payments). To spur corporate restructuring, some policymakers have recently called for an enhanced approach to bank restructuring, including "greater capital infusion from the public and private sector to weak banks" (Financial Markets Development Committee of the Pacific Economic Cooperation Council, 1999).

Provisioning and loan classification rules

Lax loan classification and provisioning rules can discourage banks from entering into loan workouts. This can arise when a bank's required provisioning at the outset of the workout is less than the loss it will have to absorb during the workout through debt forgiveness and loan reduction. Likewise, when provisioning rules are too stringent, they can also distort a bank's incentive to engage in workouts. An example might be a bank that has decided it is in its best interest to restructure a loan to a distressed but ultimately viable borrower. If the provisioning requirements for restructured loans do not allow for improved prospects of the eventual loan recovery, though, the bank may not be willing to enter into the loan workout with the borrower, especially if the workout may entail additional lending from the bank to the creditor (which may also be subject to provisioning).

Corporate governance

Improvements in shareholder protection for minority investors are important to promote debt/equity swaps. A lack of protection against self-dealing by owners and controlling shareholders serves as a "strong deterrent for creditors that might otherwise consider conversion of debt to equity stake" (IMF, 1999b). In countries like Indonesia, where reportedly 10 families accounted for more than 50 percent of market capitalization of the country's largest corporations (Iskander, and others, 1999), this can be an important consideration for the debt restructuring process. The improvement of corporate governance involves the strengthening of stock listing requirements and disclosure requirements, and the expansion of the roles of independent board members and external auditors.

Corporate restructuring vehicles

Workout often entails debt/equity swaps. This means banks sometimes become substantial, or even majority, shareholders in the firms with which they enter into a workout. This new role requires banks to become actively involved in the management of the firms, a task that in many cases banks have neither the expertise nor the resources to undertake. These considerations may be important enough to discourage the banks from entering into workouts. A unique feature of the Korean workout program is the creation of government-funded corporate restructuring vehicles that take over acquired equity from banks and, for a fee, also manage it in their stead. Professionals, many of them with international experience, staff these vehicles. So far, there is not enough evidence to evaluate their performance so as to ascertain whether they have helped move the workout process along.

Workout and nonperforming loan purchase program

Often banks are reluctant to go into a voluntary workout. This may be for lack of experience or because of the uncertainties surrounding the outcomes of a possibly lengthy process. Often banks' reluctance is further increased by any government purchase program for nonperforming loans that provides them with an easy way out of selecting the workout route. In these cases, the government may want to link the workout with the purchase of nonperforming loans by conditioning the latter on the banks' participation in the workout process. This approach entails obvious technical difficulties. Although no satisfactory design has yet been developed, the approach would require close coordination between the asset management company (which purchases the assets from the financial institutions) and the workout intermediary. One proposal is for the workout intermediary to certify the eligible banks for the sale of nonperforming loans to the asset management companies.

The role of asset management companies

Under certain circumstances, the asset management companies can play a crucial role in corporate debt restructuring. Successful debt restructuring requires negotiation between equals. In situations where most of the debtors are large corporations and the creditor banks are small, management companies that centralize the claims on the debtors can sometimes negotiate more meaningful and balanced restructuring settlements. As discussed in the third section, when necessary, asset management companies can also be given special legal power to facilitate the corporate debt restructuring process.

Legal support

Effective bankruptcy and foreclosure procedures are a crucial aspect of corporate debt restructuring. When the threat of such procedures is credible, it increases the incentives for defaulted debtors to reach out-of-court settlements with their creditors.

Legal limits on foreign ownership of domestic assets (enterprises or properties) can discourage the participation of foreign banks and other foreign creditors in the workout process by limiting the options available to them for concluding the workout (such as a debt/equity swap). In countries where foreign banks are important creditors (e.g., in Indonesia, foreign banks hold about two-thirds of all corporate debt), this can paralyze the workout process. In these cases, lifting the legal limits of foreign ownership must be a condition for the workout process.

Tax issues

Corporate debt workouts sometimes entail some form of corporate reorganization such as merger, consolidation, and stock acquisition (in addition to business restructuring) to improve the prospect of the company. For example, during the recent crisis in Korea a number of chaebols had to take over some of their subsidiaries or to swap businesses. In most tax systems, capital gains are not taxable until they are actually realized, that is, when the instruments that generate the capital gains are sold or transferred. The potential tax liabilities of companies that wish to enter into a corporate reorganization can sometimes be so substantial as to discourage the reorganization initiatives. To avoid obstructing necessary corporate restructuring, many countries have introduced the concept of tax-neutral company reorganization. This exempts companies from capital gain taxes when the reorganization takes place, provided that the stockholders and property are substantially the same before and after restructuring and that the restructuring "have some bona fide business purpose and are not principally designed to secure the tax neutral treatment." For this reason, Indonesia began to recognize mergers as tax-neutral in 1998.

Governments sometimes also introduce specific tax deductions or subsidies to create explicit incentives for debt restructuring. In Thailand, the government provided temporary tax relief on asset sales and on debt restructuring by financial institution creditors.[27] In Korea, the government provided tax breaks for the restructuring of firms, including exemption of small and medium-sized enterprises from capital gains on the sale of real estate used to repay debt to financial institutions. While the effects of tax deduction and subsidies are similar, subsidies have the advantage of being both self-terminating (to the extent that they need to be approved by the budgetary process every year) and of a finite sum in nature (with specific budgetary allocation).

Conclusion

Nonperforming assets are generally a manifestation of weakness in the corporate sector (obligor of the assets) and the immediate source of problems in the financial sector (holder of the assets). Effective asset management policies need to recognize these linkages and the interdependence between the two sectors. In this sense, asset management policies cannot be independently formulated and must be conceived in the context of a comprehensive framework for the restructuring of the financial and the corporate sectors. For a survey of the literature on the subjects of financial restructuring and corporate restructuring, see Enoch, Garcia, and Sundararajan (2001); Bank for International Settlements (1999); and Stone (2000).

This chapter has examined two asset management approaches that have been used extensively during the recent Asian crises to help facilitate the restructuring of the financial and the corporate sectors: asset management companies serving primarily as a vehicle for financial restructuring and the out-of-court centralized corporate debt workout framework for corporate restructuring. The evolution of these approaches reflects very much the circumstances of these countries during their recent crises.

Despite the advantages associated with these two approaches, they are emergency measures. This means that while they may be considered

---

[27]These include deduction of written-off debt from taxable income for the creditor; elimination or deferral of corporate income tax on written-off debt for the debtor; elimination of all taxes on asset transfer from debtor to creditor (income tax, special business tax, stamp duties, and value-added tax); elimination of taxes on accrued but unpaid interest, and the limitation of taxes on restructuring involving interest rate reductions by creditors.

the first best instruments during financial crises, they may not be under ordinary conditions. Both of these approaches have many inherent weaknesses. In particular, their dependence on government involvement is likely to lead to outcomes that are neither the most efficient nor the most optimal in normal times.

Appendix: Techniques of Asset Disposition

Asset sales, by facilitating resource and risk reallocation, are often at the core of the nonperforming asset resolution process. Many techniques, traditional and more sophisticated, have been developed for this purpose. Although so far little empirical work has been done to evaluate their relative effectiveness, it is generally accepted that this depends in large part on the type of assets for sale, the state of market infrastructure, and the objectives of asset sales. This section discusses some of the asset sale techniques for large groups of assets (asset-backed securities issues, equity partnership, and the Swedish approach).

Securitization of Assets

Traditional asset markets are often unable to digest the large stock of nonperforming assets emerging from financial crises. When this is the case, policymakers have the option of creating new markets, with the view to improving market efficiency, simplifying transaction procedures, and allowing transactions of large quantities of assets to take place at the same time. One of the markets that may be established for this purpose is the asset-backed securities market.

Securitization is the repackaging of assets with generally predictable cash flows into interest-bearing securities with marketable investment characteristics. Beginning with residential mortgages in the United States from the end of the 1970s, securitization has come to encompass pools of less homogeneous assets with uneven cash-flow characteristics and more types of collateral. The securitization of commercial mortgages is one such development.

Securitization of assets usually arises from a structured financing deal, when a company or a bank, in order to raise cash, sells some of its assets to a trust or to a special purpose vehicle, which subsequently offers asset-backed securities to investors through an underwritten public offering or a private placement. The marketability of an asset-backed securities issue is largely a function of its creditworthiness, which in turn relies on its structure and the quality of the underlying collateral. These characteristics determine the yields to investors (commonly known as the "pass-through rate"). During the lifetime of an asset-backed securities issue, the cash flows of the underlying assets are remitted to a trustee, who pays scheduled interest and principal payments to the investors.

Generally, the assets that are more suitable for securitization are those with predictable cash flows, and low delinquency rates, and whose underlying collateral has high liquidation value. Nonperforming assets usually do not have any of these characteristics, a fact that places greater demand on the design of their securitization. Below is a summary of the key issues involving asset securitization, with emphasis on nonperforming assets.

Legal issues. To obtain a high credit rating for an asset-backed securities issue, it is necessary to insulate the sold assets and the special purpose vehicle from the bankruptcy of the sellers. This is where the concept of the "true sale" enters. This is the removal of transferred assets from the originator for bankruptcy purposes. To effect a true sale, the amount of recourse on the originator, or any limited guarantee provided by the originator, should be curtailed. So should the originator's retained rights regarding the special purpose vehicle and its surplus. For a more extended treatment of this subject, see Schwarcz (1991).

Asset composition. To foster market acceptability, the structure of asset-backed securities issues must take into account the need for their tradability in the secondary markets. Standardization of securities, especially in a thin market, is therefore of extreme importance. To achieve standardization, assets to be securitized should be grouped into different classes, by type, maturity, and status. Generally, residential loans are more homogeneous than commercial mortgages (in terms of maturity and interest), which makes them better candidates for securitization. When nonperforming loans are included in the assets to be securitized, there should be detailed and regular reporting on their performance.

Credit enhancement. Credit enhancement can assist the securitization of nonperforming assets by raising the quality of the asset pool. There are two categories of credit enhancement: internal credit enhancements (reserve funds, overcollateralization, and senior-subordinated structures) and external credit enhancements (pool insurance, bond insurance, and bank letters of credit) that involve a third party assuming some of the risks in case the portfolio should underperform. Internal credit enhancements are generally favored over external ones, because the latter often are more costly and difficult to obtain. Cash reserves, funded by the proceeds from the sales of the securities, can protect investors against shortfalls and losses arising from delinquent principal and interest, and realized losses on liquidation of assets. Subordination provides some credit enhancement to the senior certificate holders by requiring that junior certificate holders (who are often the sellers themselves) absorb any shortfalls and losses. Overcollateralization can ensure steady payments in the event of some defaults. Often, sellers of assets use a combination of a reserve fund, subordination, excess interest, and overcollateralization to improve the creditworthiness of the securitized assets.

When the assets to be securitized are government-owned, governments have sometimes chosen to enhance the creditworthiness of the securities by providing some explicit guarantees. For example, the U.S. FDIC on a number of occasions provided a limited guarantee in the form of an interest-free demand note through the Bank Insurance Fund to obtain investment-grade rating for the securities offered (FDIC, 1998). Although such guarantees may have a role once all other credit enhancement options have been exhausted, the case against them is that (1) they undermine the notion of real asset sales (by forcing the government to retain some risk associated with the assets), and (2) a new security with full-faith backing by the government will compete with other government securities. Thus the appropriateness of this approach has to be determined case by case.

Market acceptability improvements. Regarding the determination of interest rates on asset-backed securities issues, a cross-index structure is sometimes used to make the securities more attractive to a wider base of investors. A cross-index structure is one in which the interest rate paid by the securities is not tied to the income of their underlying assets. The Resolution Trust Corporation (RTC) frequently issued securities bearing an interest rate tied to the London Interbank Offered Rate (LIBOR), when the interest rates on the underlying mortgage loans were tied to U.S. Treasury indexes or cost-of-funds indexes (FDIC, 1998). The use of the LIBOR index could increase the international secondary market acceptance of these securities. Of course, a cross-index structure gives rise to basis risk, which occurs when interest income of the underlying assets falls short of the interest to be paid on the securities.[28]

To broaden the investor base in developing countries, it may be necessary to issue the asset-backed securities in international currencies like the U.S. dollar, so that investors do not need to take on foreign exchange risks. In this case, the sellers need to have access to a forward or swap market in foreign exchange in order to hedge foreign exchange risks. In many developing countries, this option may be constrained by the absence of such markets.

The role of credit-rating agencies. The role of credit-rating agencies is crucial for the launching of an asset-backed securities market. This is

---

[28]The RTC sometimes covered these risks by adding additional funds to the cash reserves or by using excess interest payments to accelerate the paydown of the classes that were subject to basis risk (FDIC, 1998).

because most investors will depend on ratings issued by credit-rating agencies to determine the securities' attractiveness. Generally, rating agencies are actively involved in deciding the structure of an asset-backed securities issue (such as how many credit enhancements are needed) for these securities to obtain the sought-after rating category. The rating agencies also monitor the performance of the securities over their lifetime and adjust their credit ratings as appropriate. In countries where local credit- rating agencies lack expertise and domestic and international credibility, there may be a need to bring in international credit rating agencies either in the context of joint ventures with local firms or directly on a particular transaction or transactions.

The role of services. Services are parties who are responsible for the management and collection of the underlying assets of asset-backed securities deals. In theory, the services can be the sellers themselves, the buyers, or someone appointed by the sellers or the buyers. It is critical to ensure that incentives are in place for the services to maximize the value of the assets under their management. To do so, the issuers of the asset-backed securities can set the services' fees as a percentage of each loan that is worked out or rehabilitated.

Strengths and weaknesses of asset-backed securities. The main weakness of asset-backed securities is that they require a sophisticated market infrastructure whose development may take time. For this reason, they cannot be the primary vehicle of asset disposition during a financial crisis in most developing and emerging market economies. Another drawback is that asset-backed securities can only deal with a narrow group of nonperforming assets, such as those with at least positive cash flows. Despite these considerations, in Japan, Korea, and Malaysia efforts are under way to develop an asset-backed securities market. In November 1999, Morgan Stanley Dean Witter priced the first set of bonds linked to nonperforming Japanese real estate loans.[29] The following is a list of the advantages associated with asset-backed securities:
- The pooling nature of asset-backed securities makes them ideal for the sale of large group of assets with *irregular cash flow* characteristics. In fact, a successful issue of asset-backed securities should be large enough to ensure predictability of payment streams and dilution of default risks.
- Asset-backed securities issues allow impaired assets (with appropriate credit enhancements) to be transformed into *highly rated securities*, the main consequence being that investors can purchase

---

[29]The real estate properties are occupied and producing positive cash flows.

them without detailed knowledge of the underlying assets. This greatly accelerates the sale process.
- Asset-backed securities issues allow the sellers of the assets to gain access to an entirely *new group of investors*. These same investors, however, might not be interested in a conventional debt obligation of the same sellers.
- Asset-backed securities issues, by removing assets from bank balance sheets (provided the sale is final), increase the *lending capacity* of banks without the banks having to find additional deposits or capital infusion (Chammah, 1991).

Equity Partnership

Government-owned asset management companies often lack the experience of private firms in asset management. For this reason, they sometimes engage the expertise of private firms by entering into incentive-based contracts with them. To retain upside potential for the government-owned asset management companies and to subject the capital of private firms to downside risk according to the performance of private firms, the RTC developed the concept of "equity partnership." An equity partnership chiefly differs from conventional incentive-based contracts by preserving for the partners the profit from "improvement in inefficient markets or unpredictable returns."

Under the equity partnership program, joint ventures were created between the RTC as a limited partner and private sector investors (usually consisting of equity investors and asset management companies) acting as general partners. These deals were structured in such a way that the general partners invested equity capital and asset management services, while the RTC contributed asset pools and arranged for the financing of the partnership. The terms of these deals required that proceeds from the liquidation of assets must first retire any outstanding debt. After the debt was paid in full, the partners divided the remaining proceeds according to the percentage of ownership of each partner. Thus, unlike a direct sale, the RTC retained a residual interest that gave it some upside potential should the asset recovery rate end up being higher than initially anticipated.

Main characteristics of equity partnership programs. The RTC entered into seven types of equity partnership arrangements between 1992 and 1995. Although many of these types had different structures, they also had very similar characteristics (FDIC, 1998):
- Proceeds from the disposition of the underlying equity partnership assets were distributed pro rata to both partners. Neither party held a senior or a subordinate position.

- All deals required the general partner to acquire its interest in the partnership with cash. The RTC's capital contribution was the value of its share of assets conveyed to the partnership.
- The RTC provided the partnership with funding for interim financing or working capital.
- As the seller in the equity transactions, the RTC provided limited warranties.
- Each agreement prohibited the general partner from certain actions, including self-dealing, unless approved by the RTC.
- The general partner had full responsibility for conducting the partnership's day-to-day business affairs such as managing, servicing, and disposing of the assets in the portfolio. The partnership agreement allowed for subcontracting management, disposition, and support functions when necessary.
- The general partner was required to contract an external accounting firm to perform an annual audit and to certify the partnership's financial statements.
- Each partnership reimbursed certain general partner expenses specified in the agreement. Reimbursement was contingent upon the general partner's compliance with the partnership's policies.
- The general partner had the right to transfer its interest in the partnership upon approval of the limited partner. The limited partner, however, had the right to transfer its interest without the general partner's consent.
- The limited partner had the right to remove the general partner upon breach of certain covenants and upon occurrence of certain events and, following removal, the right to appoint a new general partner.

Strengths and weaknesses of equity partnership programs. In addition to providing the sellers an upside potential of the recovery of the assets, an equity partnership allows the sellers to transfer part of the due diligence and collection expenses. The seller financing aspect of equity partnership accelerates the bidding process, because the bidders do not have to acquire third-party financing. It also allows more investors to qualify and compete, thereby increasing demand and, as a result, prices. Like asset-backed securities, equity partnerships can handle a large quantity of assets in a short period of time. But unlike asset-backed securities issues, which are mainly suitable for homogeneous assets, an equity partnership in theory can be used for all types of assets.

The drawback of equity partnership arrangements is that they do not constitute a clean sale, and, to the extent that some of the assets transferred to the trust are still owned by the sellers and that the seller provides partial financing, the financial conditions of the seller are dependent largely on the ability of the general partner to manage the assets. While an equity partnership entitles the sellers to any upside potential of the partnership, it also exposes it to downside risks. The experience of the RTC was, based both on book value and on estimated value, that equity partnership yielded the highest recovery rate compared with other disposition strategies. This, of course, can be a reflection of the risk premium associated with the RTC taking on some of the risks.

Examples of equity partnership. In 1995 the RTC launched the SN Series of equity partnership. The SN Series transactions were legally structured as trusts, which issued bonds that were held by a trustee on behalf of the RTC. The bond debt typically represented 60 percent of the value of the trusts. The general partner owned a 40 percent interest in the trust and was a Class A certificate holder. The RTC, acting as limited partner, held Class B certificates and owned a 51 percent interest in the trust. As assets were liquidated, the trust first used the proceeds to pay off the bonds until they were retired. For the remaining 40 percent value, the trust distributed proceeds with 51 percent going to the limited partner (Class B holder) and 49 percent to the general partner (Class A holder) until all assets were liquidated. A total of $135 million in bonds was issued for the five SB Series transactions and held by the RTC.

The Korean Asset Management Company (KAMCO) has recently been experimenting with the equity partnership concept. In 1999 KAMCO sold 565 billion won (at face value) of nonperforming loans to a special purpose vehicle in exchange for 70 percent cash and a 30 percent equity stake. The vehicle, in turn, raised cash by selling the remaining 70-percent equity to the U.S.-based Lone Star Fund. The assets of the special purpose vehicle are managed by an asset management company, and any residual value arising from the asset sale is distributed to KAMCO and the Lone Star Fund with a 40/60 percent split.

The Swedish Model

Once the owner of a nonperforming asset succeeds in seizing the underlying collateral of the asset, it may sell the collateral immediately. However, because of market conditions and the possible lack of marketability of the asset, the owner may hold onto it and actively manage the collateral to maximize the price at which it can be sold later. In some cases, the seller in the holding period may try to improve the attractiveness of the asset by turning it into an income-generating asset (e.g., a rented property). Moreover, by combining the asset with other assets, the seller may be able to spin them off into a company with a steady stream of income. The seller can then sell the company, either by listing it on the stock exchange or by selling it in a bid process.

The strength and weakness of equitization. The weakness of this approach is that it cannot deal with a very large quantity of assets in the way asset-backed securities and an equity partnership can. It also requires a certain homogeneity of assets, specifically real estate properties. Its strength is that it may lead to higher returns on the sale of the assets.

An example of a strong equity arrangement of this type occurred in 1993, when Securum established four Swedish regional real estate companies in which seized real estate collateral was placed and managed. The objective of these companies was to improve their assets through active management (e.g., by reducing the vacancy rate and improving the conditions of their properties) and, once the value of the assets could not be further improved, to sell the assets. In 1994 Securum listed Fastighets AB Norrporten, formerly Securum Fastigheter Norra AB, on the Stockholm Stock Exchange. Securum made an initial public offering of 60 percent of the company to institutional investors and to the general public. To raise the price of the sale by reducing the public's uncertainties about the company, Securum guaranteed to buy back the shares at a predetermined price during the summer of that year. This guarantee helped generate interest in the sale, and the shares were substantially oversubscribed. The remaining shares in Norrporten were later sold in two stages in October and December 1996. In 1997 Securum also made a successful initial public offering of another company (Castellum).

References

Bank for International Settlements, 1999, "Bank Restructuring in Practice," Policy Paper No. 6 (Basel: BIS).

Berggren, Arne, 1996, "Establishing Asset Management Companies," paper prepared for International Monetary Fund Workshop on Systemic Bank Restructuring, Monetary and Exchange Affairs Department, Washington, unpublished.

Bernanke, Ben S., and Cara S. Lown, 1991, "The Credit Crunch," *Brookings Papers on Economic Activity*: 2, Brookings Institution, pp. 205–47.

Chammah, Walid A., 1991, "An Overview of Securitization," in *Asset Securitization: International Financial and Legal Perspectives*, ed. by Joseph J. Norton and Paul R. Spellman (Oxford: Basil Blackwell Centre for Commercial Law Studies, Queen Mary and Westfield College, University of London).

Dziobek, Claudia H., 1996, "Regulatory and Tax Treatment of Loan Loss Provision," IMF Paper on Policy Analysis and Assessment No. 96/6 (Washington: International Monetary Fund).

Enoch, Charles, Gillian Garcia, and V. Sundararajan, 2001, "Recapitalizing Banks with Public Funds," *IMF Staff Papers*, Vol. 48, No. 1, pp. 58–110.

Federal Deposit Insurance Corporation, 1998, "Other Resolution Alternatives," in *Resolutions Handbook: Methods for Resolving Troubled Financial Institutions in the United States* (Washington: Government Printing Office).

Financial Markets Development Committee of the Pacific Economic Cooperation Council (PECC), 1999, "Corporate and Bank Restructuring in East Asia," summary of a Joint PECC and World Bank conference, Singapore, April.

Ingves, Stefan, and Gören Lind, 1997, "Loan Loss Recoveries and Debt Resolution Agencies: The Swedish Experience," in *Banking Soundness and Monetary Policy: Issues and Experiences in the Global Economy*, ed. by Charles Enoch and John H. Green (Washington: International Monetary Fund).

International Monetary Fund, 1999a, *Orderly and Effective Insolvency Procedures: Key Issues*, Legal Department (Washington).

———, 1999b, "Indonesia—Corporate Restructuring—World Bank Brief," EBD/99/46 (Washington).

Iskander, Magdi, Gerald Meyermann, Dale Gray, and Sean Hagan, 1999, "Corporate Restructuring and Governance in East Asia," *Finance & Development*, Vol. 36 (March), pp. 42–45.

Kawai, Masahiro, 1998, *Financial and Corporate Sector Restructuring in East Asian Countries: Policy Development and Assessments* (Washington: World Bank).

Kent, Pen, 1997, "Corporate Workouts: A U.K. Perspective," in *Terzo Rapport sul Sistema Finanziario Italiano*, ed. by Fondazione Rosselli (Rome: Edibank).

Klingebiel, Daniela, 2000, "The Use of Asset Management Companies in the Resolution of Banking Crises: Cross-Country Experiences," Policy Research Working Paper No. 2284 (Washington, World Bank).

Liberman, Ira, and William Mako, 1999, *Korea's Corporate Crisis: Its Origins and a Strategy for Financial Restructuring* (Washington: World Bank).

Lindgren, Carl-Johan, Tomás J.T. Baliño, Charles Enoch, Anne-Marie Gulde, Marc Quintyn, and Leslie Teo, 1999, *Financial Sector Crisis and Restructuring—Lessons from Asia*, IMF Occasional Paper No. 188 (Washington: International Monetary Fund).

Schwarcz, Stephen L., 1991, "Structuring and Legal Issues in the United States," in *Asset Securitization: International Financial and Legal Perspectives*, ed. by Joseph J. Norton and Paul R. Spellman (London: Basil Blackwell).

Stiglitz, Joseph, and Andrew Weiss, 1981, "Credit Rating in Markets with Imperfect Information," *American Economic Review*, Vol. 71 (June), pp. 393–410.

Stone, Mark R., 2000, "Large-Scale Post-Crisis Corporate Sector Restructuring," IMF Policy Discussion Paper No. 00/7 (Washington: International Monetary Fund).

Woo, David, 1999, "In Search of 'Capital Crunch': Supply Factors Behind the Credit Slowdown in Japan," IMF Working Paper No. 99/3 (Washington: International Monetary Fund).

11

Recapitalizing Banks with Public Funds: Selected Issues

CHARLES ENOCH, GILLIAN GARCIA, AND V. SUNDARARAJAN

Recapitalizing banks in a systemic crisis is a complex medium-term process that requires significant government intervention and careful management at both the strategic and individual bank levels. This chapter highlights the range of operational and strategic issues to be addressed and the institutional arrangements needed to foster an effective banking system restructuring and maximize the returns on government investment. The approaches to recapitalization have varied, with countries choosing different mixes of direct capital injections and asset purchase and rehabilitation. The choice of an appropriate mix is critical, to minimize the expected present value of government outlays net of recoveries.

A banking crisis has erupted and begun to intensify and spread. In response, the government has decided to restructure and recapitalize banks to overcome the negative effects of a malfunctioning banking system on economic growth and wealth. It has made the decision because weaknesses in the financial system and the extreme uncertainty that prevail during the crisis have limited the provision of private capital, and the government fears that banks will fail in large numbers. It hopes that injecting public funds to strengthen bank capital, together with

---

This chapter was written with help from colleagues in the IMF's Monetary and Exchange Affairs Department and with able research assistance from Elena Budreckaite. It benefited from the comments of Stanley Fischer, Stefan Ingves, and Carl-Johan Lindgren. An earlier draft was reviewed by Charles Adams, Bijan Aghevli, Peter Heller, and Leslie Lipschitz of the IMF and Jonathan Fiechter, Larry Promisel, and Thomas A. Rose of the World Bank. The authors are also grateful for comments from two anonymous referees.

additional financial and operational restructuring of banks, will restore public confidence in the banking system, reduce uncertainty, accelerate resolution of the banking crisis, and promote economic recovery by overcoming the disruption of banking and payment services and by ensuring that viable businesses can fund their operations. These circumstances have recently confronted a number of countries in Asia, Central and Eastern Europe, the former Soviet Union, and the Americas.

In systemic bank restructuring, public funds may be needed to: (1) make payouts to depositors of closed banks; (2) compensate banks that agree to accept deposit transfers; (3) facilitate an acquisition, merger, or purchase and assumption; (4) help recapitalize banks; and (5) restructure assets. This chapter focuses specifically on operational and technical issues that relate to the last two items: the granting of assistance through capital injections and asset rehabilitation to facilitate the continued operation of banks that are to be kept open. The chapter examines, in sequential order, the choices that must be made and the steps that have to be taken to implement the decisions. The discussion draws on the experiences of five Asian countries, Mexico, Sweden, and the United States.

The chapter discusses preliminary considerations, and operational issues including the creation of a Bank Restructuring Agency; the terms and conditions for government support to recapitalize banks; decisions that must be made about government support; and the modalities and instruments of government capital injections and means of paying for them. Other means of support are also discussed. The chapter also focuses on rehabilitating bank assets, including through arranging debt workout, and on reducing liabilities, improving income, and granting forbearance. Appendix I contains a glossary of technical terms, and Appendix II presents a set of organizational charts for seven countries' restructuring agencies.[1]

In many of the issues covered there is no single practice that is clearly superior on theoretical or analytical grounds. Decisions are likely to have to be taken case by case, and often to be based on specific institutional factors such as the legal system in the country or the availability of skilled resources to manage problem assets. Drawing on the experience of the countries under study, this chapter therefore seeks to identify the important factors underlying the decisions in such tradeoffs, as well as the best practices that should be adopted, whichever choice the authorities make.

---

[1]The chapter does not discuss in detail certain related matters, such as the rationale for the use of public funds, the deposit insurance agency, the need for, and methods of, taking legal recourse against criminal acts, and corporate restructuring. More in-depth discussions of forbearance, asset management corporations, and lender-of-last-resort facilities are subjects of separate chapters.

Bank Restructuring Agency: Organizational Issues

This analysis starts at the point where the government intervenes in a banking/currency crisis by using public funds for bank recapitalization. Before it reaches this point, the government should have made a preliminary estimation of the costs of restoring a functional banking system.[2] The government should have formulated an overall strategy for bank restructuring, encompassing the following key elements: (1) diagnosis; (2) triage;[3] (3) prompt exit of nonviable banks;[4] (4) a well-designed recapitalization strategy for viable and essential banks; (5) operational restructuring of banks; (6) efficient management and recovery of nonperforming assets, supported by loan workouts; (7) equitable loss-sharing arrangements and containment of public sector costs; and (8) a strengthening of prudential supervision of banks to prevent further accumulation of losses.

A key limitation on the government's plans for intervention is the amount of public funds it has available. An equally fundamental constraint is the availability of human resources, which will influence the organizational structures used in the intervention. These constraints may be more binding in some countries than others.[5]

Putting a recapitalization strategy into operation will frequently require legal and institutional changes, including the possible creation of public bodies, such as a bank restructuring agency to oversee the comprehensive restructuring strategy. The agency establishes the principles for selecting the banks that will be closed and those that will be recapitalized and restructured. It may have two key components or subsidiaries: a bank support authority, which holds equity and in some cases may lend to safeguard the value of its equity holdings, and one or more asset management companies (Nyberg, 1997), which manage and restructure the assets taken from intervened banks, and which buy

---

[2]The design and sequencing of bank restructuring and prudential supervision reforms, taking into account their macroeconomic impact, are discussed in Alexander and others, (1997) and V. Sundararajan, (1999).

[3]See Appendix I for a definition of the term.

[4]The form of resolution for a problem bank—closure and liquidation, partial or complete merger, temporary "bridge bank," or support to keep the bank operating—depends on the bank's governance, its financial condition, and its franchise value.

[5]The government should appoint independent, professionally competent executives and boards to manage banks that are taken over. If it proves difficult to find such individuals, the use of international bankers, accounting firms, and investment bankers becomes critical to fill part of the human resources gap. Otherwise, human resource constraints may influence the design of the restructuring and recapitalization program and place a premium on identifying economies of scale in resolving banks and on efficient clustering of banks.

bad loans and dispose of them.[6] Sweden created an oversight board for the bank restructuring agency, with separate asset management companies as subsidiaries. Sweden has a relatively developed financial system with considerable experience of operations in a market environment but it nevertheless encountered shortages of financially skilled manpower to run these organizations. In other situations, such as in transition economies, a simpler structure with clear lines of authority and accountability may be appropriate.

The authorities must make a number of organizational decisions relating to the bank restructuring agency. The first is whether to use existing agencies or create a new organization to oversee recapitalization and restructuring, take control of funds that have already been committed, make and manage additional investments in banks, and later sell them cost-effectively (Nyberg, 1997). Where a deposit insurance agency is already in place and can be expected to manage the crises competently, it may be augmented to handle the challenge. This situation is relatively unusual. Often there is no deposit insurance agency; in some other cases the existing agency is being blamed for allowing banking problems to deteriorate into the current crisis; and typically the magnitude of the problem in the crisis is exceptionally grave, so that a new agency will be needed.[7]

The second choice is whether to make the agency independent or an integral part of the government. The agency in charge of restructuring will need clear legal authority to determine, on the basis of universally applied and transparent criteria, which banks should receive public capital assistance and which should not. It should be autonomous to make and implement resolution decisions, and it should be accountable for its actions. After decisions are implemented, they need to be made transparent and explained fully. No governments have given full independence where a large percentage of GDP is being devoted to recapitalizing banks. Accountability to parliament in most countries is achieved

---

[6]In the early stages of a bank restructuring process, provision of proper information to the public helps to restore confidence, and that information will include a brief description of the organizational structure that will be established to manage the bank restructuring and the legislative changes necessary to set up the bank restructuring agency and grant it the powers to discharge its responsibilities successfully.

[7]Indonesia, Malaysia, and Thailand have no deposit insurance agency and so required a special agency. Although it has an agency, Korea has also created a special agency to handle its bank problems. During the bank and thrift problems of the late 1980s and early 1990s in the United States, the Bank Insurance Fund was judged able to handle the banking problems and resolved 1,394 failed banks between 1984 and 1992. The thrift regulator and the insurer, though, were replaced by a new regulator, and a special temporary agency, the Resolution Trust Corporation (RTC), was created to manage the crisis (Alexander and others, 1997, pp. 86–91).

through a ministry. The ministry of finance, as guardian of the public purse, is a typical choice among government agencies to manage restructuring. The central bank or an independent bank supervisor are also possibilities. On the other hand, government agencies are not usually involved in the day-to-day business of running banks and, when they have attempted to be so, frequently the arrangement has not been very effective because of governance problems. Consequently, while it is appropriate that the government's interest in the success of the bank restructuring agency's operations be explicitly recognized in the agency's organizational structure, the structure should also protect the operating units from political interference in their day-to-day operations and allow them to be functionally independent and publicly accountable.

While there may be several ways to achieve a compromise between accountability and independence, one particular institutional model for bank restructuring is pictured in Figure 11.1. There, the bank restructuring agency is an agency that is subordinate to the ministry of finance, and separate from an independent central bank, the supervisory agency,[8] and the deposit insurance authority, where there is one.[9] It may be wise not to place the bank restructuring agency within the central bank, so as to avoid incentives to finance restructuring through money creation. It can also be argued that the supervisor should not run the bank restructuring agency because it has no sources of finance and it also may be tempted to give preferential supervisory treatment to banks that it owns. Moreover, while the deposit insurance agency could handle nonsystemic banking failures, it may lack the financial and human resources and the authority to deal successfully with a systemic crisis.

Most countries find a need for an overarching board to serve as liaison with other elements of the government and to coordinate and supervise subsidiaries' activities. The ministry of finance and the central bank should be represented on the bank restructuring agency's oversight board, together with the agency's chief executive officer and some knowledgeable

---

[8]In Figure 11.1 the supervisory agency is shown to be within the central bank. An alternative diagram could show the supervisory agency as a separate institution.

[9]Indonesia and Thailand have placed their bank restructuring agency subordinate to the ministry of finance. In Malaysia the bank restructuring agency is run by the central bank, which is only quasi-independent of the ministry of finance. Korea's bank restructuring agency is a subsidiary of its independent supervisory agency. Japan and Mexico have involved their deposit insurance agency to some extent in bank restructuring and recapitalization. The United States created an independent agency—(ie. the Resolution Trust Corporation (RTC))—to handle failed thrifts, but not failed banks. The RTC spent a smaller percentage of GDP (roughly 2 percent of GDP in the mid-1990s) on failed thrifts than the countries considered in this chapter will incur in restructuring their banking systems. Stylized models of actual experience in various countries are shown in Figures 11.3 through 11.12 in Appendix II.

Figure 11.1. Stylized Institutional Framework: Under the Ministry of Finance

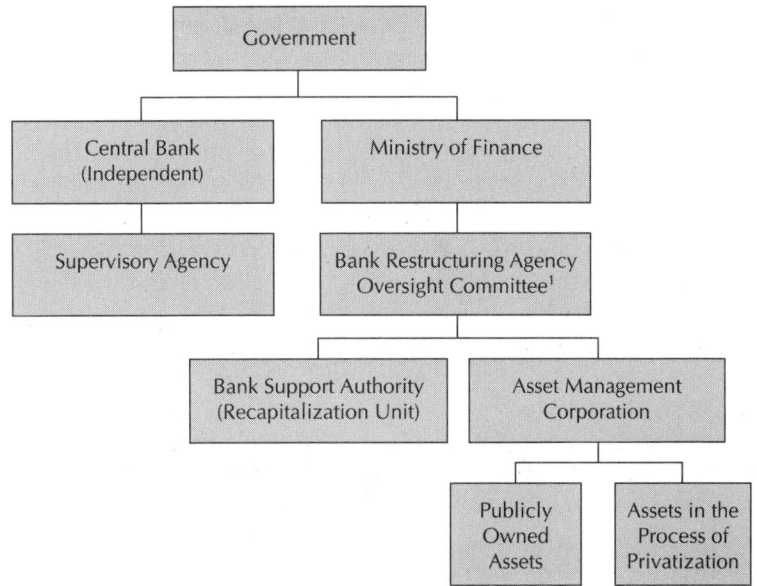

[1]Includes representatives of other agencies, including central bank, and (if separate) the supervisory agency.

and independent members of the public.[10] Such a board would strike an acceptable compromise between including all other interested parties on the board and confining membership to a manageable number. While neither the supervisory agency nor the deposit insurance agency is formally represented on the oversight board, they would need to maintain close relations with its operational arms. The supervisor must keep the bank restructuring agency informed on the condition of banks, especially those that are deteriorating toward consideration for closure or recapitalization.

The relationship of the deposit insurance agency to the bank restructuring agency depends in part on the breadth of the role the deposit agency has taken in the past. Where its role has been limited to compensating depositors in failed banks, it may continue to do so, but that task may be temporarily overridden by the comprehensive guarantee that must be funded by the government and may fall to the restructuring agency to execute. Where the deposit insurance agency has acted as the receiver/liquidator of failed banks in the past, it may continue to do so. One of many

---

[10]If the supervisory agency is outside the central bank, one may well wish to have a representative of the supervisory agency on the board of the bank restructuring agency.

organizational possibilities is that its responsibilities are temporarily taken by the restructuring agency and its staff may be reassigned there, while it itself temporarily becomes a subsidiary of the restructuring agency. These relationships are illustrated for selected countries in Figures 11.3 through 11.12 in Appendix II.

The responsibilities of the oversight board would be to plan the restructuring and recapitalization exercises, assess the appropriate level of fiscal resources for restructuring and recapitalization, and strike a balance between these needs and the fiscal constraints faced by the government. It must not only serve as liaison with the government, but also insulate its operational subsidiaries from political pressure and keep the public informed of the agency's plans and its progress toward achieving them. Transparency should be a goal and it will be encouraged by auditing the bank restructuring agency, at least annually, designing appropriate accountability and disclosure arrangements, and requiring reporting to parliament in public hearings.

Details of the institutional structures that have been established in six countries to handle bank restructuring are shown in Table 11.1.

Assistance

The bank restructuring agency needs to keep several broad considerations in mind when using public funds to recapitalize banks and administer restructuring plans. First, the strategy must hold owners of a failing bank responsible for losses, and make managers accountable for their actions, and thus put in place an incentive structure for both the public and the private sectors that discourages a recurrence of banking problems. Second, the industrial structure of the rehabilitated banking system must provide core banking services, and consideration must be given to what is a desirable long-term structure of the financial services industry. Third, the strategy should aim ultimately to turn the government's investments back into cash and return the banking sector to private control. Fourth, the restructuring agency must take control of public funds that have already been expended, for example, by converting into equity the lender-of-last-resort assistance that the central bank has given in a number of countries to not just illiquid but also insolvent institutions that are to be recapitalized.[11,12] Fifth, the restructuring strategy should

---

[11]For example, Thailand converted Financial Institutions Development Fund support into equity.

[12]Central banks rank in priority over a failed bank's assets according to whether they hold collateral against their loans to it, and the quality of that collateral.

strive to minimize the amount of public funds used (expenditures net of recoveries) to achieve the objectives of restructuring and ensure that these funds are dispensed in an efficient, equitable, and cost-effective manner, and that the government obtains securities in some form that support its right to future repayment in exchange for its investment.

In addition to providing finance directly to recapitalize the bank, the bank restructuring agency must make a judgment on the extent to which some of the impaired assets of the bank should be taken off the bank's books (for example, transferred or sold to a separate unit, such as an asset management company) so that the assets can be managed separately. Separation of these assets can help to normalize bank operations and maximize asset recovery, thereby improving the yield on funds invested in bank capital. When the problem bank is fully taken over and controlled by the government, this typically involves transferring an appropriate volume and type of assets to a separate asset management company controlled by the government or the bank restructuring agency. In some situations the government finances only a part of banks' capital needs and the private sector provides the rest and shares ownership, while at the same time it assists banks with purchases of some of the impaired assets (for example, by acting through an asset management company owned or controlled by the government or the bank restructuring agency). In these cases, the appropriate allocation of budgetary funds between direct recapitalization and financing (or facilitating) asset purchases becomes an issue. These decisions involve a number of considerations, including the degree of insolvency and government ownership, the nature of impaired assets, and the type of arrangements to manage these assets most effectively, taking into account internal governance of banks and the country's legal and institutional environment to enforce property rights and restructure assets. For instance, loans to the national airline may well be best managed centrally, while loans to local farmers may be best left on the books of the bank. Overall, a bank should not have all the problem loans taken off its books; it should be "normalized," not "supernormalized," both to ensure a level playing field with banks that do not receive assistance and to avoid excessive costs to the public sector.

The principal operational responsibility of the oversight board is to approve the conditions for eligibility for government assistance and the terms of its granting. Eligibility conditions to qualify for access to public assistance in a bank recapitalization should reflect financial and operational criteria that help assess viability and good governance. More specifically, the **eligibility conditions** include that a bank

- Has fit and proper owners and managers (including new ones) or is placed under conservatorship until they can be located;

Table 11.1. Government Agencies Associated with Bank Recapitalization

Agency Type	Indonesia	Japan	Korea
Overarching Bank Restructuring Agency	New: Indonesian Bank Restructuring Agency.	New: Financial Reconstruction Commission (replaced the Crisis Management Committee).	New: Financial Supervisory Commission.
Bank Support Authority (the recapitalization unit)	Indonesian Bank Restructuring Agency itself is the Bank Support Authority.	Existing DIA, with the approval of the CMC/Financial Reconstruction Commission.	Existing: Korean Deposit Insurance Corporation.
Asset Management Company or Asset Management Unit	New: Asset Management Unit, a division of Indonesian Bank Restructuring Agency.	Resolution and Collection Corp., includes the Resolution and Collection Bank and the Housing Loan Administration Corporation buys bad loans from any bank.	1) Korean Asset Management Corporation since 1962: 2) New: bridge bank to deal with the good assets of closed merchant banks.
Debt Restructuring Agency	New: Indonesian Debt Restructuring Agency.	No.	1) New: Corporate Restructuring Coordinating Committee.
Deposit Insurance Agency	Not yet: Indonesian Bank Restructuring Agency currently administers the full guarantee.	Yes: Deposit Insurance Corporation.	Yes: Korean Deposit Insurance Corporation, (2/97)
Government-Approved Private Initiatives	Government-set principles for loan workouts (Jakarta Initiative); the central bank issued regulations governing loan restructuring.	Cooperative Credit Purchasing Corporation.	Financial Supervisory Commission established debt resolution framework including the CRCC, which arbitrates disputes.

Source: IMF staff analysis.

Malaysia	Mexico	Thailand
Only an informal Restructuring Steering Committee under Bank Negara Malaysia.	Until 12/98: National Banking Commission and Fondo Bancario de Protección al Ahorro; now Institute to Protect Savings.	From 8/98, Financial Restructuring Advisory Committee.
Danamodal: A government agency that is a subsidiary of Bank Negara.	Fondo Bancario de Protección al Ahorro administered the PROCAPTE *recap* program; it has now been replaced by Institute to Protect Savings.	1) Financial Institutions. Development Fund has capital for intervened banks and liquidity for open banks; 2) New Financial Institutions Development Fund.
Danaharta: a government company that is owned by the Ministry of Finance, and is expected to have a lifespan of five to ten years.	1) Fondo Bancario de Protección al Ahorro 2) Valuación y Venta de Activos to appraise and dispose of assets acquired by Fondo Bancario de Protección al Ahorro 3) trust funds for bank loan workouts 4) CRB proposed under the SHCP.	1) Financial Restructuring Agency; 2) Thai Asset Management Corporation only for bad assets of intervened institutions; 3) private Financial Institutions Development Fund-funded Asset Management Company for Bangkok Bank; and 4) private tax-free Asset Management Companies.
Yes: Corporate Debt Restructuring Committee to guide private negotiations for companies in receivership or liquidation and establish negotiation practices.	A number of programs: UDI, UCABE, FINAPE, and FOPYME.	Yes: Corporate Debt Restructuring Committee uses the London Approach to establish formats for debt agreements for 200 major debtors.
No.	Yes: Fondo Bancario de Protección al Ahorro: now Institute to Protect Savings, which is to replace the full guarantee with limited deposit insurance by 2005.	No, but is currently being designed.
Banks and finance companies cooperate to acquire troubled institutions; central bank has issued regulations to govern loan restructuring.	Unidad Coordinadora del Acuerdo Bancario Empresarial to facilitate the restructuring of large, syndicated loans.	Yes. The central bank has issued regulations to govern loan restructuring.

- Recognizes the full extent of its losses, based on realistic valuation criteria;
- Submits an acceptable business plan that covers recapitalization to required capital levels and operational restructuring to assure future profitability; and
- Mobilizes private sector owners (existing or new) that put up at least a portion of the new capital in some agreed proportion and assume responsibility for operation of the institution.[13]

The **terms accompanying the provision of public assistance** to an eligible bank should ensure adequate financial and operational restructuring and provide incentives to private owners to resume efficient and profitable operations rapidly. The terms of access to a public capital facility should normally include agreements with banks to: (1) restructure operations and balance sheets, with binding performance targets in a memorandum of understanding, using proper accounting principles, if necessary through due diligence scrutiny by special auditors;[14] (2) accept specified restrictions on operations in case of noncompliance; and (3) make arrangements for the repayment of public assistance and the return of ownership to the private sector.

Although the scope and details of the terms would vary according to country- and bank-specific circumstances, these terms could include the following continuing obligations on banks:
- Suspend dividends, or be subject to other sanctions, whenever the bank is below the minimum capital adequacy ratio or violates specified performance criteria, including achievement of prudential requirements such as maximum open foreign exchange positions and operational restructuring, such as rationalizing the bank's branch structure. Accept arrangements that would trigger an intensification of government control—for example, a conversion of preferred shares acquired by the government into common stock, under one or more of the following conditions: (1) when the capital adequacy ratio falls below a specified level; (2) when the supervisor judges that the bank has otherwise failed to comply with the terms imposed upon it, and when the violations were avoidable and material; or (3) when a previously specified point in time is reached. For example, under specified conditions the

---

[13]These partners need to have sufficient capital at risk to give them a strong incentive to stay with the institution and to work for its survival.

[14]In Thailand banks' financial conditions were assessed by special audits by the banks' external auditors. In Indonesia, by contrast, all banks were audited by international accounting firms. In some former Soviet Union countries, overseas supervisors assisted in the assessment of banks' financial condition.

interest of existing shareholders would be substantially diluted and the government would obtain voting control and the right to replace management.
- Accept official oversight through regular and frequent reporting and off-site and on-site inspections to monitor compliance with time-specific performance targets for: (1) achieving loan classification and provisioning standards; (2) making improvements to procedures governing credit assessment, risk management, loan workout, and collateral control; (3) streamlining operations; (4) cutting costs; (5) bringing excessive foreign exchange positions, connected lending, and other infringements into compliance with prudential standards; and (6) arranging government representation on the board of directors where it is deemed necessary by the bank support authority and the supervisor.[15]
- Allow the public sector to obtain an increasing percentage of the bank's net income as time progresses as remuneration for its investment, and as an incentive for the bank to buy out the government's stake as soon as possible. With this design, public funds will become progressively more burdensome over time, so that the bank will seek to repay its obligation to the government and replace public funds with private capital.
- Participate in efforts to restructure corporate debt, to ensure maximization of loan payments and loan recoveries, and to minimize the capital infusion that the government and owners have to provide.

To be equitable and to allow the government to cash out of its investment, if there are private owners left, they should be given an option to redeem the government's capital either throughout the period or at a specified point in time. In general, the terms of recapitalization could also include incentives for new investors in the form of guarantee, such as stop-loss and income maintenance agreements.

Key Decisions

To achieve the objectives for efficient restructuring set by the bank restructuring agency, its operational arms—the bank support authority and the asset management company—must jointly make decisions

---

[15]While many of these functions would be part of the normal day-to-day work of the supervisors, there may well be a case for intensified supervision of recapitalized banks. In Indonesia the central bank established a special surveillance unit to focus on the largest of these banks. In Indonesia, while the government has representatives on the boards of the recapitalized private banks, it has agreed in a memorandum of understanding with the private owners not to participate in the day-to-day running of the business.

about certain operational issues related to granting capital assistance to banks. Issues discussed in this section include: (1) the valuation of individual banks' portfolios and prognosis of their future condition; (2) whether support should be uniformly available to all viable banks, or only to those institutions identified as having systemic importance; (3) the selection of individual banks that qualify for and will receive assistance; (4) whether support should be conditional on a full or partial write-off of existing shareholders' claims; and (5) the target level of capitalization that the facility should help the banks to achieve. Other operational issues such as the instruments to use and means of paying for them are discussed in the next section.

Asset Valuation and Forecasting

Realistic valuation of a bank's balance sheet and off balance-sheet exposures is a prerequisite for an effective recapitalization strategy, and for an assessment of capital shortfalls. Such valuation is difficult in a crisis environment that is pervaded by uncertainty because the usual indicators of value are not available. Market prices do not exist where trading has ceased or been disrupted. In addition, the lack of a reliable basis for estimating cash flows owing to the high volatility of exchange and interest rates in a crisis impedes valuation based on appropriately discounted present values. The valuation of classified assets, in particular, can be especially problematic, because what is needed is more than a static assessment of current conditions; a prediction of future viability is also essential for the identification of banks to be selected for recapitalization.[16] Unless carefully managed, however, self-assessment invites self-serving adoption of favorable forecasting assumptions, and external assessments may not be feasible or affordable.

Thus, given the uncertainty in times of banking crisis, alternative approaches to valuation have been used in practice to temper the assessments based on traditional valuation procedures. Banks have a continuing responsibility for valuing their assets and making provisions for losses to keep their capital intact, and external auditors and supervisors continue to challenge the banks' valuations. In an environment of banking crisis, though, the authorities in some countries have striven to ascertain realistic values for assets by requiring banks

---

[16]Sweden, for example, required banks to provide to the bank restructuring agency data based on universally applied criteria on a common date. The agency then fed the information obtained from banks and data from other sources (including macroeconomic data and predictions) into a forecasting model, which outlined each bank's likely development over the next three to five years. See Ingves and Lind (1997).

to undertake a special self-assessment of the value of their asset portfolio and future prospects, based on tightened regulations governing loan classification and provisioning, and clear guidance on the assumptions to be employed and the procedures to be followed. In other countries, the bank restructuring agency has made or checked the assessment itself using, for example, discounted present values of projected income flows. Recapitalization units have also sought to obtain an independent valuation of bank portfolios by using international accounting firms or investment banks to complement supervisory assessments and external audits.

Each of these approaches has drawbacks. Self-assessment may be biased because of conflicts of interest; other local assessments may not carry sufficient credibility in the market; government assessments may appear inflexible; and international assessors may have a less complete picture of local conditions. Moreover, critics claim that the auditors place exceptionally low values on assets, perhaps to permit the international partners to sign the audits without fearing that they would later be sued for over optimism in the uncertain environment.[17] In addition, the auditors may face a conflict of interest if other clients are in line to become the major purchasers of the banks or their assets.

Therefore, the authorities making restructuring decisions have to adopt a pragmatic and transparent approach that strives to incorporate consistent assumptions about key economic variables and best-practice accounting standards, and that, on this basis, combines and reconciles alternative valuations to formulate their own realistic judgment. In addition, prospective private investors will wish to undertake their own due diligence valuations before their decision to acquire equity stakes in banks. Where the authorities believe that banks can and will value their assets fairly and realistically, they should require banks to do so. But these valuations need to be checked either by external assessment or by the bank support authority. Where banks cannot or will not conduct a fair assessment, international accounting firms should be hired to do the valuations. In turn, their credibility will need to be checked by the bank support authority. In all cases, the authorities must clearly specify that the same date for the assessment, the same assumptions, and the same procedures be adopted for assessing asset values and forecasting bank viability.

---

[17]This criticism was made of the Big Five's work in Indonesia. Also, the Korean government wanted an assessment quickly, and the international partners of the international accounting firms declared themselves unable to sign the audits in the time frame allowed, which reduced their impact.

Which Types of Institution Should Be Eligible to Receive Government Assistance?

An important consideration is whether assistance should be confined to commercial banks or include other types of depository institutions such as savings banks and credit unions, and other financial institutions such as insurance companies, investment banks, and brokerage houses. The answer depends partly on the importance of the role of these institutions in an economy. As a general principle, commercial banks rank first in priority, because they can have systemic effects as a result of their vulnerability to runs in a financial crisis. Savings banks, which are sometimes government-owned and house the small savings of households, are usually also eligible for assistance for social and political reasons. Other types of financial institutions usually have lower priority in claiming public funds.[18]

In general, capital assistance should be available for a limited period to all commercial and savings banks that meet the established financial and operational criteria set by the bank restructuring agency, and that are both willing and able to meet the terms of assistance (laid out in the previous section) so that they can attain a specified minimum capital adequacy ratio and adequate operational restructuring. Capital assistance may also be available to banks that meet certain critical needs—for instance, a bank that is the sole provider of payments services in a particular region.

Eligibility for recapitalization should be determined primarily, but not solely, on the basis of financial and operational criteria that indicate potential viability. However, countries sometimes decide that a classification based solely on financial and operational criteria would not provide a workable resolution for banks that are weak but deemed essential, or of systemic importance to the economy. For example, it may not be feasible to close a very large bank in an orderly fashion, or one that dominates a region of the country, underpins the payments system, or has a special niche in the credit markets. Such exceptions to resolution criteria on the grounds of "essentiality" should be made only under very limited and tightly managed conditions to thwart political pressures.[19]

The resolution of both private and state-owned banks should be broadly governed by the same objectives and principles, although the resolution of state banks may often face special circumstances because

---

[18]In 1998 the near-failure of a major hedge fund in the United States prompted concerns about systemic effects on the banking system and prompted officials' efforts to preserve the institution, although ultimately exclusively through the use of private funds. Similarly, the Bank of England rescued Johnson Matthey because of its activities in the gold market.

[19]For instance, in Indonesia, the authorities declared that all the state banks were "too big to fail" and all would be recapitalized.

of their size and credit exposures. As with the private banks, recapitalization of state banks should be linked to realistic valuation based on internationally accepted accounting standards, fit and proper management, and financial and operational restructuring to ensure viability and adherence to prudential standards.

Which Banks Should Be Chosen to Receive Government Assistance?

The bank support authority needs to classify banks. In Figure 11.2, as an example, there are four categories of banks. All begin from a position of measured capital above the required capital adequacy ratio. The worst category (D), however, is projected to deteriorate rapidly into deep and irretrievable insolvency, and there seems to be no reason for direct government assistance. Where there is a blanket guarantee and the bank is small, it will be preferable to pay off the depositors and arrange to dispose of the assets, rather than recapitalize the bank. If the bank is large and systemically important, the least-cost solution may still be recapitalization. The second two categories—those banks being considered for direct assistance (B and C)—fall below the minimum required capital but ultimately are expected to recover if assisted. Bank B might recover very slowly without assistance, but bank C would not. Both of these banks are able and willing to meet the terms for and conditions of assistance laid out in the previous section. The fourth and best category (A) remains solvent unaided (Ingves and Lind, 1997).

A difficult decision is whether to aid bank B, which the valuation exercise predicts has a higher probability of recovering without aid than bank C, which is expected to become insolvent without financial assistance but could recover with aid. If the bank restructuring agency believes the country is over banked, and neither bank is systemically important, it could close both banks. If it judges that the country is over banked but that it needs to assist one bank in order to maintain sufficient competition among banks, it should aid the stronger bank and close bank C. If both banks are needed it may support both. If budgetary resources are constrained, the bank restructuring agency will need to try to spread out the necessary financing over a longer horizon or elicit greater private sector participation, including foreign investment.

Treatment of Existing Shareholders' Claims

As a general rule, the financial claims of banks' existing shareholders and subordinated debtors should be written down in accordance with their seniority in the legal system in order to cover the losses an institution has incurred. Apart from reducing the contribution of public funds needed to eliminate possibly the negative net worth, this

Figure 11.2. Expected Capital Ratios for Four Banks
(Capital adequacy ratio [CAR], %)

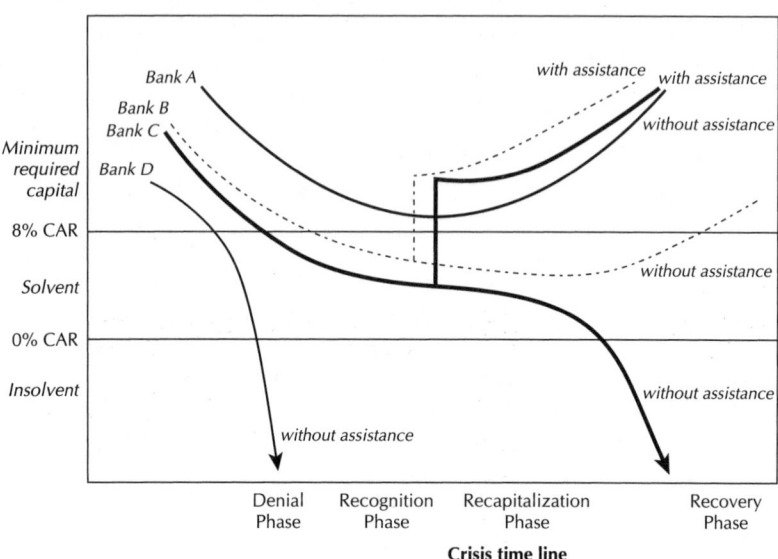

Source: Adapted from Ingves and Lind (1997).

write-down also avoids setting precedents that can result in moral hazard. Where limited liability is not in force, shareholders may also be required to subscribe additional capital.

In crisis situations, such as those in Asia, banks can fail as a result of past directed lending and exogenous factors—macroeconomic instability—despite good management, "fit and proper" owners, and initially strong capitalization. In these cases, the government may face a moral or legal responsibility to repay the losses, and may take steps to keep existing owners and managers in place and to persuade them to invest new capital.[20]

In some countries, the insolvency that is revealed from writing down owners' capital triggers supervisory action in which the bank loses its license, and is merged or closed and liquidated. In other countries, the legal system allows owners to remain in control of the bank even after

---

[20]For example, even where shares are written down to zero, human resource constraints might suggest that "fit and proper" shareholders be retained on the board of directors and be given stock options tied to future performance. Alternatively, an insolvent bank might be closed and a new charter issued to the former owners conditional on their injection of new capital. On the other hand, the mere fact that there was directed lending, or government interference, does not mean that banks' managements can necessarily walk away totally from the problems in their banks. Their "fitness and propriety" as well as responsibility for problems in the past may well be a matter of judgment for the authorities in general, and the bank supervisors in particular.

their shares have been written down to nominal values.[21] In some cases it may be necessary to allow existing shareholders to retain partial ownership rights in order to obtain their cooperation, and to avoid time-consuming and costly legal wrangles. Where the authorities are considering supporting an insolvent bank whose shareholders are protected, such support should be predicated on the shareholders themselves also providing new capital.

Experience has found that owners, especially new investors, may be induced to provide fresh capital if the uncertainty they face is reduced by instruments that guarantee outcomes. For example, the government may agree to share losses with the owner or new investor (in a "loss-sharing" arrangement); place a cap (a "stop-loss" provision) on the amount a bank may lose; agree to maintain bank income at a specified level (in an "income- or yield-maintenance" provision); or allow the bank to return some or all of the bad assets it purchases to the government (through a "put-back" provision). More specifically, such guarantees and options can be given, with appropriate safeguards, to limit an acquirer's losses during a review period during which additional "skeletons" may come to light. Such guarantees may cover asset values or yields that an institution will earn on certain assets specified in the recapitalization contract.[22] While these inducements to new investment have been used successfully in many countries, a government will need to be confident that they will convey good incentives for the new owners to maximize the value of recoveries and not abuse the guarantee by failing to make the maximum effort to maintain and improve the value of the assets acquired. Working with guarantees can create an illusion of private ownership; with guarantees, technically a bank can have private ownership while all the risk is borne by the government.

Finally, using the legal system to obtain redress for criminal acts or regulatory violations committed by owners and others may reduce the government's fiscal obligations, while preserving incentives for good governance.

The Size of the Recapitalization

When there is a blanket guarantee for depositors and other creditors, recapitalizing a bank to a zero capital adequacy ratio (bare solvency) is

---

[21]The former applies in most industrial countries; the latter, for example, in most Asian crisis countries.

[22]These techniques have all been used by the Bank Insurance Fund and the Resolution Trust Corporation in the United States. Malaysia has provided asset guarantees to acquirers of merged finance companies, Korea has given put options to acquiring banks in P&As, and Thailand has provided stop-loss guarantees and yield-maintenance agreements to new investors taking over intervened banks.

roughly equivalent to honoring the guarantee without making a pay-out to depositors and creditors. In systemic crises, recapitalizing to bare solvency, given the limited supply of private capital (domestic and foreign), may not be sufficient to establish credibility in the soundness of a recapitalized banking system, and it may well be desirable for the government to recapitalize selected banks to some positive minimum level. Where the fiscal situation permits, the government may recapitalize banks to Basel standards or even higher, while taking a commensurate ownership interest.[23] A decision in this regard will depend on competing fiscal demands, as well as the extent to which the authorities expect that such "overcapitalization" will have a beneficial effect in restoring confidence in the system among bank customers and counterparts and potential investors.

Burden-Sharing the Recapitalization

The amount of public funds needed to recapitalize the banking system depends in part on the willingness of private investors, existing and new, to put up a share of the capital needed. This willingness will depend in turn on the distribution of ownership after recapitalization, and the guarantees and contractual terms designed to reduce uncertainty and apportion losses and profits.

Where the law does not call for limited liability for bank owners, shareholders may be required to recapitalize their bank. Even where limited liability is in place, it may be possible to design the recapitalization so that the shareholders are encouraged to reduce the call on government funds in certain ways.[24] They might be induced to: (1) bear losses beyond their original capital and share with the government the financial responsibility for "filling the hole" and bringing the bank up to bare solvency; and (2) contribute additional capital to help meet the minimum capital adequacy ratio. This approach—persuading existing shareholders to "fill the hole"—is equivalent to denying limited liability, a provision that is frequently regarded as a protection to shareholders necessary to encourage them to invest in an enterprise or bank.[25]

To encourage new shareholders to participate in a recapitalization, it may be necessary to give them preference over existing shareholders.

---

[23]Korean banks have been recapitalized to 10 percent, to allow them to survive some further deterioration in asset quality.

[24]Unlimited liability is not uncommon. Before granting a license, supervisors frequently require shareholders to undertake, for example, in a comfort letter to keep their bank adequately capitalized.

[25]Nevertheless, this approach is being tried in Indonesia, where the capital support facility for private banks requires contributions from existing shareholders to "fill the hole" in return for the opportunity to buy back the government shares later and reacquire the bank under specified conditions.

Such preference could provide that old shareholders shoulder the burden of additional depreciation of existing assets before the new shareholders are called on to bear losses.[26] Any additional losses on certain specified old assets would then be underwritten by a government guarantee so that new shareholders are held responsible only for losses incurred on the other assets that are not guaranteed. Alternatively, new shareholders may receive, at least for a certain time period, a disproportionately large share of future dividends. In some countries, the law (for example, the law that governs rights issues) would need to be changed to permit such discrimination among shareholders. In other countries, it may be sufficient to persuade old shareholders to agree to the arrangement on pain of being dispossessed entirely.

Modalities of Government Support: Capital Injections

Having made the decision on which banks to recapitalize, the bank support authority must choose the best ways to provide the funding. In principle, there are a number of instruments that the government can use to strengthen a bank's capital adequacy: injecting capital with public funds rehabilitating assets reducing liabilities and improving net income (Dziobek, 1998). This section will focus on issues relating to capital injections, particularly the instruments to use and the means of paying for them. The other instruments are discussed in the following two sections.

Tier 1 and Tier 2 Instruments

An increase in paid-in equity or Tier 1 capital is the preferred form of recapitalization, because it improves the capital ratios, can enhance profitability, and is essential under the Basel Capital Accord. It does not involve immediate servicing costs, because dividend payments could and should be postponed until the bank's capital and income are fully and durably restored. In addition, the government's provision of Tier 1 capital can facilitate the bank's efforts to raise Tier 2 capital from private sources. The components of Tier 1 and Tier 2 that are recognized by the Basel Committee are listed in Box 11.1. The actions of six countries when providing Tier 1 and Tier 2 capital to recapitalize their banks are shown in Table 11.2, which reports the capital instruments used and means of payment adopted. (Table 11.3 reports other financial actions, such as granting loans and issuing guarantees.)

---

[26]The published Joint Statement of August 14, 1998, from the ministry of finance and the Bank of Thailand imposes this condition (Thailand, 1998a).

Box 11.1. Capital Instruments in Use in Banks[1]

	Characteristics	Examples of Countries
Tier 1 Instruments (Core Capital)		
Issued and fully paid ordinary shares	Must be: (i) issued and fully paid; (ii) noncumulative; (iii) permanent; (iv) able to absorb losses within the bank on a going-concern basis; (v) junior to depositors, general creditors, and subordinated debt; (vi) neither secured nor guaranteed by the issuer; (vii) publicly disclosed; and (viii) immediately and fully available without limit to the issuing bank.	Many: including Mexico, Malaysia, Finland, Sweden
Disclosed reserves from retained after-tax earnings or other surplus		Many: Mexico
Perpetual, noncumulative preference shares		Thailand, Japan
Convertible, noncumulative preference shares		Thailand, Indonesia,[2] Japan,[2] Finland, Sweden
Minority interests in equity of less than fully owned subsidiaries whose accounts are consolidated and that meet certain conditions and do not exceed 15% of Tier 1 capital		Malaysia
Innovative, synthetic, capital instruments Limited to <15% of consolidated Tier 1 capital	Not secured or guaranteed, callable by issuer only after a minimum of 5 years and with supervisory approval.	Portugal, Spain, Thailand,[3] U.S.A.
Tier 2 Instruments (Supplementary Capital)		
Undisclosed reserves	Unencumbered; immediately available	Japan, Mexico
Asset revaluation reserves	Prudently valued with a discount	U.K., Japan, Mexico
General provisions/loan-loss reserves[4]	<=1.25 % of risk-weighted assets	Many: Mexico, Malaysia
Hybrid debt/equity instruments including,	Must: (i) be unsecured, subordinated, fully paid-up; (ii) not be redeemable without the prior consent of the supervisor; (iii) be available to participate in losses without the bank having to cease trading; and (iv) allow servicing obligations to be deferred where the bank's profitability would not support payment.	Several
Cumulative long-term preference shares		Canada
Convertible cumulative preference shares		France
Titres participants and titres subordonnés a durée indéterminée		
Genusscheine		Germany
Perpetual subordinated debt		U.K., Thailand
Preference shares		U.K.
Mandatory convertible debt instruments		U.S.A.
Subordinated term debt instruments including:	Not normally available to share losses unless bank closes; thus, not to exceed 50% of Tier 1 capital.	U.S.A.; Finland
Conventional unsecured subordinated debt		
Convertible subordinated debt	Minimum original term to maturity of over five years with a discount of 20% in each of last five years to maturity.	Mexico, Thailand, U.S.A., Malaysia
Limited-life redeemable preference shares		
Deductions from capital		
Goodwill		
Investments in unconsolidated financial subsidiaries		

Sources: Basel Committee on Banking Supervision (1998, pp. 1–16, and 1999).
[1] The precise specifications vary from country to country.
[2] The Indonesian preference shares are nonvoting.
[3] Thailand, for example, issues Stapled Limited Interest Preferred Securities (SLIPS) that are attached to high-rate subordinated debt that pays interest even when there are no profits. U.S. bank holding companies can issue "trust preferred" or "capital securities" and pass the proceeds on to their banks as Tier 1 capital. European countries have issued "step-up callable preferred securities."
[4] Specific loan-loss reserves are not countable as capital under the Basel Capital Accord, although some countries do so. Japan, for example, counts reserves against substandard loans, but not doubtful or loss loans, as Tier 2 capital.

When recapitalization with public funds leads, in effect, to nationalization,[27] this should be regarded as a transitional arrangement designed to strengthen management and operations, and it should lead to reprivatization in due course—preferably according to a specific time frame. Consequently, the bank support authority needs to choose its capital instruments with regard to its ability to redeem them later. Two financing decisions need to be made—which instruments to acquire, and how to pay for them. While the government could purchase common stock, which may be more marketable than other instruments when the government wants to recover its investment, the bank support authority may wish to avoid taking voting control in circumstances where it believes that operations under private direction are more efficient, or where it feels that abstaining from asserting such control would significantly increase the incentive for the private sector to bring in more capital. In this situation, it would prefer to purchase convertible preferred shares, which count as Tier 1 capital under the Basel Committee's rules, and may be constructed to convey voting rights under a variety of restricted arrangements. Nevertheless, the government could retain veto rights on identified strategic issues relating to bank portfolios and operations.

Where the government wishes to obtain control of the bank in case the bank's condition deteriorates, it should purchase preferred stock that can be converted into common equity under certain specified conditions.[28] Convertible, preferred shares count as Tier 1 capital, provided they are undated and noncumulative.[29] They carry a prior entitlement to any income earned, but they do not give the holder voting power in normal circumstances, and so they help to reduce any potential conflict of interest for the government. The trigger for conversion could, for example, be a decline in the capital adequacy ratio below some threshold value (4 or 6 percent, for example) or other material failure to meet the terms for continued assistance listed in the section "Key Decisions." The rate for converting preferred into common shares should dilute the common stock and give the government control.

The tension between satisfying the Basel Committee's requirement that capital instruments cannot qualify as Tier 1 capital if they are

---

[27]Nationalization is the usual outcome in cases where insolvency is deep and the bank is regarded as systemically important.

[28]The government could also retain specific rather than general voting powers, to allow it to approve the details of a merger, for example.

[29]They are popular among "white knight" acquirers because they allow the acquirers to rescue a corporation, while ensuring that they can exit first if trouble occurs. Convertible preferred shares are being used by the Japanese government and also in Thailand and Indonesia.

Table 11.2. Actions by the Public Sector to Provide Tier 1 and Tier 2 Capital[1]

Instrument/Payment	Indonesia	Japan	Korea
Provide capital	Yes.	Yes.	Yes.
Tier 1:	Yes.	Yes.	Yes.
Common stock	Yes.	Yes, but rare.	Yes: government and Korea deposit insurance corporation for development, intervened, and merged commercial banks.
Pay in cash	No.	Yes.	Yes: through the Korea deposit insurance corporation; otherwise to development banks.
Pay with bonds	Yes.	Not yet. But Deposit Insurance Corporation will probably issue short-term bonds soon.	Yes: stocks in public enterprises owned by the government to nationalized banks; government-guaranteed Korea deposit insurance corporation bonds.
Preferred stock	No.	Yes; now mostly convertible; if bank raises private capital and makes new loans.	Yes: for acquirers in P&As for five commercial banks.
Pay in cash	No.	Yes.	Yes.
Pay with bonds	Yes: 1) indexed, 2) regular; both negotiable.	No: Deposit Insurance Corporation issues government-guaranteed bonds and borrows from BOJ to raise cash.	Korea deposit insurance corporation sells bonds to provide cash.
Tier 2:	Yes.	Yes.	Yes.
Subordinated debt	No: (lender-of-last-resort support converted to subordinated debt before the crisis).	Yes, more common than equity.	Yes: early P&As for five closed banks.
Pay in cash	No.	Yes.	No.
Pay with bonds	No.	Not directly, but the government issues bonds to fund the cash injection.	Government-owned exchange-quoted stocks in public enterprises.
Memo: allow more **foreign ownership**	Yes: law amended to permit up to 99% foreign ownership of banks.	There are no restrictions on the foreign ownership of banks.	Yes: have eased legal restriction, and foreigners, including the IFC, have bought stakes in four banks.

Source: IMF staff analysis.
[1]The public sector includes the government, the central bank as lender of last resort, the deposit insurance corporation, the asset management company, the restructuring agency, and any vehicle for recapitalizing banks.
[2]Aided banks must have sold their bad assets to Danaharta and have Capital Adequacy Ratios below 10 percent.

Malaysia	Mexico	Thailand
Yes, for at least 10 banks.[2] Yes. Yes.	Yes. Yes. BOM/Fondo Bancario de Protección al Ahorro in intervened and small financial institutions to end insolvency and permit private recap.	Yes. Yes. Only in intervened banks
Yes: using proceeds from issuing Danamodal bonds.	No.	Financial Institution Development Fund converted some lender-of-last-resort support into equity in intervened banks.
No.	Ten-year, Fondo Bancario de Protección al Ahorro zero-coupon, non-tradable bonds. IPAC will issue negotiable, government-guaranteed, bonds to replace Fondo Bancario de Protección al Ahorro's.	No.
Yes: bought by Danamodal.	In intervened and merging banks.	Yes: up 2.5% Tier 1, then match private contributions 1:1.
Yes. No.	No. Ten-year, Fondo Bancario de Protección al Ahorro zero-coupon, nontradable bonds. IPAC will issue negotiable bonds to replace Fondo Bancario de Protección al Ahorro's.	No. Ten-year, tradable, government, bonds with market-related interest rate.
Yes. Yes: redeemable, subordinated debt issued to nine institutions by end-1998.	Yes. Banks issued to government callable, five-year sub. debt mandatorily convertible into equity after five years or when Capital Adequacy Ratio is < 2.	Yes. Yes: to 2% of risk assets if bank restructures corporate debt and makes new loans.
Yes.	Yes, but sterilized as increased reserves at BOM.	No.
No	IPAC will issue negotiable bonds to replace Fondo Bancario de Protección al Ahorro's bonds.	Yes: Government buys bank debentures with government ten-year bonds at lower market-related rate.
Yes: for financial institutions and limits on purchase of real estate by foreigners relaxed.	Eased before, ended remaining restrictions on foreign participation in existing banks in 12/98.	Existing restrictions have been waived for ten years.

Table 11.3. Public Sector Loans and Guarantees to Support Banks[1]

Instrument/Payment	Indonesia	Japan	Korea
Provide loans	Yes.	Yes.	Yes.
Long-term	No: but de facto short-term loans are rolled over.	No.	BOK to the Bridge Merchant Bank.
Short-term	Yes: by Bank Indonesia.	Yes: the BOJ with and without collateral.	Yes: BOK loans in foreign currency are rolled over.
Place deposits	No.	The Trust Bureau places Postal Savings Bank and local government deposits.	Reported in the press.
Guarantees	Yes.	Yes.	Yes: but not including off balance-sheet items.
Bank liabilities	Yes: from 1/98 for at least two years, with six months' notice of termination; includes off balance-sheet items; not share- and sub-debt holders or connected parties.	Yes: from 1997 through 3/01, may be extended to cover subordinated debt.	11/97 until 12/00 on most liabilities (including some inter-bank claims) of all financial institutions.
Bank assets		Guarantee associations reinsure SME loans with the Small Business Credit Insurance Corporation.	Yes; 1) informal guarantee of foreign exchange debts; 2) Korean Guarantee Corp.; 3) Korean Technology Guarantee Fund; 4) up to 100% on loans to SMEs;[2] 5) put options for acquiring banks in P&As.
Borrowers	No: apart from long-standing export guarantee scheme.	No; direct government lending.	Yes: credit guarantees for SMEs.

Source: IMF staff analysis.
[1]The public sector includes the government, the central bank as lender-of-last-resort, the deposit insurance corporation, the asset management company, the restructuring agency, and any vehicle for recapitalizing banks.
[2]See Table 11.4 for the details.

redeemable and the government's wish to recover its investment over time must be handled by ensuring that there will be a secondary market where the stock can be sold. The stock can be designed to give the owners the option to redeem it, with the consent of the government, if the bank is in good condition, and if the remaining Tier 1 capital would keep the bank above the minimum requirement after redemption. The government, however, would not have the power to redeem the shares

Malaysia	Mexico	Thailand
Yes.	Yes.	Only to intervened banks and to honor the guarantee.
No.	To intervened and small banks.	No: but in fact short-term loans are rolled over.
Yes: by Bank Negara Malaysia.	Yes: BOM made LOLR loans in pesos and, via Fondo Bancario de Protección al Ahorro, collateralized loans in dollars.	Yes: from the FIDF.
Yes: of state-owned cos., and national pension fund.	Yes.	No.
Yes.	Yes.	Yes: including off balance-sheets items, but not sub-debt.
Yes: from 1/98 indefinitely.	Yes: until 2005 IPAB replaces Fondo Bancario de Protección al Ahorro's guarantee on all, including foreign exchange, debts but not sub. debt.	Yes: from 10/97 indefinitely.
Yes: for the bad assets of Banks Sime and Bumiputra.	Yes: via Fondo Bancario de Protección al Ahorro, which lent to companies that were indebted to banks.	Profit and loss-sharing, stop-loss and yield maintenance agreements for new investors in intervened banks; for example, loss-sharing for intervened Krung Thai Bank.
The government guarantees Danaharta bonds.	Yes: many, such as UDIs and preferential exchange rates.	No.

from the bank because that would disqualify the shares from inclusion in Tier 1 capital.

Forms of Payment

In terms of payment, Tier 1 capital provided by private investors should be paid for by injecting cash; submissions in kind are not acceptable. The government may contribute cash or bonds (either negotiable or nonnegotiable). Bonds and cash immediately increase net worth, and improve the capital ratios, liquidity, and potential profitability.[30] Bonds are often a convenient source of payment for the government. The downside to this convenient arrangement is that banks may prefer to retain the bonds as a risk-free source of income, rather than making loans and easing the crisis-induced credit crunch.[31] If bonds are to be used, they should pay market, not submarket, interest rates. It must be decided whether market rates will be denominated in nominal or real terms (with the principal indexed for inflation). Bonds paying fixed nominal rates will give banks greater liquidity during the early years of the life of the bond than bonds that pay real rates, but paying nominal rates increases immediate government outlays.[32]

For these reasons, direct placement of government paper with the banks is the most common practice when purchasing bank capital. As stated previously, these bonds should pay market rates. Because market rates are likely to be high initially, due to uncertainty, the bonds should carry variable rates, so that the government's debt service costs will decline as rates fall.

It might be expected that the government would opt to inject negotiable bonds, which encourage market development and also facilitate liquidity management by banks.[33] There is a risk in supplying negotiable bonds, though, that the recipient will sell the bonds and reinvest unwisely in unsafe assets in a gamble for recovery. Fit and proper owners and managers, and very close supervision, are necessary to limit this risk. It may therefore be appropriate to contain negotiability for an initial period when the management, governance, and operational restructuring plans are being strengthened as part of the terms of government assistance.

Giving Guarantees

During the recent crises, all governments in the major crisis countries have issued blanket guarantees to a bank's depositors and frequently its creditors. In addition to these guarantees on the liabilities of a bank, governments have in some cases guaranteed bank assets or income streams (Table 11.3).

---

[30]Capital adequacy ratios are improved because equity increases and the value of risk-weighted assets falls, as both cash and government bonds have zero-risk weight under the Basel standards.

[31]Authorities sometimes place indexed bonds with banks to lower the initial costs of debt service and to mask the full costs of recapitalization. However, costs to the government could rise and banks could benefit if inflation escalates.

[32]Indonesia has used indexed bonds; see Table 11.2.

[33]This has occurred in Korea and Thailand, and is in prospect in Indonesia.

Guaranteeing liabilities forestalls runs and prevents the potential losses from selling assets in a fire sale and from high-cost borrowing to repay depositors. Such a guarantee should enable a return to relative stability in the banking system, enabling the authorities to deal with the banking situation in a properly sequenced and calm manner.[34] Insofar as the holders of the deposits are other financial institutions, such a guarantee should serve to revive the interbank market, which typically dries up during a banking crisis, and thus enabling the continuation of intermediation across the banking system.

Guaranteeing income (for instance through "stop-loss guarantees") allows banks to increase capital through retained earnings. This may be particularly helpful for prospective bank purchasers, especially in cases where there is substantial uncertainty about the value of a bank's assets and prospects for recovery.[35] Guarantees are appealing politically because they appear to be a substitute for additional immediate expenditures on Tier 1 or Tier 2 capital, and they offer some protection against giving windfall gains to bank investors in the event that the bank's situation turns out better than expected. Although widely used, they are not a "free lunch" for the government, which carries contingent liabilities that it may have to honor. In the absence of proper fiscal transparency, guaranteeing income may serve to disguise the costs of handling a banking crisis. Guaranteeing assets may involve providing assistance to the borrowers of a bank, frequently the corporate sector. With increasing recognition that bank and corporate restructuring are closely intertwined,[36] support for the corporate sector may be part of the authorities' overall strategy for handling a pervasive economic crisis.

Guaranteeing assets and income—to a level beyond that otherwise projected in the market—increases asset values, which improves the balance sheet and measured capital.[37] Not only will such guarantees

---

[34]The government of Thailand charges banks 0.4 percent of liabilities annually for the guarantee it is providing. Indonesia charges the banks 0.25 percent of liabilities.

[35]Among the Asian crisis countries this technique has been used in particular in Thailand, where banks have not all been subject to audit by international accountants and where the authorities have been particularly aggressive in seeking new private investors at an early stage.

[36]Corporate restructuring is beyond the scope of this paper. It is becoming increasingly recognized that bank restructuring without corporate restructuring may be self-defeating, because if banks' problems are derived from problems with their customers, addressing the problems of the customers will be critical to remedying the underlying situation facing the banks.

[37]There are obvious moral hazard effects here if the original owners stand to benefit from these guarantees. Hence there is a strong case that the granting of such guarantees should be conditional on the fulfillment of conditions similar to those discussed above for government assistance with bank recapitalization.

raise the market value of the assets covered, but—if they guarantee a return greater than the written-down value of the return—they also enable the bank to recover any provisions that it has previously made against the no longer impaired assets. Both effects boost capital. On the other hand, with proper fiscal accounting the contingent claims on the government will need to be shown at once, as would be immediate expenditure on capitalizing the banks; the suspicion exists, therefore, that those countries that pursue this route may not be pursuing full fiscal transparency. In any case there seems very rarely if ever to be a full and realistic estimate of the potential cost of these guarantees at the time they are given; they may be a major factor in the continuing escalation of costs of bank restructuring long after the authorities seem to be handling the situation.

Supporting Banks by Transferring Their Assets

In addition to injecting various forms of capital with public funds, the government can purchase and rehabilitate bank assets and facilitate business- and household-debt workouts to aid banks. It can also reduce bank liabilities, raise income, and grant forbearance. Such actions by six countries are shown in Table 11.4. This section discusses asset rehabilitation and debt workouts. The remaining actions are reviewed in the section that follows.

Asset rehabilitation is an important concomitant reform that either is operationally linked to capital assistance programs or otherwise strongly influences the effectiveness of such programs in supporting economic recovery, thereby reducing the net cost to the government. It is both a substitute for, and a complement to, capital injections. In principle, bad assets can be: (1) retained and managed by banks themselves at appropriately written-down values, while receiving financial assistance from the government for recapitalization; or (2) relocated or sold to one or more decentralized "bad banks" or loan recovery companies or privately owned asset management companies that specialize in the management of impaired assets; or (3) sold and transferred to a centralized asset management company, which is typically state-owned. In the recent Asian crisis all countries have accorded a significant role to this last option.

The government can purchase some or all of banks' impaired assets outright. This can help under certain conditions. The value of loans (good or bad) on the bank's books will decline and the amounts of cash and government (or government-guaranteed) bonds will rise. This substitution lowers the value of risk-weighted assets and raises the risk-weighted capital adequacy ratio.[38] It thus facilitates compliance with prudential requirements. Moreover, by reducing the riskiness of a bank's overall portfolio, it may change the incentive structure for banks' managements. Asset purchases should be supported by appropriate institutional arrangements for the resale of assets, debt workouts, and loan recoveries, however, so as to maximize the market value of purchased assets and reduce the ultimate cost to the government. For this reason the crisis countries have typically created a special agency—an asset management company—to acquire and handle bad assets (see Table 11.1).

Certain decisions must be made before the creation of an asset management company for this purpose. For example: (1) Do the advantages of asset purchases by a government agency outweigh the disadvantages and warrant establishment of a centralized asset management company? (2) Should it buy only from banks that are to be liquidated, or also from banks that are being assisted, or from any bank that wishes to sell its assets, regardless of that bank's condition and whether the government has taken over the bank? (3) Will the asset management company buy both good and bad assets? (4) Should the asset management company warehouse assets (that is hold them over a longer period without trying actively to restructure or dispose of them)? (5) What prices should it offer for the assets it purchases? (6) What are the best institutional and operational arrangements for the asset management company? (7) Should the government encourage corporate debt workout and restructuring? Countries are taking different positions in answering these questions. This section touches on some aspects of these issues that have a direct impact on the success of bank recapitalization.

The Purchase Price

In general, the authorities should not buy impaired assets at their book value to help recapitalize the institution, because this in effect conceals the cost of recapitalization from the public.[39,40] Such a transaction subsidizes banks, can be used to bail out owners and

---

[38]Under the Basel Capital Accord, loans carry a 100-percent weight, while cash and government bonds carry a zero or 20-percent weight.

[39]An exception to the general rule may occur where the government buys banks' loans to public enterprises. Where these loans have received an explicit or implicit public guarantee, the government may, with justification, choose to buy the loans close to book value.

[40]A question arises about provisions that have been taken against assets that are purchased by the government. If the provision is greater than the loss, if any, on the sale of the asset to the government, then the bank will benefit from the transaction. If the excess provisions are reversed in the profit-and loss-accounts, the government may recoup some of its outlays in the form of additional taxes on bank profits. This would happen, for example, when provision had been made for an asset that the government buys at book value.

Table 11.4. Public Support to Enhance the Value of Bank Assets[1]

Action	Indonesia	Japan	Korea
Aid assets	Yes.	Yes.	Yes.
Revalue assets	No.	Yes: real estate, value shares at cost if market.	Yes: Korean Land Corporation buys land to support prices.
Buy bad assets	Loss loans only in recapitalized banks; assets of closed banks.	Resolution and collection corporation buys bad assets from failed and operating banks.	Yes: initially from all banks; now less often and only to aid restructuring deals.
Pays with	Buys at zero value.	Cash (obtained from bond issues)	70% in government-guaranteed KAMCO bonds, 30% cash.
Other actions	1) Loan-loss provisions made tax-deductible; 2) publication of list of large delinquent borrowers.	As no automatic tax deduction for LLP, banks created the Cooperative Credit Purchasing Company; deferred taxes.	Removed limit on tax deductibility for LLP. Put options in P&As for acquiring banks.
Restructure debt	Yes: Indonesian Debt Restructuring Agency (INDRA); and the Jakarta/London Initiative. IBRA and the state banks in restructuring discussions, beginning with the 20 largest borrowers.	Can now tax-deduct debt forgiveness in a comprehensive restructuring plan. Limits on bank ownership of equity have been raised to facilitate debt equity swaps. There are also private initiatives; and restrictions on the foreign purchase of automobile companies, real estate, and brokerage houses have eased.	Yes: the FSC's Corporate Restructuring Agreement uses a modified London Approach to guide restructuring. Private (Corporate Restructuring Coordination Committee), arbitrates disputes for all but the five largest chaebols; for these, it is proposed to concentrate ownership where there is excess capacity under a Structural Improvement Plan. The CRA has been signed by 200 financial companies. Rescheduling involves interest rate reductions, debt forgiveness, and exchanging debt for equity or convertible bonds.

Source: IMF staff analysis.

[1]The public sector includes the government, the central bank as lender-of-last-resort, the deposit insurance corporation, the asset management company, the restructuring agency, and any vehicle for recapitalizing banks.

Malaysia	Mexico	Thailand
Yes.	Yes.	No.
No.	Yes: mortgage principal indexed to inflation.	No.
Yes: since 8/98 buying large bad loans from 18 banks by year-end 1998.	Yes; 1) Fondo Bancario de Protección al Ahorro buys 2 pesos of bad loans for every peso of additional private capital; 2) banks' UDI loans and foreclosed real estate transferred to trust funds	In principle, the asset management company buys only from intervened institutions.
Cash or zero-coupon, government-guaranteed, Danaharta bonds.	Five-year or ten-year, variable-rate, non-negotiable, zero-coupon Fondo Bancario de Protección al Ahorro bonds.	Five-year bonds without a government guarantee.
LLP tax-deductible; national pension fund bought "under-valued" shares; eased reserve and liquidity requirements and loan limits; credit floor.	1) 25:75 loss-sharing (bank: government) on bad loans; 2) facilitate the creation of credit bureaus.	Tax deductibility for LLP, stop-loss and yield maintenance guarantees for new investors taking over intervened banks.
Yes: Corporate Debt Restructuring Committee had received 42 applications for aid by end-1998; more in 1999; works with creditors and debtors to effect workouts. Banks threaten to sell delinquent loans to Danaharta, which has extensive powers over the borrowers of any loans it buys.	1) Unidad de Inversion (UDI) converted floating rate peso and dollar loans into long-term, fixed-rate loans denominated in UDIs for household mortgages, loans of corporations, states and municipalities and development banks; 2) Programa de Apoyo Inmediato a Deudores de la Banca, provided an interest subsidy to small borrowers that remained or became current; 3) assistance for highway concessionaires that restructured their loans in UDIs; 4) discount on payments to mortgage debtors that restructured their loans in UDIs and remained or became current; 5) FINAPE's discount on monthly payments for borrowers in the agricultural and fishery industries that restructured their debts or remained current; 6) FOPYME gave assistance to micro, small, and medium-sized firms; 7) the Punto Final offers rebates on mortgage loans to borrowers whose loans are current.	Corporate Debt Restructuring Advisory Committee uses the Bangkok/London Approach for workouts; classification standards for restructured loans were relaxed and tax impediments removed temporarily; tax exemptions are granted; a draft law establishes centralized credit bureaus; legal amendments will facilitate greater foreign ownership of property; bank ownership of equity easier to permit debt- to-equity swaps; the BOT is trying to facilitate loan workout for the 200 largest debtors; the state-owned Bank of Agriculture and Cooperatives permitted to give debt relief case by case.

managers, and violates the principle of transparency and accountability.[41] A realistic valuation/pricing of assets based on market pricing, sound accounting norms, strong loan classification and provisioning standards, or discounted present values is crucial, as discussed earlier. The rigorous recognition of loan losses is the first and most important element of an effective strategy for dealing with problem assets, because it creates the right incentives for banks to restructure their loans, foreclose on collateral, and precipitate bankruptcy reorganizations. The sellers of problem assets may be persuaded to accept conservative valuations if the asset purchase contract allows them to share unexpectedly good recovery values.

Do the Advantages of Asset Purchases Outweigh Their Disadvantages?

Asset purchases by a separate government agency may have a number of advantages that can aid bank recapitalization and restructuring and, if supported by proper incentives for loan workout and recovery efforts, could control fiscal costs. Because banks' problems are often derived from a deterioration in their loan portfolios, measures directed to the loan portfolios come closest to the source of the problems and may therefore be the most efficient form of remedial action, enabling banks to resume their normal operations quickly.

Such asset purchases achieve economies of scale in asset management, particularly by centralizing scarce human resources; foster the development of secondary markets for bank assets; and allow the bank to focus on managing its good assets during its recovery. Handling assets through a centralized asset management company is most appropriate when the banks originally holding the assets have been closed, where open banks holding the assets have no specific expertise in managing them, and where many banks may have claims on the same entity (e.g., a national airline or a major conglomerate).[42] In addition, asset purchases (and recapitalization with public funds generally) can be made conditional on participation by banks in debt workouts for borrowers and the achievement of performance targets for loan recovery for the assets retained in banks. Indeed, asset purchases/transfers complement a recapitalization package, for reasons already mentioned earlier, with the allocation of funds between asset purchases and direct recapitalization varying among

---

[41]There are examples in Asia and elsewhere of assets purchased at inflated prices. In Indonesia and Malaysia, however, the asset management agency has stated that asset purchases would be based on realistic values.

[42]Legal deficiencies may also be handled more easily through a centralized agency. See Stone (1998).

countries, according to specific institutional circumstances.[43] They can serve as an additional inducement to a bank to comply with the conditions for a recapitalization package.

Problem assets should be purchased, with bonds or cash, at realistic and fair prices. As pointed out above, cash and bonds have lower risk-weights than loans and will thus raise the bank's risk-weighted capital adequacy ratio, and will change operating incentives for banks' managements. A swap of classified assets whose yields are uncertain for bonds that carry market rates may also reduce bank's funding costs by decreasing uncertainty. An exchange for cash or bonds, which are negotiable or can be discounted at the central bank, improves bank liquidity and permits banks to make loans or other investments, and increase income.[44]

Asset purchases by a separate asset management company have several important potential disadvantages though. First, they do not raise banks' net worth unless the operation is done at above-market prices, which should be avoided as discussed above. Asset purchases thus do **not** solve a problem of lack of capital in the banking sector. Second, the government needs to consider the overall cost of this form of assistance, because the expenses it incurs in disposing of the troubled assets may be high and difficult to estimate, depending on the legal and operational environment for loan recovery and the likelihood of being subject to political pressure. Third, asset purchases may provide liquidity if purchased, for example, with cash or negotiable bonds. As with a direct capital infusion, this additional liquidity would need to be managed to avoid any potential conflict with the monetary stance. Moreover, again as with capital infusions, asset purchases can distort incentives if banks come to expect that the government will bail them out in the future by repeatedly buying their bad assets. Again, in this case, the pricing of the assets is the key issue.[45]

Overall, while one cannot draw universal conclusions, there do seem to be conditions under which the advantages of asset purchases by a separate

---

[43]By mid-1996, Mexico had spent two-thirds of its projected net outlays to purchase bad loans and support debtors; only one-third went to recapitalize banks. See pp. 114–16, Ito and Folkerts-Landau (1996). Countries typically purchase bad loans and support debtors when banks' internal governance is weak and property rights are poorly defended by the legal system.

[44]If the assets are purchased at written-down values, and if banks have already provisioned to those values, the sale of the assets should have no direct impact on a bank's profitability.

[45]If the centralized asset management company is dealing with private banks, it is particularly important to determine transfer prices that do not involve an implicit subsidy, and such determination is quite complex in times of uncertainty, as discussed earlier.

asset management company can outweigh the disadvantages. The company should be staffed by financial experts who are both honest and skilled in asset management and sale and its operations should be transparent and cost-effective for the government. It should have, if necessary, special legal powers to expedite loan recovery and loan restructuring. It should be constructed as a temporary agency for handling a special situation, and not as a permanent arrangement to preserve a good incentive structure.

Should the Asset Management Company Buy Assets from All Banks?

Some countries have chosen to acquire and sell assets only from banks that are being resolved by liquidation or merger.[46] Other countries also provide assistance to banks that are to remain open by buying their bad assets.[47]

When the asset management company purchases assets from open banks, a potential conflict arises between economizing limited resources and being fair to all banks. To buy bad assets only from troubled banks that are to receive government assistance could prejudice the survival of those better banks that are still struggling unaided to handle their portfolio of bad loans. One way for the government to resolve this dilemma is to buy some, but not all, of the bad assets of assisted banks. The assisted banks should be left with roughly the same proportion of bad loans as the rest of the surviving industry.[48]

Should the Asset Management Company Buy Only Impaired Assets?

The answer in general is "yes," given the purpose of the exercise, which is to restore banks to health and promote corporate restructuring. Good assets left with banks, and those transferred to banks in exchange for bad assets, are the means to rehabilitate bank profitability and soundness.

When banks have a choice as to which assets are to be transferred, they may seek to "cherry pick" and just provide the worst ones; by analogy, if the asset management company can choose its assets, it will choose those where it sees the best possible returns.[49] This problem can be avoided to some extent by ensuring that sales are at a "fair" price, and by defining classes of assets—such as all assets classified as "loss" or "doubtful" by the bank's auditors—that are to be transferred in their entirety.

---

[46]Thailand and the United States have taken this approach.

[47]Indonesia, Japan, Korea, Malaysia, and Mexico have bought bad assets from open banks.

[48]This was the approach adopted by Sweden. See Ingves and Lind (1997).

[49]Where governance problems have been associated with some assets, the bank may be reluctant to transfer them for fear that these problems would come to light. This has arguably been one of the factors explaining the protracted nature of the process for transferring loans to the asset management company in Indonesia.

Should the Asset Management Company Warehouse Assets?

There is disagreement on this issue. Some analysts believe that selling assets as soon as they have been catalogued and adequately serviced in preparation for sale will establish a floor for asset prices in the economy. Establishing that floor will provide a turning point for economic recovery. They argue that warehousing assets prevents price adjustments, particularly where markets have ceased to function in the crisis, and the overhang of the stored assets impedes price discovery and market recovery and prolongs the recession. Finding the price floor, on the other hand, will promote a speedier recovery. Proponents of prompt sale also point to the danger of asset deterioration while under government control and claim that restoring assets to the private markets will ensure better maintenance. Others disagree; they believe that a "fire sale" will accentuate the depth of the recession. Thus, they argue that assets should be warehoused and released for sale slowly so that they do not flood the market. Such warehousing, they assert, will increase the net present value of the amount that the government will receive when it sells the assets and reduce the taxpayers' ultimate costs. The balance struck between these two possibilities varies from country to country. The United States was particularly active in quickly on-selling assets taken over during the savings and loan crisis, although commentators suggest that the far greater depth of the markets in the United States means that the country is not an appropriate model for countries elsewhere. Among the Asian crisis countries, Thailand has been the most forceful in quickly selling the assets taken over by the public sector.

Institutional and Operational Arrangements[50]

There are a variety of institutional structures that will permit the asset management component of the bank restructuring agency to accomplish its tasks. Institutional arrangements to work out or recover problem assets could involve a mixture of roles for governments to ensure adequate flexibility to respond to different bank circumstances and market requirements (Nyberg, 1997). As discussed earlier, a proactive and centralized role for governments (such as government-owned asset management units) could be desirable in some circumstances (to deal with a large volume of problem assets acquired in facilitating mergers, bank closures, and recapitalizations, for example, or to deal with large, legally complicated exposures). In contrast, an enabling role for governments that involves decentralized arrangements (debt workout units within banks themselves, for example, or separately capitalized

---

[50]Berggren (1996) discusses establishing and operating asset management companies.

loan recovery and asset management companies) is the most appropriate in many circumstances. Most impaired loans where the borrower itself has value as an ongoing concern, and where there is a likelihood that the borrower can pay after some financial restructuring, should remain with the originating bank or its successor. But some small and medium-sized loans or some insider loans where value lies mainly in recovery from underlying assets or collaterals are often handled by separate loan recovery companies outside the banks.[51]

Operational aspects of the asset management company are largely beyond the scope of this paper, but they are pertinent to the curtailment of the government's costs in bank recapitalization. In its activities, the asset management company will rely on the valuation that has already been made of bank assets, the prognosis previously made for recovery by individual banks, and the identification already made of those banks deemed eligible for government assistance. The asset management company's tasks are to ensure performance of the loans; take control of the assets, including legal title to collateral; protect real assets from deterioration; improve them if possible; prepare them for marketing; sell them at the best possible price; and go out of business when it has fulfilled its obligations. There are two extreme approaches to asset management. One is to treat each asset separately, selling real property item by item and holding individual loans to maturity while pursuing legal options to force borrowers to service their debts.[52] The opposite end of the spectrum on approaches is to package the assets and sell them by auction in bulk.[53] This distinction reflects the choice whether the asset management company should **own** the assets or merely act as **agent** handling the assets. The latter approach was used by the Federal Deposit Insurance Corporation (FDIC) in the United States, but in other countries the authorities have preferred direct ownership so as to be able more fundamentally to regroup and reorganize the assets before selling them. Again, no overall preference can be determined ex ante. Different tools may be appropriate in different cases.[54]

Contractors from the private sector can assist regardless of which approach is adopted; they can ensure performance of the loans. They can design and maintain a computerized database of assets acquired and

---

[51]Existing bank-client ties may in fact reflect a "cozy" relationship that could impede an aggressive liquidation process.

[52]This is the approach adopted in Lithuania, as described by Maldeikis (1998) at the FDIC International Conference on Deposit Insurance.

[53]This approach is being used in Thailand, as described by Vichit-Vadakan (1998) at the FDIC International Conference on Deposit Insurance.

[54]For instance, it may be particularly productive to hold and repackage property companies before seeking to sell them.

an electronic system for tracking loan condition and disposition. Investment bankers and other financial experts can design classification criteria for packaging assets, prepare the assets for marketing as securities, and conduct asset auctions.

Encouraging Loan Workouts

Asset management companies and banks can facilitate debt workouts and debt restructuring of potentially viable corporate borrowers. Countries have taken widely disparate approaches to this tool. During the course of bank restructuring, some leave it to banks themselves and to the private sector.[55] Other countries have been more active in working out and restructuring loans, especially where they believe that the legal system is inadequate to support purely private negotiations or where there are market failures.[56] If carefully constructed, however, debt workouts can support recapitalization efforts, whether done through capital injections or asset purchases. They should reduce debt or debt service burdens and improve borrowers' ability to repay their loans, thereby reducing the volume of nonperforming assets on banks' books, without destroying, in the long run, the incentive structure that expects borrowers to repay their loans.

The enabling role of governments in facilitating loan-workout arrangements can take several forms, and it can be an important component of bank recapitalization. Appropriate legal frameworks for bankruptcy and dealing with collateral are necessary of course, whatever the institutional mechanisms for handling problem assets. Possible governmental actions range from the informal and decentralized to the formal and centralized (see Stone, 1998). In the informal, decentralized approach the government provides incentives to encourage, and offers guidance on conducting loan workouts. Taking a more active stance, it might arbitrate disputes among private negotiators. The ultimate interventionist action is to form a centralized asset management company and have the government buy banks' bad debts to renegotiate, manage, and sell them. The proper choice varies depending in part on the seriousness of the problem. In cases of deep insolvency and ultimately government ownership of banks, a government-owned asset management company (or companies) is the likely outcome, while in less severe cases a privately owned asset management company may be more feasible.

---

[55]Japan and the United States have followed this approach.

[56]Indonesia, Korea, Malaysia, Mexico, and Thailand have assisted in the restructuring of private debt. The government of Mexico has been particularly active in providing support to households, and small and medium-sized businesses of all sizes. Corporate restructuring is being done privately with government encouragement.

In many cases, both types will be needed to maximize loan recovery in addition to building up effective loan-workout capacity within banks themselves to deal with normal credit risks.

Governments have often played a catalytic role in fostering corporate debt restructuring, either as a component of bank recapitalization or as a separate complementary policy in times of banking distress.[57] One framework for debtor-creditor negotiations in which the government encourages corporate restructuring is the "London Approach," which has no direct link to capital support facilities (see Kent, 1987, and 1997). When advising the parties or arbitrating disputes between private negotiators, the government can encourage banks or other acquirers to restructure loans, and retain and recover impaired loans of uncertain value through government guarantees under income-maintenance, loss sharing, stop-loss, or put-back provisions during a specified period.[58] There could also be arrangements for acquirers and sellers to share profits, if assets are sold or recovered for more than a specified amount.

In summary, the choice of institutional and regulatory arrangements for asset management, loan recovery, and corporate debt restructuring is among the most critical aspects of successful bank recapitalization. The design of these arrangements should ensure realistic valuation of impaired assets, prompt recognition of loan losses, and a balanced and pragmatic approach to asset disposition that is neither too rapid nor too delayed to avoid losses on assets. Specific institutional choices to achieve these goals will depend also on the legal and governance constraints, the nature of the problem assets, and the size and distribution of these assets among banks. As indicated above, one cannot state ex ante which specific measures should be adopted. The authorities will need to determine their policies on a case-by-case basis.

Other Actions to Aid Bank Recapitalization

Governments frequently try to aid banks in recapitalizing by reducing their liabilities, improving their income, and granting forbearance. Many of the techniques employed disrupt monetary and fiscal management, distort incentives, and reduce transparency. When they do so, they should be adopted only cautiously, if at all. Nevertheless, they are being used (see Table 11.5).

---

[57]Examples of the former approach are bank recapitalization schemes linked to bank conciliation agreements in Poland, or to debt workout and restructuring in Thailand. See Montes-Negret and Papi (1997), and the capital support schemes announced by the Ministry of Finance in Thailand, on August 14, 1998 (Thailand, 1998b).

[58]These techniques have been used, for example, in Malaysia and the United States.

Reducing Liabilities

Rather than increasing the assets of a bank to match its liabilities, the authorities may seek to reduce the liabilities to the level of the assets. A program like this is, however, often constrained by the comprehensiveness of guarantees already given to depositors and creditors (for example, in the Asian crisis countries and Mexico), and the legal framework governing their rights under bank-bankruptcy laws. Even where there is a comprehensive guarantee by the government or the central bank, though, it may be possible to reduce the size of the bank's balance sheet by converting liquidity support from the central bank into bank capital, thereby changing the incentive structure of management in particular as with respect to the size and the riskiness of the bank's portfolio.

Improving Income

The authorities sometimes assist banks through measures to improve the income stream of banks, which include more lenient tax treatment of banks in various forms, and public sector loans or deposits at below-market interest rates to improve income and liquidity. Such measures are not transparent, they do not adequately address the problem of capital shortage, and they distort monetary and fiscal management.

Granting Regulatory Forbearance

Measures of regulatory forbearance[59] adopted in six countries are shown in Table 11.5. They range from counting certain items as capital in violation of the Basel Capital Accord, to relaxing loan classification and provisioning standards, to phasing in the minimum capital adequacy ratio. Forbearance can be hidden or explicit, and concealed forbearance should be eschewed. Forbearance that allows banks to disguise their losses and recognize them only slowly over time is particularly objectionable. However, in a crisis one form of explicit regulatory forbearance—phasing in prudential and regulatory standards—can be a useful tool that facilitates recapitalization. The capital adequacy standard can be explicitly and temporarily reduced to some positive number below the desired standard, such as the Basel Committee's recommended 8 percent or a larger ratio. Banks, under closely monitored conditions, can then be allowed to raise capital over time on a

---

[59]Regulatory forbearance is used here in the sense of adopting a time-bound and internally consistent strategy for achieving prudential standards rather than being required to achieve those standards immediately. It is not the same as neglecting prudential standards in the hope that conditions will simply improve.

Table 11.5. Other Actions by the Public Sector to Recapitalize Banks[1]

Action	Indonesia	Japan	Korea
Burden-sharing	Shareholders and connected lenders.	Shareholders, and some junior creditors.	Shareholders.
Assume debts (full guarantee)	Yes.	Yes: regular and call deposits, trusts, bonds.	Yes.
Reduce claims	The losses imposed on depositors in 16 closed banks were later retroactively fully guaranteed.	Shares, convertible bonds and subordinated debt.	All shareholders in intervened banks.
Other actions	Loan-loss provisioning made tax deductible	No automatic tax deduction for LLP: so banks created the Cooperative Credit Purchasing Co.; loan-loss carry forwards.	Removed limit on tax deductibility for LLP. Put options in P&As for acquiring banks.
Forbearance	Yes	Yes.	Yes.
Capital Adequacy Ratio	Capital Adequacy Ratio temporarily lowered to 4%; will gradually increase to 8%; have limited to 1.25% the general provisions to be included in Tier 2 capital (previously all general and specific provisions were allowable in Tier 2).	1) Permit international banks to convert to domestic status to lower their Capital Adequacy Ratio to 4%; 2) grace period for compliance with even this low Capital Adequacy Ratio; 3) excessively count deferred taxes; 4) some provisions against substandard loans as capital; and 5) can value securities at book, not the lower of book or market.	1) Phased for commercial and merchant banks; 2) for others 8% would rule only in year 2000; 3) loan losses deferred for three years for merchant banks; 4) additional provisions required as a result of forward-looking criteria can be phased over two years.
Other	International loan classification and provisioning rules have improved, but recognition of the loss (in excess of provisions) on special-mention and substandard loans can be deferred for up to four years; losses on other loans are recognized immediately.	Accounting; LCP tightened, but not always enforced; unconsolidated subsidiaries hold bad loans; some banks do not classify or provision to until loan is overdue six months and they may lend unpaid interest to enable the borrower to keep the loan current; banks have been allowed to revalue property and equities.	Yes: for merchant banks; otherwise accounting is improving and the timetable for phasing in the regulations serves accelerate the process; ceased including special provisions for NPLs in Tier 2 capital in 1999.[1]

Source: IMF staff analysis.

[1]The public sector includes the government, the central bank as lender of last resort, the deposit insurance corporation, the asset management company, the restructuring agency, and any vehicle for recapitalizing banks.

Malaysia	Mexico	Thailand
Shareholders.	Shareholders.	Shareholders.
Yes.	Yes.	Yes: to honor the guarantee.
Shareholders.	Maturities extended.	For some closed finance companies.
LLP already tax-deductible; national pension fund bought "undervalued" shares; lowered reserve and liquidity requirements.	25:75 loss-sharing on bad loans.	Tax deduct LLP, profit and loss-sharing; stop-loss and yield maintenance guarantees for new investors in intervened banks.
Yes.	Yes.	Yes.
Loan classification and provisioning firmed, then relaxed then firmed again; Capital Adequacy Ratio remains at 8%; supervision tightened; watch lists formalized.	The tightening in 1997 was reversed in 1998: restructured loans now count as performing even when nothing is paid up front; bonds have been reclassified from the trading to hold-to-maturity portfolio; subordinated debt counts as base capital and specific provisions as regulatory capital; write-down on banks 25% in loss-sharing can be phased over eight years.	In exchange for restructuring corporate debts; either LCP to be phased in gradually until year 2000 or cost of debt restructuring can be deferred over five years.
For loans sold to Danaharta, banks have up to five years to recognize the difference between book value and selling price.	1) Grace period for loan repayment; 2) the limit on shareholding raised from 10% to 20% of capital; 3) market share limitations were waived; 4) interest rate swap engineered in 9/98 to pay banks higher rates on their treasury securities; 5) banks could pledge non-negotiable Fondo Bancario de Protección al Ahorro bonds as collateral; and 6) IPAB notes are negotiable.	No.

specified and uniformly applicable schedule toward a desirable capital adequacy ratio.[60]

Sometimes countries choose to tighten loan loss provisioning standards gradually over time, rather than opting for a gradual approach to reaching desired capital ratios combined with full compliance with provisioning rules. The gradual approach to desired capital ratios is preferable to the gradual increase in provisioning because it is more transparent. Moreover, the latter can reduce incentives for prompt recognition of asset values that are needed to support loan workout and efficient asset management arrangements.

Concluding Remarks

Recapitalizing and restructuring banks in the aftermath of a systemic crisis is a complex process that typically requires significant government intervention and takes several years to design and implement. To be effective, it must be carried out in a coordinated, prompt, but carefully prepared manner that reconciles financial and human resource needs with resource constraints, and that provides an incentive structure that will foster financial stability in future years. It requires careful management both at the strategic level and at the individual bank level to ensure that government investment in banks yields the maximum return and that an efficient and sound banking system emerges at the end of the process.

The achievement of the objectives above requires effective institutional and organizational arrangements to make recapitalization and restructuring decisions, to manage impaired assets, and to foster rapid corporate restructuring. The approaches to recapitalization have varied, with countries choosing different mixes of direct capital injections and asset purchase and rehabilitation. In an effective recapitalization process, the two approaches are generally complementary, but a balance between the two approaches (which differs from country to country) becomes necessary to minimize the expected present value of government outlays net of recoveries.

---

[60]For example, Chapter 6, "Other Resolution Alternatives" of the FDIC's *Resolutions Handbook* (1998), takes the position that regulatory forbearance can be a useful tool when recapitalizing banks. A number of Asian countries have been transparently allowing their troubled banks to fall temporarily below minimum capital standards, while adhering to a schedule for restoration of capital standards. In Indonesia, for instance, the minimum capital requirement was temporarily reduced to 4 percent in the crisis, with banks having until the end of 2001 to achieve the 8 percent standard.

New investment in banks may also be encouraged by government efforts to aid the restructuring of corporate and consumer debt so that loan quality can improve. For example, lengthening maturities or debt-to-equity conversions can enable some borrowers who would otherwise default to repay their debt and reduce uncertainty in the market.

As the restructuring and recapitalization proceeds, and financial stability is restored, the activities of the agencies established to handle these functions will change. They will shift from planning and implementation to preparation for cessation and closure. The bank restructuring agency, the bank support authority, and the asset management company will complete their assigned tasks and close down. As their termination approaches, the authorities must prepare to replace the full guarantee, if any, with a limited deposit insurance system, and ensure that the traditional mechanisms for effective corporate governance are firmly in place to preserve financial stability.

Appendix I: Glossary

Asset-backed bonds. Income from a homogeneous bundle of assets can be used to pay the interest on collateralized bonds sold to pay for the purchase of the assets. The bonds may be sold in several tiers depending on the priority of their claim over the income from the assets. The claims with the highest priority have the least risk, and those holding residual claims after all other bond holders have been paid are the most risky. Financial institutions have widely used this technique to sell their mortgages to a mortgage banker who securitizes the loans. It is now being adapted for marketing impaired assets. The issuer of the bonds may offer an interest guarantee on some tranches of the debt.

Asset management company. A separately capitalized institution, owned privately, publicly or jointly, that is established for a limited period of time to restructure, manage, and sell the problem assets acquired during bank closures and restructuring. A country may establish one centralized asset management company or a number of decentralized ones.

Bad bank. The portion of a troubled bank that represents the "bad" assets. Sound assets and often some of the liabilities, particularly the insured deposits, go to the "good bank," for example, in a purchase and assumption transaction. The nonperforming assets go to the "bad bank," which typically does not accept deposits from the public. The bank's principal liability is likely to be the equity of its public or private owner.

Bank restructuring agency. A lead agency, often created specifically to design and coordinate the implementation of the comprehensive strategy for bank restructuring and recapitalization. This agency coordinates with other government agencies and is accountable to the government for the restructuring process.

Bank support authority. The subsidiary of the bank restructuring agency that provides financial support to banks that continue to operate.

Bridge bank. A newly chartered, nationalized bank established and operated by the authorities on an interim basis to acquire the assets and assume the liabilities of failing institutions until final resolution can be accomplished. The use of bridge banks is generally limited to situations in which more time is needed to permit the least costly resolution of a large or complex institution.

CAMELS rating. The quality rating for banks that typically ranges from 1 for the best banks to 5 for the worst. CAMELS stands for **c**apital, **a**sset quality, **m**anagement capacity, **e**arnings, **l**iquidity, and **s**ystemic risk.

Centralized approach to asset management. A single centralized asset management company, which is common to all banks and may be government- or privately owned, recovers value from troubled assets individually or in bulk through debt servicing, debt renegotiations, asset swaps, liquidations, and sales of collateral. The asset management company may also be involved in corporate restructuring.

Comfort letter. A letter from the owners and managers indicating their willingness to perform certain actions required by a supervisor, such as being prepared to recapitalize a bank when instructed.

Debt auction. A debtor asks individual creditors to submit bids indicating the percentage repayment they would be willing to accept in settlement of their debts. The debtor then repays those submitting the smallest percentages, probably paying a uniform, cut-off price.

Debt workouts. Agreements between borrowers and lenders to restructure the debts of heavily indebted borrowers. Restructuring a loan for a financially distressed borrower can be more productive for a bank than foreclosing on the collateral or initiating lawsuits to collect on the debt.

Decentralized approach to asset management. Each bank retains financial responsibility for working out its problem assets. Its workout unit may be run as a separate department of the banks or as a wholly owned subsidiary.

Due diligence. The on-site inspection of the books and records of a failing institution. Before an institution's failure, the authorities invite potential purchasers to the institution to review pertinent files so they can make informed decisions about the value of the failing institution's assets. Such potential purchasers must sign a confidentiality agreement. In addition, contractors may be hired to perform due diligence on assets that are earmarked for multi-asset sales initiatives.

Essentiality. An exception to the financial criteria that should usually govern eligibility for recapitalization with public funds may be made when a bank provides essential, irreplaceable services to the economy or is too large to be closed.

Fit and proper test. An evaluation of the competence, integrity, qualifications, and experience of the owner, senior managers, and directors of a bank. This evaluation involves background checks on whether previous activities, including adverse regulatory or judicial decisions, raise doubts about competence, sound judgment, or honesty.

Franchise value. The franchise value is the discounted present value of the bank's future profits. Thus, a bank with zero net worth could have a positive franchise value, which an acquirer would be willing to buy. Deposits that can be invested at a positive profit have a positive franchise value.

Good bank. A bank whose bad assets have been removed.

Income-(or yield) maintenance agreement. A resolution method used by the authorities to guarantee a market rate of return on certain assets of troubled banks. For example, the authorities may pay the holder the difference between the current yield on assets and the bank's average cost of funds. These agreements can also be used to facilitate mergers and purchase and assumptions (often called P&As) between troubled banks and healthy institutions.

Intervention. The intervention may take several forms. An insolvent bank may be closed; an undercapitalized bank may be nationalized, placed in conservatorship, or given capital assistance while under close supervision.

Loss-sharing agreement. An agreement between the acquiring bank and the authorities about the sharing of losses in a failed bank. Loss sharing aims to sell as many assets of a failed bank as possible to the private sector and align the interests and incentives of the acquiring bank and the authorities so that the assets are well-managed and maximum recoveries are obtained. Under loss sharing, the authorities agree to absorb a significant portion of the loss, perhaps 80 percent, on a specified pool of assets while offering even greater loss protection in the event of financial catastrophe. The acquiring bank is liable for the remaining portion of the loss.

Memorandum of Understanding. A written statement indicating agreement between a bank and its supervisor that the bank will perform certain actions.

Noncumulative preferred shares. A perpetual component of Tier 1 capital that provides the owners with special voting rights as well as a fixed amount of dividends, where the bank's financial results permit.

Open-bank assistance. A term used especially in the United States to indicate financial assistance to a bank that will be allowed to continue in business. That bank may be briefly closed and its shareholders wiped out to be reopened as a temporary bridge bank or, as in the case of Continental Illinois National Bank, shareholders may be allowed to retain some residual ownership rights.

Options. A call option gives the right, but not the obligation to purchase an asset at an agreed-upon price at a specified date (European option), or within a specified period (American option). A put option conveys a similar right, but not the obligation to sell.

Profit-sharing. This gives the government an opportunity to share in the upside potential when the economy recovers. A government-owned asset management company, for example, may lend funds to a private sector acquirer to enable the acquirer to purchase restructured assets. In addition to paying interest, the acquirer may agree to convey, for instance 20 percent of the profits earned on the acquisition, to the asset management company.

Purchase and assumption (P&A). An acquiring bank purchases the assets and assumes the liabilities of a failed bank. The transaction may cover all of the assets (whole bank P&A), or the best part of the assets ("good bank" P&A).

Put-back provision. A provision under which an assuming institution has the option of returning to the authorities, within a specified time period, certain assets that have been transferred to the acquiring institution.

Risk-weighted capital adequacy ratio. The Basel Capital Accord assigns risk-weights to on and off balance-sheet exposures, according to broad categories of relative riskiness. The Accord sets minimum capital ratio requirements for internationally active banks of 4 percent for Tier

1 capital and 8 percent for total capital in relation to risk-weighted assets.

Securitization. The asset management company can hire an expert investment bank to set criteria for packaging a bundle of impaired assets into a relatively homogeneous group. Asset-backed bonds are then sold to finance the asset purchase. These assets will be serviced either by the asset management company or by the expert in this task, and the income received will be used to pay the interest owed on the bonds.

Stop-loss agreement. A "stop-loss" agreement imposes limits on the acquirer's exposure to unanticipated losses on the shared loss-assets. If asset losses exceed the authorities' best estimate of the loss, their percentage coverage is then increased, for instance to 95 percent, and the acquiring bank's exposure is reduced to 5 percent of the loss.

Triage. The division of institutions between those that need no help, those that are worth helping, and those that are beyond help.

Warrants to purchase. Securities that give their holders the right to purchase a certain number of the shares of common stock in a corporation, at a preset price and under predefined conditions.

Yield-maintenance agreement. See income maintenance agreement.

Appendix II: Organizational Charts

Figure 11.3. Institutional Framework: Indonesia

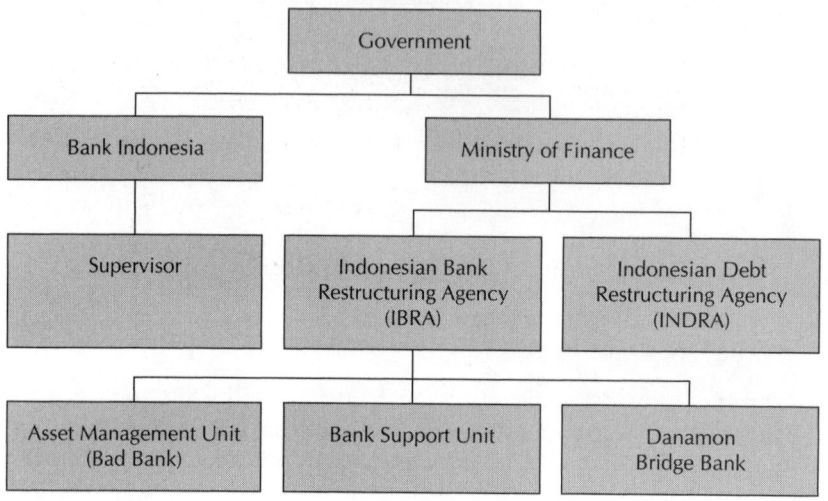

Source: IMF staff analysis.

Figure 11.4. Institutional Framework: Japan[1]

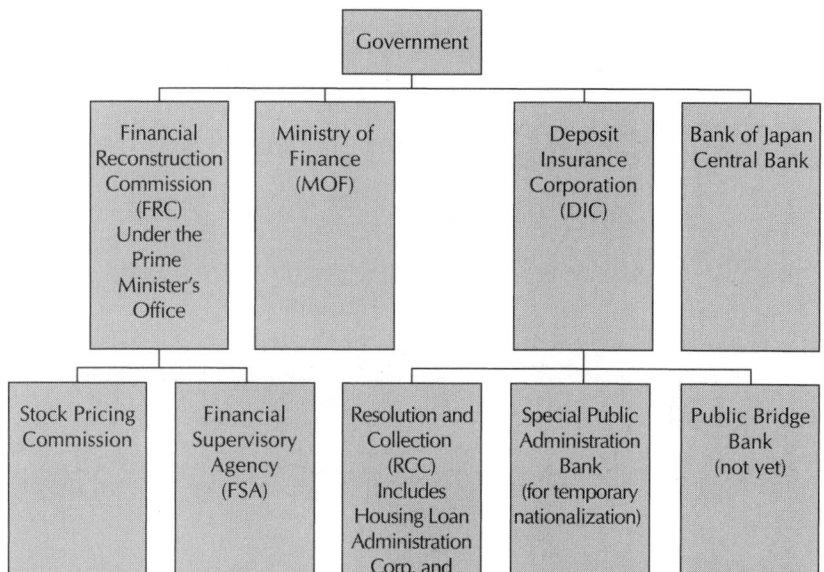

Source: IMF staff analysis.
[1]Since April 1, 1999.

Figure 11.5. Institutional Framework: Korea

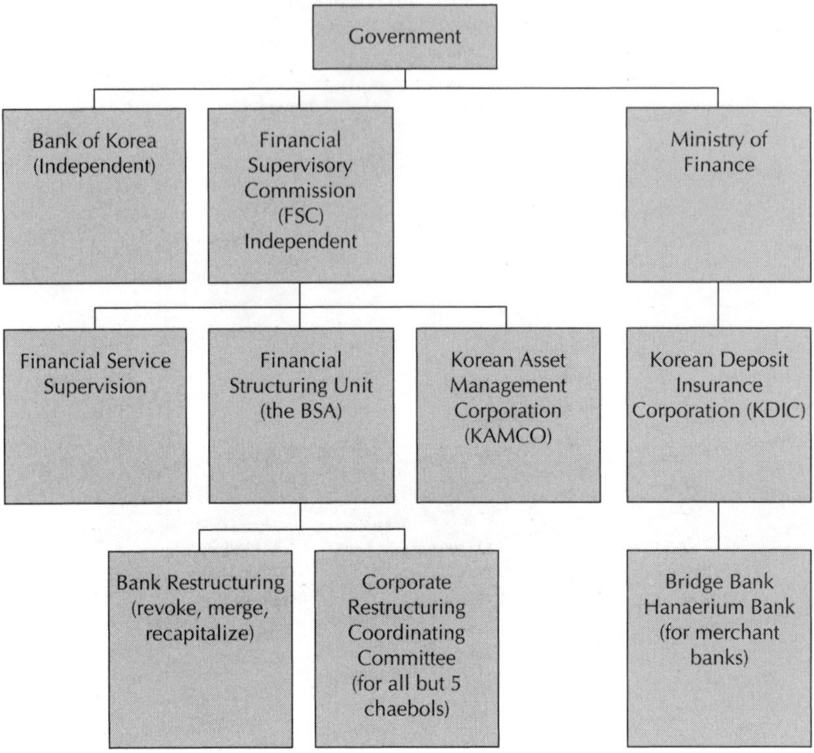

```
                          Government
          ┌─────────────────┼──────────────────┐
   Bank of Korea      Financial          Ministry of
   (Independent)      Supervisory         Finance
                      Commission
                      (FSC)
                      Independent
          ┌───────────────┼──────────────┐         │
   Financial Service  Financial      Korean Asset   Korean Deposit
   Supervision        Structuring Unit  Management    Insurance
                      (the BSA)      Corporation    Corporation (KDIC)
                                     (KAMCO)
                   ┌─────┴─────┐                      │
            Bank Restructuring  Corporate         Bridge Bank
            (revoke, merge,     Restructuring     Hanaerium Bank
            recapitalize)       Coordinating      (for merchant
                                Committee          banks)
                                (for all but 5
                                chaebols)
```

Source: IMF staff analysis.

Figure 11.6. Institutional Framework: Malaysia

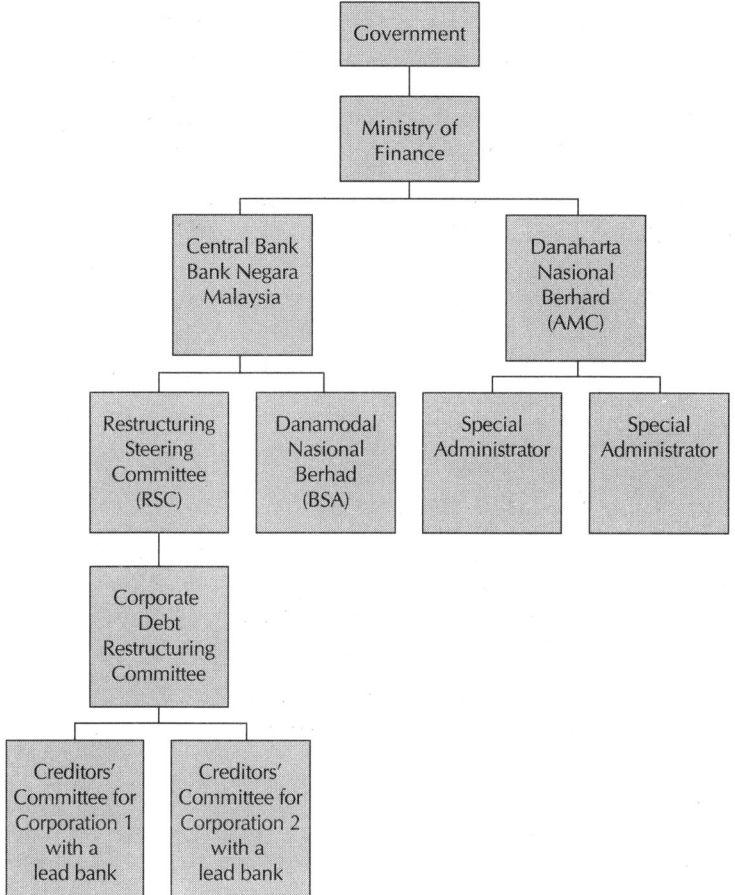

Source: IMF staff analysis.

Figure 11.7. Institutional Framework: Mexico Before December 1998

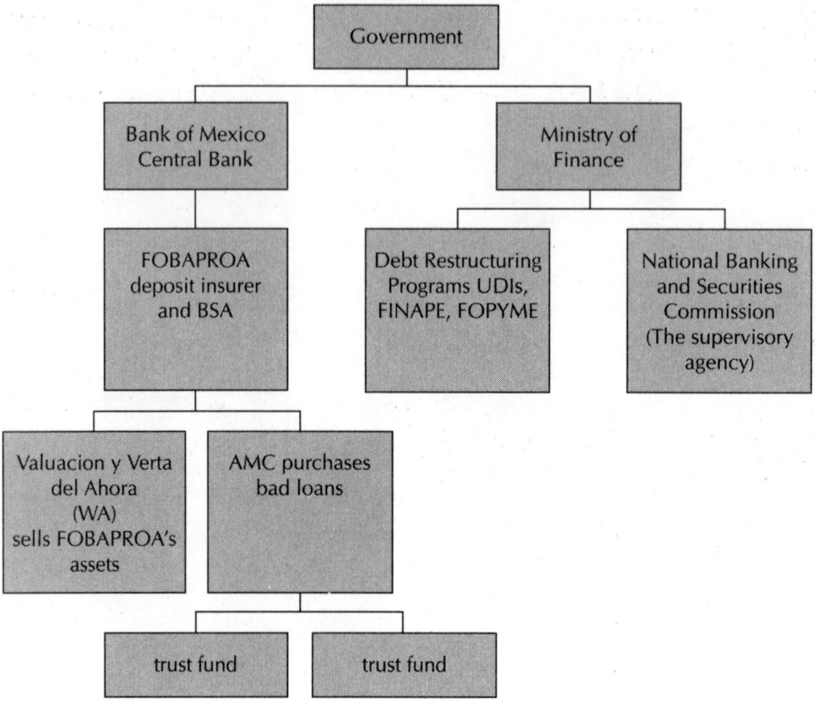

```
                          Government
                    ┌──────────┴──────────┐
          Bank of Mexico            Ministry of
           Central Bank               Finance
                │              ┌────────┴────────┐
            FOBAPROA    Debt Restructuring   National Banking
         deposit insurer  Programs UDIs,     and Securities
            and BSA       FINAPE, FOPYME       Commission
                │                             (The supervisory
       ┌────────┴────────┐                         agency)
  Valuacion y Verta   AMC purchases
    del Ahora          bad loans
      (WA)                 │
  sells FOBAPROA's    ┌────┴────┐
      assets       trust fund  trust fund
```

Source: IMF staff analysis.

Figure 11.8. Institutional Framework: Mexico in 1999

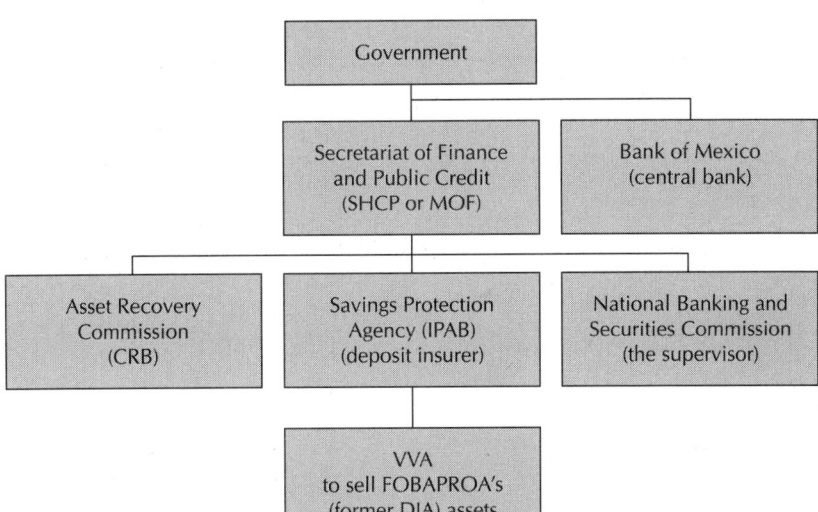

Source: IMF staff analysis.

Figure 11.9. Institutional Framework: Sweden

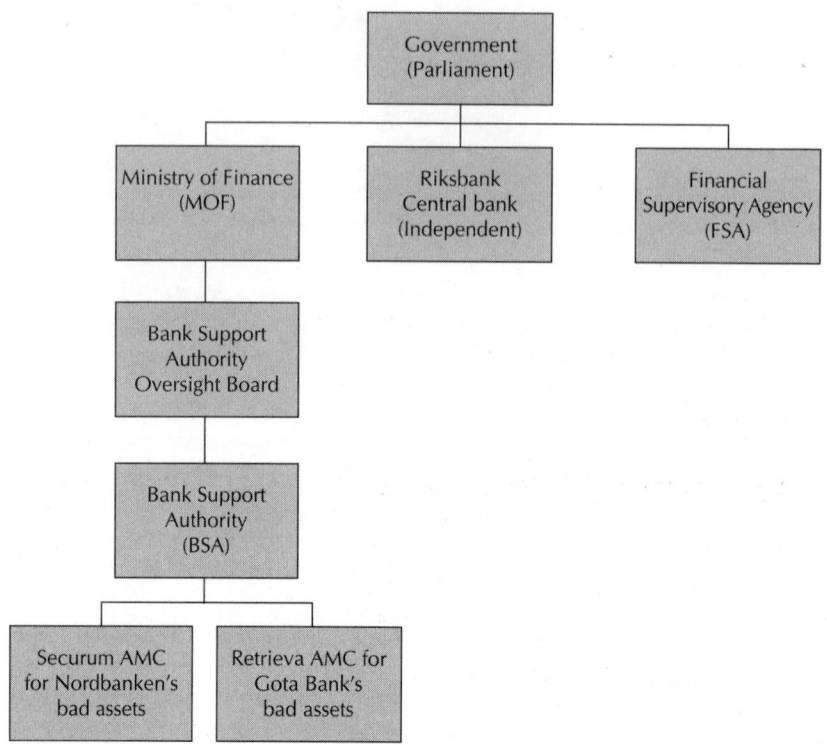

Source: IMF staff analysis.

Figure 11.10. Institutional Framework: Thailand

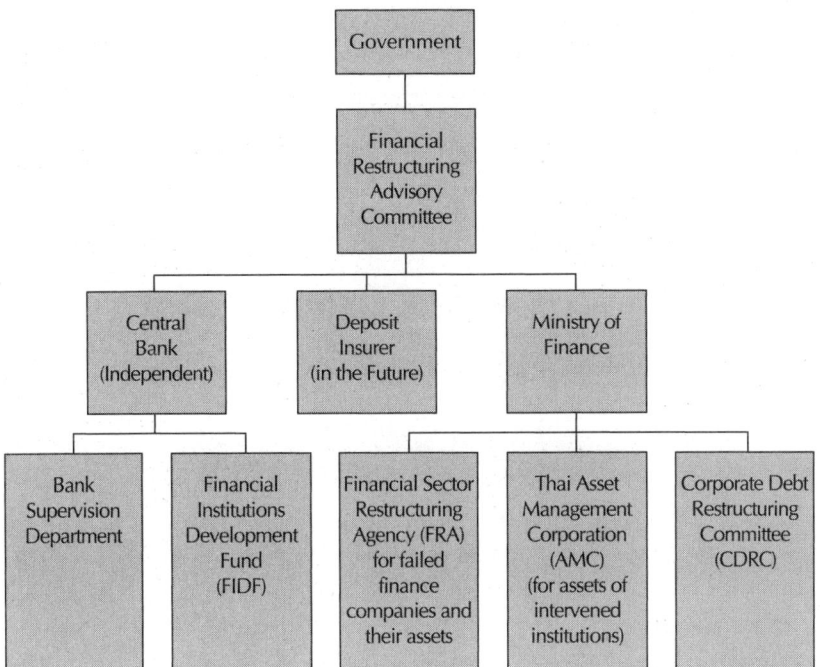

Source: IMF staff analysis.

Figure 11.11. Institutional Framework: the U.S. FDIC Model

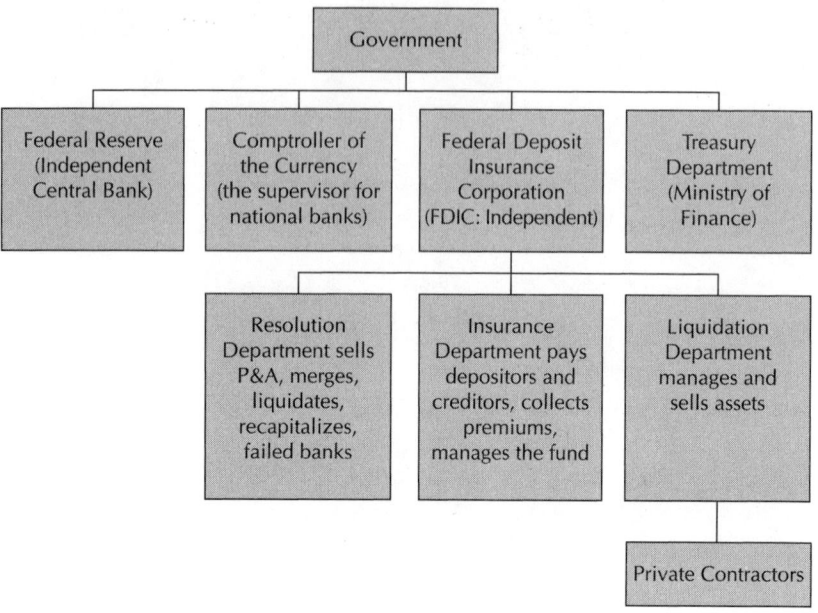

Source: IMF staff analysis.

Figure 11.12. Institutional Framework: the U.S. RTC Model

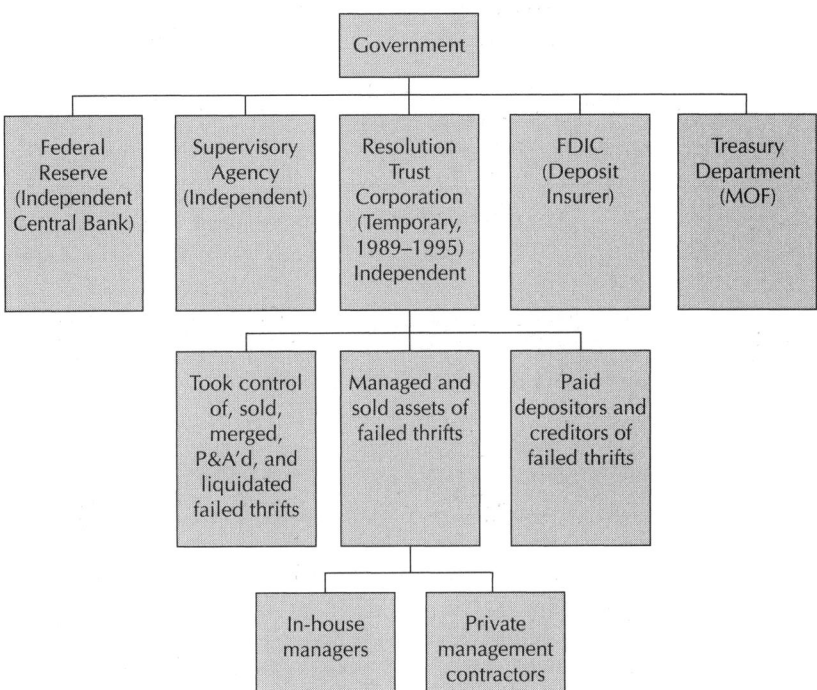

Source: IMF staff analysis.

References

Alexander, William E., Jeffrey M. Davis, Liam P. Ebrill, and Carl-Johan Lindgren, 1997, *Systemic Bank Restructuring and Macroeconomic Policy* (Washington: International Monetary Fund).

Basel Committee on Banking Supervision, 1997, *The Compendium of Documents Produced by the Basel Committee on Banking Supervision* (Basel: Bank for International Settlements).

———, 1998, "Instruments Eligible for Inclusion in Tier 1 and Tier 2 Capital," Press Release, October 27 (Basel: Bank for International Settlements).

———, 1999, *The Compendium of Documents Produced by the Basel Committee on Banking Supervision*, February (Basel: Bank for International Settlements).

Berggren, Arne, 1996, "Establishing Asset Management Companies" paper prepared for Workshop on Systemic Bank Restructuring (unpublished; Washington: IMF Monetary and Exchange Affairs Department).

Dziobek, Claudia H., 1998, "Market-Based Policy Instruments for Systemic Bank Restructuring," IMF Working Paper No. 98/113 (Washington: International Monetary Fund).

Federal Deposit Insurance Corporation, 1998, "Other Resolution Alternatives," in *Resolutions Handbook: Methods for Resolving Troubled Financial Institutions in the United States* (Washington: Government Printing Office).

Ingves, Stefan, and Göran Lind, 1997, "Loan Loss Recoveries and Debt Resolution Agencies: The Swedish Experience," in *Banking Soundness and Monetary Policy: Issues and Experiences in the Global Economy*, ed. by Charles Enoch and John H. Green (Washington: International Monetary Fund).

Ito, Takatoshi, and David Folkerts-Landau, 1996, *International Capital Markets: Developments, Prospects, and Key Policy Issues* (Washington: International Monetary Fund).

Kent, Pen, 1987, "International Debt: The Case-by-Case Strategy," *Banking World*, No. 5 (May), pp. 13–16.

———, 1997, "Corporate Workouts: A U.K. Perspective," in *Terzo Rapporto sul Sistema Finanziario Italiano*, ed. by Fondazione Rosselli (Rome: Edibank).

Maldeikis, Eugenius, 1998, "Asset Disposition in Lithuania," paper presented at the FDIC International Conference on Deposit Insurance, *Conference Papers, Volume II*, Washington, September.

Montes-Negret, Fernando, and Luca Papi, 1997, *The Polish Experience with Bank and Enterprise Restructuring*, Policy Research Working Paper No. 1705 (Washington: World Bank).

Nyberg, Peter, 1997, "Authorities' Roles and Organizational Issues in Systemic Bank Restructuring," IMF Working Paper No. 97/92 (Washington: International Monetary Fund).

Stone, Mark R., 1998, "Corporate Debt Restructuring in East Asia: Some Lessons from International Experience," IMF Paper on Policy Analysis and Assessment 98/13 (Washington: International Monetary Fund).

Sundararajan, V., 1999, "Prudential Supervision, Bank Restructuring, and Financial Sector Reform," in *Sequencing Financial Sector Reforms: Country Experiences and Issues*, ed. by R. Barry Johnston and V. Sundararajan (Washington: International Monetary Fund).

Thailand, Ministry of Finance and Bank of Thailand, 1998a, *Joint Statement of August 14, 1998.*

———, 1998b, Capital Support Schemes announced on August 14.

Vichit-Vadakan, Vicharat, 1998, "Thai Financial Crisis and Reform," paper presented at the FDIC International Conference on Deposit Insurance, *Conference Papers, Volume II*, Washington, September.

12

An Operational Framework for Addressing the Public Costs of Systemic Bank Restructuring

PRIYA BASU

Systemic bank restructuring entails high costs, which are borne largely by governments and funded through the issuance of vast quantities of public debt. Cross-country estimates show that the stock of public debt issued in the context of recent systemic bank restructuring programs has ranged from single digits to 50 percent or more of GDP. While government support to bank restructuring through the issuance of public debt can help address the immediate crisis, it can result in escalating costs to the government, raising significant, and often unanticipated, medium-term risks related to fiscal and debt sustainability and financial stability. This chapter presents a simple operational framework for quantifying, analyzing, and reducing such costs, on an ex post basis.

In recent decades, a large number of countries—both developed and developing—have experienced systemic banking crises requiring a major—and expensive—overhaul of their banking systems, with the costs of bank restructuring shouldered largely by governments (and thus, ultimately, by taxpayers). These public costs of bank restructuring have arisen from the need for solvency support to ailing banks through the recapitalization of these banks, the purchase of nonperforming

---

The author would like to thank the staff of the IMF's Monetary and Exchange Affairs Department for their comments and assistance, in particular David Hoelscher, Claudia Dziobek, Oliver Frécaut, Yuri Kawakami, Delisle Worrell, and Mark Zelmer.

loans from banks, the paying out of the guaranteed liabilities of banks that are closed, and the provision of liquidity support. The bulk of these costs have been borne through the issuance of domestic public debt in the form of government bonds, issued directly to ailing banks for recapitalization or in exchange for nonperforming loans. Governments have also issued bonds to central banks and other government agencies to compensate them for past liquidity support to ailing banks. In recent episodes of financial crises, for example, the governments of Ecuador, Indonesia, Jamaica, Korea, Mexico, Romania, and Thailand have shouldered the costs of bank restructuring almost entirely by issuing government bonds, with the stock of bonds issued estimated to range from single digits to 50 percent or more of GDP (Table 12.1).[1]

While government support for bank restructuring can help address the immediate crisis, the public costs of bank restructuring—manifested in the vast quantities of public debt issues and the servicing of this debt—can raise significant, and often unanticipated, risks to macroeconomic and financial stability, contributing to increased country vulnerability and to macroeconomic and financial shocks.[2] Servicing this debt may contribute to chronic fiscal imbalances,

---

[1]These estimates represent the *gross* costs to the government. The *net* costs can be known only after proceeds from (re)privatization of banks and recoveries of assets accruing to the government have been taken into account. A more complete picture of the costs would also involve indirect effects of the crisis and subsequent reforms. For a detailed discussion of the costs of restructuring, see Lindgren, and others (1999) and Honohan and Klingebiel (2000).

[2]This chapter does not attempt to address the theoretical debate on the relevance or welfare implications of debt management. It may be useful to note, however, that there is a rich theoretical literature on the relevance of public debt management, stemming from the debate over the validity of the "Ricardian Paradigm." In its purest form, Ricardian equivalence would render irrelevant the level and composition of government debt and its management. Whether or not Ricardian equivalence is a good approximation has received considerable attention in the empirical literature. Papers by Plosser (1982) and Giavazzi and Pagano (1990), for example, have lent support to Ricardian equivalence, while several other papers, for example, by Feldstein (1982) and Bernheim (1987), have argued against Ricardian equivalence. On balance, empirical work does not appear to support the idea that the private sector systematically offsets changes in the government's net debt position. Moreover, there are several theoretical frameworks in which government deficits do matter. Blanchard, Dornbusch, and Buiter (1986), for example, present an intertemporal model in which deficit finance can make an important contribution to stability and growth. Suffice to say that deviations from the assumptions underlying Ricardian equivalence do suggest that debt management is important, particularly in light of its implications for financial stability. For an excellent discussion on the role of sound debt management policies in reducing the susceptibility of countries to contagion and financial risk, see the *Guidelines for Public Debt Management* prepared by the International Monetary Fund and the World Bank (IMF/World Bank, 2000).

Table 12.1. Public Costs of Systemic Bank Restructuring: Selected Country Estimates
(as a percentage of GDP in 2000)

	Gross Public Costs Incurred as of Mid-2000	Government Bonds Issued as of Mid-2000	Estimated Additional Costs for FY 00/01
Ecuador (1998–mid-2000)	12.3	12.0	7.7
Indonesia (1997–mid-2000)	n.a.	55.0	3.0
Jamaica (1996–mid-2000)	45.0	40.6	3.0
Korea (1997–mid-2000)	20.4	12.2	9.5
Mexico (1994–mid-2000)	19.0	19.0	0.3
Romania (1997–mid-2000)	4.7	4.7	n.a.
Thailand (1997–mid-2000)	n.a.	10.0	0.02

Sources: Lindgren and others (1999); Enoch and others (2001); Becker (1999); Honohan and Klingebiel (2000); IMF staff estimates.

necessitating distortionary taxation.[3] A high public debt burden may also limit the monetary authorities' ability to pursue price stability by putting pressure on the central bank to monetize some debt to alleviate the burden.[4] If debt dynamics become unsustainable, some policy change will eventually be needed, and this can take the form of fiscal consolidation, inflation (and attendant currency depreciation), or—under extreme circumstances—default.[5] Addressing the public debt arising from systemic bank restructuring can thus become an important item on the agenda of policymakers in the aftermath of a banking crisis.[6]

The specific nature and purpose of the debt issued in the context of bank restructuring, and the lack of transparency surrounding the issuance and accounting of such debt, highlight the need for an explicit operational framework for quantifying, monitoring, and reducing the debt and its associated debt servicing burden. This chapter attempts to present such a framework. The framework recognizes that any strategy for addressing the public debt arising from a banking crisis must balance the specific objectives of bank restructuring with the government's broader macroeconomic objectives. It emphasizes that the results of any strategy to address such debt must be integrated with the

---

[3]For a discussion on the possible real effects of public debt, see Lane (1997).

[4]In an extreme case of "unpleasant monetary arithmetic," monetary policy is fully determined by the debt dynamics; see Sargent and Wallace (1981).

[5]In most industrialized countries, inflation and depreciation are the most likely alternatives (see Giovannini and Piga, 1992). In developing countries, the risk of default presents a more realistic possibility (see Dooley, 1998).

[6]While the focus of this chapter is on addressing public costs on an ex post basis, this should not be seen to undermine the importance of the ex ante containment of the public costs arising from systemic bank restructuring programs.

overall government debt management effort[7] and linked to a clear macroeconomic framework under which governments seek to ensure that the level and rate of growth in public debt, and the servicing of that debt, are sustainable.

The Specific Nature of Public Debt Issued for Bank Restructuring

Two main features distinguish the public debt issued for bank restructuring from other forms of public debt. First, unlike most government debt, which is floated with the objective of raising cash to help finance the fiscal deficit, the primary purpose of most of the debt issued for systemic bank restructuring is to provide solvency support to ailing banks, and may be viewed largely as an exercise in creative accounting. Second, and related to the first point, government bonds—which are the main *instruments* through which public debt is issued for the purposes of bank restructuring—are not issued and sold through the standard market-based (auction) system, but rather are placed directly on the books of the recipient institution (appearing on the "assets" side of the recipient institution's balance sheet). The interest paid by the government on these bonds is often the main source of liquidity for the bank after it has been recapitalized. Therefore, in restructuring these bonds to reduce the government's debt burden and servicing costs, the authorities have to balance macroeconomic objectives with the objectives of bank restructuring, namely, recapitalizing banks, covering losses, and bringing a troubled banking system back to soundness and profitability. For example, restructuring all bonds into zero coupon bonds can help reduce the medium-term fiscal burden associated with bank restructuring—because the government would not have to provide immediate cash in the form of interest payments. But this can also slow down the process of restoring ailing banks to health, because a bank that has a large part of its assets in the form of such bonds would likely continue to suffer severe cash-flow constraints. Converting bonds into fixed coupon bonds with coupon rates lower than prevailing market interest rates may ease short-term fiscal constraints, but it may present a problem over the longer term, to the extent that if banks want to sell down these bonds, they may be forced to do so at a discount and bear the capital loss.

Bank restructuring bonds may be *issued* either directly by the central government (as in Thailand) or by government agencies such as bank

---

[7]For a broader discussion on issues concerning the strengthening of public debt management, see IMF/World Bank (2000).

Figure 12.1. Issuers and Holders of Bonds

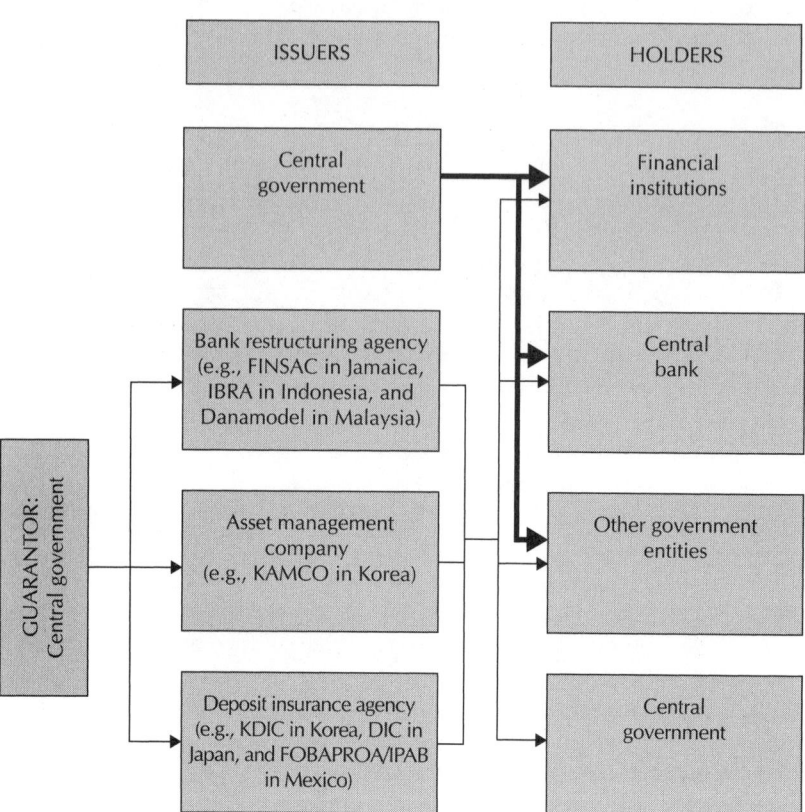

restructuring agencies (as in Indonesia, Jamaica, and Malaysia), asset management companies (as in Korea), and deposit insurance agencies (as in Mexico). Bonds that are issued by a government agency, rather than directly by the central government, are typically guaranteed by the central government. The *holders* of the bonds may include intervened financial institutions; the central bank—in cases where the government issues bonds to the central bank to compensate it for past liquidity support to banks; other government entities; and the central government—in cases where the bank restructuring agency issues debt to the central government in exchange for initial cash support provided to assist in covering the operational expenses of the restructuring agency (Figure 12.1).

The bonds issued include a mix of fixed coupon, variable coupon, zero coupon (i.e., bonds issued at a discount, earning no interest but redeemable at par value), and index-linked bonds, which may be tradable or

Table 12.2. Types of Bonds

	Debt Instrument Issued	Received
Indonesia	• Variable and fixed coupon bonds • Variable coupon bonds • Index-linked bonds; tradable	• Equity • Nonperforming loans • Equity
Jamaica	• Fixed and variable coupon bonds; tradable • Fixed and variable coupon bonds; nontradable (allowing for interest capitalization)	• Equity • Equity, subordinated debt, nonperforming loans
Korea	• Variable coupon bonds; tradable • Fixed and variable coupon bonds	• Equity or preference shares • Nonperforming loans
Malaysia	• Zero coupon bonds; not easily traded • Zero coupon bonds	• Convertible preference shares or subordinated debt • Nonperforming loans
Mexico	• Ten-year promissory notes, nontradable (allowing for interest capitalization)	• Nonperforming loans
Thailand	• Fixed coupon bonds; tradable • Fixed coupon bonds; nontradable	• Equity • Subordinated debt

Sources: Based on Lindgren and others (1999).

nontradable, denominated in domestic or foreign currency. In exchange for the bonds issued, governments may receive equity or subordinated debt in the intervened institution, or nonperforming loans (Table 12.2).

Key Steps in Addressing the Public Costs of Bank Restructuring

Addressing the public costs of bank restructuring involves a series of steps, including cost recognition and quantification of the total costs, the specification of alternative scenarios to reduce the costs, and determination of the preferred strategy. Each step requires the concerned authorities—in most cases the ministry of finance, in coordination with the bank restructuring agency—to make difficult decisions, as illustrated in Figure 12.2.

Cost Recognition and Quantification of the Debt Problem

The first step is to assess the magnitude of public costs, to serve as a basis for projecting the evolution of costs over time and assessing their impact on medium-term debt and fiscal sustainability. This requires a

Figure 12.2. Decision Sequence

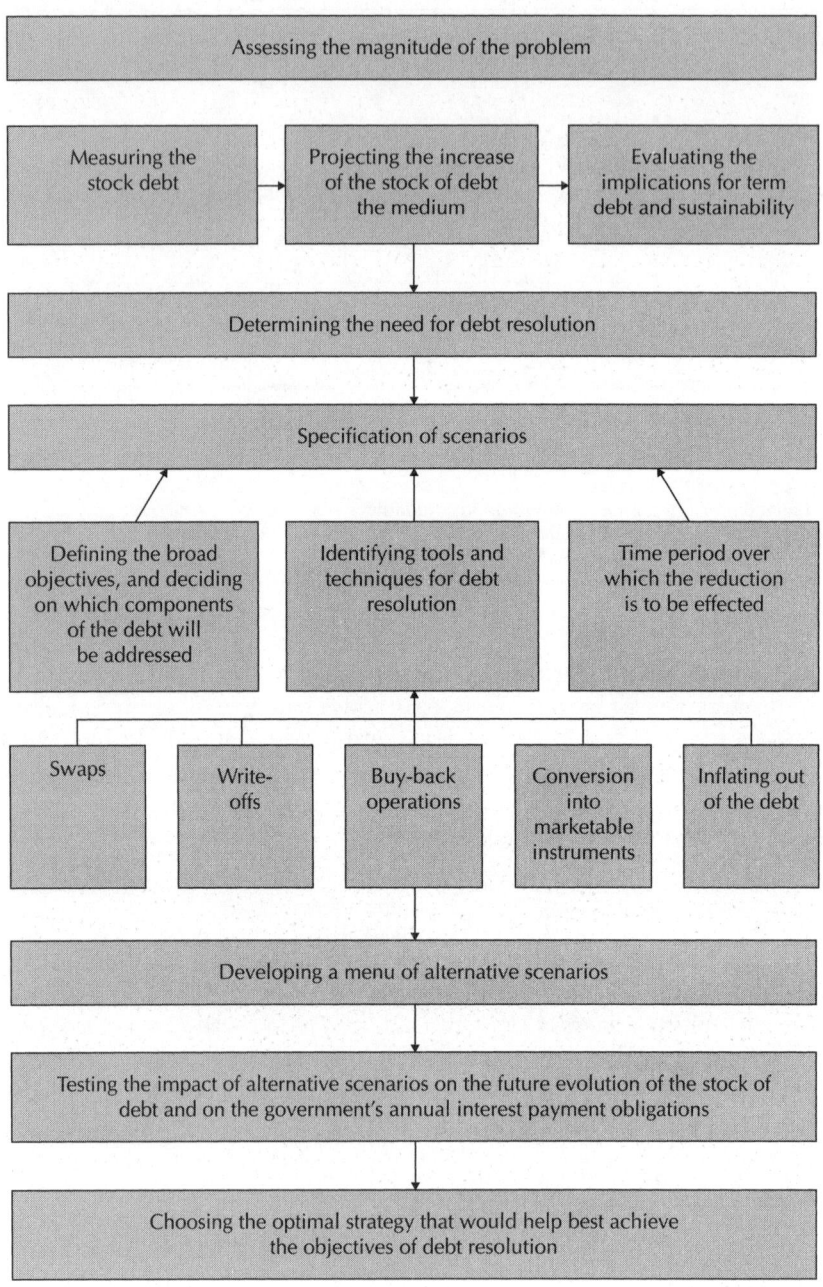

full and transparent accounting of the total public costs of bank restructuring and the incorporation of these costs into the budget.

Because the current guidelines for classifying government costs in bank restructuring are founded on the use of the cash-based balance of the general government, as described in the 1986 Manual on Government Finance Statistics, and do not allow for the explicit inclusion of the stock of debt issued for bank restructuring, it may be misleading to follow these guidelines in quantifying the total magnitude of the public costs.[8] An "augmented fiscal balance" approach, involving the explicit recognition of all the major quantifiable budgetary and quasi-fiscal costs of bank restructuring, is more appropriate for gaining an accurate picture of the total public costs of bank restructuring.[9] Under this approach, the public costs would be defined as the entire stock of debt issued in support of bank restructuring, plus the costs of servicing that debt. The approach requires identifying each and every bond issued and gathering information on the maturity, currency, interest rates, schedule of coupon payments, and amortization schedule of each bond.

Once the stock of debt has been calculated, projections need to be made on the *future evolution* of this stock, over the medium term (generally defined as the next three to four years). Preparing accurate stock projections requires that the following key issues be considered:
- The stock projections should properly reflect whether any (or all) of the bonds allow for the capitalization of interest accrued. If so, all bonds to be issued over the medium term in lieu of interest

---

[8]Under the existing guidelines, the fiscal balance is affected only by financial assistance that involves cash operations by the general government. Noncash expenditures and quasi-fiscal operations associated with bank restructuring are *not* accounted for in the overall fiscal balance. Thus, for example, recapitalization via the issuance of government bonds to troubled banks affects the standard fiscal balance only through interest payments, not through the principal, even if the bank immediately sells the debt. Likewise, in circumstances where the government issues bonds to compensate the central bank for past liquidity support, or where the bank restructuring agency or deposit insurance agency issues government-guaranteed bonds for bank restructuring, then only the interest accrued by these bonds (and not the principal) would be included in the budget. Furthermore, quasi-fiscal operations such as the extension of credit to troubled banks by the central bank or other public agencies (e.g., bank restructuring agencies or deposit insurance funds) are either entirely excluded from the government budget or their inclusion comes indirectly. If, on the other hand, governments were to float the debt and transfer proceeds to ailing banks and other financial institutions, that debt would be classified as government budgetary expenditure. A new manual, the *2001 Government Finance Statistics Manual*, which is likely to take several years in many countries before it is adopted, takes an accrual-based approach to the recording of government transactions which therefore addresses the issues raised here.

[9]For a detailed discussion of the augmented fiscal balance approach, see Daniel, Davis, and Wolfe (1997).

payments must be fully reflected in the stock projections, based on thorough information about the coupon payment schedule of each bond. For variable coupon bonds on which interest is being capitalized, assumptions need to be made about the projected interest rate path so that the amount of future bonds to be issued in lieu of interest payments can be measured accurately. For foreign exchange–denominated bonds on which interest is being capitalized, medium-term exchange rate projections need to be made so that the amount of future bonds to be issued in lieu of interest payments can be estimated accurately.

- A clear understanding needs to be reached on the government's *existing commitments* to issue new bonds to support financial restructuring; the level of commitments, types of bonds to be issued, and details of the proposed coupon payments need to be defined.
- Estimates also need to be made of the *likelihood of any additional bonds* that may be required to provide solvency or liquidity support to financial institutions over the medium term. This requires an assessment of the current and future soundness and stability of the financial system, including capital adequacy, asset quality, management, liquidity, and profitability. In cases where the assessment suggests that financial institutions are likely to require solvency or liquidity support in the future, estimates need to be made of the extent of such support needed, and of whether this would need to be funded through the issuance of new government bonds (as opposed to funds raised by the private sector). These estimates must be factored into the stock projections.

Based on the stock projections, an assessment has to be made of whether the government has the capacity to sustain the projected debt burden and the attendant fiscal costs of servicing the debt. If the debt burden and its carrying costs are deemed to be unsustainable, then a strategy for addressing the debt problem would clearly be warranted.

Scenario Specification

Any strategy for debt reduction must begin with the specification of alternative scenarios under which the problem may be addressed. A starting point in the scenario specification exercise is to define the objectives of the strategy. While the specific objectives would vary depending on the nature and the extent of the problem at hand, and the particular circumstances of the country in question, it is reasonable to assume that the strategy would aim, at the very minimum, to reduce the stock of debt and associated debt servicing costs to levels that are sustainable over the medium term, while ensuring that the objectives of the bank restructuring program are not jeopardized.

Once the objectives of the resolution strategy have been defined, the authorities have to make a number of decisions (Figure 12.2). They must first decide on which components of the debt will be addressed through the strategy (e.g., whether debt issued both to the public and private sectors should be reduced/eliminated). Next, the amount by which the various components of the debt will be reduced needs to be determined (e.g., in the case of debt issued to public sector entities, will all of the debt be eliminated, or will debt owed to certain entities be eliminated selectively; similarly, by how much will the debt issued to various private institutions be reduced?). The period over which the reduction will be implemented also needs to be determined. These decisions tend to be guided mainly by the specific policy goals of the authorities. For example, if the goal is to privatize the recapitalized banks as soon as possible, and if a certain recapitalized bank is considered to be potentially more "salable" than others, with the main obstacle to its sale being the large portfolio of nonmarketable recapitalization bonds on the asset side of its balance sheet, the authorities may decide to buy back the bonds of that bank (in exchange for cash) on a larger scale than bonds held by other banks in the system.

The next steps involve selecting the appropriate financial engineering techniques. The available techniques typically include (1) write-offs, (2) debt buy-back operations, (3) swaps, (4) debt restructuring through a conversion of the debt instruments (e.g., the conversion of nonmarketable debt into marketable instruments, which make regular coupon payments, based on market-determined interest rates), and (5) simply "inflating out" of the debt problem, so that real interest rates on the debt can be significantly reduced without actually implementing a systematic debt reduction program (Table 12.3).

Not all of these techniques are equally preferable. For example, writing off debt issued by the government carries the important risk of moral hazard, creating disincentives for the government to honor its debt obligations in the future. Moreover, if governments use write-offs for dealing with intragovernment debt (e.g., debt issued by the treasury to the central bank, or by a government-owned bank restructuring agency to the treasury), this could send adverse signals to the private sector, which may be led to believe that such write-offs are also an option for dealing with government bonds held by private institutions. If governments use write-offs for addressing debt issued to selected private institutions, this could also have systemic implications on the private sector's perception of the government. In general, writing off debt

Table 12.3. Objectives and Techniques

Objectives	Financial Engineering Techniques
• To reduce the stock of debt to a level that is sustainable over the medium term • To ensure that the fiscal burden (i.e., the debt-servicing costs) is sustainable and in line with the overall macroeconomic program	• Write-offs • Debt buy-back operations • Swaps • Conversion of debt instruments • Inflating out of the debt problem

issued by the government may contribute to a loss of credibility for the government, which risks generating panic on the part of private holders of government debt. Similarly, the option of inflating out of the debt problem carries serious adverse consequences, not least of which is the risk of macroeconomic instability. On the other hand, debt buy-back operations, swaps, and improvements in the marketability of bonds are associated with fewer obvious adverse consequences.

Governments may not always have the luxury of being able to choose from among the various alternatives presented above. The choice of techniques is limited by a number of factors, including the composition of the debt, time constraints for debt resolution, and perhaps most important, the resources available to the government to implement the selected techniques. The use of debt buy-back operations, for example, is constrained by the budgetary or extra budgetary resources available for such purposes. Governments may wish to use resources from asset recovery to finance debt buy-back operations, which would imply that the scale of buy-back operations would be constrained by the success with which governments are able to recover value on "core" assets (i.e., the equity of various ailing financial institutions that is transferred to the government/government entities in exchange for the bonds issued to those institutions) and "noncore" assets (i.e., nonperforming loans and collateral transferred to the government/government entities in exchange for the bonds issued).

The techniques chosen may be combined in different ways, under varying assumptions about interest payment and accrual, resources available to reduce the stock of debt, and changes in the stock of debt held by the public and private sectors, so as to specify a menu of alternative scenarios for debt resolution. In theory, available techniques may be combined in an infinite number of ways—under different assumptions—to develop a menu of scenarios. A set of scenarios, based on rather simplified assumptions, is presented below.

Assume that the stock of debt, issued in the context of the bank restructuring program, is defined as follows: $D = D_{pb} + D_{pv}$, where D is the total stock of public debt issued by the government in the context of a systemic bank restructuring program, when D_{pb} is the stock of debt held by other public sector entities, that is, intragovernment debt (e.g., debt held by the central bank), and D_{pv} is the stock of debt held by the private sector.

Assume further that the debt burden and associated fiscal costs are unsustainable over the medium term and that the authorities have determined the need to design a debt resolution strategy, with the objectives of reducing D, so that both D, and the annual costs of servicing it, are sustainable over the medium term.

It is agreed that the strategy should be implemented over a period, say, from t through $t+3$. It is also decided that the reduction in D will be implemented through efforts to eliminate D_{pb}, and to reduce D_{pv} by as much as possible, given available resources.

Having agreed on these definitions, the authorities need to identify appropriate techniques to develop alternative scenarios. Let us assume that the preferred tool to bring about a reduction in D_{pb} is an intragovernment debt **write-off**. Changes in D_{pb} are determined by a parameter δ, which denotes the government's ability to negotiate write-offs: if $\delta = 0$, D_{pb} remains unchanged; if $\delta = 1$, D_{pb} is fully retired.

Let us also assume that the preferred tool to bring about a reduction in D_{pv} is a debt **buy-back operation**, and that the *only* resources available to fund this buy-back operation are proceeds from the sale of "core" or "noncore" assets transferred to the government in the course of bank restructuring. Core assets comprise the government's equity in the recapitalized financial institutions (often representing 100 percent of the equity of the institution concerned), while noncore assets comprise nonperforming loans, real estate assets, and similar instruments purchased by the government in the restructuring process. It follows that the amount by which D_{pv} can be reduced through a buy-back operation is determined by the amount that can be recovered through the sale of core and noncore assets, with the assumption that proceeds from asset recovery would be devoted entirely to buying back D_{pv}.

Recovery on *core assets* is denoted by a value parameter α: if $\alpha = 0$, this would mean that there is no recovery on core assets for any given year, and therefore that no resources are available from the sale of core assets to reduce D_{pv}; if $\alpha = \alpha^*$, this would mean that some amount is recovered from the sale of core assets, which the government would use toward buying back an equivalent amount of D_{pv}.[10]

---

[10]In practice, scenario specification should involve assigning a variety of different values for α, based on different estimates of recovery values on core assets—ranging from pessimistic to optimistic estimates.

Recovery on *noncore assets* is denoted by the value parameter γ: if $\gamma = 0$, this would mean that the recovery value on noncore assets for any given year is zero; if $\gamma = \gamma^*$, this would represent (in present value terms) the government's recovery value from the sale of its noncore assets, which it would then use toward achieving a reduction in D_{pv} by an equivalent amount.[11]

The cost to the government of servicing the debt (i.e., interest payments) is denoted by parameter i: if $i = 0$, this would mean that all interest on outstanding debt in any given year is capitalized; if $i = 1$, this would mean that cash interest would be paid out on the debt outstanding as of year $t+1$, commencing in $t+1$; if $i = 2$, this would mean that cash interest would be paid out on the debt outstanding as of year $t+2$, commencing in $t+2$.

Based on the above, various alternative scenarios for debt resolution may be developed. Table 12.4 presents some of these scenarios.

The final step is to evaluate the effectiveness of each scenario in meeting the predefined objectives of the strategy to address the public costs of bank restructuring, so that a preferred or "optimal" strategy may be selected. This requires estimating and analyzing the impact of each scenario on the evolution of the stock of debt, on the government's annual interest payment obligations for the period t through $t = 3$, on other predefined macroeconomic goals, and on the bank restructuring program. The optimal strategy would be one that would best achieve the predefined objectives of debt reduction and fiscal sustainability while assisting the banking system to return to soundness and profitability. It is also important that the strategy does not jeopardize the government's credibility vis-à-vis the market. Thus, before the optimal strategy is chosen, it would be necessary to consider, for example, how the private sector would perceive a debt write-off. At the same time, the impact on banks' balance sheets of buying back the recapitalization bonds issued to troubled banks, swapping those bonds, or converting them into marketable instruments would need to be carefully evaluated—with a view to ensuring that a debt resolution strategy involving such measures does not in any way jeopardize the solvency, liquidity, or profitability of the banks in question.

---

[11] In practice, scenario specification should involve assigning a variety of different values for γ, based on different estimates of recovery values on noncore assets—ranging from pessimistic to optimistic estimates.

Table 12.4. A Menu of Alternative Scenarios

Policy Variables		Examples of Alternative Strategies
$\delta = 0$ or 1	$\alpha = 0$ or α^*	**Baseline:** $\delta = 0$, $\alpha = 0$, $\gamma = 0$, $i = 0$ for each year from t through $t + 3$
$I = 0, 1$ or 2	$\gamma = 0$ or γ^*	
		Scenario 1: $\delta = 0$, $\alpha = 0$, $\gamma = 0$ for each year from t through $t + 3$; $i = 1$
		Scenario 2: $\delta = 0$, $\alpha = 0$, $\gamma = 0$ for each year from t through $t + 3$; $i = 2$
		Scenario 3: $\delta = 1$, $\alpha = \alpha^*$, $\gamma = 0$ for each year from t through $t + 3$; $i = 1$
		Scenario 4: $\delta = 1$, $\alpha = \alpha^*$, $\gamma = \gamma^*$ for each year from t through $t + 3$; $i = 1$

A Numerical Example

This section provides a numerical example to illustrate the steps involved in developing a strategy to address the public costs of bank restructuring.

Assumptions

Consider an economy where the government has financed a systemic bank restructuring program entirely through the issuance of bonds. All bonds have been issued by the government-owned bank restructuring agency and are guaranteed by the government. The total stock of public debt (bonds) issued (D) is $100. Bonds issued to, and held by, the public sector (D_{pb}) amount to $40 of this (comprising a combination of bonds held by the central bank to compensate it for past liquidity assistance provided to troubled banks, and bonds held by the central government to compensate it for cash support provided in the past to help cover operational expenses). Bonds issued to, and held by, the private sector (D_{pv}) amount to $60 (comprising a combination of bonds held by troubled banks and other financial institutions, including nonbank financial institutions).

The bonds are denominated in domestic currency, are nontradable, and have a maturity structure in the 3–15 years range, with interest payable on a biannual basis, either at a fixed rate or at a floating rate (typically, at the six-month treasury bill interest rate plus 100 basis points). Interest on bonds is capitalized through the issuance of new bonds.

The majority of the bonds issued carry variable interest rates; therefore, projections on the future evolution of the debt stock require

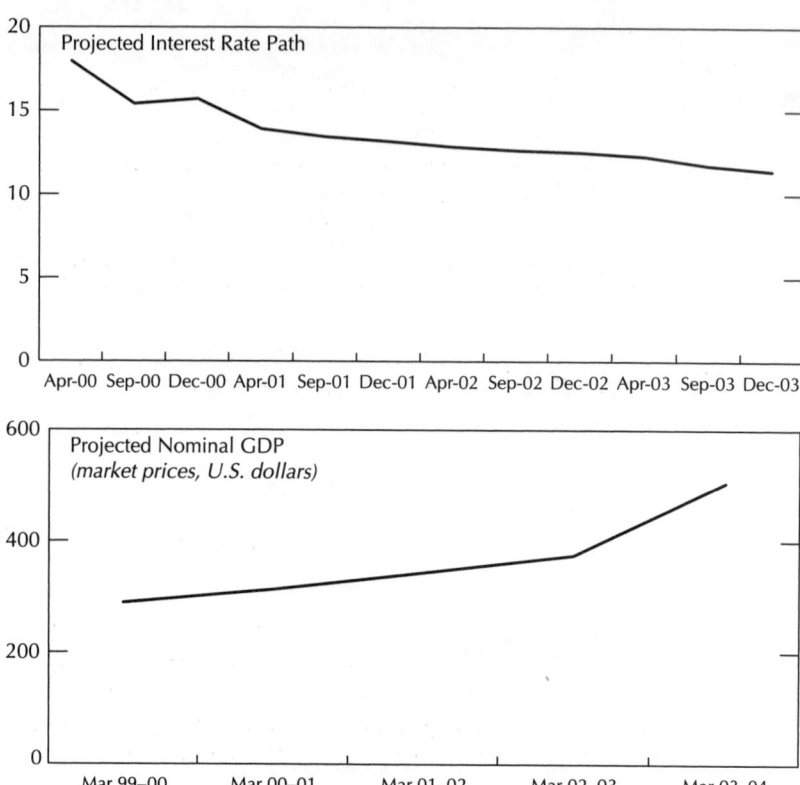

Figure 12.3. Illustrated Interest Rate and Exchange Rate Projections (baseline scenario)

assumptions about the nominal interest rate path. Nominal interest rates are projected to decline over the medium term, and GDP is assumed to increase over the medium term (Figure 12.3).

Assume also that the government does *not* need to issue any additional bonds to meet liquidity or solvency needs of the banking system over the medium term, but that all interest is capitalized through the issuance of new bonds.

Quantifying and projecting the stock of debt

The first step for the authorities would be to quantify the existing debt problem. With interest capitalized, and with no reductions in the stock of debt, the total stock of debt is estimated at $100, and it is projected to evolve as shown in the baseline scenario (Figure 12.4)—

Figure 12.4. Evolution of Public Debt (Baseline Scenario)
(In U.S. dollars)

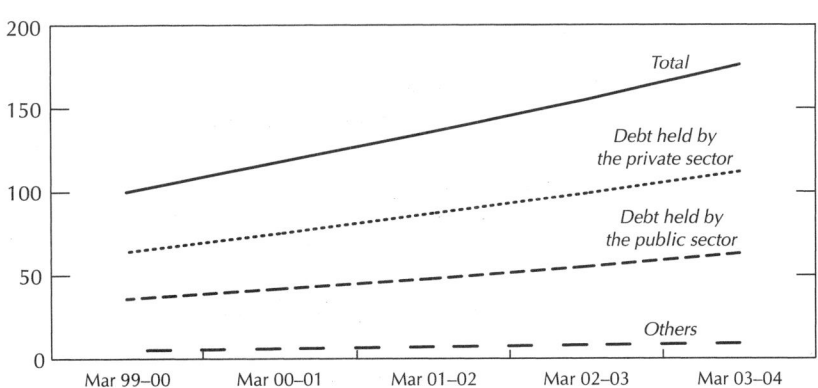

increasing from $100 in base year FY1999/2000 to about $175 by FY2003/2004, or an annual growth rate of about 15 percent. Based on these estimated projections, let us assume that the authorities determine that the debt problem would become unsustainable, and that a strategy for addressing this debt is therefore warranted.

Scenario specification

Now assume, as before, that the only technique available to the authorities for reducing D_{pb} is a write-off: if $\delta = 0$, there is no write-off; if $\delta = 1$, this means that the entire amount of D_{pb} ($40) is written off. Also, assume that the only technique available for reducing D_{pv} is a buy-back operation—funded through proceeds from the sale of core assets (α) or noncore assets (γ), where the maximum recovery from the sale of core assets (α^*) is $10 and the maximum recovery value on noncore assets (γ^*) is estimated at $5, in present value terms. Against this background, the scenarios defined in the section on the public costs of bank restructuring can be developed, based on alternative combinations of key choices on interest accruals and payments, changes in the stock of debt held by the public sector effected through a write-off of public debt, and changes in the stock of debt held by the private sector effected through debt buy-backs, funded by proceeds from the sale of core assets and noncore assets. Summary results of the impact of each scenario on the stock of debt, and on the government's debt-servicing costs (shown as a percentage of GDP, on an annual basis for the period FY 1999/2000 through to FY 2002/2003) are presented in Figure 12.5.

Figure 12.5. Illustrated Evolution of Debt Stock and Debt Servicing Costs

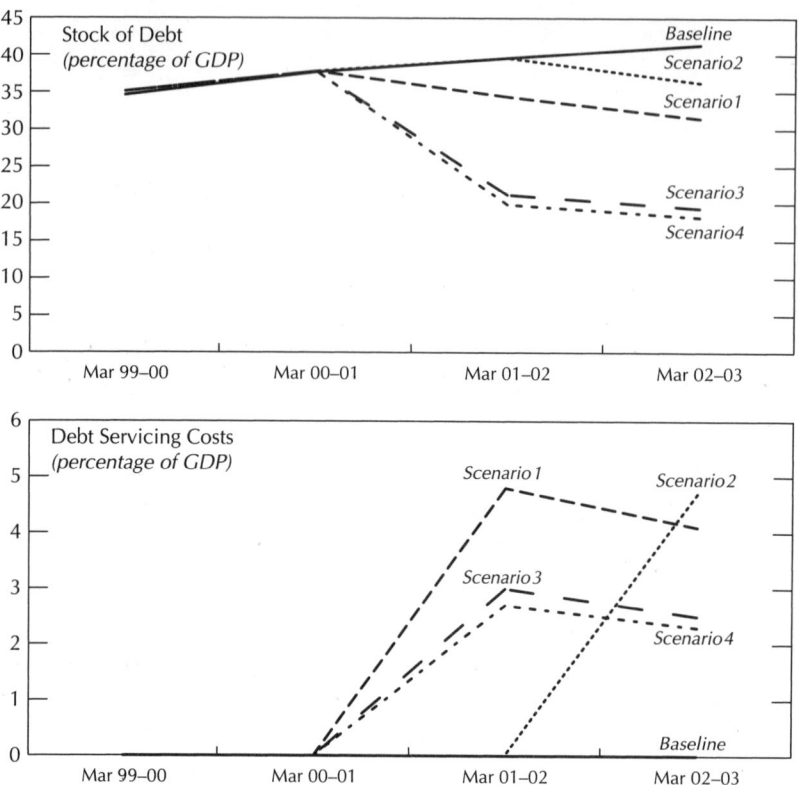

Assessment[12]

Figure 12.5 (top panel) shows the impact of the various scenarios on the evolution of the total stock of debt over the medium term. Scenarios 1, 3, and 4 each result in stock reductions over the medium term, in varying degrees, achieved through different combinations of policy tools to reduce the stock of debt held by the public sector and the private sector and assumptions about the capitalization of interest on the debt. In contrast, Scenario 2 results in an increase in the stock of debt as a percentage of GDP, with the ratio being higher for 2002–2003 than for 1999–2000, because it assumes that interest would continue to be capitalized up until FY 2001/2002, resulting in a sizable increase in the

---

[12]The model showing details on the evolution of debt and debt-servicing costs, under each scenario, is available from the author on request.

stock of debt, and that no reductions would be made in the stock of debt held by the public or private sector.

Figure 12.5 (bottom panel) shows the impact of the various scenarios on the evolution of the government's interest payment obligations, and hence on the fiscal balance, over the medium term. Scenarios 1 and 2 result in the maximum drain on government cash resources in the outer years, but a minimum drain in the initial years. These scenarios assume that the government would commence cash interest payments on the debt in FY 2001/2002 and 2002/2003, respectively. Furthermore, they assume that the government would *not* be able to recover any value on core or noncore assets, and therefore would have no resources available to bring about a reduction in the stock of private sector debt (which is predicated on the availability of resources to buy back the debt); and that the government would *not* be able to reach an agreement on the write-off of debt held by other public sector entities. Scenarios 3 and 4 show the impact on the government's cash flow of different degrees of realization from core and noncore assets.

In this hypothetical case, Scenario 4 presents an optimal strategy for addressing the public debt problem, with optimal recoveries on the sale of both core and noncore assets, which would help provide significant resources for the buy-back of private sector debt. It also assumes a resolution/write-off of debt held by the central government and public sector entities. The scenario would represent a "first best" strategy, in terms of both its impact on the government's debt servicing burden and the stock of debt. Interest payments at the nominal rate of interest would yield a cost to the government of about 2.7 percent of GDP for 2001–2002, trending down to 2 percent of GDP for 2002–2003. At this level of effort, the government would be lowering the stock of debt in real terms. The stock of debt would decline from 35 percent of GDP in FY 1999/2000 to 18 percent in FY 2002/2003.

Some Caveats

This chapter has aimed to present an operational framework for quantifying, analyzing, and addressing, on an ex post basis, the public costs arising from systemic bank restructuring. The framework developed in this chapter is based on a set of simplified assumptions on the composition of public costs, on how the debt is structured in terms of its maturity, currency, and interest rate composition, on the specifics of the debt problem, and on the factors guiding both the specification of various alternative resolution scenarios and the choice of an optimal strategy. In practice, developing a strategy for addressing the public costs of bank restructuring is likely to be more complex, requiring governments to make difficult, and often competing, choices at various stages. Because no decision on an optimal strategy can be made independently of its potential impact on medium-term macroeconomic and financial stability, its implications for the bank restructuring program under way, and the perceived impact on the government's credibility vis-à-vis market participants, each of these factors needs to be carefully considered in selecting the preferred strategy.

Finally, while the chapter focuses on addressing public costs on an ex post basis, this should not be seen to undermine the importance of the ex ante containment of the public costs arising from systemic bank restructuring. Indeed, decisions on the extent of public costs, the types of instruments to be used to finance these costs, and the pricing and marketability of those instruments, have important implications for the medium-term debt and fiscal dynamics and, more generally, for the overall macroeconomic and financial stability of the country in question. They should be addressed up front in the design of a systemic bank restructuring program.

References

Becker, Torbjörn, 1999, "Public Debt Management and Bailouts," IMF Working Paper No. 99/103 (Washington: International Monetary Fund).

Bernheim, B. Douglas, 1987, "Ricardian Equivalence: An Evaluation of Theory and Evidence," NBER Working Paper No. 2330 (Cambridge, Massachusetts: National Bureau of Economic Research).

Blanchard, O., R. Dornbusch, and W. Buiter, 1986, "Public Debt and Fiscal Responsibility," in *Restoring Europe's Prosperity: Macroeconomic Papers from the Centre for European Policy Studies*, ed. by Olivier J. Blanchard, Rudiger Dornbusch, and P. Richard G. Layard (Cambridge, Massachusetts: MIT Press).

Daniel, James A., Jeffrey M. Davis, and Andrew M. Wolfe, 1997, "Fiscal Accounting of Bank Restructuring," IMF Paper on Policy Analysis and Assessment 97/5 (Washington: International Monetary Fund).

Dooley, Michael P., 1998, "Government Debt and Asset Management in Financial Crises: Sellers Beware," Department of Economics Working Paper No. 409 (Santa Cruz: University of California).

Enoch, Charles, Gillian Garcia, and V. Sundararajan, 2001, "Recapitalizing Banks with Public Funds," *IMF Staff Papers*, Vol. 48, No. 1, pp. 58–110.

Feldstein, Martin, 1982, "Government Deficits and Aggregate Demand," *Journal of Monetary Economics*, Vol. 9 (January), pp. 1–20.

Giavazzi, Francesco, and Marco Pagano, 1990, "Can Severe Fiscal Contractions Be Expansionary? Tales of Two Small European Countries," NBER Working

Paper No. 3372 (Cambridge, Massachusetts: National Bureau of Economic Research).

Giovannini, Alberto, and Gustavo Piga, 1992, "Understanding the High Interest Rates on Italian Government Securities," CEPR Discussion Paper Series No. 720 (London: Centre for Economic Policy Research).

Honohan, Patrick, and Daniela Klingebiel, 2000, "Controlling Fiscal Costs of Banking Crises," Policy Research Working Paper No. 2441 (Washington: World Bank).

International Monetary Fund, 2001, *Guidelines for Public Debt Management* (Washington: IMF). Available via the Internet at http://www.imf.org/external/np/mae/pdebt/2000/eng.

———, 2001, *Government Finance Statistics Manual* (Washington).

———, 1986, *A Manual on Government Finance Statistics* (Washington).

IMF/World Bank, 2000, *Draft Guidelines on Public Debt Management* (Washington: International Monetary Fund).

Lane, Timothy, 1997, "High Public Debt: Consequences for Investment and Growth," in *Banking, International Capital Flows, and Growth in Europe: Financial Markets, Savings, and Monetary Integration in a World with Uncertain Convergence*, ed. by Paul J.J. Welfens and Holger C. Wolf (New York: Springer Verlag).

Lindgren, Carl-Johan, Tomas Baliño, Charles Enoch, Anne-Marie Gulde, Marc Quintyn, and Leslie Teo, 1999, *Financial Sector Crisis and Restructuring—Lessons from Asia*, IMF Occasional Paper No. 188 (Washington: International Monetary Fund).

Plosser, Charles I., 1982, "Government Financing Decisions and Asset Returns," *Journal of Monetary Economics*, Vol. 9 (May), pp. 325–52.

Sargent, Thomas J., and Neil Wallace, 1981, "Some Unpleasant Monetarist Arithmetic," *Federal Reserve Bank of Minneapolis Quarterly Review*, Vol. 9 (Winter), pp. 15–31.

List of Authors

Richard K. Abrams
Advisor, Monetary and Exchange Affairs Department of the IMF.

Michael Andrews
Financial Sector Advisor, Monetary and Exchange Affairs Department of the IMF.

Priya Basu
Senior Economist at the World Bank in India. Previously Economist in the IMF's Monetary and Exchange Affairs Department.

Luis Cortavarria
Senior Economist in the Systemic Banking Issues Division in the IMF's Monetary and Exchange Affairs Department.

Fernando Delgado
Senior Economist in the Systemic Banking Issues Division in the IMF's Monetary and Exchange Affairs Department.

Claudia Dziobek
Assistant to the Director of the Statistics Department of the IMF. Previously Senior Economist in the Monetary and Exchange Affairs Department of the IMF.

Charles Enoch
Senior Advisor in the Statistics Department. Previously Assistant Director of the Systemic Banking Issues Division of the Monetary and Exchange Affairs Department of the IMF.

Gillian Garcia
Previously Senior Economist in the IMF's Monetary and Exchange Affairs Department.

Peter Hayward
Financial Sector Advisor in the Banking Supervision and Regulation Division of the Monetary and Exchange Affairs Department of the IMF.

Dong He
Senior Economist in the Systemic Banking Issues Division of the Monetary and Exchange Affairs Department, IMF.

List of Authors

J. Kim Hobbs
Director of Financial Risk Management at Capital One in Virginia. Previously consultant for the IMF.

David Hoelscher
Division Chief, Systemic Banking Issues Division, Monetary and Exchange Affairs Department of the IMF.

Akihiro Kanaya
Investment Banking Division at Morgan Stanley Japan Ltd. Previously Economist, Monetary and Exchange Affairs Department of the IMF.

Daniel Kanda
Economist in the IMF's Asia and Pacific Department. Previously in the Monetary and Exchange Affairs Department of the IMF.

David Marston
Division Chief, Banking Supervision and Regulation Division, Monetary and Exchange Affairs Department of the IMF.

Greta Mitchell
Senor Economist, Banking Supervision and Regulation Division, Monetary Affairs and Exchange Department of the IMF.

Armando Morales
Senior Economist, Monetary and Exchange Policy Review Division, Monetary Exchange Affairs Department of the IMF.

Inwon Song
Senior Economist, Banking Supervision and Regulation Division, Monetary and Exchange Affairs Department of the IMF.

Michael Taylor
Financial Sector Issues Representative in Indonesia of the IMF's Monetary and Exchange Affairs Department. Previously Senior Economist in the IMF's Monetary and Exchange Affairs Department.

V. Sundararajan
Deputy Director of the Monetary and Exchange Affairs Department of the IMF.

David Woo
Vice President of the Economic and Market Analysis Department of Citigroup. Previously Economist in the IMF's Monetary and Exchange Affairs Department.